FOLKLORE FROM KANSAS

FOLKLORE FROM KANSAS

Customs,
Beliefs,
and
Superstitions

WILLIAM E. KOCH

THE REGENTS PRESS OF KANSAS
Lawrence

Library of Congress Cataloging in Publication Data
Main entry under title:

Folklore from Kansas.
1. Folk-lore—Kansas. 2. Superstition—Kansas.
I. Koch, William E.
GR110.K2F64   390'.09781   79-20197
ISBN 0-7006-0192-9

The photographs on pages 95, 175, 198, and 235 are from the Kansas State Historical Society, Topeka.

The photographs on pages 317, 348, 370, and 380 are from the collection at Kansas State University in Manhattan.

The photographs on pages 21, 59, 77, 112, 158, 169, 221, 249, 265, 295, 360, 363, and 405 are from the Pennell Collection at Spencer Research Library at the University of Kansas, Lawrence.

Each of these institutions has graciously given its consent to the Regents Press so that those photographs could be used in this book.

And the rain descended, and the floods came, and the winds blew, and beat upon that house; and it fell not; for it was founded upon a rock.

Matthew 7:25

Contents

Preface

THE STATE OF KANSAS IS A 200 BY 400 MILE PORTION OF land in the exact center of the United States. Most of this state is a part of America's Great Plains region, which means that it is semiarid. The population of 2.5 million is concentrated mostly in the eastern half. Unlike its sister states, Kansas has always had a very low percentage of foreign-born citizens, less than 12 percent, and that was before the turn of the century.

Kansas' statehood came early—for this part of the nation at least—1861. Because of its centrality, it has been and is a crisscross state, from the time of the early explorers and mountain men to the present era of car, truck, train, and air travel. For a brief period of time the horsemen-cowboys crisscrossed Kansas and left an indelible mark for the world's romanticists. Although Kansas is rich in some minerals, it is basically a livestock- and grain-raising state, and for many years it has been the nation's most productive wheat state. Also, and significantly, Wichita has the distinction of being the nation's leader in aircraft production.

Because of its relatively early statehood and its crisscross character, the people of Kansas constitute a mosaic society. Old-timers say, "We're a mixture of everything." But a few pockets of distinctive European folk cultures, a residue of migrations that took place before the turn of the century, still are in evidence, and some have been the subject of folkloric studies.

Kansas has, from its very beginnings, nurtured a society composed of a great many ethnic heritages that had already adopted a full American life style. Therefore, I have made no attempt to consciously isolate particular beliefs, customs, or superstitions to old world influences, although these influences do exist quite noticeably in a few counties, especially where Swedish, German, German-Russian, and Czech heritages are predominant.

This book is the result of a careful statewide survey of folk beliefs, customs, and superstitions as told to college students, acting generally on volunteer assignments. These students, who were enrolled in folk-loric and folk-life classes at Kansas State University, in Manhattan, and Fort Hays, Kansas, State College, in Hays, completed over seventeen thousand 3 x 5 "informational" cards, which form the basis for these listings, gathered mostly during the years 1956 through 1963. Vacation times such as Christmas, Thanksgiving, and Easter provided the students with the opportunities to reach people living in the 105 counties in the state. More often than not the student collectors were residents of the county in which they searched for the folk knowledge of their relatives, neighbors, and acquaintances.

The impetus for this collection arose during my formal academic study of Comparative Folklore at Indiana University, 1952-54. My teachers, Dr. Stith Thompson and Dr. Warren Roberts, who were not especially interested in this type of lore then, stressed that surveys and studies of this kind were needed in the light of an America that was rapidly changing from rural to urban.

The complexity of coping with this need, as far as actual collecting in the field was concerned, lessened when I realized that literally everyone has at least a dozen folk beliefs or has direct knowledge of customs in his immediate consciousness and that these are usually expressed in one sentence. I was not then interested in searching for informants with lots of special knowledge; they are the exceptions! Rank-and-file people were my interest! In a collection of this kind, in which some statistical considerations are included, this is obviously important for reliability of diffusion and for frequency of duplication of the particular items submitted.

My teachers at Indiana University referred me to Dr. Wayland D. Hand, of UCLA, who was then editing the volumes on this subject for Frank C. Brown's North Carolina collection, which appeared from 1961 to 1964. This scholar became my advisor and friend, and I thank him most heartily; for without his encouragement and aid on this subject, I doubt that I would have spent so many years pursuing it.

In 1958 I acquired a copy of Ray B. Browne's *Popular Beliefs and Practices from Alabama* (Berkeley and Los Angeles: University of California Press, 1958). This collection stirred me to reach my goal of collecting at least one hundred beliefs from each of the 105 counties in Kansas. In about 1960 Professor S. J. Sackett of Hays, Kansas, agreed to assist in directing further collecting by students in the far-western part of the state.

In 1965, when the collecting project had been completed, the challenge of utilizing modern automation methods and techniques to handle the problems of sorting and arranging for a convenient print-out arose.

This challenge was intriguing but theoretical at best. Dr. Sackett arranged a coding system and spent considerable time and effort in coding and having IBM cards cut. Unfortunately, for purposes of publication, Dr. Sackett's endeavor presented too many problems and obstacles. So, beginning in the spring of 1977, I struggled to arrange the collection into a more traditional approach. This explains the time lag between the end of the field-collecting project and this publication.

The complete collection, amounting to twelve cases of 3 x 5 file cards and several boxes of IBM cards, is now stored in "The William E. Koch Folklore Collection" at the Kansas State Historical Society Library in Topeka, Kansas. The information written on these specially prepared 3 x 5 collectors' slips includes the folklore item itself and arrangement for three classifications: primary, secondary, and tertiary. The primary classification had to fall under one of twenty listed subject areas, which were included in small print on the slip itself. Information provided on the other side of this slip consisted of the contributor's name, age, current address, birthplace, number of years on a farm or ranch, and, if he remembered, from whom this particular item was learned. Most people did not remember this last bit of information, but it was apparent in this collection that the mother was the main source. The contributor was also asked where his paternal grandfather and grandmother were born. The collector's name, home address, and the date that the item was recorded were also entered on these slips. Fortunately, over two thousand people of all ages and from all counties contributed. Forty years was the average age of the contributors, 70 percent of whom were women, 30 percent men. About 50 percent had spent all or part of their lives on farms or ranches.

The 450 or so collectors did their work efficiently and accurately. To keep the statewide collection project in balance, it was necessary to maintain careful tabulations county by county. In spite of this, a few counties soon exceeded the desired goals. Since my classes in "American Folklore and Folkliterature" at Kansas State average over one hundred students per semester, including summer school, there was no problem in utilizing volunteer collectors. These student collectors were trained in the technique of collecting this type of folklore. I wanted only what would come quite spontaneously from our contributors. No "bleeding," as they say; just what came naturally and quickly.

Names of the contributors are listed at the end of this volume. Their identification with the numbered folklore items in the text is merely by sex, age, whether rural or not, and the year in which the item was collected. For example, F, 74, R, 1961, means that this item is from a seventy-four-year-old farm lady, who gave the information in

1961. If more than one individual gave exactly the same item, then the youngest contributor is recorded, as above, and the additional contributors are noted by sex only. For example, F, 20, 1961, + 12 F and 5 M means that 18 identical items came from a female who was twenty years old in 1961 and did not live on a farm and from 12 more females and 5 males, all of whom were more than twenty years of age. The decision not to list after each particular item the names of individuals who contributed it was arbitrary.

Identifying an individual item of folklore specifically as a "belief," a "custom," or a "superstition" depends on several variable factors and was not considered in preparing this book. Justification for such classification, unless the item is patently one of the three, depends a great deal on the individual. What is a superstition to one person may not be a superstition to another person. Behavioral patterns and individual beliefs, which are often entrenched in early life, are complex indeed. To the folklorist, a prime requisite is that the items have lived in oral tradition. Truth, validity, and even psychological implications are obviously important, but the folklorist must be detached from these aspects, or he is likely to give up his concern for the "force of oral tradition" and be concerned too much with patterns that are not actually folkloristic.

Broadly speaking, the overall function of folk beliefs and superstitions is to assist in overcoming physical and psychological hazards. More specifically, they can be listed functionally as providing a set of rules to keep one from harm, providing a set of rules to assist one in having good luck, providing a set of rules to assist one in making prophecies, and providing a pseudo-scientific rationale for attempting to understand life and nature. Additionally, there is much concern for corrective action after the fact and for the power that "thinking" gives. Recommended actions are traditionally quite voluntary, as opposed to the involuntary treatment of the professional.

Folk customs—which are sometimes termed "mores"—are important in the traditions of all peoples and are concerned very much with the social, both calendric and noncalendric. Some are rites of passage; some are of the ethnic; some are occupationally related. Most Kansas communities revere the customs of pioneer settlers in that they add to the understanding of that life and assist in maintaining historical and family heritages.

It is surprising that nearly 50 percent of the items in this collection of over five thousand are concerned with the general categories of health, weather, and luck. As far as the cures for illnesses and injuries are concerned, one can say only, without going into detail, that the strategies involved range all the way from the psychosomatic to the ancient primitive. The folklore of weather lives on and is a very important part of the American heritage, with the wind, the sky, and animals aiding in prognostications. It should be mentioned that weather specialists generally have respect for rural folk who will pinpoint the weather after a sniff of the breeze and a look at the sky.

Neither the Alabama nor the North Carolina collections, mentioned above, treat luck in separate chapters. In our collection it was mandatory to do so, because there are 730 separate items, 87 of which had a frequency of five or more duplications. This fact, and the range of thirty subject classifications, indicates that luck enjoys a deeply rooted knowledge and that it has influence on human thought and action. Attribution of success or failure to luck rather than to ability or hard work is apparently not an indifferent state of affairs in Mid-America.

A great many people have assisted me with this book, either as contributors or collectors, and I acknowledge their help most gratefully. The more than 2,800 people who are listed in the back of this book are those who generously offered their knowledge and supportive help in the initial fieldwork.

Other individuals who were involved deserve special mention and credit for aid and encouragement: Dr. Richard McGhee, head of the English Department; Dr. Robert Kruh, dean of the Graduate School and chairman of the Bureau of General Research Committee; and Dr. Mike Finnegan—all of Kansas State University, Manhattan; and Dr. Paul Gatschet of Fort Hays, Kansas, State College.

Special assistance with some knotty problems was given by Lynn Hoyt and Dave Albracht, students. Other students who were especially helpful through these years include Jane Koefod, Dixie Des Jardins, Pat Sawyer, Mina Jones, Jean Koernet, Virginia Haun, Ann Cook, and Emily Hinkhouse. Typists Gail Leis, Joni Berry, Cheryl Burleson, and Karen Caffrey deserve many thanks.

Although I have mentioned them before, I must again acknowledge the help of Dr. Wayland D. Hand of the Center for the Study of Comparative Folklore and Mythology, University of California, Los Angeles; and Dr. Sam Sackett, formerly a member of the English Department of Fort Hays, Kansas, State College.

Courtship and Marriage

CUSTOMS AND BELIEFS WITH REGARD TO COURTSHIP AND marriage depend primarily upon the particular society in which the people live. Social sanctions within the society rely on a succession of factors, ranging all the way from the religious, the economic, and the legal to a host of particular national and local traditions. Some of these traditions seem absurd and silly and no doubt are partly for fun. Yet implicit belief is the case for many of these traditions, and in effect, they are testimonials. It is important, however, to note that in whatever society these courtship preliminaries and marriage ceremonies are held, they are universally geared to the idea that the process is intended to mean persistence with "This right one" throughout the entire duration of their joint lives. Social norms are strictly monogamous in these times, and the courtly love traditions of the middle ages are necessarily long gone.

Our St. Valentines Day, Mother's Day, and Father's Day are folksy, festivallike days, which are intended to remind everyone again that love in all its ramifications is to be tenderly observed by everyone from third graders to octogenarians. One community used, as its 1977 Harvest Festival theme, "Love and Marriage." On that occasion at Cuba, Kansas, which has a population of three hundred, over five thousand people gathered to view Cupid floats, to honor all couples who had celebrated fifty or more years of marriage, and to celebrate generally in other activities such as a horse show, tractor pulls, and an icecream social.

Some favorite taboos on the courtship and marriage procedures are: "Don't sing at the table, or sit on the table" and "Don't eat the last bit of food from a plate" (or you'll be an old maid). Also: "Don't be married in green (brown, yellow, red, or black)" and "Don't be a bridesmaid very often." If one can predict the weather, avoid rain.

On the positive side, we have: "Red and yellow will catch a fellow" and "Making a neat bed foretells a handsome husband." Good luck and happiness may be assisted by wearing a penny in the shoe before marriage and, at the wedding, by wearing "Something old, / Something new, / Something borrowed, / Something blue." The latter is probably one of the most forceful wedding-dress traditions in America.

Dress for the bridegroom, unless he is of the affluent elite, has traditionally been a good quality, contemporary styled dark suit. In earlier days, the wedding suit might also be the coffin suit. Since World War II, men's apparel for weddings has taken a surprising turn. Today, even those from very humble circumstances often get married in outlandishly styled rented suits of various colors. Ruffled shirts, massive bow ties, and patent-leather shoes of late design are all included in this rental process. Conceived by creative entrepreneurs in the big city for their folk, it supplies a surprising bit of dash for the usually conservative Midwestener.

Where population is sparse and the towns small, there are certain groups that have kept alive the traditional "chivaree" and "wedding dance," the purpose of which may be to raise some extra cash for the newlyweds. But the routine of old shoes and rice and decorated getaway cars with pebbles in the hubcaps is sustained everywhere. The dictates of Emily Post have been cast aside, or she has never been heard of: "Who is this Post woman?" asked the young rancher.

The coding beneath individual items is to be interpreted thus: F = female; M = male; R = rural. The age of the youngest contributor and the year in which the item was collected are also indicated; additional contributors are noted by sex only.

CATCHING A SWEETHEART

1   If you wear red and yellow, you will catch a fellow.
      (F, 21, 1950, + 13 F and 3 M)

2   If a maiden will pray to Saint Barbara on December 4, she will have a lover.
      (F, 50, 1961)

3   If you get an ash an inch long on your cigarette, you can have any girl in town.
      (M, 20, R, 1960)

4   When you see the first star in the evening, say the name of the one you love and then say this rhyme: "Star, star, shining star, / All flowing in a stream. / If you love me like I love you, / I'll meet you in a dream."
      (F, 69, R, 1962)

5   When a girl is sitting on a table, she is looking for a husband.
    (M, 70, 1959)

6   When a family has a single daughter of marriageable age, it paints its gate blue to show that she is available.
    (M, 50, R, 1959)

7   A girl for whom a fire burns well will get a good husband.
    (F, 59, R, 1957)

8   If you break a needle while sewing on a garment, the owner of the garment will have a new love before the garment is worn out.
    (F, 20, R, 1958)

9   If you can tie a lover's vine, you'll get the girl you want.
    (M, 74, 1959)

10   If you find a red ear while you are shucking corn, kiss any girl you desire.
    (M, 22, R, 1959, + 2 F)

11   If you put a stamp on an envelope upside down, this means you are saying "I love you" to the recipient.
    (F, 20, 1957, + 1 F)

12   If you kiss the turned-up hem of your dress, you'll get a new sweetheart.
    (F, 60, R, 1960)

13   If the hem of a woman's skirt is turned up and she kisses it, she will see her boyfriend before night.
    (F, 20, 1960, + 1 F)

14   If the hem is turned up on your skirt or dress, the next person you see will be your true love.
    (F, 29, R, 1958, + 2 F)

15   If the edge of a lady's dress is turned up and she does not turn it down, but shakes it down, she is sure to catch a beau.
    (F, 80, R, 1959)

16   If part of the hem on your dress is turned up, be sure to kiss it; otherwise someone will steal your boyfriend.
    (F, 54, 1959)

17   If the hem of your dress is turned up, it means that you have a boyfriend. You should say his name and turn the hem down.
    (F, 50, 1959)

18   Make a good bed, and you will get a handsome husband.
    (F, 42, R, 1958)

19   Make an untidy bed, and you will marry a lazy man.
    (F, 81, 1959)

20   Count ninety-nine white horses and three white mules. When you have this total, the next boy you meet will be your intended.
(F, 40, 1957)

21   When on a trip, stamp all the white horses you see. When you have stamped one hundred, shut your eyes. Then open your eyes and note the first color you see. The first man you see wearing a necktie of that color will be your husband-to-be.
(F, 60, 1959)

22   After you have seen one hundred white horses, you will marry the next man you see.
(F, 20, R, 1958, + 1 F)

23   Count white horses until you reach fifty; if you see a white mule, count it ten. When you have reached fifty, if you see a red-headed girl, you will marry the next person of the opposite sex that you meet.
(F, 70, 1958)

24   If you see three convertibiles, you will marry the first red-headed girl you see.
(F, 19, 1957)

25   Count one hundred red convertibles; after that, the first man you see will be your husband.
(F, 20, 1959, + 3 F)

26   If you get the big piece of the wishbone and hang it over the kitchen door, you will marry the first man to walk in.
(F, 18, 1955, + 3 F)

27   When breaking the breastbone of a chicken, the person who gets the smallest half will marry first.
(M, 30, R, 1959, + 1 M)

28   If a girl hangs a wishbone over her door, the first gentleman to enter will be her husband.
(F, 30, R, 1962, + 3 F and 4 M)

29   Tall women make good lovers.
(M, 1950)

30   If your shoestring comes loose, your sweetheart is thinking about you.
(M, 80, 1959)

31   Girls at home often say this on straws: "He loves me; he don't; he'll date me; he won't; he would if he could; he could if he would; he will; he won't." This series will end at a different place each time and will predict the future.
(F, 19, 1958)

32 Take a soda straw. Using the thumb and forefinger of one hand, then the other, start squeezing at the bottom of the straw. Do this alternately until you reach the top of the straw, saying, "Date, call, letter, kiss." Then do the same thing to determine on which day you will get whatever you ended with, saying, "Sunday, Monday," and so forth.
(M, 20, 1957)

33 Take a straw; and using your hands alternately, go down the straw, saying: "He loves me; he loves me not." Whichever one you are saying when you reach the end of the straw indicates the feelings that your lover has for you.
(F, 21, 1957, + 1 F)

34 If an older sister is still single when a younger one gets married, the older girl should go dance in a hog trough on her sister's wedding day to ensure that she will have a wedding someday.
(F, 40, R, 1957, + 1 F)

35 If you can peel your apple without breaking the peeling, the first girl you speak to will be your sweetheart. (The contributor's grandfather told this to her many years ago. The young people who worked in a jewelry factory used to try to peel their apples during lunch without having the peeling break so that they could get a sweetheart.)
(F, 50, R, 1957)

36 If you peel an apple at one peeling, you may kiss the first girl that smiles at you.
(F, 20, 1958)

37 If a girl wants to find out if a boy loves her, she should pull off the petals of a daisy one by one, saying: "He loves me; he loves me not." If the last one is "He loves me," he loves her; if it is "He loves me not," he does not love her.
(F, 21, R, 1957, + 7 F and 2 M)

38 If one picks the petals off a flower, saying alternately, "She loves me; she loves me not," the last petal will tell whether she really does or not.
(F, 21, R, 1958, + 3 F and 2 M)

39 Sunflower Petal Rhyme (use a sunflower):
   One, I love; two, I love;
   Three, I love, I say;
   Four, I love with all my heart;
   Five, I cast away.
   Six, he loves;

Seven, she loves;
Eight, they both love.
Nine, he comes;
Ten, he tarries;
Eleven, he courts;
Twelve, they marry.
(F, 60, R, 1962, + 1 F)

40   Stub your toe, kiss your thumb, turn around, and you'll see your boyfriend before day is done.
(F, 44, R, 1957, + 5 F and 1 M)

41   When I my true love want to see, I put my shoes in the shape of a T.
(F, 20, R, 1957, + 1 F)

42   If you swallow a raw chicken heart, you will marry the next person that you shake hands with.
(M, 17, R, 1959)

43   The number of kinks that a girls' strand of hair shows when drawn between her fingernails indicates how many boyfriends she has.
(F, 21, R, 1958)

44   If a fellow sees a car coming with only one light and says "padiddle," he may kiss his girl. If she sees it first and says "padiddle," she may slap the boy.
(F, 19, 1959, + 4 F)

45   If you see a car coming at you that has only one light functioning, you may kiss the driver if of the opposite sex.
(F, 20, 1958, + 4 F and 1 M)

46   If you see a rabbit while you are driving a car, you may kiss the driver.
(F, 20, 1958, + 1 F and 1 M)

47   If the first glimpse of a new moon is over the left shoulder, it is favorable to love. If seen over the right shoulder, it means disappointment in love.
(F, 70, R, 1958)

48   Counting the white places or spots in your fingernails will tell you how many boyfriends you will have.
(F, 40, R, 1963)

49   Where cobwebs grow, boys won't go.
(F, 40, R, 1962, + 1 F)

50   Opposite likes and interests attract people to one another.
(F, 20, 1957, + 1 F)

51 People who are born in April are most attractive to the opposite sex.
   (F, 53, 1959)

52 If the nerve in your eye twitches, you will get a letter from
your boyfriend.
   (F, 1962)

53 When a girl sticks her tongue out at a boy, she wants to be
kissed.
   (F, 27, 1957)

CHARACTERISTICS OF ONE'S FUTURE SWEETHEART
OR SPOUSE

54 Don't iron the tail of a shirt; for if you do, you'll marry a
drunkard.
   (F, 18, 1962)

55 People used to say that if a woman washing on a washboard
got her belly wet, she would marry a drunkard.
   (F, 59, 1959, + 1 F)

56 If a young girl splashes dishpan water on the floor, she'll
marry a drunkard.
   (F, 14, R, 1959)

57 One contributor's mother used to tell her that she was going
to marry a drunkard when she stood so close to the dishpan
while washing dishes that she got her dress or apron wet.
   (F, 60, R, 1962, + 1 F and 1 M)

58 Don't swig at the table, or you'll marry a drunkard.
   (F, 19, R, 1958)

59 If you eat in the bathroom, you will marry a tramp.
   (F, 50, R, 1957)

60 If you have a white string hanging on you, you will marry a
widower.
   (F, 23, R, 1963)

61 Sit on a table, and you'll marry a crazy man.
   (F, 50, R, 1963)

62 Pull petals off flowers to see if you'll be married in silk, satin,
calico, or rags.
   (F, 40, R, 1963)

63 If you want to discover what type of man you will marry, start
at the top of your shirt with the top button, and go down,
touching each button and saying, "Richman, poor man, beg-

gar man, thief, doctor, lawyer, merchant, chief." The one that you are saying when you touch the last button will indicate the type of person you will marry.

    (F, 30, R, 1959, + 5 F)

64   To decide what profession one's future husband would follow, people used to pull petals from a flower, saying, "Rich man, poor man, beggar man, thief, doctor, lawyer, merchant, chief." This sequence was repeated until all the petals were gone. The last one determined the facts.

    (F, 62, 1957, + 2 F)

65   If you sing at the table, you will marry a crazy fellow.

    (F, 19, R, 1957, + 2 F and 3 M)

66   If you sing at the table, you'll have a dumb husband.

    (F, 20, 1962, + 1 F)

67   If your nose itches, your boyfriend is coming.

    (F, 19, R, 1959, + 1 F)

68   If your nose itches, you're going to kiss a fool.

    (F, 22, 1959)

69   If your nose itches, you are going to get married.

    (M, 45, R, 1958)

70   If your ear itches, you have a secret lover.

    (F, 20, R, 1963)

71   Green eyes—grand lover; brown eyes—sweet and gentle.

    (M, 21, 1950)

IDENTIFYING ONE'S FUTURE SWEETHEART

72   In the olden days, when beds had four tall corner posts, a girl would give each post the name of a boy before going to bed; the one that she looked at first in the morning would be her future husband.

    (F, 50, 1959, + 2 F)

73   The first night that you sleep in a strange bedroom, give each corner a different boy's name, and the first corner that you look at in the morning will tell you the name of the boy you will marry someday.

    (F, 1957, + 2 F)

74   Sleep on a piece of wedding cake, cut it in seven pieces, put the names of seven boys on the pieces, draw one each morning, and the one that you draw on the last day will tell you the name of your husband.

    (F, 75, R, 1957)

75   A girl should have someone secretly name the three corners
of a piece of pie for her favorite swains. The corner that she
eats last will bear the name of her future husband.
(F, 50, 1962, + 4 F)

76   On a stone, place one apple seed for each suitor. The one that
pops first will indicate whom you will marry.
(F, 58, 1958)

77   As you look over your left shoulder, say: "New moon, new
moon, tell me true the very color of my true love's hair."
(M, 65, R, 1959)

78   Turn over a rock in order to find out the color of your lover's
hair.
(F, 70, R, 1959)

79   Take three steps forward, turn on your heel, and look in the
footprint that you have left; if you find a hair, it will be the
color of the hair that your husband will have.
(F, 20, R, 1959)

80   If you look through a silk scarf at the full moon, you will see
your lover's face.
(F, 19, R, 1956)

81   To find out about your prospects for marriage, recite:
New moon, true moon, happy may I be;
Let me tonight my true love see.
If I shall marry near; let me hear a bird cry.
If I shall marry far; let me hear a cow low;
If I shall never, never, marry at all,
Let me hear a hammer blow.
(F, 60, R, 1962)

82   After you have turned one hundred rings on the fingers of one
hundred different people, the next boy who speaks to you will
be your future husband.
(F, 21, 1957)

83   If you see a strange man three times in a row, you will marry
him.
(F, 20, R, 1958)

84   If a handkerchief is placed where the dew can fall on it on the
morning of the first day in May, the name of the person you
are going to marry will appear on the handkerchief.
(F, 77, R, 1961)

85   Boil an egg, fill the space of the yoke with salt, and go to bed.
Whoever you dream about will be your spouse.
(F, 82, R, 1959)

86   If an unmarried person throws a shoe over his left shoulder,
his lover will come from the direction in which the shoe
points.
(F, 50, 1961)

87   If a girl sits before the mirror with a lighted candle beside it
at midnight on Halloween, she will see the face of her future
bridegroom in the mirror.
(F, 60, 1959)

88   On Halloween, hold a mirror over your head, and look into a
well. Your future mate's picture will be reflected in the mirror.
(F, 70, R, 1957)

89   At high noon on a sunshiny New Year's Day, take a looking-
glass to an open water well, turn your back to the well, hold
the glass so that you can see the bottom of the well, and you
will see your future companion's face.
(F, 60, 1959)

90   If you look into a mirror at midnight on New Year's Eve, you
will see the face of the man that you will marry.
(F, 76, 1957)

91   If you count seven stars each night for seven nights in a row,
you'll dream of the man you're going to marry.
(F, 26, 1958)

92   Count nine stars for nine consecutive nights, and on the ninth
night, you will dream of the person you are to marry. But if it
rains before you finish counting, you will have to start over.
(F, 20, R, 1959)

93   A girl will marry the first man that she sees on May Day
morning.
(F, 50, 1958)

94   Look into a mirror at midnight on May 1, and you will see in
the mirror the man you will marry.
(M, 65, R, 1956)

95   If you look down a well at noon on May Day, you will see the
image of your future husband.
(F, 60, R, 1958)

96   If you find a four-leaf clover, put it in your shoe, put the shoe
back on, and the first boy you meet will be your future husband.
(F, 45, 1957, + 1 F)

97   Strike a match, then blow it out; the direction in which the

smoke blows will indicate the direction in which your true love lives.

(F, 40, 1957)

98   Hold a burning match to determine the direction in which your lover lives. As the flame burns out, the charred head will point in that direction.

(M, 40, R, 1962, + 4 F and 2 M)

99   If you drop a spoon, your love will come soon.

(F, 20, 1958)

100   When you drop a knife, it will fall so as to indicate the direction from which the man that you will marry will come.

(F, 20, R, 1959)

101   If a girl drops a knife while she is eating, her boyfriend will come to see her from the direction in which the knife points.

(F, 40, 1957)

102   If an unmarried person drops a fork at the table, its points will indicate the direction to go in order to find his or her future mate.

(M, 62, R, 1958)

103   One contributor reported that when he was a boy on the farm, there was a girl in his neighborhood who was in love with two boys. Both had proposed to her. One of the boys, Sam, lived east of her house. The other boy lived west of her house. She did not know which one of the two she really wanted to marry. To decide the matter, she took a broom out to the road in front of her house, stood it up on its brush end, and then let loose of it. It fell over toward Sam's house, and the girl ran back to the house shouting, "I'll take Sam." And she married him.

(M, 60, R, 1960)

104   If you find a straight pin, the head will point in the direction where your boyfriend lives.

(F, 40, R, 1961, + 1 M)

105   After you drink a soda, take your straw and pinch it in alternate directions. Then go down it, saying "A, B, C," etc. The last letter that you come to will be the first letter of your last name after you are married.

(F, 19, R, 1962)

106   One can foretell the initial of the person whom he or she will marry by twisting an apple stem and starting to say the ABC's. The letter that one is saying when the stem breaks will be the initial of the intended.

(F, 20, R, 1959, + 8 F and 3 M)

107   Throw apple peelings over your left shoulder; the letter that they form as they land will be the initial of the person you are going to marry.
  (F, 20, R, 1959, + 25 F and 2 M)

108   Cut the letters of the alphabet out of the newspaper, put them in a pan of water face down, go to bed, the letters that have turned over by morning will be the initials of your future marriage partner.
  (F, 82, R, 1959)

109   Wash a handkerchief, and hang it on the line on April 30; on May 1 it will have the initials of the man you are to marry.
  (F, 19, R, 1959)

110   If the hem of your dress is turned up, you will soon have a beau. If you take hold of your dress about hip high and gently shake the fold out while saying the alphabet, the letter on which the fold falls out will be the initial of your beau.
  (F, 50, 1959)

111   As you pull out each grey hair, say the alphabet—the letter that you end with will be the first letter of the name of the man you will marry.
  (F, 70, R, 1960)

112   You can find the initials of your future husband in a spider web.
  (F, 80, R, 1960)

113   Twirl a lover's knot (flower) around your shoulder three times; then let it fall over your shoulder. It will form the initial of your future husband.
  (F, 35, 1958)

114   To find the initial of one's future spouse, one should count the seeds in an apple. The number will correspond with the correct letter of the alphabet.
  (F, 56, R, 1963, + 1 F)

115   If you walk backwards down the cellar stairs on Halloween while looking into a mirror, the first face that you see reflected will be the face of the person you will marry.
  (F, 69, R, 1958)

116   If you go down the cellar steps backwards, you will marry the next person you see.
  (F, 23, 1956)

117   If you eat a thimbleful of salt before going to bed at night, you will dream about your true love giving you a drink of water.
  (F, 50, 1958, + 2 F)

118   Sleep with a piece of wedding cake under your pillow, and you will dream about the man you are to marry.
       (F, 20, 1959, + 2 F and 3 M)

119   To find out who your true love will be, say:
       New moon, true moon, come unto me.
       Tell me who my true love shall be.
       Right to me—sure to be.
       Left to me—soon to be.
       Back to me—never to be.
       (F, 35, 1956)

120   After a man has buried his first wife, the first woman whose eyes meet with his will be his second wife.
       (F, 44, R, 1956)

KEEPING ONE'S SWEETHEART; BREAKUPS; AND QUARRELS

121   Raise your feet up when you cross a railroad track in a car; otherwise you'll lose your girlfriend or boyfriend.
       (F, 17, R, 1959, + 4 F and 2 M)

122   A woman should never remove her engagement or wedding ring, because this might cause trouble with her fiancé or husband.
       (F, 20, 1965)

123   If two people who are walking become separated by an object, it will cut their love in two unless they quickly say "Bread and Butter."
       (F, 20, 1957, + 1 F)

124   A woman is for sale if she is on the street side when walking with a man.
       (F, 40, R, 1957, + 2 M)

125   If you sing while you are single, you will cry after you are married.
       (F, 70, R, 1959)

126   If you cry during the year before your wedding, you should never need to cry again.
       (F, 15, R, 1958)

127   If you wear blue and white, you'll hold your fellow tight.
       (F, 54, 1959)

128   If you can light a kitchen match and hold it until it is

completely burned all the way down the matchstick, your fellow is true to you.
(F, 47, 1958)

129   Stepping on a manhole will cause one to lose one's boyfriend.
(F, 20, 1961, + 1 F)

130   If your girlfriend's skirt hem is turned up and you turn it down for her, you're going to steal her boyfriend.
(F, 20, 1958, + 1 F)

131   If you sit on the table when talking to your boyfriend, you will never marry him.
(F, 19, R, 1956)

132   If you have a pearl engagement ring, your marriage won't last.
(F, 19, 1959)

133   Give your love a new penny on New Years; it will keep him or her happy throughout the year.
(F, 21, 1957)

134   You should never loan pens to your girlfriends or boyfriends, because if you do, you'll lose them (that is, you'll lose your friend, not the pen).
(F, 1963)

135   Lovers are inclined to quarrel when there is a full moon.
(M, 20, 1957)

SIGNS OF ROMANCE;
PROPOSALS; AND WEDDINGS

136   This may be superstition's aftermath,
But the old wives told me this.
If a redbird flies across your path,
Your lover will bring you a kiss.
(F, 1960)

137   A redbird to your right; you'll see your lover before night.
(F, 28, 1958)

138   To determine what the future holds for a couple, write the girl's full name, write the boy's full name, then cancel out all the letters that are the same. On the remaining letters say, "Hate, love, friendship, courtship, marriage."
(F, 40, R, 1962, + 2 F)

139   If you sit on the table, you will marry before you are able.
(F, 19, R, 1957, + 5 F and 3 M)

140 If you sing at the table, you will get married before you're able.
   (M, 60, R, 1959, + 1 F)

141 If a girl sings at the table, she is sure to marry soon.
   (M, 63, R, 1963)

142 If you sneeze in the morning, you will see your sweetheart before night.
   (F, 70, R, 1962)

143 If you whistle at the table, you'll marry before you're able.
   (F, 20, R, 1963)

144 If you spill salt on the table, you'll marry before you're able.
   (F, 75, R, 1956)

145 You'll get married tonight if the new moon shines over your shoulder in a water trough.
   (M, 45, 1958)

146 Friday, being Venus's day, is the best day for proposals and marriage.
   (F, 40, R, 1961)

147 If a girl's engagement ring sparkles, the girl is happy.
   (F, 22, 1954, + 1 F)

148 If a young man raps on the door while a lady is sweeping her house, she should say, "You'll soon get married."
   (M, 69, R, 1956)

149 If a boy gives a girl white heather, he is proposing (white heather is very rare and is found only high up on the mountains).
   (F, 50, 1957)

150 If two people see two falling stars at the same time, they are going to marry.
   (F, 20, R, 1956)

151 If you see a shooting star, you will be kissed.
   (F, 70, R, 1962)

152 If you see a ring around the moon, you'll soon marry.
   (F, 20, 1958).

153 If someone falls upstairs, there will be a wedding.
   (M, 56, 1958)

154 If a person at a table receives two dishes of food from opposite directions, he will marry soon.
   (F, 81, 1955, + 1 F)

155 You will be married soon if you meet a friend who does not recognize you.
   (M, 84, R, 1956)

156   You will be married as many times as you miss when trying to blow out a coal-oil lamp.
(F, 68, 1954)

157   When you receive roses, a bud is a sign of affection, a half-open bud is a sign of love, and a full-blown flower is an open proposal of marriage.
(M, 22, 1955)

158   A gift of red roses is a declaration of love.
(F, 35, 1956)

159   If someone mistakenly places two knives, two forks, or two spoons at a place setting, there will soon be a wedding.
(F, 50, R, 1957)

160   Finding a red ear while husking corn foretells a lover.
(F, 77, R, 1965)

161   If you find a red ear while shucking corn, you will be married soon.
(F, 80, R, 1960)

162   A sure sign of an approaching wedding is the incidence of four people shaking hands with the two pairs of hands crossed.
(M, 1962, + 1 F)

163   If two people reach for food at the table and happen to cross hands, there will be a wedding in the family.
(F, 62, R, 1962, + 1 F)

164   If you bump heads, you are supposed to sleep together.
(F, 21, R, 1956, + 6 F)

165   If two people dry their hands on the same towel, they'll be sleeping together within the year.
(F, 30, 1959)

166   When you want to get married, pull petals off a flower, saying, "This year, next year, now, or never."
(F, 40, R, 1963, + 1 F)

167   "In February, birds do mate; / You may wed or mourn your fate."
(F, 53, 1959)

168   A penny in your shoe means that you don't date. A nickel means that you date some. A dime means that you are going steady. A quarter means that you are engaged to be married.
(M, 22, R, 1963)

169   When a girl laces her tennis shoes or other laced shoes from top to bottom, it signifies that she is going steady.
(F, 20, 1962)

170   If you see a face in the moon, you're in love.
       (F, 20, 1962)
171   A few years ago, girls used to wear identification bracelets on their left legs to indicate that they were going steady; on their right to indicate that they were not going steady.
       (F, 20, 1957)
172   If you drop your dishcloth, your sweetheart is coming.
       (F, 50, R, 1958, + 1 F)
173   "Make a rhyme; I'll bet a dime / I'll see my sweetheart before bedtime."
       (F, 60, R, 1962)
174   When you see a star fall, someone in your family is going to get married.
       (F, 23, 1950)
175   If you are ticklish, you have a boyfriend.
       (F, 20, R, 1957, + 1 F)
176   When one tickles the palm of the hand of another person of the opposite sex with one's finger, it is a sign of passion and of sexual desire for that person.
       (F, 1962)
177   If you drop a spoon, you are going to get a kiss.
       (F, 23, 1954)

SPINSTERHOOD AND BACHELORHOOD

178   As long as the wedding dress is in the family, the daughter will not get married.
       (F, 50, 1961)
179   If you don't touch glass when going over railroad tracks, you'll lose your boyfriend.
       (F, 16, R, 1967)
180   If you wear a lilac on any day except May Day, you will never marry.
       (F, 96, R, 1954)
181   If you upset a chair, you won't get married for a year.
       (F, 75, R, 1956)
182   The third person to light a cigarette on one match will die an old maid.
       (F, 19, 1960)
183   If you touch a baby kitten before its eyes are open, you will be an old maid or a bachelor.
       (F, 85, R, 1960)

184   If you eat the unpopped kernels in a dish of popcorn, you'll never marry.
 (M, 49, 1958)

185   You'll never get married if you boil water in a teakettle with the spout turned toward the wall.
 (F, 19, R, 1956)

186   If a young girl sasses her grandma, she will be an old maid.
 (M, 62, R, 1959)

187   If a young girl watches a chicken die, she will be an old maid.
 (M, 62, R, 1959)

188   If you fall up the stairs, you'll never get married.
 (F, 67, 1967)

189   If you fall out of bed on your face, you'll never be married. If you fall on your back, you'll marry someone who is very handsome or pretty.
 (M, 45, R, 1959)

190   If you don't marry by the same age that your mother married, you'll be an old maid.
 (F, 50, 1960)

191   You will never marry if you sweep a broom to only one side as you use it.
 (F, 70, R, 1959)

192   If you put anything with butterflies on it in your hope chest, you will be an old maid.
 (F, 1959)

193   If the moon shines through your window at night and onto your bed, you'll never marry.
 (F, 20, R, 1960)

194   Sit on a table, and you'll be an old maid.
 (F, 21, 1950)

195   Young girls ruin their chances for marriage if they scrape the breadboard.
 (F, 50, R, 1957)

196   A girl who drops a dishrag will be an old maid.
 (F, 72, R, 1958)

197   If you drop a knife or fork, you will never marry.
 (F, 84, 1958)

198   If you try on an engagement ring before you are engaged, you will never become engaged.
 (F, 46, R, 1958)

199   You will never marry if you try on anyone else's engagement ring.
 (F, 20, 1959)

200 If you sweep under a bed while someone is lying on it, that person will never get married.
    (F, 21, 1956)

201 If someone sweeps under your chair, you won't get married.
    (F, 21, 1958, + 1 F)

202 If you sweep under someone's feet, he'll never get married.
    (M, 30, R, 1954, + 2 F and 1 M)

203 If you upset a chair, there will be no marriages in that household for one year.
    (M, 70, R, 1959)

204 She who takes the last bit of food from a plate will be an old maid.
    (F, 20, R, 1957, + 7 F and 2 M)

205 Hold up your feet when going under a viaduct, or you will be an old maid.
    (F, 20, 1959)

206 You will be an old maid if you don't pick up your feet when crossing a county line.
    (F, 56, 1952)

BRIDESMAIDS AND THE BRIDE'S BOUQUET

207 The single girl who catches the bride's bouquet will be the next to marry.
    (F, 20, R, 1957, + 23 F and 1 M)

208 Whoever catches the bride's bouquet will marry within the next year.
    (F, 20, 1957, + 2 F)

209 Three times a bridesmaid; never a bride.
    (F, 19, R, 1956, + 7 F)

210 Often a bridesmaid; never a bride.
    (F, 50, 1958, + 4 F)

211 Always a bridesmaid; never a bride.
    (F, 40, R, 1959, + 1 F)

212 If a girl serves as a bridesmaid seven times, she will never find a husband.
    (F, 70, R, 1959)

213 A boy and his girlfriend should never both be in someone else's wedding together, because if the boy should be, for example, the best man and the girl should be the maid of honor, they themselves will never marry.

(F, 20, 1963 [learned from one of her neighbors, a lady who had come from Germany])

214   The pins used about the wedding toilet should all be thrown away; if the bridesmaid keeps them, she will not marry before Whitsuntide.

(F, 75, 1962)

GIFTS, RICE, AND CAKE

215   Rice thrown at newlyweds will ensure their fertility.

(F, 50, R, 1959)

216   The throwing of rice signifies that the newlyweds will have many material goods in the future.

(F, 21, 1955, + 1 F)

217   After a wedding, throw rice on the newlyweds to wish them well in their married life.

(F, 23, 1957, + 4 F and 2 M)

218   Don't give sharp instruments for a wedding present; for if you do, you will sever your friendship with the couple.

(F, 70, 1957)

219   If you get knives for wedding presents, blood will be shed.

(F, 22, 1954)

220   If any of the gifts at a bridal shower are cutlery, the bride-elect should return to the giver a similar gift to prevent her engagement from being severed.

(F, 22, 1955, + 1 F)

221   If a ribbon on a wedding-shower gift is broken, it will bring bad luck.

(F, 60, 1952)

222   It is bad luck to cut the ribbon on gifts at bridal showers.

(F, 40, 1960, + 3 F)

223   At a bridal shower, the giver of the seventh gift that is opened will be an old maid.

(F, 30, 1957)

224   At a bridal shower, the giver of the seventh gift to be opened will be the next to be married.

(F, 50, R, 1952, + 2 F)

225   Bake a ring, a thimble, and a dime in a wedding cake. Whoever gets the ring will be the next to wed; the one who gets the dime will be rich; and the one who gets the thimble will be an old maid.

(F, 65, R, 1957)

226   It is bad luck to eat a piece of your wedding cake before you feed one to your mate.
        (F, 90, 1958)

227   Pinning money on the bride at the wedding dance will bring good luck.
        (F, 20, 1950)

228   Someone should place money in the hand of the bride just before she leaves home.
        (F, 50, 1957)

WEDDING CLOTHES

229   "Marry in pearl; / You will live in a whirl."
        (F, 30, R, 1956, + 1 F)

230   "Marry in brown; / You'll live out of town."
        (F, 20, 1959, + 11 F and 2 M)

231   "Marry in brown; / Act like a hound."
        (F, 79, R, 1962)

232   "Marry in brown; / You'll live in town."
        (F, 21, R, 1957, + 2 F and 1 M)

233   "Marry in green; / Ashamed to be seen."
       (F, 21, 1950, + 8 F and 1 M)
234   "Married in May and kirked in green; / Both bride and bride-
       groom won't long be seen."
       (F, 75, R, 1965)
235   "Marry in green; / He'll always be mean."
       (M, 43, 1958, + 1 F)
236   "Marry in white; / You marry all right. / Marry in black;
       / You wish yourself back. / Marry in red; / Wish yourself
       dead. / Marry in green; / Ashamed to be seen. / Marry in
       blue; / You'll marry a-true."
       (F, 60, R, 1959 [her parents])
237   "Marry in blue; / You'll always be true."
       (F, 21, 1950, + 24 F and 2 M)
238   "Marry in pink; / Your spirits will sink."
       (F, 39, R, 1956, + 6 F and 1 M)
239   "Marry in pink; / Your fortune will sink."
       (F, 30, R, 1962, + 2 F)
240   "Marry in pink; / Your marriage will sink."
       (F, 21, 1954, + 1 F)
241   "Marry in pink; / You'll live in a stink."
       (F, 75, 1956)
242   "Marry in pink; / Your husband will stink."
       (F, 80, R, 1962)
243   "Marry in gray; / You'll live far away."
       (F, 30, 1962, + 5 F)
244   "Marry in gray; / You'll rue the day."
       (F, 21, 1950, + 1 F)
245   "Marry in gray; / You'll always be gay."
       (F, 54, 1955)
246   "Marry in red; / You'll wish yourself dead."
       (F, 20, 1959, + 38 F and 1 M)
247   "Marry in yellow; / Ashamed of your fellow."
       (F, 39, R, 1956, + 11 F and 1 M)
248   "Marry in yellow; / You've got the wrong fellow."
       (F, 60, R, 1962, + 1 F)
249   "Marry in yellow; / He'll be a jealous fellow."
       (F, 20, 1959)
250   "Marry in yellow; / He's the right fellow."
       (F, 45, R, 1957)
251   "Marry in yellow; / You'll be jealous of your fellow."
       (F, 103, R, 1966)

252   "Marry in black; / Wish yourself back."
        (F, 19, R, 1959, + 38 F and 2 M)

253   "Marry in tan; / Get a good man."
        (F, 40, R, 1958)

254   "Marry in white; / Live in delight."
        (F, 60, R, 1957, + 2 F and 1 M)

255   "Marry in white; / Life will always be bright."
        (F, 23, 1957)

256   "Marry in white; / Heart's delight."
        (F, 21, 1950)

257   "Marry in white; / Future is bright."
        (F, 59, R, 1957)

258   "Marry in white; / You've chosen right."
        (F, 20, 1959, + 16 F and 1 M)

259   "Marry in white; / You'll always be right."
        (F, 21, 1950, + 7 F)

260   "Marry in white; / You'll always live right."
        (F, 40, R, 1958)

261   "Marry in white; / You'll quarrel and fight."
        (F, 60, 1960, + 2 F)

262   If you're married in white, you'll live like a queen.
        (M, 81, R, 1958)

263   A bride is supposed to wear something old, something new,
        something borrowed, and something blue.
        (F, 20, 1959, + 45 F and 3 M)

264   It's good luck for a bride to wear something old, something
        new, something borrowed, something blue, and a penny in
        her shoe.
        (F, 20, 1959, + 45 F and 3 M)

265   A bride should wear something old, something new, some-
        thing borrowed, something blue, and a sixpence in her shoe.
        (F, 21, 1950, + 2 F)

266   A bride should always wear something old and something
        new, something borrowed and something blue, and a four-
        leaf clover put in her shoe.
        (F, 75, R, 1962)

267   Putting a penny in your shoe before you get married will
        bring good luck.
        (F, 21, 1950, + 8 F)

268   A bride puts a penny in her right shoe to ensure happiness.
        (F, 20, R, 1951, + 2 F)

269   Put a penny in your shoe on your wedding day, and you will be blessed with good luck.
        (F, 27, R, 1959, + 1 F)
270   A bride should wear a penny in her shoe for prosperity.
        (F, 55, 1958)
271   Put a dime in your left shoe for a happy marriage.
        (F, 21, 1950, + 1 F)
272   You'll never be rich until your wedding clothes are worn out.
        (F, 70, R, 1960, + 1 F)
273   Regarding the dress of the bride, she must wear three rings—a ring on her finger; a brooch on her heart, signifying maidenly innocence; and a garland on her head, signifying the gladness and dignity of wedlock.
        (F, 75, R, 1962 [her parents])
274   The groom should wear a bachelor's button on his wedding day.
        (F, 20, 1958)
275   It is bad luck for a groom to wear new socks that have not been washed or rinsed out.
        (F, 20, R, 1961)
276   A woman who is not being married for the first time should not wear white during the ceremony.
        (F, 29, 1959)
277   You should add something to your bridal clothes after you have looked in the mirror for the last time.
        (F, 21, 1950)
278   Salt in a bride's glove is a sign of purity.
        (F, 20, R, 1963)
279   You should wear a blue garter for good luck when you get married.
        (F, 21, 1950, + 1 F)
280   Don't wear black shoes on your wedding day, or you will have bad luck.
        (F, 21, 1956)
281   A marriage will never last if the bride makes her own wedding dress.
        (F, 1961)

WHEN TO HOLD THE CEREMONY

282   "In February, when the birds do mate, / You may marry and not dread your fate."
        (F, 71, R, 1958)

283   "Marry in March when winds do blow; / Over land and sea you'll go."
      (F, 71, R, 1958)

284   Marriage in May will end in dismay.
      (F, 20, R, 1957, + 2 F)

285   "Marry when the June roses bloom; / Your life will be one long sweet tune."
      (F, 71, 1958)

286   "They who in July do wed / Must always labor for their bread."
      (F, 71, 1958)

287   "Monday for wealth; / Tuesday for health; / Wednesday, the best day of all; / Thursday for losses; / Friday for crosses; / Saturday, no luck at all."
      (F, 21, 1950, + 5 F)

288   Don't get married on Friday; that's hangman's day.
      (F, 65, R, 1960, + 2 F)

289   It is good luck to have a marriage take place on a Sunday.
      (F, 58, R, 1958, + 1 F)

290   Couples that get married after sundown willl have unhappy marriages.
      (F, 50, R, 1951)

291   Bad luck will follow your married life if you are late to your own wedding.
      (F, 51, R, 1957)

292   The practice, the wedding, and the reception must start right on time; otherwise the marriage will be a failure.
      (M, 20, 1957, + 1 F)

293   Start the wedding as the clock is on its upward climb.
      (F, 21, 1950, + 4 F)

294   When a man marries within a year after the death of his wife, people say, "I'm glad the wind blew hard enough to blow his wife's foot tracks out of the backyard before he brought his new wife home."
      (F, 80, 1962 [her mother])

295   Marry in haste; repent at leisure.
      (F, 58, R, 1958)

296   Marry in Lent; live to repent.
      (F, 75, R, 1957)

297   It's bad luck to change a wedding date.
      (F, 40, R, 1957, + 8 F and 2 M)

298   It is bad luck to set your wedding date on a birthday or anni-
       versary of anyone in your family.
           (F, 30, 1951)
299   It is most fortunate to be married on the groom's birthday.
           (F, 75, 1962)

WEATHER ON THE WEDDING DAY

300   The weather on your wedding day will foretell the kind of life
       you will have.
           (F, 21, 1950, + 3 F and 2 M)
301   The kind of weather on the day of a wedding determines the
       type of life a bride will lead; that on the second day, the
       groom's life.
           (F, 50, R, 1961)
302   Happy is the bride that the sun shines on.
           (F, 19, 1956 [her mother], + 36 F and 3 M)
303   Blest is the bride that the sun shines on.
           (F, 76, R, 1956)
304   If it rains on the bride's veil, she is bound to get rich.
           (F, 40, R, 1960)
305   For every raindrop that a bride gets on her gown on her wed-
       ding day, she will someday have a thousand dollars.
           (F, 1965)
306   Rain on your wedding day foretells that your marriage will go
       on the rocks.
           (F, 19, 1959, + 10 F and 2 M)
307   If you get married when it's raining, you will have showers of
       blessings for the rest of your life.
           (F, 19, R, 1959, + 2 F and 1 M)
308   If it rains on your wedding day, you will go all through life
       crying, as many tears as there were drops of rain.
           (F, 19, R, 1959, + 14 F)
309   There is an old Chinese proverb: "Every drop of rain on the
       wedding day is a pearl."
           (F, 60, 1957)
310   If the wedding day is windy, the bride will be a grouchy wife.
           (M, 52, R, 1958 [his mother])
311   If the wedding day is stormy, the marriage will be a success.
           (F, 21, 1950)

SIGNS OF SUCCESS OR FAILURE

312   "Change the name and not the letter; / Change for worse and not for better."
      (F, 32, 1959, + 14 F and 1 M)

313   If you dream of your bride or groom on the eve of your wedding, you will have an unhappy marriage.
      (F, 49, 1958)

314   A good cry on your wedding day means that you will never have to cry after you are married.
      (F, 14, 1959, + 1 F)

315   It is bad luck for a bride to shed tears on her wedding day.
      (F, 70, R, 1960 [her mother])

316   If a bride laughs on her wedding day, she will weep ever after, and the marriage will be a failure.
      (M, 74, R, 1971)

317   There must be two members of the bride's immediate family in the wedding party; otherwise the marriage will be a failure.
      (M, 20, 1957)

318   An insecure marriage will result if the bride sees the groom on the night before the wedding.
      (F, 21, 1950)

319   On his wedding day it is bad luck for the groom to see his bride before the ceremony, and vice versa.
      (F, 20, R, 1957 [her grandparents and relatives], + 65 F and 10 M)

320   It is bad luck if the groom sees the bride in her wedding dress before the wedding.
      (F, 60, R, 1958, + 9 F and 2 M)

321   The bride's dress should not be seen by anyone before the wedding.
      (F, 20, 1958)

322   It is bad luck for the bride to rehearse her part in the wedding.
      (F, 52, R, 1958, + 5 F and 1 M)

323   If the bride or the groom drinks any liquor from the time of the wedding rehearsal until the end of the wedding reception, the marriage will be a failure.
      (M, 20, 1957)

324   If the groom doesn't stay with the bride till midnight on the eve of the wedding, the marriage will not last six months.
(M, 20, 1957)

325   One should tie tin cans on the car of a newly married couple.
(F, 28, 1956)

326   If someone secretly wishes you bad luck on your wedding day, yours will be an unhappy marriage.
(F, 60, R, 1957)

327   Double weddings always end unhappily.
(F, 76, R, 1955, + 2 F)

328   If a girl likes cats, she will have a nice wedding day.
(F, 60, R, 1958)

329   Kissing wears out; cooking doesn't.
(F, 20, 1957)

330   If the farmer's daughter cuts the bread thick, she'll be a good wife.
(F, 20, R, 1952)

331   No matter what you are working at, if you have just enough material to complete the job and have nothing left over (be it sewing, canning, wallpapering, painting, or whatever), you will hear of a wedding.
(F, 52, 1954)

332   Always leave the crumbs of a wedding cake.
(M, 81, 1958)

333   If a wedding cake does not crumble when it is being cut, the marriage will be without trouble or argument.
(F, 1957)

334   The groom should give the bride a string of pearls for a wedding present.
(F, 70, R, 1957)

335   If the groom drops the knife while cutting the wedding cake, the marriage will end in divorce in less than ten years.
(F, 40, 1958)

336   Bad luck will follow both the bride and her friend if the friend tries the bride's wedding ring on her left hand before the wedding.
(F, 90, 1958)

337   Dropping the wedding ring or trying it on before the wedding is bad luck.
(M, 22, 1955)

338   It is bad luck to take your engagement ring off before you are married.
(F, 90, 1958)

339   It is a sign of good luck for the groom to carry the bride over
        the threshold.
                (F, 20, 1959 [her parents], + 9 F and 1 M)

2

Pregnancy, Birth, and Infancy

BELIEFS AND CUSTOMS REGARDING PREGNANCY, CHILD-birth, and the care and rearing of children are matters of great cultural concern everywhere. For the parents, it is an awesome responsibility to bring into being children whose life will have significance in this world. Generally, parents make resourceful efforts in carrying out their responsibility for the healthy growth, happy home-life, and future success of their children, as can be noted in this chapter. Historically, some beliefs are associated with those of primitive cultures and may interfere with modern circumstances.

Of the 312 items in this chapter, 25 percent have to do with what might affect the unborn baby; 19 percent are about methods of determining sex; and 15 percent deal with predicting the child's future appearance, because of whether or not he sucks his thumb or walks too early, for example.

The variety of behavorial taboos on physical exertion, food, and even certain "thoughts" may not be explained easily, but at least the cautionary aspect may make sense for an expectant mother. While birthmarks are not much in evidence these days, every community used to have a few people with birthmarks, to the wonder of children and teenagers.

The age-old beliefs in sympathetic and homeopathic magic still arise, such as putting sharp tools under the bed to "cut the pain" of childbirth or putting a four-leaf clover in the shoe so that "You'll get a baby brother." The five items on babies who are born with a "caul," signifying unusual psychic powers, show the persistence of this old belief; as does the widow's peak or sharp dip of hair on the forehead, or being the seventh son of the seventh son.

Only one item refers to midwifery, a practice that is either frowned on in modern America or is actually a legal crime in some states. In 1977 a Lincoln, Nebraska, woman was convicted and fined $100 for practicing midwifery, that is, for practicing medicine without a license. A county nurse recently explained that "we are in a transitional phase back to semiofficial midwifery."

31

THINGS THAT WILL AFFECT
THE UNBORN BABY

340   If during the first three months of pregnancy a woman is frightened by an animal, wherever she touches herself at the time, there will be a similar marking on the baby in that exact place.
(F, 40, 1959, + 6 F and 1 M)

341   If a pregnant woman is frightened, her child will carry the mark of what frightened her.
(F, 22, 1963 [her grandmother] + 14 F)

342   If something scares the mother before her baby is born, the baby will be marked.
(F, 21, 1950 [her mother], + 9 F and 3 M)

343   If a pregnant woman has been badly frightened by an animal, her child will have one of that animal's physical characteristics.
(F, 30, 1958, + 3 F and 3 M)

344   Never look at a deformity; for ugly things or anything that scares a pregnant mother will mark the baby.
(F, 70, 1962 [her mother])

345   When a pregnant woman craves some food, but the craving is not satisfied, this will cause a birthmark on the child.
(F, 60, 1961, + 2 F)

346   If a pregnant woman has a craving for a certain food, the child will be marked with that thing.
(F, 1962)

347   If a pregnant woman craves strawberries, her child will have a strawberry-shaped birthmark.
(F, 24, 1957, + 8 F and 1 M)

348   A mother can "mark" a baby, for example, cause a birthmark, by sitting on a strawberry.
(F, 21, 1950 [the contributor did not actually believe this, of course])

349   If a pregnant woman eats strawberries, her baby will be born with red spots on his face.
(F, 19, 1957)

350   A pregnant woman was thrown a strawberry by her husband. It struck her in the face, and when their baby was born, the baby had a strawberry birthmark on his face.
(F, 46, 1960)

351   If a pregnant woman looks at a snake, the baby will be
        marked.
          (F, 50, 1959)

352   To prevent a baby from being marked, a pregnant woman
        must be careful about what she sees.
          (F, 21, 1961)

353   If a heavy crop of tomatoes grows in the summer season, the
        unborn child will have a tomato (birth) mark.
          (F, 46, 1958)

354   If an expectant mother burns herself and then touches the
        burn, her child will have a birthmark.
          (F, 50, R, 1960)

355   While some children were playing with a big bullsnake, one
        of the contributor's neighbor ladies said: "My, what if an ex-
        pectant mother should touch that snake? It would mark her
        baby."
          (F, 70, R, 1962)

356   A birthmark in the shape of a snake on the infant means that
        the mother was scared by a snake.
          (F, 72, 1957)

357   If a pregnant woman sees a dead person before he is in his
        coffin, there will be a mark on her baby.
          (F, 50, R, 1961)

358   Never let a pregnant woman look upon anything evil, or there
        will be a mark on the child.
          (F, 30, 1960)

359   If something unusual happens before a woman gives birth to
        her child, it will mark the baby. (The person who told this said
        that some woman's dress sleeve had caught fire, she had
        jerked the sleeve from her dress, and her baby had been born
        without an arm.)
          (F, 60, R, 1959)

360   If the mother injures herself during pregnancy, the child will
        have a birthmark in the same place.
          (F, 1961)

361   An old woman told me that she knew a child who had a small
        birthmark like the skin of a hog (bristle) because someone had
        slapped the mother on the back while she was looking at the
        hogs in a pen.
          (F, 1961)

362   A pregnant woman can mark her baby by things that she sees
        when under great emotion.
          (F, 35, 1956)

363   When a pregnant woman is frightened and touches a part of her body in fear, the baby will have a birthmark on his body at the place where the mother touched her body.
(F, 20, R, 1958, + 1 F)

364   One contributor reported that when her cousin's cousin was pregnant, she looked through a keyhole, and when her baby was born, there was the shape of a keyhole in his eye.
(F, 1962)

365   If a pregnant woman is scared by a black cat, her baby will be marked.
(F, 19, 1961)

366   If a pregnant woman looks at a deformed person, her baby may be marked unless she thinks about her child.
(F, 43, R, 1961)

367   A birthmark is caused by something that the mother has done during the pregnancy. All pregnant women should avoid bucking horses and should never go to the circus. If one fails to take these precautions, one's child is sure to be marked.
(F, 72, 1957)

368   If you see a spider, snake, or like creature, keep your hands off yourself, or your baby will be marked in the same spot.
(F, 60, R, 1968)

369   Feeling sorry for one's condition during pregnancy will mark one's child.
(F, 1962)

370   One contributor reported that before her sister was born, her brother went out of the house, yelling, "Fire, fire, the barn is on fire!" Their mother was frightened, and when her sister was born, there was a red streak going across her face, resembling the flame of a fire.
(F, 50, R, 1961)

371   Don't reach over your head when you are pregnant; this will tie the cord around the baby's neck.
(F, 28, 1956, + 9 F)

372   If a woman crawls under a fence when she is pregnant, the child will be born with the cord wrapped around his neck.
(F, 40, R, 1958 [her aunt])

373   A pregnant woman should never walk under a clothesline, or the cord will be wrapped around the baby's neck when he is born.
(F, 60, R, 1960)

374   When a baby is born, the cord must be burned; otherwise the baby will die within a year.
(F, 40, R, 1958)

375   If you scrub floors when you are pregnant, the cord will choke your unborn infant.
(F, 20, R, 1958)

376   If an expectant mother walks under a clothesline without saying, "I walk and you walk," the child will have the umbilical cord wrapped around his neck.
(F, 40, R, 1960 [her parents])

377   Some of the German immigrants believe that when a baby is "lying" in an adverse position before birth, if one takes the father's cap or hat, places it over the position of the child's head, and rotates the cap over the mother's abdomen, the ·child will follow the hat to the right position.
(F, 50, 1950, + 1 F)

378   If a pregnant woman plays the piano, the child will be musically inclined.
(F, 21, 1950, + 1 F)

379   If you want your child to be musical, listen to music during your pregnancy.
(F, 21, 1957, + 1 F)

380   If a pregnant woman sings the day before her child is born, the baby will be blessed with a beautiful voice.
(F, 42, 1961 [her mother])

381   A pregnant woman shouldn't have a permanent, because it won't take.
(F, 28, 1956)

382   A pregnant woman shouldn't have her teeth worked on, because the fillings will fall out.
(F, 28, 1956)

383   A mother can mark her child or cause it to be talented in a particular field by her activities and associations previous to the child's birth.
(F, 22, 1956)

384   If a mother stares at a person, her child will look and act like that person.
(M, 24, R, 1951)

385   A pregnant woman should always eat with a knife or small spoon so that the child will have a rosebud mouth.
(F, 1961)

386   If a pregnant woman is listening to a record that sticks just before she gives birth to her baby, the baby will stutter.
(F, 53, 1955)

387   If a pregnant woman sees a lot of water, her baby will drown.
(M, 20, 1961)

388   If a pregnant woman looks at a cripple, her child will be crippled.
(F, 45, R, 1961, + 1 F)

389   If a woman gets a wart during pregnancy, her child will be born very homely.
(F, 42, 1961 [her mother])

390   It has been said that a pregnant woman who smokes will tend to have a baby with yellowish skin.
(F, 35, 1961)

391   A pregnant woman shouldn't go to a funeral, because her child might be born dead.
(M, 20, R, 1960)

392   If a pregnant woman goes to a funeral, her baby will be born with red eyes.
(F, 20, R, 1957)

393   If a woman drinks alcoholic beverages while she is expecting a baby, the baby will be mentally retarded.
(M, 20, R, 1958)

394   A pregnant woman should not think any evil thought; or if she does, her child will think evil all his life.
(M, 22, 1961)

395   If an expectant mother thinks wrong thoughts, her child's personality will be marred.
(F, 50, R, 1960 [her mother])

396   If a woman is happy while she is carrying her baby, the baby will be a happy one; if she is unhappy, the baby will also be unhappy.
(F, 20, 1955)

397   If a pregnant woman is frightened, the child will have a natural tendency to fear something.
(F, 21, 1950)

398   If a mother sees something frightening before the baby is born, this will affect the child.
(F, 21, R, 1956)

399   If a pregnant woman desires a certain kind of food, she should eat it. Otherwise her child will always cry, and it will be hard to tell why. It will be because he desires this food.
(F, 50, R, 1957 [her mother])

400   A child will like the food that his mother craved.
         (F, 50, 1961)

401   A pregnant woman should do the things that she wants her child to excel in.
         (F, 21, 1950, + 1 F)

402   If a woman who is pregnant concentrates on beautiful pictures, she will have a beautiful baby.
         (F, 46, 1958)

403   A pregnant woman should keep a picture of a beautiful child before her so that her baby will look like the picture.
         (F, 90, 1957)

404   If you want a child to be very well educated, read a lot before your baby is born.
         (F, 80, R, 1960 [her mother])

405   If you hold someone else's baby while you're pregnant, something bad will happen to your own.
         (F, 1962)

406   If a pregnant woman likes strawberries, her child will like strawberries.
         (F, 45, R, 1961)

407   The contributor's mother told her that the reason the contributor hated peanut butter was because her mother craved it and ate it in vast quantities while she was pregnant.
         (F, 1963)

408   The contributor's grandmother had a defective left eye. Her grandmother's mother firmly believed that this was due to the fact that a tramp with a patch over his eye stopped at their house one day while she was carrying the child.
         (F, 30, R, 1957)

409   If a woman is frightened when she is pregnant, something will be mentally wrong with the baby.
         (F, 19, R, 1959)

410   A pregnant woman shouldn't handle meat that is to be cured or canned.
         (F, 50, R, 1961)

411   A woman who is pregnant is very likely to miscarry if she is around a woman who is having her monthly period.
         (F, 46, 1958)

412   If an expectant mother is threatening to lose the baby, have her drink a glass of tea made of grape leaves. This will stop the pain.
         (F, 1962)

413   If you don't have heartburn while you're pregnant, your baby
       will be born baldheaded.
            (F, 20, 1960)

414   A pregnant woman with excessive heartburn will bear a
       hairy baby.
            (F, 50, 1961 [her mother])

415   The disposition of a pregnant woman determines the dis-
       position of the child.
            (F, 1962)

416   A woman should be polite and even-tempered during her
       pregnancy so that her child will be sweet-tempered and will
       grow up to be polite.
            (F, 22, 1958)

417   If a light is on when woman conceives, her baby will be red-
       headed.
            (M, 20, 1957)

DETERMINING THE SEX AND NUMBER
OF CHILDREN

418   A pregnant woman who is carrying her child high will have a
       girl.
            (F, 1961, + 1 F)

419   If the mother carries the unborn baby high in her body, it will
       be a boy; if low, it will be a girl.
            (F, 40, 1960, + 2 F)

420   A baby carried low is supposed to be a boy.
            (M, 20, 1956, + 6 F)

421   To determine the sex of an unborn baby, observe the manner
       in which the mother carries it. If the mother is big all over,
       the baby will be a girl. If the mother is large just at the bot-
       tom, the baby will be a boy.
            (F, 1962)

422   A pregnant woman can find out what the sex of her baby will
       be by holding over her wrist a string with a pencil attached to
       its end. If the pencil swings diagonally across her wrist, she
       will have a boy; if it swings horizontally, she will have a girl;
       and if it goes in a circle, she will have twins.
            (F, 21, R, 1965 [her aunt])

423   One should hang a key in front of a pregnant woman to de-

termine the sex of the child according to the movement and direction in which the key swings.

(M, 48, 1958)

424 The sex of an unborn child can be told by tying a needle on a thread. When the needle is held over the mother, the needle will spin if the child is a boy; if a girl, the needle will stand still.

(F, 40, R, 1958 [her mother])

425 To determine the sex of an unborn child, hold a gold wedding ring, tied to a string, over the palm of a pregnant woman. If it swings back and forth, the child is a boy; if it circles, a girl.

(F, 82, 1958, + 2 F)

426 Hold a string with a wedding ring on it over the hand of a pregnant woman. If it swings from side to side, the baby will be a girl. If it swings to and fro it will be a boy.

(F, 40, R, 1957)

427 You can tell the sex of an unborn child by the heartbeat. The male heartbeat is supposed to be faster.

(F, 19, R, 1962)

428 If an expectant mother wants a boy, she should rest more and eat better.

(F, 20, R, 1959 [her mother])

429 If two stones are placed under the pillow of a woman in labor, her child will be a boy.

(F, 1961)

430 If a man's family is all girls, he should go to bed with his boots on in order to have a boy.

(M, 80, R, 1957)

431 An unborn baby that is full of life will be a boy. One that shows little activity will be a girl.

(F, 20, 1961 [her mother])

432 The first baby kissed by a newly married girl will tell her whether her first child will be a boy or a girl.

(F, 70, 1961 [her parents])

433 If a woman wants to be sure to have a boy baby, she should put something sharp under the mattress (such as a knife or spear). A child conceived in that bed will be a boy.

(F, 60, 1959)

434 A baby's sex depends on the position of the moon at the time of conception.

(F, 1962)

435   If an expectant mother has a great deal of heartburn during pregnancy, her baby will be a boy.
           (F, 40, 1960)

436   Use a vinegar douche to have a girl; a soda douche to have a boy.
           (F, 28, 1956)

437   If both of a pair of twins are male, they will never have any girls when they get married.
           (F, 71, R, 1958)

438   If a pregnant woman wears red, the child will be a boy.
           (F, 1961 [heard as a child])

439   A child conceived in an even month will be a girl, while one conceived in an odd month will be a boy.
           (F, 30, R, 1962 [her mother])

440   A woman who conceives in the sunlight will bear a son.
           (M, 1961 [heard as a young boy])

441   If you drop a knife, you will have a boy.
           (F, 42, 1958)

442   If you drop a fork, you will have a girl.
           (F, 42, 1958)

443   To keep from having the same sex of child every time, turn the mattress over.
           (F, 40, R, 1959)

444   If you hang a turkey bone under your bed while you are pregnant, the baby will be a boy.
           (F, 22, R, 1959 [her friends])

445   If the mother craves sweets before the baby is born, the baby will be a girl; if she craves sour things, she will have a boy.
           (F, 50, 1961)

446   If a baby says "mama" first, the next child in the family will be a girl. If a baby says "daddy" first, the next baby will be a boy.
           (F, 20, 1958, + 5 F and 1 M)

447   A baby that is born late will be a boy; one that comes early will be a girl.
           (F, 20, 1961, + 2 F and 1 M)

448   To tell the sex of a baby, have the expectant mother lie flat and hold over her abdomen a string with a dime tied to it. If the string swings back and forth, the baby will be a boy; if it swings around and around, a girl.
           (F, 1962)

449   If a pregnant woman walks up steps with her right foot first, she will have a girl. If she steps up with the left foot first, she will have a boy.
(F, 20, 1964, + 1 F)

450   If conception takes place just before the menstrual period, the child will be a boy; if immediately after, a girl.
(F, 60, 1959)

451   If you wish to have a boy, hang a man's hat on the bed post.
(M, 60, R, 1961 [his father])

452   A baby that was conceived in the light of the moon will be a boy; in the dark of the moon, a girl.
(F, 60, R, 1958)

453   If while you are pregnant, your navel turns inside out, you will have a girl.
(F, 20, 1960)

454   The contributor's parents said that if you want a boy, you should do outside work; if you want a girl, you should do inside work.
(F, 40, R, 1960)

455   If a pregnant woman sees twin cucumbers, she will bear twins.
(M, 50, 1957)

456   If, when stirring coffee or tea, one accidently puts two teaspoons in the teacup, one will have twins.
(F, 20, 1960 [her mother])

457   In the second generation after a pair of twins has been born, another pair will be born.
(M, 22, 1961)

458   "Needles and pins, triplets and twins. / When a man marries, his troubles begin. / When a man dies, his troubles end."
(F, 43, 1971 [her parents])

459   Eat the first ripe apple in the spring. The number of seeds you find will determine the number of children you will have.
(F, 72, 1957)

460   Count the seeds of an apple to foretell how many children you will have.
(M, 60, R, 1959, + 1 F)

461   Count the number of tea leaves in the bottom of the cup; that is the number of children you will have.
(F, 21, 1955)

462   The number of ribbons that are broken by a bride-to-be at a shower indicates the number of children she will have.
(F, 21, 1950, + 18 F)

463   The number of blue ribbons that are broken at a bridal shower indicates the number of boys that the bride will have; pink ribbons, the number of girls.
(F, 20, R, 1959)

464   The number of towels that you get at a bridal shower will be the number of children that you will have.
(F, 53, 1960, + 1 F)

465   If a child steps in the aisle during a marriage ceremony, the bridal couple will have a large family.
(F, 60, 1957)

466   The number of washcloths you receive at your shower will be the number of children you will have.
(F, 21, 1955)

467   Blow the white fluffy particles off a dandelion; the number that are left will indicate how many children you will have.
(M, 20, R, 1956)

468   When you pull your fingers, the number of knuckles that you pop will determine the number of children that you will have.
(F, 19, R, 1956)

469   Girls with wide hips will have large families, because their babies will come easily.
(M, 24, R, 1957)

470   When you clinch your fist, the number of wrinkles made by your little finger will indicate how many children you will have.
(F, 1961)

471   The number of fingers you put on the roof of the car while driving under a bridge indicates the number of children you will have.
(M, 1962)

472   If you drop a spoon, you will have a lot of children.
(F, 42, R, 1958)

473   Poor families have more children than rich ones.
(F, 60, R, 1957)

474   When the moon is full, more babies are born.
(F, 28, 1956, + 2 F)

475   A common belief found in hospitals is that on the day of a full moon, more babies will be born than at any other time.
(F, 21, R, 1957)

CAUSES FOR AND PREVENTION OF PREGNANCY

476   As long as you are nursing a baby, you can't get pregnant
       again.
              (F, 35, 1958)
477   Babies often used to be breast-fed until they were two or
       three years old because it was believed that a nursing mother
       was not likely to become pregnant.
              (M, 62, 1959)
478   If you swallow a watermelon seed, you'll get pregnant.
              (F, R, 1960, + 1 F)
479   If you help someone make her bed, she will have a baby.
              (F, 30, 1961)
480   If you drop a spoon, there will be a baby in the house.
              (F, 75, R, 1956)
481   If a four-month-old baby has four teeth, another baby will
       soon be on the way.
              (F, 59, R, 1957)
482   If a baby gets a tooth early (three or four months), another
       baby will soon be on the way.
              (F, 20, R, 1962 [her mother])
483   If you find a four-leaf clover and put it in your shoe, you'll get
       a baby brother.
              (F, 50, R, 1960 [her mother])
484   If a woman sits on a chair where a man has been sitting, and
       it's still warm, she will soon have a baby.
              (M, 19, 1958)
485   Never give away your baby's clothes, or you'll have another
       baby within a year.
              (F, 68, R, 1958)
486   Folks in Kansas commonly believe that a severe storm will
       precede the arrival of a blessed event—a baby, a colt, a calf,
       etc.
              (F, 40, 1959)
487   Babies grow in tree stumps.
              (F, 70, 1961)
488   Babies grow in the cornpatch.
              (F, 70, 1961)
489   If you take a new baby to another home, that home will soon
       have a new baby.
              (F, 40, R, 1960 [her mother])

490   If you lay a baby on someone else's bed, that person will get
one soon.
(M, 20, R, 1961, + 5 F)

491   If a baby wets on your bed, you will be the next one to have a
baby.
(F, 74, R, 1958)

492   If a diaper is left at your home by a visiting baby, your family
will soon have a new member.
(F, 25, 1959 [her aunt], + 3 F)

493   If someone leaves a baby's dirty diaper at your house, you
will have the next baby.
(F, 80, R, 1963 [her parents], + 2 F)

494   If you leave wet diapers at someone's house, that person will
have a baby soon.
(F, 42, R, 1958, + 2 F)

495   When a young baby leans forward so as to look behind the
person who is holding him, this is a sign of an oncoming pregnancy for his mother.
(F, 1962)

496   When a woman serves the same food in two ways at a meal, it
is a sign that she is pregnant.
(F, 21, 1956)

497   To bring about a miscarriage, take turpentine.
(F, 40, R, 1961 [her father])

LABOR AND DELIVERY

498   A woman who has painful cramps during menstruation will
have an easy labor, and vice versa.
(M, 23, 1957)

499   Boil eggshells, and have the mother drink the water. This will
make delivery easier.
(F, 78, R, 1959 [her aunt])

500   If a woman has slender ankles, she'll have an easy birth.
(F, 28, 1956)

501   If a woman has a difficult time during pregnancy, the birth
will be easy.
(F, 1962)

502   If a woman has an easy time during pregnancy, the birth will
be difficult.
(F, 1962)

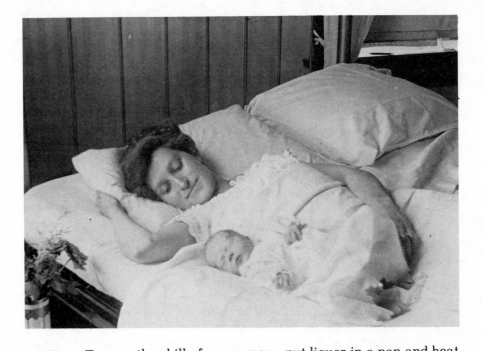

503   To cure the chill of pregnancy—put liquor in a pan and heat
        it. Then dip sheets in the liquor. Wrap the patient in the hot
        sheets. Then hold a hot iron right over her spine.
                (F, 72, 1957)

504   Expectant French mothers used to wear a belt of human skin
        to help ease their labor pains.
                (F, 60, R, 1957)

505   If a pregnant woman turns her shoes upside down under her
        bed, she won't have cramps.
                (M, 50, R, 1957)

506   If you put an empty pea pod over the door, you will be assured
        of a safe delivery.
                (F, 35, 1958)

507   If scissors are put under the mattress of a woman in labor,
        they will cut her pains.
                (F, 50, 1960, + 1 F)

508   Put an axe under the bed of a woman in childbirth to cut the
        pain.
                (F, 21, 1950, + 2 F)

509   Midwives used to put a knife under the bed to "cut the pain"
        of childbirth.
                (F, 50, 1959, + 2 F)

510   Anything sharp under the bed of a woman in labor stops the labor (cuts the pain and the labor).
       (F, 40, 1957, + 1 F)

511   One's first baby often comes prematurely.
       (F, 50, 1958)

512   A seven-month baby will have a better chance of living than an eight-month baby.
       (F, 50, R, 1959 [her mother])

513   Premature babies do not have fingernails, eyelashes, or eyebrows.
       (F, 45, 1957)

THE DATES AND DAY OF BIRTH

514   Monday's child is fair of face.
       Tuesday's child is full of grace.
       Wednesday's child has far to go.
       Thursday's child will have sorrow and woe.
       Friday's child is Godly given.
       Saturday's child must work for a living.
       The child that is born on the Sabbath day
       Will always be happy, merry, and gay.
       (F, 20, 1959, + 15 F)

515   A mother's belief is that the day on which her child is born determines what the child's prospects for the future will be, such as "Born on Wednesday, it will never be in want."
       (F, 60, 1961)

516   Thursday babies are cry babies.
       (F, 20, R, 1961 [her mother])

517   If you are born on Thursday, you will be hungry; Friday, rich; Saturday, lazy.
       (F, 21, R, 1957)

518   A child who is born on Sunday will be able to talk to animals on Christmas.
       (F, 60, R, 1959)

519   If you are born on Sunday, your life will be full of grace and happiness.
       (M, 73, R, 1957)

520   A baby who is born on New Years Day will cause his mother no tears.
       (F, 1961)

521   A baby will be born on the same day of the week that he was conceived; also at the same time of the day.
      (F, 1960)

522   Babies conceived in the fall are healthiest and heaviest.
      (F, 20, 1958)

523   Winter babies are healthiest.
      (F, 21, 1950)

524   Babies born in winter will be smarter than those born in summer.
      (F, 48, 1964 [her mother])

525   The stars that you are born under determine the type of person you will be.
      (F, 20, 1955)

526   More geniuses and insane people are supposed to be born in the fall.
      (F, 21, 1950)

527   A child born under Cancer will be courageous.
      (F, 60, 1961)

528   A child born when Mars ascends will be pugnacious and violent.
      (F, 70, 1961)

529   A child born when Jupiter ascends will be jovial.
      (F, 70, 1961)

530   A child of Saturn will be gloomy.
      (F, 70, 1961)

PREDICTING THE FUTURE

531   A baby born with brown eyes will bring particularly good luck to his family.
      (F, 40, 1961)

532   A baby born with a double crown will be rich.
      (F, 74, 1969 [a friend])

533   A baby born without hair will have lots of hair as an adult.
      (F, 21, 1950)

534   Baldheaded babies are supposed to have curly hair later.
      (F, 21, 1950)

535   Children who are born with a widow's peak or a dip of the hair in the forehead rather than straight across are supposed to be very fortunate in later life. They are considered to be lucky.
      (F, 40, 1961)

536   A baby who has soft hair will be poor; one who has hard hair will be rich.
    (M, 70, R, 1959)

537   A baby with a high forehead will be intelligent.
    (F, 21, 1950)

538   A baby who is born feet first will be low in intelligence.
    (F, 60, R, 1958)

539   A baby who is born with its eyes crossed, will be very smart.
    (F, 60, R, 1958)

540   A baby who cries when he is being christened, will be a good singer.
    (M, 62, 1958)

541   A baby who has long fingers will be a musician.
    (F, 20, R, 1958, + 1 F)

542   A baby who has small ears will be miserly.
    (F, 20, R, 1958)

543   A child carrying the name of Mary will be unhappy.
    (F, 30, R, 1961 [her mother])

544   If a pregnant woman has heartburn, her baby will have lots of hair.
    (F, 27, 1957, + 2 F)

545   A baby born with a caul (part of the placental tissue on his face) will have second sight and will be able to see into the future.
    (F, 40, 1959 [her mother], + 6 F)

546   A baby born with a caul will be a genius or have psychic powers.
    (F, 35, 1956, + 2 F)

547   Babies born with a veil on or over their heads will be great or outstanding in their life's work.
    (F, 30, 1957, + 2 F)

548   If a child is born with a veil on his face, place the veil in a fruit jar, and close the lid tightly. The veil will change color, no matter what distance the child is away.
    (F, 40, 1959 [her mother])

549   A child who is born with a veil over its face will be very intelligent. If the veil is saved, it will foretell many things during the child's life, such as sickness, by giving off a peculiar odor.
    (F, 60, 1959)

550   The seventh son of a seventh son has the ability to prophesy.
        (F, 40, 1959 [her grandmother])
551   The seventh son in the family will make a successful doctor.
        (F, 54, R, 1957, + 1 M)
552   The thirteenth child will not live.
        (F, 60, R, 1957)
553   The first-born is more apt to be like the father than the
        mother.
        (F, 63, 1950)

LOOKING IN MIRRORS

554   A baby who sees himself in a mirror before he is a year old
        will stutter.
        (F, 20, 1959 [a nurse])
555   Do not permit a baby to look in the mirror before he is a year
        old, or he will become a monkey.
        (F, 25, 1958)
556   If a baby sees himself in a mirror before he is one year of age,
        he will be silly.
        (F, 60, 1961)
557   Don't let children look at themselves in mirrors, or they will
        be vain.
        (F, 40, R, 1957 [her mother], + 2 F and 1 M)
558   Don't let a baby look into a mirror before he is one year old,
        or he will be cross-eyed.
        (F, 60, R, 1958, + 1 F)
559   If you let a baby see himself in a mirror, he will die before he
        is one year old.
        (F, 50, R, 1961 [her mother], + 19 F and 2 M)
560   Don't let a baby see himself in a mirror until he is a year old,
        or he will not live long.
        (F, 50, R, 1960 [her parents])
561   Don't let a baby look into a mirror until he is a year old, or he
        will be afraid of water.
        (F, 40, 1963)
562   Don't let a small baby look into a mirror; if you do, his
        teething will be difficult.
        (F, 40, 1962)

APPEARANCE AND GROWTH

563   A baby who walks too soon will be bowlegged.
        (F, 58, R, 1958)

564   A dark-haired baby can make great wealth.
        (F, 60, R, 1957)

565   If you make bad faces when you are growing up, your face
        will grow that way.
        (F, 60, R, 1958)

566   If it rains on a child's face before it is one year old, the child
        will have freckles.
        (F, 40, 1961)

567   Ugly babies make beautiful and handsome adults.
        (M, 20, R, 1957, + 9 F and 1 M)

568   A fat baby makes a slender adult.
        (M, 21, 1950)

569   "Cute in the cradle; / Ugly at the table."
        (F, 30, R, 1958)

570   "Pretty in the cradle; / Homely at the table."
        (F, 82, 1957)

571   Walking in back of a child, thus causing him to look over his
        head, will make him cross-eyed.
        (F, 1961 [her great-aunt, who heard it about 1860])

572   Look at a baby too close, and he will be cross-eyed.
        (F, 20, R, 1958)

573   Turn a child's head often while in a crib, or his head will be-
        come misshapen.
        (F, 46, R, 1958)

574   When a child's canine teeth are pulled, the teeth must be bur-
        ied or burned, because if a wolf or coyote finds one of these
        teeth, the child will grow a wolf tooth.
        (M, 62, R, 1959)

575   A baby who sucks his thumb will have a big mouth.
        (M, 21, 1950)

576   A baby who sucks his thumb will have buck teeth.
        (M, 31, 1955 [his friends])

577   If a baby has small feet and hands, he will have large feet and
        hands as an adult.
        (M, 21, 1950)

578   Every child must have a "spring tonic" in order to grow properly.
      (M, 60, R, 1963 [his father])

579   So that your baby will grow straight and strong, always wrap him in a quilted feather quilt—bring the left tip over first, bottom tip next, and right tip last. This must be wrapped snugly, so that he has to lie straight while asleep.
      (F, 52, R, 1958 [her mother])

580   Colicky babies grow faster.
      (F, 1962; the informant was convinced that this is based on truth, claiming that the muscular activity in response to the discomfort of the colic condition promotes growth.)

581   If a baby has the hiccups, he is growing.
      (F, 80, R, 1958)

582   Picking children up by the head during the day of the Gloria is supposed to cause a child to grow a little extra taller.
      (M, 40, R, 1961)

583   A child at the age of two and one-half years will measure one-half its height when full grown.
      (F, 30, R, 1962)

584   If a child's hair is not cut by his parents until he is past one, it will be curly.
      (F, 1962)

585   If a baby's soft spot on his head is pressed, he will become a lunatic.
      (F, 1961 [heard during her childhood])

586   The moon's shining in a baby's face will cause it to be feeble-minded.
      (F, 80, R, 1960 [her parents])

587   When a baby is baptized, he must always cry, or he will not live out the year. In the past, babies were often pinched to be sure that they would cry.
      (F, 40, 1960)

588   Never put a baby's dress on over its head first, or the baby won't live a year.
      (F, 70, R, 1961 [her father])

589   Feed a newborn baby a tablespoonful of water before he is one hour old. This will prevent his death before he is two years of age.
      (F, 40, R, 1958 [one of her neighbors])

590   "Dimple in the chin; / Devil within."
      (F, 30, R, 1958)

591   If a baby has blue eyes that are rimmed with white, it is a sign that he won't be bright.
(F, 60, R, 1958)

592   If you stand a baby on its feet too early, he will have bowlegs.
(F, 20, R, 1958, + 1 F)

593   If you tickle a baby's feet, he will grow up to be flatfooted.
(F, 22, 1958)

594   Tickling a baby's feet will make the child stammer in later years.
(F, 20, 1955 [her mother], + 4 F and 1 M)

595   If you tickle a baby, he will stutter.
(F, 20, R, 1958, + 5 F and 2 M)

596   If a baby laughs aloud before he is six weeks old, he will be "foolish."
(M, 80, R, 1957)

597   A baby will grow up to have a disposition like that of the first person you take him to visit.
(F, 54, 1959)

598   A baby will be like the first person to carry him.
(F, 25, 1958)

599   When you have a new baby, the first of his two hands that you wash will be the hand he uses (that is, he will be right-handed or left-handed).
(E, 28, 1959 [her mother])

600   A child who is born after his father's death has the power to heal.
(F, 71, 1961, + 1 F)

601   Do not cut a babies fingernails the first time, instead chew them. If you cut them, the baby will steal.
(F, 20, R, 1961, + 8 F)

602   It's bad luck to cut a baby's fingernails—it will cause him to be a thief.
(F, 21, 1950 [her mother], + 1 F)

603   If a baby does not grasp a coin that is placed in his hand, he will become a spendthrift when he grows up.
(F, 60, 1961 [her mother])

604   If a baby clutches a coin that is put in his hand, he will save money when he grows up.
(F, 1961)

605   Give a newborn baby, or one who is still very young, a penny. If he clutches it tightly, he will be wealthy.
(F, 43, R, 1961)

606   Place items to represent occupations before a baby: a book for teacher, money for banker, and so forth. What the baby reaches for will foretell his future occupation.
      (M, 50, R, 1960 [his mother])

607   On the day that a baby is a year old, place before him a hammer, a Bible, and a silver dollar. Whichever he picks up first will determine his career, such as a carpenter, preacher, or banker.
      (F, 50, R, 1961 [an aunt])

608   On a child's first birthday, place a purse, a book, and a liquor bottle in his reach. If he takes the purse, he will gain wealth; if he takes the book, he will be a scholar; but if he picks up the bottle, he will be a drunkard.
      (F, 50, R, 1962 [her mother])

609   One contributor, Mrs. Strothman, said that her father would always lay his finger in a new baby's palm to see if the baby would grasp it. If the baby did, her father would always say that the baby was bright. Every time that her father went to see a new baby, he would test the baby in this way about the first thing.
      (F, 55, 1957)

NURSING, WEANING, AND TEETHING

610   A baby nurses nervousness off its mother.
      (F, 28, 1956)

611   The reason for a new mother not having enough milk for her newborn child is because of a moth nursing at the mother's breast without her knowing it.
      (F, 50, 1961 [her mother])

612   Don't get chilled when you nurse a baby; this makes the milk bad.
      (F, 28, 1956)

613   Drink beer to make plenty of milk.
      (F, 28, 1956)

614   To dry up breasts, rub them with spirits of camphor.
      (F, 78, R, 1959)

615   For caked breasts, make a poultice with hot pancakes that have had a lot of salt and a tablespoonful of turpentine baked into them.
      (F, 78, R, 1959)

616   Fry pancakes and put them on the breast after nursing a
        child to dry up the milk and relieve caking and pressure.
            (F, 20, 1961 [a friend])

617   To cure "caked breasts" while nursing a child, bake hot pan-
        cakes and place them over your breasts.
            (F, 57, R, 1957, + 1 F)

618   Good Friday is the best day of the year for the weaning of
        babies.
            (F, 40, 1962 [her grandmother firmly believed this])

619   Wean a baby when the sign of the zodiac is in the thighs and
        the wind is in the north.
            (F, 30, R, 1957)

620   If you wean a baby when the following signs of the zodiac are
        present, the baby will have no trouble changing over: Capri-
        corn, the Goat; Sagittarius, the Archer.
            (F, 65, R, 1961)

621   Babies will wean from the breast or bottle easier in the right
        sign of the moon.
            (F, 30, R, 1958 [her mother-in-law], + 1 F)

622   You must wean a baby in the light of the moon (time of the
        month), or the child will be badly affected psychologically.
            (F, 40, 1959 [one of her neighbors])

623   If you take the bottle away from a baby when there is a new
        moon, the baby won't want it again.
            (F, 20, R, 1956)

624   Never trim a baby's fingernails, or he will cut his teeth hard.
            (F, 60, R, 1959 [her grandmother])

625   Rub a silver thimble on a baby's gums to help him cut his
        teeth.
            (F, 40, 1962)

626   If you put a string of Job's-tears on a baby's neck, he will have
        no trouble cutting teeth.
            (F, 60, 1959 [her parents])

627   Put a dime around a baby's neck to help his teething to be
        easy.
            (F, 40, 1962)

628   If a baby is having trouble cutting teeth, rub oil from the hide
        of a pinto horse in the gums of the baby, and he won't have
        any more trouble.
            (M, 40, 1962 [a friend])

629   If your children have trouble cutting teeth, kill a rabbit or a

chicken, and rub the child's gums with the warm brains—
they will have no more trouble cutting teeth.
> (F, 50, 1958)

630   An eye tooth (not tusk) of a dog can be used to prevent teething problems among babies. A pouch containing the tooth
should be attached to a ribbon, and the ribbon should be
placed around the child's neck so that the pouch may dangle
freely.
> (F, 78, 1963)

631   Don't ever put a man's hat on a baby, as this will make his
teething hard.
> (F, 40, 1962)

632   If a baby has difficulty in teething, sew a rattlesnake's rattle
in a piece of cheesecloth, and hang it around the baby's neck.
> (F, 60, R, 1957)

633   A baby will cut his teeth easily if the baby is not allowed to
look at himself in the mirror.
> (M, 64, 1957)

THE BABY'S HEALTH, MISCELLANEOUS

634   Beets are poisonous to children under two years of age.
> (F, 80, R, 1964 [her mother])

635   If you can't find anything that will agree with a new baby,
give it mare's milk.
> (M, 87, 1959 [his mother])

636   A child will die if he is named after someone who is dead.
> (F, 40, 1959 [her grandparents])

637   If you name a child for a dead relative, he won't live beyond
twenty-five years.
> (F, 75, 1959)

638   A child has worms if it picks its nose.
> (F, 42, 1958)

639   A white ring around a child's mouth is a sign of worms.
> (F, 42, 1958)

640   An elderly person will, when sleeping with a child, sap the
child's strength and cause his complexion to darken.
> (F, 50, 1961 [her mother])

641   If you let a baby's clothes freeze, the baby will have colic.
> (F, 43, R, 1961)

642   If an east wind blows on a baby's bare chest, the baby will
always have stomach trouble.
(F, 50, R, 1963 [her grandmother])

643   Never leave a cat in the room with a baby. The cat will suck
the baby's breath away, and the baby will die.
(F, 60, 1959, + 1 F)

INFANCY, MISCELLANEOUS

644   Hang bacon fat from a string, and let the baby chew on it to
keep him happy.
(F, 28, 1956)

645   A baby who sleeps with his fists clenched is happy.
(F, 28, 1959 [her mother])

646   Lots of boys being born is a sign that there will be a war.
(F, 1959 [her grandparents])

647   To pacify a crying baby, make a sugar tit from a handkerchief
and a lump of sugar. The baby will stop crying.
(F, 79, R, 1957)

648   A baby should be carried upstairs before he is carried down-
stairs.
(F, 21, 1950)

649   Psychologists' kids are always mean.
(M, 30, R, 1964)

650   When a baby smiles in his sleep, he is talking to the angels.
(F, 60, R, 1958)

651   Old folks say that if young people play with fire, they will wet
the bed.
(F, 78, 1962, + 1 F)

3

The Prevention and Cure
of Illnesses and Injuries

FOLK-ADMINISTERED MEDICINE HAS A PLACE IN OUR SOCI-
ety today, but its scope is far less than it was during our comparatively
recent period of frontier development of one hundred years ago. As has
been the case through the centuries, dire necessity made folk application a serious and immediate matter, so the curing of illnesses, injuries,
and ailments was woven into the family or community unit. Someone
had to take charge, and so someone did—the mother, the father, a relative, or a friend. Sometimes it was a hit or miss matter, but reliance on
traditional cures was the only alternative. It was inevitable that old
primitive practices would creep in; but few of these are actually harm-
ful; in fact, they may even be beneficial in overcoming psychological
hazards.

Information on the efficacy of nonprofessional folk treatment is
amply taken care of by countless newspaper columnists, magazines,
books, which sometimes are best sellers, and organized classes of all
kinds. It should be noted also that the medical profession itself credits
folk medicine with some important contributions to scientific medicine,
although it also points out potentialities for harm.

Traditionally there have evolved two branches or areas of approach for treatment of the ill or ailing by the nonprofessional. One is
use of the natural world's plants, herbs, animal products, and the like.
The other is the magico-religious. Judgment on the curative values for
whatever approach is a matter of one's point of view.

This chapter comprises 20 percent of our collection, the highest
percentage for the total of items in any of the twelve chapters. Of the
twenty-eight categories—excluding the miscellaneous section—cures
for the common cold, warts, bleeding, and the hiccups rank highest. Dr.
Jan H. Brunvand, an American folklorist, has noted, "The less that
medical science knows about an ailment, the more likely it is that folk
remedies will survive." He further states that the common cold, hiccups, warts, fever blisters, and rheumatism are the ailments that are
most frequently treated with folk cures. This observation is accurate,

since concern for these particular ills rank high in frequency and/or duplication in this collection. In fact, the common cold—with its sometimes accompanying ills such as coughing, sore throat, hoarseness, croup, the flu, or pneumonia—accounts for twenty percent of the 1,018 items listed in this chapter. Other ills that rank high in kinds of treatments are boils, infections, insect and snake bites (11 percent); bad digestion, hangovers, and dog bites (8 percent); how to stay well and how to treat and keep a "beautiful skin" (10 percent).

On the matter of health care and cures, folk opinions and ideas are never lacking. And periodically there is an extra wave of fascination for remedies that grandma used, while at the same time Americans are quick enough to consult their academically trained doctors.

ACHES

652   If you have cramps in your feet at night, put your shoes under your bed upside down, and your cramps will end.

(M, 42, R, 1957, + 3 F and 2 M)

653   Two teaspoonfuls of honey three times a day will keep away cramps in feet and legs.

(F, 82, 1958)

654   Tie a cord string around your legs. Wear it all the time. This will cure the cramps in your legs.

(M, 50, R, 1961 [his mother])

655   Douse your legs before going in swimming to prevent cramps.

(M, 86, 1959)

656   If you have a pain in your side, spit under a clod of dirt, and the pain will go away.

(M, 40, R, 1960 [his grandfather], + 2 F and 1 M)

657   To get rid of an ache in your side when you walk or run rapidly, pick up a stone, spit on the underside, put it back in the same position and on the same spot where you found it, and your side ache will disappear.

(M, 26, R, 1957, + 1 F and 3 M)

658   If a man has a toothache, he should put a chaw of tobacco on the sore tooth, and the pain will go away.

(M, 55, R, 1958, + 3 F and 1 M)

659   To cure a toothache, insert in the cavity the trimmings from the hoof of a "critter."

(F, 83, 1962 [her grandmother])

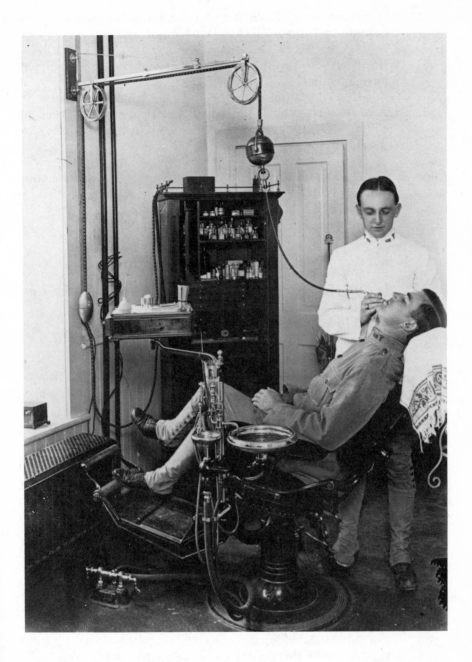

660   If you are often troubled with a toothache, cutting your fingernails on Friday will cause the toothache to recur.
(M, 50, R, 1957)

661   If you cut your fingernails and toenails on Friday, you will not
have a toothache.
(F, 77, 1960 [her mother])

662   A cure for toothache: Put salt and pepper on a piece of
cotton, soak it in camphor, and place it in the ear that is on
the side of the toothache.
(M, 60, R, 1962)

663   Rattlesnake oil used to be considered a cure for toothaches
and severe headaches.
(F, 60, R, 1960)

664   Put kerosene in your mouth for the toothache.
(M, 56, 1962)

665   Use a teabag on a sore tooth for toothache.
(M, 23, 1964)

666   In case of an earache, blow smoke in your ear, and the ache
will cease.
(F, 40, 1962, + 3 F and 4 M)

667   Blow smoke from pipe into the ear to cure an earache.
(F, 50, R, 1959, + 3 F and 4 M)

668   To cure an earache, blow cigar smoke into the aching ear.
(F, 20, R, 1959, + 1 F)

669   To stop an earache, put warm raisins in the ear.
(F, 50, R, 1957 [her parents])

670   To cure an earache, spray the ear with ice water.
(F, 50, R, 1957)

671   For earaches, clean the ears out with peroxide to clear up the
infection.
(F, 60, R, 1958)

672   Use a hot sock for an earache.
(F, 50, 1957)

673   Put black pepper on a piece of cotton, and place it in the
aching ear.
(F, 50, R, 1962)

674   To cure an earache, rinse the ear with fresh urine from a
virgin.
(M, 50, R, 1957)

675   Putting a child through a horse collar will cure his earache.
(M, 48, R, 1958)

676 Warmed rabbit wine placed in the ear will cure an earache.
      (M, 51, R, 1956)

677 Putting cow urine in the ear will cure an earache.
      (F, 40, R, 1957)

678 For an earache: crack a peach seed; use the center. Get it hot
      with butter, put it on cotton, and use it in the ear.
      (F, 40, R, 1959)

679 To cure an earache: Bake an onion with its peeling on. Take
      the peeling off, put in a cloth, and squeeze the juice into the
      ear.
      (F, 60, R, 1959)

680 Drip juice from a roasted onion into an ear for earache.
      (F, 1959)

681 For earache, heat the bulb end of a young onion or the heart
      section of a big onion and put it in the ear, reheating the onion
      frequently.
      (M, 62, R, 1959)

682 To cure an earache, pack the ear with tobacco juice.
      (M, 50, R, 1957)

683 Spit tobacco juice into the ear for earache.
      (F, 80, 1960)

684 Olive oil will cure earaches.
      (M, 50, 1959, + 1 F)

685 Blow in your ear to get rid of an earache.
      (M, 50, 1956)

686 Piercing the ear lobes will cure an earache.
      (M, 69, 1955)

687 To cure a headache, place a bag of peeled raw potato on the
      painful area.
      (M, 70, R, 1958 [her mother])

688 Let your head get wet during a first May rain, and you will
      not have a headache for the year.
      (F, 50, 1962)

689 To cure a headache, place a band of wet paper around your
      head.
      (M, 72, R, 1956)

690 Put goose grease on your head, then wrap a dirty stocking
      around your head to cure a headache.
      (M, 70, R, 1963)

691 For a sick headache, lay cold, wet cloths on your head, chang-
      ing them every fifteen minutes.
      (M, 60, R, 1964)

692   Rub your eye in a certain spot; this will make your headache
go away.
(F, 50, 1964)

693   Soak up some vinegar in brown absorbent paper, then apply
it to your forehead.
(F, 60, R, 1960 [her mother])

694   Never get a haircut in March, or you will have headaches for
the rest of the year.
(M, 70, R, 1959 [his mother])

695   You'll have a headache if you throw any hair outside and the
birds use it in a nest.
(F, 50, R, 1959, + 5 F and 1 M)

696   Hair combings should be burned; otherwise, birds will make
nests out of them, and the person will have headaches.
(F, 40, R, 1958, + 1 F)

697   Rattlesnake rattles worn in the sweatband of a hat will prevent headaches.
(M, 50, R, 1956, + 2 M)

698   Kill a snake and wrap it around your head; this will cure a
headache.
(F, 30, R, 1957)

699   A cabbage leaf in your hat will cure a headache.
(F, 40, R, 1955)

700   Headaches may be cured by going to the woods and finding a
heart's-leaf plant, then digging up the roots and chewing
them.
(F, 57, 1957)

701   To get rid of a headache, stick your head under a pillow and
count to a hundred.
(M, 1962)

For the prevention and cure of stomach aches, see the section entitled
"Advice about the Digestive Tract."

APPENDICITIS AND KIDNEY PROBLEMS

702   Fingernails, if swallowed, will cause appendicitis.
(M, 50, R, 1958, + 1 F)

703   Frequent chewing of the fingernails will cause an attack of
appendicitis.
(F, 20, R, 1961)

704   If you swallow any kind of seeds, you will have appendicitis.
        (F, 60, R, 1958)
705   If you eat strawberries, you will have appendicitis.
        (M, 64, 1957)
706   If you eat cherries and then drink milk, you will have
        appendicitis.
        (F, 40, R, 1961)
707   To cure appendicitis: Stand up on your head as long as you
        can, so that your appendix will drain. Then lie down, and if
        the pain doesn't stop, stand on your head again.
        (M, 70, R, 1962)
708   Tea made from watermelon seeds is good for kidney
        disorders. Pour water on the watermelon seeds, and bring it
        to a boil. Cool and drink.
        (F, 50, R, 1961 [her mother])
709   One contributor reported that her aunt was very economical.
        Back long ago, extravagance had to be justified. She justified
        paying ten cents for a twenty-five-pound watermelon by say-
        ing, "Watermelon is sure expensive to eat, but it sure flushes
        the kidneys."
        (F, 57, R, 1957)
710   Alfalfa tea is good for the kidneys.
        (F, 49, R, 1961 [her mother])
711   Steep the berries from a cedar tree for kidney disorders.
        (M, 40, R, 1961)
712   Use flaxseed tea for kidney trouble.
        (F, 71, 1961)

ARTHRITIS AND RHEUMATISM

713   Put a teaspoonful of salt in your shoe in order to relieve
        arthritis.
        (F, 1959)
714   One contributor reported that her father carried a buckeye
        in his pocket all his life to prevent arthritis.
        (F, 47, 1958)
715   To cure arthritis, attach a potato to the affected part of the
        body and go to bed with a potato in each hand.
        (M, 30, R, 1957)
716   One should hold a potato in an arthritic hand as much as
        possible, because this will cure the hand.
        (F, 50, 1961)

717   Carry a potato in your pocket to relieve arthritis. (This must be German, as the contributor's father, who was German, spoke of this being common in the old country.)
(M, 50, 1959, + 1 F)

718   Wearing a copper band around your arm or leg will help to relieve arthritic pains.
(F, 19, 1956, + 5 F and 8 M)

719   If afflicted with rheumatism, sleep with a dog wrapped around your feet, and the rheumatism will drain into the dog.
(M, 55, 1961)

720   When taking your shoes off at night, take care to put the heels next to the wall. This will prevent rheumatism.
(M, 60, R, 1959 [his parents])

721   A string of glass beads will keep off rheumatism.
(F, 28, 1956)

722   Wear red flannels to rid yourself of rheumatism.
(F, 70, 1960)

723   One contributor reported that her grandmother always wore a woolen string just below her knee; this was to ward off rheumatism.
(F, 1961)

724   Use venom from bees to cure rheumatism.
(M, 70, R, 1963 [his father], + 1 F)

725   Alfalfa tea is good for rheumatism.
(M, 22, 1961)

726   Ragweed tea—made when the weed is just turning green and the leaves are tender—is an excellent cure for rheumatism and lumbago.
(F, 1963)

727   Carry an acorn in your pocket in order to ward off rheumatism.
(M, 40, R, 1959 [his father])

728   A rock carried in one's pocket becomes even harder, because it is absorbing the rheumatism.
(F, 67, R, 1960 [her father])

729   Carry a double cedar knot in your pocket to cure rheumatism.
(F, 70, R, 1959)

730   If you wear a copper band or wire around your wrist or arm, it will cure you of rheumatism.
(F, 20, R, 1956, + 17 F and 17 M)

731   Wear a brass band around the affected member, and your rheumatism will be cured.
(M, 25, R, 1959, + 5 F and 1 M)

732   Carry a chestnut in your pocket to keep from having rheumatism.
       (F, 40, R, 1962, + 1 F)

733   To cure or prevent rheumatism, carry a buckeye in your pocket.
       (M, 40, R, 1957, + 13 F and 7 M)

734   If you carry a potato in your pocket, you will ward off rheumatism.
       (F, 19, 1956, + 17 M and 18 F)

735   To cure rheumatism: add one ounce of pulverized sulfur and one ounce of Seneca snake root to one quart of whiskey; drink over a period of four or five days.
       (F, 50, 1963 [her grandfather])

736   An old remedy for rheumatism was yellow dirt made like a dough.
       (M, 70, R, 1962)

737   Some people still believe that the drinking of kerosene will cure rheumatism or stiffness of the legs.
       (F, 60, R, 1957)

738   Tennessee mountaineers say that painting the body with vinegar will stop rheumatism.
       (F, 60, R, 1957)

739   Put dry rose leaves on a smoldering fire and then breathe the odor. This will cure rheumatism.
       (F, 60, 1961 [her mother])

740   To make liniment for rheumatism: take one pint of good cidervinegar, add one heaping teaspoonful each of salt and pepper, boil down to one-half pint, and use.
       (F, 70, R, 1962)

741   Dust a little sulfur in each shoe to cure rheumatism.
       (M, 1954)

742   To cure rheumatism: put a beef's gall into a quart of rum, and rub the affected part with this.
       (F, 50, 1963 [her grandfather])

743   Drink one-half teaspoonful of soda in the juice of one lemon every day to cure rheumatism.
       (F, 70, 1961)

744   To cure rheumatism: take four lemons, squeeze out the juice, put the juice and rinds into one quart of water—add four heaping tablespoonfuls of epsom salts, and boil for a few minutes—let this mixture cool, then drink it.
       (F, 20, R, 1963)

745   Tie a bullsnake around your waist to cure rheumatism.
         (M, 50, R, 1958 [a hired hand])
746   Cure rheumatic fever by smoking the patient with rye straw.
         (F, 40, R, 1963)
747   Use powdered rhubarb for colds and rheumatism.
         (M, 70, R, 1963)
748   Catch an eel, skin it, and wrap the skin around your left ankle
         and left wrist to drive out rheumatism.
         (F, 1962)
749   Wear a wire wrapped with yarn as a bracelet to cure rheu-
         matism.
         (F, 70, 1958)

ASTHMA, HAY FEVER, AND CROUP

750   Two or three drops of kerosene taken in a small amount of
         sugar will cure asthma.
         (M, 50, R, 1959 [his mother])
751   To cure asthma, hang a nutmeg around your neck on a string.
         (F, 54, R, 1963 [her grandmother])
752   One contributor reported that her grandmother suffered ter-
         ribly from asthma. She used to smoke snuff to help it. She had
         to keep moving farther west to be able to get along.
         (F, 40, R, 1962)
753   A gold ring worn through the nose will prevent asthma.
         (F, 1962)
754   One should smoke dried mullein leaves for asthma.
         (F, 61, R, 1957)
755   Take a teaspoonful of honey a day to cure arthritis, asthma,
         coughs, and so forth.
         (F, 1962)
756   If you have a sinus condition or hay fever, you can get rid of it
         by urinating and then smelling the urine.
         (M, 1963)
757   A remedy for hay fever and other allergies is as follows: Boil
         clean, fresh hay in water. Allow it to cool, and take it often.
         Some people substitute ragweed for hay.
         (F, 1963)
758   Alderberry leaves, dried, fixed into a pillow, and slept on,
         will relieve hay fever.
         (F, 50, 1963)

759   To cure croup, tie a cold cloth around your throat and cover it with a towel.
(F, 75, R, 1956)

760   If you have a croupy child, tie a black silk ribbon around his neck, and he will be cured. It must be black silk.
(F, 50, 1958, + 1 M)

761   A crocheted string of black silk thread worn around the neck will keep the croup away.
(F, 80, R, 1960)

762   Tie a black string around the child's neck, so that he won't have the croup.
(F, 53, R, 1958 [her grandmother], + 1 F)

763   A drop of coal oil and sugar is good for the croup.
(F, 49, R, 1961 [her mother], + 2 F)

764   Croup may be cured by applying skunk oil and goose oil.
(F, 57, R, 1957)

765   Skunk grease used to be rendered and used, mixed with sulfur, to rub on the chest and throat. A piece of flannel was put over it. This was considered to be good for the croup and colds.
(F, 1962)

766   Render the grease from a skunk for treating croup. Rub it on, or swallow a little bit of it.
(F, 40, R, 1961 [her mother], + 2 F and 1 M)

767   To cure croup, take one tablespoonful of goose grease and alum internally.
(F, 60, R, 1959 [her mother], + 1 F)

768   Use a mixture of turpentine and lard to cure the croup.
(F, 92, R, 1957)

769   Kerosene and lard will cure croup.
(F, 44, R, 1956, + 2 F)

770   For croup, take a teaspoonful of white sugar with two or three drops of kerosene in it.
(F, 50, R, 1960, + 2 F)

771   Give heated honey for croup.
(F, 75, R, 1961)

772   Amber beads cure croup.
(F, 80, R, 1964)

773   Fry onions, put them in a bag, and put the bag on the chest for the croup.
(F, 1962 [her mother])

774   When a child was ill with croup, feathers or other pungent

substances used to be burned, and the child was held where he had to inhale the smoke or vapor.
(M, 62, 1959)

BLOOD AND BLEEDING

775   Drink sassafras tea in the spring to thin the blood. (The informant said that at her home this was done without fail every spring.)
(F, 1962, + 2 F)

776   Take sulfur and molasses or sassafras tea to thin your blood.
(M, 70, R, 1961)

777   Sassafras tea in the spring will build up your blood.
(F, 49, R, 1961)

778   To stay healthy in the winter, you should eat plenty of molasses to keep your blood thick.
(F, 19, 1957)

779   Poisoned blood may be removed by using a leech.
(F, 65, 1957)

780   Raisins are supposed to purify the blood.
(F, 1962)

781   Put a cigarette paper under your upper lip to stop a nosebleed.
(F, 1962, + 1 M)

782   To stop a nosebleed, roll a small roll of paper, and place it between the upper lip and the gum.
(F, 20, 1962, + 7 F and 1 M)

783   A piece of brown paper on the back of the neck will stop a nosebleed.
(F, 78, 1959)

784   A cold knife on the back of your neck will stop a nosebleed.
(M, 29, 1956, + 1 M and 1 F)

785   To stop a bleeding nose, place a silver knife against the nape of the neck, and stop the nose up with cotton.
(F, 75, R, 1950, + 1 F)

786   A silver spoon held against the back of the neck will stop a nosebleed.
(F, 50, 1959 [her parents], + 1 M)

787   Hold a key at the back of the neck to stop a nosebleed.
(F, 70, 1958)

788   A nosebleed can be stopped by placing a pair of scissors in an open position, with points upward, on the back of the neck.
(M, 50, R, 1959 [his grandmother], + 1 F)

789   To stop one's nose from bleeding, one should lie on one's stomach and place a pair of scissors downward toward one's feet in the flat of one's back. This used to be guaranteed to stop a nosebleed.
(F, 1963)

790   To stop a nosebleed, put an iced towel on the back of your neck, and lie down.
(F, 20, 1969, + 9 F and 3 M)

791   Put your arms above your head, put ice or cold water between your shoulders, and then snuff very hot or very cold water in order to stop a nosebleed.
(F, 50, 1963 [her grandmother])

792   For nosebleed, put ice packs on your nose, and tilt your head back.
(F, 19, 1969, + 11 F and 2 M)

793   To stop a nosebleed, tilt your head back, and put a cold, wet rag on your forehead.
(M, 22, 1969, + 2 F and 1 M)

794   To stop a nosebleed, have the person place his head between his legs, with a cold, damp cloth on his nose and the back of his neck.
(M, 33, 1969, + 1 F)

795   Nosebleed remedy: put your head back, put a cold compress on your neck, and then put cotton in your nose.
(M, 1969 [his mother], + 2 M)

796   For nosebleed: lean your head back, and pinch each side of your nose close to the eyes. Use an ice pack on the back of your head.
(F, 21, 1969, + 1 F)

797   Cure for nosebleeds: lean your head back.
(F, 20, 1969, + 8 F and 9 M)

798   A cure for nosebleed is to put a penny or a piece of metal under the upper lip (between lip and gum).
(M, 21, 1959, + 5 F and 2 M)

799   To stop a nosebleed, place a coin under the upper lip.
(F, 50, 1959 [her parents], + 1 M and 1 F)

800   To stop a nosebleed, put a match stick, broken in half, under the upper lip, and press tightly; a dime will also work.
(M, 1959 [his parents])

801   If you wear a strand of red beads around your neck, you will never have a nosebleed.
(F, 75, R, 1960 [her mother])

802   Tie a string around your little finger; this will cure a nosebleed.
(F, 60, R, 1961 [her mother], + 1 F)

803   Wearing a chain around one's neck will cure nosebleeds. It
puts pressure on the blood vessels at the back of the neck.
(M, 50, R, 1960)

804   Cure for a bloody nose: take the lead end off a bullet, hammer
it out flat, punch a hole in it, and insert a string so that you
can hang it around your neck and wear it as a necklace.
(F, 20, R, 1961)

805   To heal a cut, take the membrane from an eggshell, and apply
it to the cut.
(M, 60, R, 1959 [her mother], + 1 F)

806   A cobweb placed over a wound will stop the bleeding.
(F, 35, 1956 [her parents], + 5 F and 3 M)

807   Make a poultice of some moistened tobacco and salt, and tie
it on a wound.
(F, 69, R, 1963)

808   Chewing tobacco rubbed on a wound will stop the bleeding
and help the healing.
(M, 60, R, 1954, + 1 F and 1 M)

809   When you cut your hand, spit tobacco juice on it, and your
hand will be all right.
(M, 22, 1965)

810   One way to stop bleeding is to place the fine silks of corn
upon the wound.
(F, 1963)

811   Pure salt will stop bleeding.
(F, 80, R, 1960 [her parents])

812   Smell vinegar to stop bleeding.
(M, 1962)

813   A way to stop bleeding: Place soot on the wound, and bind it
with a cloth.
(M, 1962)

814   One contributor reported that when one had an accident, cut,
or bruise that started to bleed, some people just used to take
an old shoe sole, scrape it off real fine, then put that fine
scraped leather on the place where the blood came out; the
bleeding stopped in no time.
(F, 72, R, 1962)

815   For severe bleeding, shave the flesh side of sole leather and
bind the shavings on the cut.
(F, 69, R, 1963 [one of her neighbors])

816   Dried toadstools will cause blood to clot.
        (M, 81, R, 1958)

817   Soot out of the chimney stopped one informant's foot from
        bleeding.
        (M, 48, R, 1958 [her mother])

818   To stop a bleeding wound, cover the wound with sugar.
        (F, 25, R, 1956)

819   Lie on your back, and apply a cold washcloth to your fore-
        head to stop bleeding.
        (M, 1962)

820   Always run cold water on a bleeding cut; this will actually
        help the clotting of blood.
        (M, 1964)

821   When one cuts one's hand or finger, one should pour kero-
        sene on it.
        (M, 1964)

822   If you cut your hand, cover the wound with black pepper.
        Contrary to belief, this will not burn and is most healing; it
        forms a crust to keep out infection.
        (F, 50, 1963)

823   To stop bleeding, place a coin on the wound.
        (M, 21, R, 1961)

824   Some people always used to keep some sponge that grew
        around the farm, and when dried out, it was good to stop the
        bleeding.
        (M, 72, R, 1962)

825   To stop bleeding, repeat Ezekiel 16 silently three times.
        (F, 50, R, 1961)

826   Stop bleeding by opening to a passage in the Bible, then put
        the Bible under your pillow and sleep on it that night.
        (F, 1962)

827   Put flour on a cut to stop the bleeding.
        (F, 30, 1957 [her mother], + 1 F and 1 M)

828   To stop the bleeding, put either flour or baking soda on the
        wound.
        (F, 20, R, 1961)

829   If a woman hemorrhages after childbirth, get a piece of
        heavy steel, an ax head, or a maul. Put it on the floor under
        her bed, and this will check the hemorrhage.
        (F, 60, 1959)

BOILS AND COLD SORES

830   Make a poultice of laundry soap and sugar to cure a boil.
(F, 58, 1958, + 1 F)

831   For a boil: apply old-type laundry soap to the boil, holding it in place with a bandage. This will draw the boil to a head.
(F, 60, R, 1960 [her mother])

832   To cure a boil, one informant had discovered three separate remedies. In every instance these are applied directly to the boil. 1. Fifty percent laundry soap, and fifty percent sugar. 2. Fat pork. 3. Enough milk added to bread to render it pastelike.
(F, 1963)

833   Put fresh pork on a boil, and the pork will draw the boil to a head.
(M, 50, 1960 [his father])

834   Place bacon on a boil in order to bring it to a head.
(F, 35, 1958, + 2 F)

835   For carbuncles: Wrap sausage around the infected area, and it will draw out the poison.
(F, 80, R, 1963 [his mother])

836   Boils may be cured by tying a beefsteak to them.
(F, 57, R, 1957)

837   Use a bread-and-milk poultice for boils.
(F, 30, R, 1957, + 5 F and 4 M)

838   Eat raisins to cure boils.
(M, 60, R, 1957, + 2 M)

839   Eat raisins to prevent boils.
(F, 45, R, 1958 [her grandfather])

840   Put a poultice of roasted onions on a boil to bring it to a head.
(F, 1951)

841   In order to draw out the poison, scrape a raw potato, and apply the scrapings as a poultice. This is good for boils.
(F, 1962, + 1 F)

842   A poultice made from ground up elm-tree bark used to be put on boils and abscesses to draw out the impurities.
(M, 62, R, 1959)

843   A poultice of flaxseed, made into a paste and placed over a boil, will bring the boil to a head.
(F, 30, 1957)

844   Put a raw egg on a boil; this will make the boil go away.
(F, 1952)

845   The lining of an eggshell will draw a boil to a head.
        (F, 40, R, 1960, + 1 F)

846   The white of an egg will cure a boil.
        (F, 52, R, 1956)

847   Mix an egg yolk with flour to make a paste for taking the
        infection out of boils and carbuncles. Another mix for this is
        sugar and lathered soap in a paste form.
        (F, 58, 1954)

848   Put fresh cow manure on a boil to bring the infection out.
        (M, 56, R, 1960, + 1 F and 1 M)

849   Apply wagon grease or chewing tobacco to boils to cure
        them.
        (M, 60, 1963 [her grandmother])

850   Sulfur and molasses will clean up your blood so that you
        won't have boils.
        (F, 1962)

851   To cure boils, take pipe tobacco, and apply it to them.
        (F, 79, 1957)

852   If one does not have a boil at least once a year, there is
        something wrong with one's blood.
        (M, 25, 1957)

853   A boil destroys twenty dollars' worth of disease germs.
        (F, 27, 1952)

854   Place a dry fig on a boil to cure it.
        (F, 1962 [her mother])

855   You may get rid of a boil by placing a leech on it.
        (M, 1963)

856   A way to get rid of boils: take the BBs out of a shotgun shell,
        and put them in a bandage over the boil.
        (F, 60, R, 1961 [her grandmother])

857   Boils or bites may be treated by following cattle until they
        void, and then applying the fresh urine to the boils or bites.
        (F, 57, R, 1957)

858   Break open a cactus, and use the pulp in a poultice in order to
        cure boils.
        (F, 40, 1958 [her grandfather])

859   Make a prickly-pear poultice by burning the thorns off a
        prickly pear; then roast it, open it up, and apply it to boils or
        abscesses.
        (F, 79, R, 1957)

860   Use alum or pickle juice to cure cold sores.
        (M, 50, R, 1960 [his grandparents])

861   If you feel a fever blister coming on, rub it with a gold coin or ring, and it won't get any bigger.
(M, 76, R, 1959)

862   Do not kiss anyone with a fever blister, or you will get one.
(F, 40, R, 1960)

863   A cold sore on the lips is a sign that one has been kissed by a fool.
(F, 40, R, 1960)

BUNIONS AND CORNS

864   A mixture of laudanum and camphor ice will get rid of bunions.
(F, 73, R, 1959)

865   To remove bunions, rub them with caster oil.
(F, 82, R, 1957)

866   To get rid of corns, soak your feet in hot water, and then put castor oil on them.
(M, 50, 1960 [one of his friends])

867   If you have a corn on your toe, spit on the corn as soon as you wake up for seven mornings, and the corn will disappear.
(M, 62, R, 1959)

868   Place a piece of old rubber bath sponge between your corns, and if you wear the sponge long enough, the corns will go away.
(F, 82, R, 1957)

869   If you paint corns with ink, they will go away.
(F, 82, R, 1957)

870   A cure for a soft corn between the toes: tear the piece of margin from a newspaper; place between the toes; change every day. This will dry up the corn, and you will soon be able to pull it out.
(F, 60, 1959 [her parents])

871   Soak bread in vinegar, bind it on corns day and night, and the corns will come out by the roots.
(F, 71, 1971)

872   To get rid of a corn, one should wrap a kernel of corn in a handkerchief and bury it.
(F, 22, 1958)

873   A cure for corns is to walk on dewy grass early in the morning.
(F, 20, R, 1957)

874   The way to get rid of callouses on your feet is to take some hair oil and put it on the callouses every day for a while; they will come off after a while.

(M, 70, 1959)

875   A mixture of turpentine and lard rubbed into sore feet soothes them very effectively. This mixture was used by settlers moving westward who had to walk all day herding cattle.

(F, 73, R, 1959)

BURNS

876   You can take the pain out of a burn and help it to heal quickly by dousing it in vanilla extract—it works!

(F, 1963)

877   Mrs. George Neely reported that at Camp Point, Illinois, there were some people who believed that burns could be cured by reburning. Mrs. Neely remembered that when she was a small child, she heard a girl scream from several miles away when the girl's father held her over the fire to reburn her after she had been scalded with water.

(F, 80, 1963)

878   To help a burn, hold it over a red-hot coal.

(F, 1962, + 1 F)

879   If a burn blister is opened up after sundown, it won't make a sore.

(M, 1962)

880   Put a raw potato on a burn to make it stop hurting.

(F, 20, R, 1961 [her mother], + 1 F and 1 M)

881   If you burn your finger, place it behind your ear, and it will not blister.

(M, 20, R, 1957, + 1 F and 1 M)

882   Use pickle juice for a burn.

(F, 50, R, 1950)

883   Put egg whites on a burn to stop the pain; never use grease.

(F, 50, R, 1962 [her mother])

884   Contrary to the common belief that water is very bad for burns, it is now advocated that the immersion of a burned limb or area in ice-cold water is excellent for drawing out the pain of the burn.

(M, 1962)

885   Use soda for burns.
        (F, 1962)

886   Put baking soda on a burn to make it stop hurting.
        (F, 20, R, 1961 [her mother])

887   For burns: gather winter fern, strip off the leaves, and fry
        them in lard till they turn black. Strain while hot. This will
        heal the burns in a few days.
        (M, 60, R, 1964 [his mother])

888   Butter is good for a burn.
        (F, 1962)

889   Take a cattail (the plant), strip it off, place it in pure lard, and
        bind it to the burn.
        (F, 75, R, 1956)

890   Put strong tea on a sunburn to make it stop hurting.
        (F, 20, R, 1961 [her grandmother], + 1 F)

891   Sweet cream is good for a sunburn.
        (F, 1962 [her parents] + 1 F)

892   Put vinegar on a sunburn to help cure it.
        (F, 1976 [her mother])

THE COMMON COLD

893   If you put camphor on the "soft spot" of your baby's head, he
        won't catch a cold.
        (F, 50, 1950)

894   You won't catch cold if you wear a black silk ribbon around
        your neck.
        (M, 23, R, 1956)

895   Eat at least one or two oranges a day to prevent the flu or a
        cold. If you get either one, go to the drug store or the student
        health service.
        (F, 23, 1969)

896   If you hang a bag of onions in the house, you won't catch a
        cold.
        (F, 80, R, 1961 [her parents], + 1 M)

897   Feed a cold; starve a fever.
        (F, 21, 1950, + 12 F and 5 M)

898   Wear asafetida around your neck to cure a cold.
        (F, 21, 1950, + 12 F and 10 M)

899   A bag of garlic worn around the neck will help to cure colds.
        (M, 50, 1957, + 2 F and 1 M)

900   Goose grease rubbed on the soles of a child's feet will cure
      his chest cold.
          (M, 60, R, 1959, + 1 F)
901   To cure a cold, mix goose grease and turpentine, rub it into
      the chest thoroughly, and cover with a flannel cloth.
          (M, 40, R, 1957, + 3 M)
902   Goose grease rubbed on the chest will cure a cold.
          (F, 50, R, 1959 [her aunt], + 4 F and 1 M)
903   Melt skunk grease, and rub it on the chest for colds.
          (M, 50, R, 1959 [his father, who came from Germany], +
          10 F and 5 M)
904   Kill a skunk and render out the fat (in wintertime). Mix it with
      a little coal oil, and use it for a chest rub.
          (M, 60, R, 1960 [his mother], + 1 F and 1 M)
905   Rub a mixture of coal oil and lard on your chest to relieve
      chest colds.
          (F, 80, 1954, + 1 F)
906   To cure a cold, rub lard and mustard seed on your chest.
          (M, 22, R, 1959)
907   To cure a cold, rub sheep grease on your chest.
          (F, 55, 1958)
908   For a cold, drink coal oil and sugar.
          (F, 20, R, 1958 [her mother], + 2 F)
909   Rub turpentine and lard on the chest to cure a chest cold.
          (F, 50, R, 1960, + 10 F and 7 M)
910   Use a lard and nutmeg poultice to break up a congested lung
      cold.
          (F, 1961)
911   Use lamb tallow for chest colds. Use a mustard plaster mixed
      with egg white for colds, and use flaxseed poultices for draw-
      ing out infection.
          (F, 40, R, 1960)
912   One remedy for colds and sore throats used to be skunk
      grease and a wool sock.
          (F, 40, R, 1958 [her mother])
913   Skunk oil and turpentine used to be rubbed on a child's chest
      when he had a chest cold.
          (F, 78, R, 1959 [her grandmother])
914   To cure a cold, go to bed, covering up with an excess of
      blankets so that you will sweat.
          (F, 1965 [her mother], + 1 F)
915   To cure a cold, put on lots of clothes, and work up a good

sweat; then take a hot shower, and go to bed with lots of blankets.

(M, 1964 [one of his buddies], + 2 F and 2 M)

916   Put fried onions between two pieces of wool, and apply this to the chest to cure colds or pneumonia.

(F, 43, R, 1963 [her schoolmates], + 10 F and 1 M)

917   Eat onions in order to get rid of a cold.

(F, 21, R, 1969, + 1 F and 1 M)

918   To cure a cold, wear red flannel around the neck.

(F, 21, 1950 [her mother], + 3 F and 1 M)

919   Wear new flannel on the chest to cure a chest cold.

(F, 50, R, 1961 [her parents])

920   To relieve a chest cold, rub the chest with Vicks (the informant's grandma used lard) and cover it with a warm flannel cloth.

(F, 22, 1969, + 7 F and 5 M)

921   To treat a cold: rub in an abundance of Mentholatum on your chest, throat, and upper lip. Next, take a hot towel and wrap it around your neck. Use a warm washcloth on your chest, go to a cold bedroom, and sleep under many covers.

(M, 21, R, 1971)

922   Tie a dirty sock around your throat to cure a cold.

(F, 30, R, 1958, + 2 F and 2 M)

923   A mustard poultice will break up a cold when it is applied to the back or chest.

(F, 30, R, 1960, + 1 F and 2 M)

924   Use warm salt water in the nose for a cold.

(M, 50, R, 1960)

925   A favorite cure for a cold is to breathe in the steam from hot water.

(F, 20, R, 1969 [her father], + 3 F and 1 M)

926   To cure a cold, take aspirin.

(F, 20, 1973, + 13 F and 7 M)

927   Rest and consume lots of vitamin C in order to cure a cold.

(F, 20, 1973, + 7 F and 2 M)

928   To treat a cold, take a cold tablet, and go to bed.

(F, 21, 1961 [her family doctor], + 6 F and 4 M)

929   To cure a cold, get more rest than usual, and stay in bed.

(F, 20, 1973 [her mother], + 9 F and 8 M)

930   When you have a cold, drink plenty of liquids, and get lots of rest.

(F, 19, 1969 [her mother], + 18 F and 22 M)

931   Drink a large amount of orange juice (at least two large glasses each day) when you have a cold.
       (F, 19, 1973 [her mother], + 9 F and 4 M)

932   You are guaranteed to wake up the next morning without your cold if your drink four quarts of orange juice, take two aspirin, set the thermostat up, and put on three or four wool blankets.
       (F, 21, 1971)

933   To cure a cold: gargle with Listerine, take aspirin, drink fluids, stay in bed, turn on a vaporizer, watch TV (drink 7-up), and keep warm; it is mainly a matter of time.
       (F, 19, 1973)

934   One contributor said that to cure a cold, one should drink a concoction of her grandmother's spiced tea, take a hot bath, and stay in a small steamy room, with a hot towel wrapped around one's neck.
       (F, 20, 1969)

935   To kill a cold, soak your feet in hot water, drink sage tea, and go to bed.
       (F, 70, 1955)

936   For colds, drink red-pepper tea.
       (M, 1961 [his father])

937   Cure green alfalfa leaves, boil them with sugar, and mix them with hot tea. Take this for colds.
       (M, 21, R, 1971 [his grandfather])

938   When you have a cold, take a warm bath, drink some hot tea, and go to bed.
       (M, 21, 1971 [his mother], + 4 F and 1 M)

939   To help relieve a common cold, drink hot tea with honey as an additive.
       (M, 21, 1973 [his mother])

940   Drink honey and vinegar once in the morning and at night when you have a cold.
       (F, 21, 1961, + 1 M)

941   When you have a cold, drink hot lemonade and get lots of rest.
       (F, 21, 1971 [her parents], + 10 F)

942   Drink honey with lemon juice in it when you have a cold.
       (F, 21, 1971, + 3 F and 3 M)

943   When you have a cold, drink lots of grape juice, lie in bed, and watch TV.
       (M, 22, R, 1969 [his mother])

944   To treat a cold: fix hot tea or coffee; add a double shot of bourbon, lots of lemon juice (to mask the taste), and a couple of tablespoonfuls of honey; stir well; and drink it. Then go to bed, and keep well covered.
(F, 21, 1973, + 1 F and 1 M)

945   When you have a cold, drink a hot mixture of two shots of brandy, some lemon juice, and two tablespoonfuls of honey.
(F, 21, 1971, + 2 M)

946   The best cure for a cold is to drink a hot toddy made of honey and whiskey just before you go to bed.
(F, 19, R, 1973 [her grandmother], + 2 F and 10 M)

947   Mix whiskey, lemon juice, and sugar, and heat. Drink this while it is hot to break a cold.
(M, 40, R, 1961, + 3 M)

948   Indulge in alcoholic beverages for a whole day to get rid of a cold quite readily.
(F, 20, R, 1971)

949   A hot toddy before going to bed is a real cure-all for colds.
(F, 21, 1969 [her parents], + 13 F and 16 M)

950   When you have a cold, drink a shot of whiskey, and go to bed.
(F, 20, R, 1973 [her father], + 1 F and 8 M)

951   To cure a cold, take a shot of Old Crow every morning, either straight or in a cup of coffee.
(F, 21, R, 1971)

952   When you have a cold, drink two or three jiggers of whiskey every three or four hours while getting lots of rest.
(M, 21, R, 1971 [his father], + 1 M)

953   To treat a cold, take a fifth of whiskey, and go to bed.
(M, 21, 1969, + 2 M)

954   If you have a cold, drink a pint of whiskey shortly before bedtime.
(M, 21, R, 1971, + 2 M)

955   Advice for treating a cold: go to the candy store, and buy a pound of rock candy. Then, go to the liquor store, and purchase a fifth of your favorite brand. On the way home, throw the candy away, and drink the fifth. When you wake up, your cold will be gone.
(M, 25, 1969 [his father])

956   When you have a cold, drink approximately twenty double screwdrivers. The orange juice helps to cure the cold, and the vodka alleviates the pain.
(M, 24, 1973 [learned while serving in the army])

957   One contributor said that when he had a cold, his grandma
        used to go to the pantry, get some corn whiskey, and have him
        drink some; after this, she'd rub some on his chest, which she
        said had great penetrating power. He then went to bed and
        slept well.
        (M, 20, R, 1969)

958   To treat a cold, mix equal parts of orange juice and whiskey,
        heat, and drink in one gulp.
        (M, 21, 1971, + 1 M)

959   When you have a cold, drink hot brandy or whiskey with
        lemon and peppermint.
        (M, 23, R, 1969 [his grandmother], + 1 F)

960   Drink whiskey and sugar in hot water before going to bed
        when you have a cold.
        (M, 20, R, 1969, + 2 M)

961   For a cold, take two teaspoonfuls of vodka straight, and then
        drink a cup of hot black coffee.
        (M, 22, 1969)

962   If you have a cold, mix rum, hot water, and some melted
        butter. Drink this as rapidly as possible; then go to bed and
        sleep.
        (M, 21, 1969 [his father], + 1 M)

963   Drink some apricot brandy, and don't get your feet wet when
        you have a cold.
        (F, 21, 1971)

964   Drink a mixture of brandy and honey before going to bed
        when you have a cold.
        (F, 21, 1971)

965   Drink peppermint schnapps; it will almost relieve a cold for
        about two hours.
        (M, 22, R, 1971, + 2 M)

966   Drink lemon juice and gin to treat a cold.
        (M, 20, 1969)

967   To cure a cold, drink hot eggnog before and after going to
        bed.
        (M, 21, 1969)

968   Drink this prescription when you have a cold: two jiggers of
        Scotch and one tablespoonful of honey; add these to a glass of
        milk, and stir.
        (M, 1962)

969   Drink whiskey and eat rock candy for a cold.
        (M, 65, R, 1958)

970   The best way to cure a cold is to buy a bottle of whiskey, hang
       your hat on the bedpost, and crawl in. When you can see two
       hats on the post, cover up and go to sleep. In the morning your
       cold will be gone.
           (M, 63, 1955)
971   To treat a cold, drink an Irish toddy made of: one-half cupful
       of hot water; the juice of one-half lemon; one jigger of Irish
       whiskey.
           (F, 1962)
972   A spoonful of brandy is the best medicine for colds, tummy
       aches, rheumatism, and everything up to the measles.
           (M, 1963)
973   If you have a cold, burn the alcohol out of some whiskey, and
       then drink it.
           (M, 20, 1960)
974   To treat a cold, heat beer that is much like ale, and drink it till
       you are warm all over or drunk, whichever the case may be.
           (M, 20, R, 1969 [his grandmother], + 1 F)
975   When you have a cold, apply a heating pad or hot water over
       your nose and sinus passages.
           (F, 1966)
976   When you have a cold, do not eat any supper. Do not overeat,
       and avoid meats and pastries. A cold should be starved.
           (M, 26, 1956)
977   Food for a cold: beat the yolk of an egg with a tablespoonful of
       sugar; beat the white separately; add a teacupful of boiling
       water to the yolk; then stir in the white—add any seasoning.
           (F, 70, R, 1960)
978   Make tea from the bark of slippery elm: break the bark; pour
       on boiling water to cover; let it infuse until cold; sweeten, ice,
       and take it for a summer disorder; or add lemon juice, and
       drink it for a bad cold.
           (F, 70, R, 1960)
979   Recipe for sea-moss farina: mix one dessertspoonful of sea-
       moss farina with one quart of boiling water; steep a few min-
       utes, sweeten, and flavor with a slice of lemon. This is a very
       pleasant drink, and it is good for colds.
           (F, 70, 1960)
980   Use lots of honey when you have a cold.
           (M, 26, R, 1971)
981   Wrap raw beefsteak against the bottoms of your feet. It will
       draw a cold out.
           (F, 50, R, 1958)

982   Melt Laundry (bar) soap; make a poultice by spreading this melted soap on a cloth; and apply it to your chest. This will relieve a tight bronchial chest cold.
      (F, 60, R, 1962)

983   One contributor said that when butchering time came, hogs hooves used to be saved, cleaned, dried, and powdered. This powder was made into a poultice to put on the chest for deep colds and pneumonia.
      (F, 80, 1959)

984   Eat horehound candy to cure a cold.
      (F, 57, R, 1957)

985   To cure a cold, put a live spider in a thimble and tie it around your neck.
      (M, 19, 1955)

986   To treat a cold, soak your feet in hot water.
      (M, 60, R, 1961)

987   Jerk out the crown hairs of your head to cure colds and other minor ailments.
      (F, 20, R, 1957)

988   To cure his cold, an adult should throw black pepper on a hot stove and inhale the fumes.
      (M, 62, R, 1959)

989   To cure a cold, hang a sack of sassafras around your neck.
      (F, 21, 1950)

990   Rub liniment on the bottom of a baby's feet to relieve cold congestion.
      (F, 70, R, 1955)

991   Hanging a bag of sulfur around one's neck will help to cure colds.
      (F, 60, R, 1957)

COUGH REMEDIES

992   Gargle with a mixture of one teaspoonful of sugar soaked with coal oil.
      (M, 50, R, 1958 [his mother], + 2 F)

993   Eat loaf sugar with turpentine dripped on it.
      (F, 70, 1960 [her mother])

994   Drink a syrup made of kerosene and lard!
      (F, 56, 1962)

995   Drink whiskey, and eat rock candy.
      (M, 50, R, 1957, + 1 M)

996   Take whiskey and sugar.
        (F, 60, R, 1960)

997   Take a syrup made of sliced onion and sugar. (The informant
        remarked that her mother kept this syrup on the back of their
        wood stove all during the winter.)
        (F, 50, 1952, + 1 F)

998   Eat ginger and sugar.
        (F, 30, R, 1958)

999   Make a syrup by heating together lemon juice and brown
        sugar.
        (M, 23, 1964)

1000   Make a syrup by boiling down the bushy part of broomweed
        until it becomes thick.
        (F, 1963)

1001   Mix equal parts of sugar and butter with water.
        (F, 1962)

1002   Mix the juice of six lemons with one pint of strained honey.
        Take one teaspoonful as often as necessary.
        (M, 60, R, 1964 [his mother])

1003   Take a mixture of kerosene and sugar.
        (F, 1962, + 1 F)

1004   Take a simple cough medicine made with five teaspoonfuls of
        vinegar, six teaspoonfuls of sugar, and one tumblerful of
        water. Stir until the sugar is dissolved. Then take one or two
        swallows each time you cough or once every ten or fifteen
        minutes until you get relief.
        (F, 69, R, 1963)

1005   Take a preparation made from honey, vinegar, butter, and
        cooked onion juice.
        (M, 60, R, 1961)

1006   Take a syrup made of horehound candy, mistletoe, and whis-
        key, boiled together.
        (F, 56, 1962)

1007   Use cough drops made from horehound root.
        (F, 50, 1958)

1008   Drink the liquid from boiled horehound leaves.
        (F, 61, R, 1957)

1009   Boil horehound leaves; then mix this liquid with syrup.
        (F, 80, R, 1960.)

1010   Take cough syrup made from two tablespoonfuls of vinegar,
        three tablespoonfuls of sugar, and one teaspoonful of butter,
        warmed together.
        (F, 72, R, 1959)

ADVICE ABOUT THE DIGESTIVE TRACT

1011   One informant said that she was never allowed to eat bread
        the day it was baked, because it was supposed to be bad for
        you—it was too doughy in your stomach. Her grandma's
        bread always had some rye flour in it.
        (F, 60, R, 1959)

1012   Parsnips used to be considered poisonous if eaten by humans
        unless the parsnips had first been allowed to freeze in the
        ground before they were dug up.
        (M, 62, 1959)

1013   Cherries and milk eaten at the same meal are poisonous.
        (F, 50, 1957)

1014   You shouldn't eat citrus fruit and milk together, because they
        will surely sour in your stomach and make you sick.
        (F, 57, R, 1957)

1015   Eating pickles and ice cream together will upset your
        stomach.
        (F, 28, 1956)

1016   Your life will be prolonged if you don't drink ice-cold water.
        (F, 60, R, 1959)

1017   Do not eat oysters in months that don't contain an r, or you
        will become ill.
        (M, 40, R, 1960)

1018   Don't eat rabbits in any month other than the ones that are
        spelled with an r.
        (F, 30, 1958)

1019   Never drink milk when you eat fish; they don't mix.
        (F, 20, 1969, + 10 F and 5 M)

1020   If you drink milk and chili at the same time, you will get sick.
        (F, 23, 1959, + 4 F)

1021   Sugar and turpentine will kill roundworms in children.
        (F, 60, R, 1960, + 1 F)

1022   Swallowing a cat's hair will cause you to have tapeworms.
        (F, 30, R, 1957, + 1 M)

1023   Children pick their noses when they have worms.
        (M, 39, R, 1963, + 3 F and 1 M)

1024   Crushed eggshells and molasses make a cure for worms.
        (F, 50, R, 1962)

1025   If you get worms, just drink garlic juice once a day for a month.
        (F, 57, R, 1957)

1026   Sassafras tea (made by boiling roots of the sassafras bush) will purify the blood and remove any worms from the body.
        (F, 50, R, 1959)

1027   Take sassafras bark sprinkled in dry fruit to keep out worms.
        (F, 82, R, 1957)

1028   To cure worms, take three drops of turpentine a day for three days.
        (F, 56, 1962)

1029   A person will get worms if he eats a raw potato.
        (M, 30, 1958)

1030   If a child eats dirt, he has worms.
        (F, 20, 1958)

1031   If a child grinds his teeth at night, he has worms.
        (F, 24, R, 1956)

1032   Turpentine or coal oil with sugar is a remedy for worms.
        (F, 1962)

1033   A cure for worms is one teaspoonful of sugar with two or three drops of turpentine.
        (F, 1962)

1034   To cure worms, drink small doses of sugar and turpentine or sugar and kerosene daily until the worms disappear.
        (M, 1963)

1035   Eating just before you go to bed will give you worms.
        (F, 20, R, 1961)

1036   Drink tea to stop diarrhea.
        (M, 60, 1967)

1037   Use coltstail tea for "summer complaint" (diarrhea). (Coltstail is a common Kansas weed that looks like a colt's tail.)
        (F, 50, R, 1958)

1038   The lining from chicken gizzards used to be saved, dried, and steeped into tea. This was given to babies, and others, for "summer complaint."
        (F, 80, 1959 [her father])

1039   To prevent diarrhea, give babies catnip to make them break out in hives.
        (F, 22, 1958)

1040   To cure diarrhea: brown flour in a skillet; add water to make a thick gruel; then eat it.
        (F, 50, R, 1961)

1041   A tea made by steeping dried nightshade vine plant in hot water used to be considered a cure for "summer complaint" in babies.
(F, 80, R, 1960)

1042   Dice jelly; add one tablespoonful of rice flour, mixed with cold water, and a scant pint of boiling water; sweeten. Boil until quite clear. This is good for "summer complaint."
(F, 70, R, 1960 [her mother])

1043   Cinnamon tea: to a half pint of new milk, add stick cinnamon to flavor and white sugar to taste; bring to the boiling point. Taken either warm or cold, it is excellent for diarrhea in adults or children.
(F, 70, R, 1960)

1044   Dysentery may be cured by eating the lining of a chicken gizzard that has been ground up.
(F, 57, R, 1957)

1045   Peppermint extract in water will relieve a baby's gas.
(F, 50, 1960)

1046   It used to be thought that if one's stomach was upset, his navel was out of place. The cure was to lay the patient on his back, place a coin on his navel, and stick a lighted candle onto the coin. Then an inverted water glass was placed over the candle. The candle would soon go out. The water glass was left over the candle until it fell off. The navel was now in place, and one was cured.
(F, 40, R, 1960)

1047   If you have chronic pains in your stomach, it may be a sign that you are liver-grown, which is supposed to mean that your liver is stuck down. The cure is to get down on the floor on your hands and knees and crawl under the dining table. First crawl through from east to west, and then from north to south, forming a cross. You will probably laugh enough at this undignified procedure to shake your liver loose.
(M, 60, 1954)

1048   Peach-leaf tea, given every two hours, will relieve inflammation of the stomach.
(F, 50, R, 1959)

1049   The lining from an eggshell is good for the stomach.
(F, 49, R, 1961)

1050   Burned toast is good for a stomach ache.
(F, 60, R, 1960)

1051   Take peppermint drops mixed with sugar to cure a stomach ache.
        (M, 80, R, 1960 [his mother])

1052   A mixture of sulfur and molasses is good for a stomach ache or anything else (such as unruly kids).
        (M, 23, 1964)

1053   When you have a pain in your stomach, sleep with your hand over it, and it will get better.
        (F, 93, R, 1963)

1054   When one informant had a pain in her stomach, two pieces of cloth were cut. One was placed on her stomach, and the other on the back of her neck. Then she got better. (They looked like cheesecloth. She attributed this custom to the Bible verse about healing with the laying on of hands.)
        (F, 93, R, 1963)

1055   Use mule's tail tea to stop stomach aches in children.
        (F, 58, 1958)

1056   To cure a stomach ache, place a half dollar over your navel; then turn a glass upside down over it, and leave it for a few minutes (an old custom).
        (F, 80, R, 1960)

1057   If you're sick at your stomach, take a white rag, ring it out in vinegar water, and put it around your throat in order to settle your stomach.
        (F, 60, R, 1958)

1058   Germans and Russians used to believe that stomach cramps in the daytime were just that. But stomach aches at night were believed to be caused by little black devils jumping up and down on one's stomach. The only way to get rid of these little black devils was to fumigate the house with sulfur the next day.
        (M, 40, 1964)

1059   Skunk meat is a good cure for stomach disorders.
        (M, 40, R, 1963 [learned in Mexico])

1060   For the "bellyache," people used to take soda mixed with hot water. Most got relief.
        (F, 71, R, 1958)

1061   Calamus roots are good for stomach trouble.
        (F, 49, R, 1961)

1062   Drink tea made from senna leaves as a laxative.
        (F, 60, R, 1961, + 3 F)

1063   One contributor reported that he used to work on the section (on the railroad). He had heartburn and couldn't get rid of it. Another man had a bacon rind, which he carried, and told him to chew it. It helped, and thereafter he carried a bacon rind. He believed in it.

(F, 70, R, 1962)

1064   To cure heartburn, rub your fingers in your armpit; then smell them; and the heartburn will be gone.

(M, 80, R, 1957)

1065   Chew peach seeds for indigestion.

(F, 82, R, 1957)

1066   If you always drink a glass of hot water in the morning, you will not have to worry about constipation.

(M, 1962)

1067   One contributor said that he had never seen this done, but he had been told that when some of the old people used to have the piles (hemorrhoids), all they did was take a dry cow chip (cow dropping), start a fire, burn the cow chip till no flame was left, and then put it on a tin bucket and sit on the bucket as long as there was any heat left in the cow chip. They said they cured their piles that way. He himself had never tried that old remedy.

(M, 62, R, 1962)

1068   Take the lining of a chicken gizzard, and let it dry till it is brittle. Crush it with a rolling pin, and use it for a laxative.

(F, 1962)

DOG BITES

1069   The hair of the dog is good for healing a dog bite.

(F, 80, R, 1957, + 1 F)

1070   People used to think that you could heal a dog bite by boiling a madstone—a smooth round stone—in sweet milk and putting it on the dog bite while the stone was still hot.

(F, 60, R, 1960)

1071   Rabies can be prevented by placing a madstone on a dog bite. (A madstone here is a hard rocklike substance that the animal has spit out; it is collected and formed by an animal's licking its hair.)

(M, 70, R, 1957, + 1 F)

1072   A madbone is a bone taken from near the stomach of a deer. It is used to draw the poison from the bite of a mad dog. The bone is placed in the bite and then put into milk; if the poison

is present, the milk will turn black. The bone is then boiled,
and the process is repeated until all the poison has been
drawn out.

(F, 1962)

1073   If a mad dog bites you, then rub the wound with a madstone
taken from the pit of a cow's stomach. It will cure you.

(F, 50, 1957)

FLU, PNEUMONIA, COLIC,
AND WHOOPING COUGH

1074   As a preventive for the flu, eat a Bermuda onion at dinner
every night.

(M, 50, 1964)

1075   To avoid getting the flu, keep an open bottle of carbolic acid
in the house, and touch your tongue to turpentine every night
before you go to bed.

(M, 50, 1964 [his family])

1076   Garlic hung in a sack around the neck will cure the flu.

(M, 21, 1955)

1077   To treat the flu, take hot tea with honey.

(M, 1964 [his mother])

1078   To cure a case of the flu, use some hot water and some Old
Crow.

(M, 1964 [his parents])

1079   A cure for flu: slice one-half of a lemon and one-half of an
orange; boil in one cup of water for five minutes; mix with
two teaspoonfuls of honey and one ounce of whiskey; drink
immediately.

(F, 1962)

1080   The treatment for lung fever used to be turpentine and lard
mixed and applied to the chest and back.

(F, 71, R, 1958)

1081   To relieve congestion in the lungs, make a mustard plaster of
one tablespoonful of flour and two tablespoonfuls of mustard
(dry); moisten this with water and spread it on a cloth that is
large enough to cover the entire chest. Put the cloth on the
chest, and cover it up. Leave the plaster on until the chest is
good and warm.

(F, 50, R, 1959)

1082   Another cure for lung fever used to be a paste of mustard and flour. This was smoothed on two pieces of old muslin and was bound on the soles of a person's feet.

(F, 71, R, 1958)

1083   To check a cold in the lungs, cook onions and put them between two layers of cloth. If the cloth turns green, then you have a lung cold.

(F, 30, R, 1959)

1084   Lung congestion should be treated as follows: Roll onions in cornmeal, and fry them until they are well done. Place the onions in a salt sack, and apply it to the chest. In severe cases, camphor should be added to the mixture.

(F, 1963)

1085   A common idea used to be that skunk's oil applied to the throat and lungs was a good remedy for a cold on the lungs. Sometimes it was given internally in small doses.

(F, 69, R, 1963, + 1 F)

1086   Give a baby a teaspoonful of water when it is first born, and it will never have the colic.

(M, 22, R, 1958)

1087   To cure a baby of colic, feed it liquid from the food that the mother craved most during her pregnancy.

(F, 29, R, 1963 [her grandmother])

1088   Give the baby some onion tea for colic; this is also good for a fretful baby.

(F, 80, R, 1961 [her mother])

1089   Mix asafetida and whiskey together, and let it stand. Give a small dose to the baby for colic.

(F, 50, R, 1961 [her mother])

1090   Catnip tea is good for colic. Make it by boiling the leaves of the catnip plant.

(F, 50, R, 1961 [her mother])

1091   Always sleep in your own bed in the winter; or you will catch pneumonia.

(M, 22, R, 1958)

1092   Use skunk grease to make a poultice for pneumonia.

(F, 80, R, 1958 [her mother])

1093   Skunk oil, made by rendering the fat from a skunk, used to be rubbed on the chest and throat to cure croup and pneumonia.

(F, 80, 1959 [her father])

1094   Fry onions in fat until they are soft and yellow. They make a good poultice for pneumonia. Or you can use a mustard poultice.

(F, 60, 1962, + 5 F)

1095   To prevent whooping cough, wear asafetida around the neck.
        (F, 1961, + 1 F)

1096   Wear amber beads around your neck to ward off whooping
        cough.
        (F, 19, 1956)

1097   If your child has the whooping cough, get some warm milk
        from a mare that has recently foaled, give the milk to the
        child, and he will cease whooping.
        (F, 50, 1958, + 1 M)

1098   Skunk grease is a good cure for whooping cough and colds.
        (M, 50, 1963 [his mother])

1099   To cure whooping cough, tie a piece of buckskin around the
        neck. This will stop the whooping.
        (F, 75, R, 1956)

1100   For whooping cough, thoroughly mix equal parts of strained
        honey, olive oil, and whiskey. Give one teaspoonful three
        times a day.
        (F, 60, R, 1962)

1101   Bake a field mouse, and feed it to the patient to aid in curing
        whooping cough.
        (F, 50, 1959 [her aunt])

1102   One contributor reported that her Irish grandfather used to
        urge mothers of young children suffering from whooping
        cough to put a small live fish in the child's mouth and to hold
        it there for three minutes, then to put the fish back in the
        creek. He claimed that if this were done, the fish would swim
        away with the disease.
        (F, 40, R, 1959)

                            GOITERS

1103   Nutmeg worn on a chain around the neck will keep one from
        having a goiter.
        (F, 40, R, 1963 [her grandmother])

1104   Tie a black silk thread around your neck if you want to keep
        from having a goiter.
        (M, 19, 1958)

1105   A live garden snake wrapped around your neck will cure a
        goiter.
        (M, 60, R, 1960 [his parents])

1106   To cure a goiter, let a pup sleep by your neck one night, and he'll get the goiter.
(F, 40, 1961 [her mother])

1107   To cure a goiter, soak a dirty stocking in vinegar, and wrap it around the afflicted area.
(M, 19, 1958)

1108   In order to rid oneself of a goiter, it used to be thought that one had only to rub one's hands over the neck of the corpse of someone who had a goiter. One then immediately massaged one's own neck.
(F, 1963)

1109   If a woman has a goiter, she should take the left hand of a male corpse, and put it on her throat. A man should do the same thing with a woman's corpse.
(F, 60, 1959)

1110   Wear amber beads to cure an enlarged thyroid.
(F, 1961)

HANGOVERS

1111   To avoid having a hangover, take two aspirins with a glass of milk before you go to bed. (This always worked for the informant.)
(F, 1962)

1112   If you have had a lot to drink, avoid a hangover by drinking a glass of milk when you get in.
(F, 1961)

1113   To keep from getting sick, mix one-half a glassful of cold milk and one-half a glassful of cold Coca Cola, and drink it quickly. (The informant said that, speaking from experience, this really works and doesn't even taste bad.)
(M, 1962)

1114   If you are going to drink but don't want to get drunk, you should drink at least three glassfuls of milk before you even start.
(M, 1962)

1115   To keep from getting drunk, eat several extra-greasy Maid-Rites (hamburgers) with extra salt before drinking.
(F, 20, 1968)

1116   An egg in a glass of tomato juice is a good cure for a hangover.
(M, 1962)

1117   If you have a hangover, drink a raw egg mixed with orange juice and whiskey. This will relieve it.
        (F, 1962)

1118   If you have a hangover, a glass of tomato juice and gin will fix it.
        (M, 1962)

1119   For a hangover, drink strong sugar water.
        (M, 30, R, 1958)

1120   Eat a raw turnip to abolish the mouth aroma after drinking alcoholic beverages.
        (M, 70, 1957)

1121   Cure for a hangover: one-half part tomato juice, one-fourth part Tabasco sauce, and one-fourth part Worcestershire sauce.
        (F, 1962)

1122   Cure for hangovers: in an old-fashioned glass, put one-half a lump of sugar, one teaspoonful of Tabasco sauce, one and one-half jiggers of rye, and one lump of ice. Fill the glass with champagne. Top this with two dashes of absinthe.
(M, 1962)

1123   Hangover remedy: one glassful of buttermilk, one dash of Tabasco sauce, one dash of Worcestershire sauce, one dash of salt and pepper. Sprinkle with nutmeg for seasoning.
(M, 1962)

1124   Mix tomato juice with salt, pepper, and Worcestershire sauce to cure a hangover.
(M, 20, 1960)

1125   The best cure for a hangover is to take "hair of the dog" that bit you. That is, drink some more.
(M, 60, R, 1960 [his father])

REMEDIES FOR HICCUPS

1126   Take one teaspoonful of sugar, and swallow it as slowly as you can.
(F, 20, 1969, + 2 F and 1 M)

1127   Take sugar and water.
(M, 1959 [his grandmother])

1128   Take one teaspoonful of sugar, covered with vinegar.
(F, 20, R, 1960 [her father])

1129   To stop hiccups for a baby, put a pinch of sugar on his tongue.
(M, 35, R, 1958 [his parents])

1130   Drink water while hiccuping.
(F, 19, 1969, + 10 F and 12 M)

1131   Drink nine swallows of water without taking a breath.
(F, 21, 1950, + 7 F and 2 M)

1132   Take ten swallows of water without taking a breath.
(M, 19, 1969, + 4 F and 2 M)

1133   Take thirteen swallows, and you'll be rid of them.
(M, 1961)

1134   Drink a glass of water with your head upside down. (It runs down your throat slowly that way.)
(F, 1969 [her mother], + 3 F)

1135   Bend over at the waist, with your head low. Drink three or four swallows of water with your head in this position.
(F, 20, 1969)

1136   Place a silver knife in a glass of water; then drink the water.
(F, 1962)

1137   Drink nine cupfuls of water through a tea towel.
(M, 20, 1961 [his mother])

1138   Drink water while holding your nose.
(F, 21, 1969)

1139   Have someone cover your ears while you drink water.
(F, 1962 [her parents])

1140   Place a sack over your head while you drink water.
(F, 1962)

1141   Run a mile in less than five minutes; then drink a quart of
wine.
(M, 19, 1969)

1142   Hold your breath as long as you can.
(M, 19, 1969, + 2 F and 8 M)

1143   Hold your breath while you count slowly to thirty, then sixty.
(M, 21, 1969, + 1 F and 2 M)

1144   Hold your breath till you turn blue in the face.
(F, 20, 1969)

1145   Hold your breath while you count to ten.
(F, 20, 1969, + 12 F and 4 M)

1146   Take three deep breaths. Hold the third one, tuck your chin
down against your chest, and stick out your stomach. Hold
that third breath until you have to let go of it.
(F, 21, 1969)

1147   Take a deep breath; then stand on your head.
(M, 20, 1969, + 1 F)

1148   Take a deep breath, and start counting out loud until you are
out of breath.
(F, 19, 1969)

1149   Hold your breath, and think of ten white horses.
(F, 1961 [her parents])

1150   Bend forward, and inhale deeply twenty-five times.
(M, 23, 1959)

1151   Breathe as fast as possible for thirty to forty-five seconds,
and concentrate on not hiccuping.
(F, 20, 1969)

1152   Blow in a paper sack without inhaling.
(F, 20, R, 1962 [her parents])

1153   Put a paper bag over your head, and breathe into it.
(M, 20, R, 1961 [his father], + 11 F and 1 M)

1154   Scare the person who has hiccups.
(F, 19, 1969, + 8 F and 11 M)

1155   Make the person who has them mad.
(F, 1962 + 1 F)

1156   Make this suggestion to a person who has hiccups: "Hic for me." This will generally stop the hiccups.
(F, 1962)

1157   Look at someone and say "Hiccup for me" in a serious tone.
(F, 20, 1969, + 1 F)

1158   Close your eyes, place your right thumb in your mouth, and blow as hard as you can. While you are doing this, you must think about an ocean.
(M, 21, 1969)

1159   Lie down on your back; then have someone sit on you.
(F, 20, 1969)

1160   Very deep and passionate kissing.
(F, 19, 1969)

1161   Lie on a table with your head hanging down for three minutes.
(F, 1962)

1162   Have someone hold you upside down by the feet and shake you up and down.
(M, 21, 1969)

1163   Pull your tongue out as far as possible for one minute.
(F, 60, R, 1957)

1164   When you have the hiccups, someone is thinking about you. If you can think of the person who is thinking about you, the hiccups will stop.
(F, 50, R, 1957)

1165   With your elbows bent and pointing out to each side, try touching your two little fingernails together and hold them together for ten seconds.
(F, 18, 1969)

1166   Put your fingertips together, and think of the last time you saw an old gray horse.
(F, 50, R, 1957)

1167   Put all your fingers together—thumb to thumb, and so on.
(F, 60, R, 1962)

1168   Say in one breath seven times, "Hiccup, sneacup, rise up, Jacob."
(F, 50, R, 1961)

1169   Bite the ends of your little fingers till they hurt.
          (F, 50, R, 1961)
1170   Swallow a gulp of air; then try to belch.
          (F, 20, 1969)
1171   Eat a piece of dry bread. Don't chew it up very well.
          (M, 21, 1969)
1172   After your last hiccup, yell for as long and as loudly as you
          can.
          (M, 21, 1969)
1173   Forget about them, and they will usually stop.
          (F, 20, 1969)
1174   Drink lots of bourbon.
          (M, 21, 1969)
1175   Think of your best girlfriend.
          (M, 1962)
1176   Swallow a piece of ice.
          (F, 20, R, 1963)
1177   Hiccups are the sign of a healthy baby.
          (F, 50, 1961 [her mother])

HOARSENESS

1178   If you are hoarse, take the stocking that you have been
          wearing, put the dirty foot against your throat, and then
          wrap the rest of the stocking around your neck; in the morn-
          ing you will have your voice back.
          (F, 58, R, 1958)
1179   One informant reported that some of the old-timers in her
          community used to say that a mixture of honey and vinegar
          was good for coughs and hoarseness. Milk and red pepper
          was also used for hoarseness.
          (F, 69, R, 1963)
1180   Sugar and kerosene is good for hoarseness.
          (M, 1962)

INFECTION

1181   To take out infection, mix a bread-and-milk poultice and
          place it on the infected area.
          (F, 20, R, 1961, + 4 F)

1182   Flaxseed meal makes a good poultice.
          (F, 50, R, 1957)
1183   Pulp from a cactus can be used as a poultice.
          (F, 50, R, 1961 [her mother])
1184   If you have a cut on your foot or finger that won't heal
          because of infection, go out and get fresh cow manure, place
          it on a cloth, then bandage the injury in it. Leave for at least
          twelve hours, or longer if needed.
          (F, 20, R, 1962, + 3 F and 5 M)
1185   A sliced-beet poultice can be used to draw out infection.
          (F, 1961)
1186   To remove infection, make an egg-skin poultice.
          (F, 1962 [her grandfather])
1187   Freshly chewed tobacco makes an effective poultice for in-
          fected sores.
          (F, 1962)
1188   To draw out infection, use a poultice of raw grated potato.
          (F, 50, R, 1961 [her grandparents], + 2 F)
1189   For inflamed eyes, scrape a raw potato and apply as a poul-
          tice on the eyes. Renew as it gets dry.
          (F, 70, R, 1962 [her mother])
1190   For any sore or inflammation, rub the area with a potato
          covered with finely pulverized charcoal. Keep the area moist
          for three to four hours, and the skin will become free from
          sores.
          (F, 70, R, 1960 [her parents])
1191   Use fat meat to make a poultice for infection.
          (F, 44, R, 1957, + 1 F)
1192   To remove infection, use a bacon poultice.
          (F, 1962)
1193   If you have stepped on a nail, bind a piece of the rind of salt
          pork on the part; then keep quiet until the wound heals.
          (F, 69, R, 1963 [her grandfather], + 1 F and 1 M)
1194   Hot pitch pine, applied when you have stepped on a nail, will
          take out the soreness.
          (F, 82, R, 1959)
1195   If you run a nail into your foot, soak your foot in coal oil.
          (M, 50, R, 1959, + 1 F)
1196   Use kerosene as a disinfectant and cure-all.
          (M, 23, 1964 [his grandfather], + 2 F)
1197   To alleviate pain from stepping on a rusty nail, apply a poul-
          tice of peach leaves and turpentine.
          (F, 60, R, 1958, + 1 M)

1198   Turpentine and laundry soap make a good paste for curing in-
        fection.
                (F, R, 1960)
1199   In order to prevent infection, use turpentine when you have
        stepped on a nail or gotten a cut.
                (F, 45, R, 1960, + 1 F and 1 M)
1200   To cure a nail puncture in your foot, get an old woolen rag,
        burn it, and then put it around your foot.
                (F, 35, 1958)
1201   Use turpentine and hot water to soak a wound from a rusty
        nail. This will draw out the soreness.
                (F, 40, R, 1962)
1202   When someone steps on a rusty nail, hang three onions above
        the door, and have the victim walk through the door back-
        wards three times. Soak his foot in pure vinegar, then remove
        the nail. There won't be any infection.
                (F, 20, 1959)
1203   For nail wounds, soak the foot in very hot water to which car-
        bolic acid has been added.
                (F, 50, 1958)
1204   Coal oil used to be put on cuts and nail wounds to heal them.
        (F, 50, 1958)
1205   If you step on a rusty nail, pull the nail out, grease it with
        lard, and put it in an east window; your foot will heal and will
        not be sore.
                (F, 42, R, 1957)
1206   In order to counteract the poisons caused by stepping on a
        nail, let the smoke of a burning wool rag enter the wound.
        This will draw out both the pain and the poison.
                (F, 65, R, 1958)
1207   If you step on a nail, the nail must be put in a window so that
        the infection will go away. It must be left there until your foot
        is well.
                (M, 1956 [his grandmother])
1208   If someone steps on a sharp object, grease the object and
        bury it to prevent the wound from becoming sore.
                (F, 33, 1962)
1209   Lick a sore with your tongue, and it will heal quickly.
                (M, 50, R, 1957)
1210   Let a dog lick your sores to cure and heal them.
                (M, 49, R, 1963 [his mother])

1211   If you have gangrene, cure the infected part of the body by putting it in boiling or near-boiling water.
   (M, 1960 [his grandfather])

1212   Put moldy bread on a cut or sore.
   (M, 81, 1958)

1213   Use chicken heart or liver to draw out poison.
   (M, 81, 1958)

1214   Use egg white to draw out infection.
   (F, 58, 1958)

1215   Wood ash is a disinfectant home remedy.
   (F, 49, R, 1956)

1216   Soak the inflamed part of the body in hot "salts" water to draw out soreness.
   (F, 70, R, 1957)

1217   To heal a cut on your toe, tie red yarn around the toe so that the yarn covers the cut.
   (F, 70, 1963)

1218   To prevent bed sores, place a pail of water under the bed of the sick person.
   (M, 73, R, 1959)

1219   "Comfy"—a type of melon—used to be raised in gardens. The roots were dug and eaten to cure abscesses.
   (F, 57, R, 1957)

1220   Coffee grounds or chimney soot will kill infections.
   (F, 75, R, 1958)

INSECT BITES AND STINGS

1221   Place cow manure on a bee sting to relieve the pain and cure it.
   (F, 50, R, 1960, + 1 M)

1222   If a bee stings you, urinate on the ground, pick up some of the mud that has thus been made, and rub it on you where the bee has stung you; then the place will not become swollen. (This is a Spanish home remedy from Puerto Rico.)
   (F, 56, 1963)

1223   Put a potato on a bee sting; it will take the sting out.
   (F, 50, 1962)

1224   Use lard or drippings for a bee sting.
   (M, 55, R, 1959)

1225   Put vinegar on a bee sting.
          (F, 20, 1959)

1226   To cure the sting of a bee or wasp, mix common earth with water to about the consistency of mud. Apply it at once.
          (M, 20, 1955, + 4 F and 5 M)

1227   A poultice of mud is good for bee and wasp stings.
          (M, 25, 1954, + 2 M)

1228   The best cure for a wasp sting is mud from a hog wallow.
          (F, 60, R, 1960 [her mother])

1229   A chewed wad of chewing tobacco will take the sting out of a wasp or bee sting. Put the tobacco on the sting.
          (F, 20, 1958, + 2 F and 2 M)

1230   Put a poultice of baking soda on bee and wasp stings.
          (F, 91, 1954, + 2 F)

1231   The juice from green grass mixed with mud will keep the swelling and pain from occurring when one is stung by a bee or hornet.
          (F, R, 1954 [her mother])

1232   Put kerosene on bee and wasp stings; put turpentine on nail punctures and cuts.
          (F, 98, R, 1963)

1233   If you get stung by a wasp, put a copper penny on the bite. It will take the poison out.
          (M, 76, R, 1959)

1234   If a spider bites you, catch a live chicken, split it open, and put it on the wound to draw out the poison.
          (F, 40, R, 1961)

1235   For bedbug poisoning, take egg whites or milk.
          (F, 50, 1963)

1236   Put a madstone on a bite, and the bite will go away.
          (F, 1962)

1237   Black mud applied to bites and stings is one of the best remedies; it is also easily obtained.
          (F, 69, R, 1963 [her grandfather])

1238   To take the sting out of insect bites, apply blueing.
          (F, 21, R, 1958, + 1 F)

1239   To kill chiggers that burrow into the skin, apply kerosene and salt in equal parts.
          (F, 60, 1963)

1240   If you put a piece of tape over a chigger bite and leave it there a while, the chigger will come with the tape when you pull it off.
          (M, 50, R, 1961 [his parents])

1241   For poisonous bites, mix table salt with the yolk of an egg, and bind it on four times a day. This is said to be a cure for cancer also.
(M, 60, F, 1964 [his mother])

1242   A mixture of flour and honey will take out the swelling from stings and insect bites.
(M, 20, R, 1963 [his grandmother])

MEASLES, MUMPS, AND FEVERS

1243   Children often used to be taken to visit other children who had measles, mumps, whooping cough, or chicken pox in order to expose them to the disease, so that they could catch the disease and get it over with.
(M, 62, R, 1959)

1244   People used to drink tea made from sheep manure to get measles to break out.
(F, 80, R, 1960)

1245   Give the patient a hot bath to help the measles to break out.
(F, 47, R, 1961)

1246   Give hot ginger water to help measles break out.
(F, 47, R, 1961)

1247   Bake an onion, peel it, and put sugar on it. Have the child drink the juice. This will bring the hives of the measles out.
(F, 1962)

1248   Some people used to think that when a person had measles, he had to decide to drink only hot liquids or only cold liquids for the entire duration of the illness; changing from one to the other would prove fatal.
(M, 62, R, 1959)

1249   To keep the mumps from "going down," tie a string around the patient's neck.
(F, 30, R, 1957 [her mother], + 1 F)

1250   Tie a silk thread from one ear to the other when you have the mumps, so that you will be sure to have them on both sides.
(F, 35, 1962)

1251   The cure for mumps in adults is to rub sardine oil over the area of the mumps.
(F, 1962 [her mother])

1252   Your jaws will "lock" if you eat ice cream when you have the mumps.
(M, 30, 1958 [her mother])

1253   One contributor reported that when she was a child, she had brain fever following scarlet fever. After the doctor had given up, an old Dutch neighbor told her mother to kill a chicken, split the chicken, and wrap the patient's head in it. The heat from the chicken drew out the fever.
(F, 60, R, 1958)

1254   A person who is suffering from scarlet fever should drink warm lemonade and keep a hot cloth on his stomach. This will rid the person of this disease.
(F, 70, R, 1969 [her parents], + 1 F)

1255   After a person has recovered from a severe case of a fever such as typhoid, all his hair must be cut off very close. Otherwise it will not grow again, and he will be bald.
(M, 62, R, 1959)

1256   It used to be thought that typhoid fever could be cured by never giving the patient a drink from spring water that had been taken out more than thirty minutes before.
(F, 72, 1957)

1257   Great care must be taken when skinning a rabbit to avoid scratching your fingers on the bones. If you are scratched, rabbit fever will result.
(M, 51, R, 1965)

1258   Fevers and chills may be cured by drinking catnip tea every hour until the fever or chill leaves.
(F, 57, R, 1957)

1259   A refreshing drink for fever patients: put one-half teaspoonful of currant, lemon, or cranberry jelly into a goblet; beat it well with two tablespoonfuls of water; and fill with ice.
(F, 70, R, 1960)

1260   Pour cold water on wheat bran; let it boil for one-half hour; strain; add sugar and lemon juice. This is a good drink for a fever patient.
(F, 70, R, 1960)

1261   A tub of water placed under the bed will cure an attack of malaria.
(F, 40, R, 1957)

1262   If a live spider is shut up between the halves of a walnut shell that have been glued back together, and if the shell is worn as a locket, it will cure a fever.
(M, 62, R, 1959)

1263   Give quinine for a temperature.
(F, 83, R, 1963 [her mother])

1264   To break a fever, put seven buttons on a string, and tie it around the feverish person's neck. His fever will go away.
(F, 50, 1958)

1265   Convulsion fits sometimes follow feverish restlessness; in such cases, a hot bath should be administered without delay, and the lower parts of the body should be rubbed, the bath being as hot as it can be without scalding the tender skin.
(F, 70, R, 1962)

1266   Bleed the bad blood in order to cure a fever.
(F, 63, 1958)

1267   To break a fever, take a hot bath; drink three shots of rum or whiskey; then climb under a stack of blankets, and sweat it out.
(M, 1961)

1268   Malaria may be cured by eating a piece of ironweed once a day. (Cures you if it doesn't kill you.)
(F, 57, R, 1957)

POULTICES AND HEALING CURES

1269   Chew tobacco and put it on a sore or wound to cure it.
(F, 40, R, 1958, + 1 F and 3 M)

1270   Fresh cow manure makes a good poultice.
(M, 50, R, 1957, + 2 M)

1271   Let a dog lick a wound to heal it.
(F, 60, R, 1964 [her mother], + 1 F and 1 M)

1272   Use kerosene as a disinfectant for cuts and sores.
(F, 50, R, 1958 [her mother])

1273   Among the early-day Mennonites of Pawnee Rock, kerosene and turpentine were used as home remedies, especially for cuts.
(F, 70, R, 1962)

1274   The remedy for any mashed part of the body is to soak it in kerosene.
(M, 80, R, 1960 [his father])

1275   If you bathe a wound in clean water from a river, it will cure the wound.
(F, 45, 1958)

1276   Use garlic to heal wounds that are hard to heal.
(F, 50, R, 1962)

1277   In the early days of Kansas, lampblack was used for healing cuts. (There are many old-timers who still carry black scars from this.)

(F, 1962)

1278   Use axle grease and sulfur to heal bad cuts.

(F, 1962)

1279   Fungus off an old tree stump will heal wounds.

(F, 80, R, 1960 [her parents])

1280   To relieve a sore spot or injured area, rub it and say: "Heile, Heile. Drei tage rege. Drei tage schnee. Morgen hast——— (your name). Nimmer weh." Essentially this means: Heal, heal. Three days rain. Three days snow. Tomorrow you will no longer hurt.

(F, 50, 1961)

1281   Coal oil is a good disinfectant for all kinds of cuts and scratches. It is also very good for burns and snake bites.

(F, 70, R, 1958)

1282   Let flies get into an open sore; after the maggots have appeared, get rid of them, and the wound will heal clean.

(M, 50, R, 1957)

1283   Granulated eyelids may be treated with a mixture of fresh butter and nutmeg (the butter should be free of salt). Massage the eyelids with the mixture before retiring.

(F, 1963)

1284   The Negroes of Louisiana used to mix cow manure, spider webs, and soot with hog lard. This was placed on any cut or sore to heal it.

(M, 40, R, 1957)

1285   Moldy bread and water will kill infection when used as a poultice.

(M, 50, R, 1957)

1286   A bread-and-milk poultice will draw out all kinds of poisons.

(F, 79, R, 1957, + 1 F)

1287   An Indian remedy for taking the sting out of a minor injury is to take three different kinds of leaves, crush them together, and rub them over the injured area.

(M, 1962)

1288   Use the inside white skinlike part of a raw egg as a poultice to draw out a sticker or sliver.

(F, 80, R, 1958 [her mother])

1289   Make a poultice of bread, cream, and sugar. Use it for drawing stickers out or to the surface so that they can be gotten to more easily.

(F, 85, R, 1962 [her mother])

1290   A peach-leaf poultice will draw poison out of a wound.
          (F, 48, R, 1958)
1291   A slice of cured fat pork will act as a poultice when put on an
          infected wound.
          (F, 60, 1959)
1292   A piece of fat meat like bacon bandaged to the foot will draw
          out a piece of glass or splinter. Bread and milk will also work.
          (F, 1962 [her mother])
1293   Fat bacon will draw a splinter out of the skin.
          (F, 1962)
1294   A fat piece of uncooked pork will draw out a splinter.
          (F, 54, R, 1958)
1295   To remove a splinter from under a finger nail: Hold the finger
          in the top of a bottle that is partially filled with hot water. As
          the contents of the bottle cool, the splinter will be drawn out.
          (M, 50, R, 1957)

SKIN PROBLEMS

1296   One contributor reported that she had had an itch that was
          caused by little blisters. She had tried to scratch it away for
          three days, but it wouldn't go. So her mama mixed sulfur and
          lard, in equal parts, and rubbed it all over, in her hair and
          everywhere. She did this one night; then the next night the
          child had to take a bath. The mother just about scalded the
          sulfur and lard off the child; but the itch was cured.
          (F, 60, 1961, + 1 F and 1 M)
1297   For the itch, lard and sulfur should be mixed together and
          applied to the infected spot.
          (F, 1962)
1298   Make a salve of sulfur and gunpowder with lard for the itch.
          (F, 60, R, 1955)
1299   To cure the itch, boil pokeweed root and swab it on the itch.
          (F, 70, R, 1963 [her mother])
1300   Warm vinegar applied to the scalp will remove dandruff.
          (F, 50, 1963 [her mother])
1301   The scaly encrustation called cradle cap that often appears
          on the scalp of young babies used to be cured by rubbing the
          scalp with a wet diaper when a baby was being changed.
          (M, 62, R, 1959)

1302   To cure athlete's foot, tie a wool string around each toe that is dry and cracking.
       (M, 24, 1960, + 1 F and 1 M)

1303   Sugar or lead is good for poison ivy.
       (F, 50, R, 1957)

1304   Laundry soap will prevent poison ivy if it is used soon after a person has been exposed.
       (F, 50, R, 1957, + 1 M)

1305   Eat some poison ivy in order to make yourself immune to poison ivy.
       (M, 52, R, 1958)

1306   If you get poison ivy, rub it with "crayfish meat," and it will be cured.
       (F, 21, 1952)

1307   One contributor reported that her sister had had poison ivy. Indian tobacco was cooked in milk and put on her legs. (Indian tobacco is a weed with a whitish-looking leaf.)
       (F, 40, R, 1961)

1308   Another contributor reported that once, when she had had poison ivy, gunpowder was mixed with vinegar to doctor it.
       (F, 40, R, 1961)

1309   Lysol is a good cure for poison ivy.
       (F, 50, R, 1957)

1310   Putting a green walnut on a ringworm will heal it.
       (M, 30, R, 1959, + 3 F)

1311   Put copper pennies in vinegar, then rub the solution on the affected areas to cure ringworm.
       (F, 26, R, 1958 [her mother], + 4 F)

1312   Put a copper penny in vinegar, then rub the penny on ringworm to cure it.
       (F, 58, 1951, + 1 F)

1313   To kill ringworms, rub the places with a silver dollar.
       (F, 82, R, 1957)

1314   Immerse the affected areas in sheep dip as a cure for ringworm.
       (F, 26, R, 1958)

1315   Use hog lard and sulfur to cure ringworm.
       (M, 50, R, 1959)

1316   Place cigar ashes on a ringworm to cure it.
       (F, 65, R, 1959 [her mother])

1317   To cure a ringworm, put the leftovers of burned tobacco (nicotine) from a pipe on it.
       (M, 39, 1963 [his father])

1318   Use warm water and axle grease for ringworm.
         (M, 81, R, 1959)

1319   Use urine for ringworm.
         (M, 81, R, 1959)

1320   For ringworm, use a paste made of gunpowder.
         (F, 80, 1959 [her father])

1321   A sure cure for ringworm: burn a piece of white paper on an
         ax, then rub the ashes on the sore.
         (F, 25, R, 1961 [her sister-in-law])

1322   Too much pork causes ringworms or boils.
         (F, 40, R, 1962 [her mother])

1323   Soda and water will relieve hives.
         (F, 1962)

1324   Give catnip tea to a baby to make him break out in hives, or
         the hives will stay on the inside, and the baby will have a
         fever.
         (M, 23, 1957)

1325   To prevent hives, one has only to put several buckshot into a
         glass of water and then drink a spoonful of the water every
         two hours.
         (F, 80, 1959)

1326   Red saffron is good for hives.
         (F, 82, R, 1957)

1327   Give your baby some catnip tea with three drops of whiskey
         in it every day for a year, and it will never have hives.
         (F, 50, 1958)

1328   To cure chapped hands, wrap them in a cloth that has been
         saturated with urine.
         (M, 80, R, 1957)

1329   To treat chapped skin, melt the fat of a lamb, and use it as a
         lotion.
         (F, 60, R, 1960 [her mother])

1330   White wax, one ounce; strained honey, two ounces; juice of
         lily bulbs, two ounces. The foregoing, melted and stirred to-
         gether, will remove wrinkles.
         (F, 70, R, 1962)

1331   On the first day of May, wash your face in the dew before the
         sun comes up, and your face blemishes will disappear.
         (F, 25, 1961 [her grandmother], + 2 F)

1332   In the past, when children's feet became cracked from going
         barefoot and wading in mud, buttermilk was used to soak the
         feet and to smooth the cracked skin.
         (F, 80, 1959 [her father])

1333   People used to think that real sour buttermilk was a good bleach for suntan—it also softened the skin.

        (F, 80, R, 1960 [one of her neighbors], + 2 F)

1334   When used as a lotion, vinegar will keep the skin soft.

        (F, 80, 1960)

1335   The skin can be bleached by a liberal application of cow manure.

        (F, 50, 1961 [her brother])

1336   Eat raisins to clear up your complexion.

        (F, 40, R, 1961 [her father])

1337   To have a lovely complexion, wipe your face daily with a wet diaper.

        (F, 60, 1959)

1338   Put unsalted, freshly churned butter on scars to make them go away.

        (F, 58, 1958)

1339   Eat molasses and sulfur to cure skin diseases.

        (F, 70, 1961)

SNAKEBITES

1340   For snakebites, place a wet-mud pack over the wound.

        (M, 50, R, 1957, + 3 F and 1 M)

1341   Cut the thigh from a freshly killed chicken, and then put it on a snakebite to draw out the poison.

        (F, 50, R, 1961, + 2 M)

1342   Apply a chicken's heart to a snakebite, so that it will pump the blood out.

        (M, 60, R, 1959)

1343   To cure a snakebite, apply the liver of a chicken.

        (M, 25, 1960)

1344   If a poisonous snake bites you, grab a chicken and cut it in half. Place half the chicken over the bite, and the chicken will turn green because it has absorbed all the poison. The poison will no longer be in your system, and you will suffer no ill effects.

        (F, 50, R, 1959 [her father], + 5 F and 3 M)

1345   When one informant's uncle was bitten by a snake, his grandmother took baby chicks, cut them in half, and placed them on the bite. Later a doctor told her that this had saved his uncle's life.

        (M, 20, 1960, + 1 F)

1346   Whiskey, taken internally, will cure a snakebite.

(F, 50, R, 1962 [her mother], + 3 F and 1 M)

1347   Use a tobacco-plug poultice to draw out snake poison.

(M, 20, 1959, + 2 F and 3 M)

1348   Coal oil, when poured on a rattlesnake bite, will draw out the poison.

(F, 50, R, 1961, + 2 F and 2 M)

1349   Men used to always carry strong cord with them in case of a rattlesnake bite. Then, if someone were bitten, they would tie the cord tightly between the bite and the person's heart until the bite could be lanced and the poison drawn from it.

(M, 60, R, 1962)

1350   If a snake should bite you, make a slit where the snake has bitten, and suck it. Chew tobacco while sucking so as not to get poisoned.

(M, 79, R, 1962)

1351   If you should be bitten by a poisonous snake, put an onion on the bite, and it will clear up right away.

(F, 40, 1959)

1352   Ingredients of remedy for snakebite: two ounces of iodide of potassium; two ounces of iodine; add enough ammonia to mix this; shake this mixture well. Cut cross marks across the bite. Wet a ball of cotton well with the solution, and hold the cot-

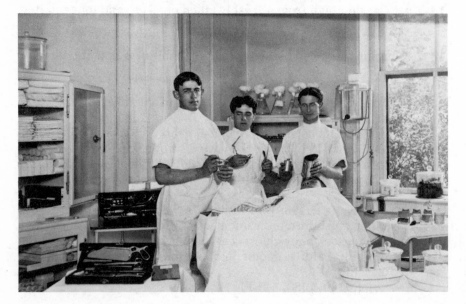

ton in the cut for thirty minutes, keeping it well saturated all the time. Then bathe the swollen area with ammonia.

(F, 70, R, 1963 [her mother])

1353   Egg white used to be used for rattlesnake bite.

(F, 80, 1959 [her father])

1354   Cure for snake, spider, or other poisonous bites: take the yolks of eight or ten eggs. Put them in a dish, stir in enough salt to thicken to the consistency for a poultice. Spread on a cloth one-quarter-inch thick; let this remain on the bite for about twelve hours. This is a perfect cure—it never fails.

(F, 60, 1963 [her grandfather])

1355   One person said that if a dog were bitten by a rattlesnake and if it were fed a large quantity of butter, it would recover from its poisonous bite.

(F, 50, 1958 [her mother])

1356   Treatment for snakebite: immerse the bite in kerosene to draw the poison out. Cut a chicken in half, and apply the warm, cut side to the wound. Give the victim a large quantity of whiskey. Give snakebitten dogs fat meat that has been liberally sprinkled with gunpowder. Put a wet-mud poultice on the leg of a snakebitten horse.

(F, 50, 1960 [her father])

TREATMENTS FOR A SORE THROAT

1357   Mix one drop of kerosene with a little sugar, and eat it.

(F, 50, R, 1963)

1358   Kerosene and sugar are good. Mix the kerosene with the sugar, and take a small amount in the mouth.

(F, 50, R, 1958 [her mother])

1359   Grease your throat with coal oil, and wrap it with an old sock.

(F, 52, 1963)

1360   Give the patient two drops of kerosene (coal oil).

(M, 62, R, 1959, + 1 F)

1361   Put a bacon rind around your neck.

(F, 58, 1955, + 1 M)

1362   Gargle with a mixture of red pepper, vinegar, and salt.

(F, 70, R, 1963)

1363   Gargle warm salt water.

(M, 26, 1956 [his mother], + 1 F and 1 M)

1364   Blow sulfur on your throat.
        (M, 40, R, 1961 [his father], + 1 F)

1365   Take gunpowder and sulfur for a putrid sore throat.
        (F, 80, 1959 [her father])

1366   Skunk oil, which had been rendered from the fat of skunks,
        used to be considered good for sore throats or lungs. Some
        people took it for colds.
        (F, 69, R, 1962 [her mother])

1367   Rub skunk grease on your neck.
        (F, 50, R, 1963 [her mother], + 1 F and 1 M)

1368   For a sore throat or chest cold, smear on a mixture of tur-
        pentine and goose lard.
        (M, 50, R, 1961 [his parents], + 1 F)

1369   A mixture of turpentine and lard is the best cure for sore
        throats and chest colds. It should be rubbed on the throat.
        (F, 40, R, 1960 [her mother])

1370   Give the patient two drops of turpentine on a spoonful of
        sugar.
        (M, 62, R, 1959)

1371   One contributor's mother used to take a large piece of pork
        fat; heat it in a pan on the stove until it was very hot; then
        wrap it in a piece of red flannel. This was then placed around
        the throat. That greasy mess seemed to have some effect on
        the sore throat, too.
        (F, 50, 1952, + 1 F)

1372   Wear strips of bacon around the neck.
        (F, 50, R, 1961 [her parents])

1373   Take a piece of fat, and tie it around your neck.
        (M, 60, R, 1961 [her mother])

1374   A pinch of salt held on the end of the tongue is good for a sore
        throat.
        (F, 85, R, 1959)

1375   Suck rock salt.
        (M, 48, R, 1962 [his mother])

1376   Put a dirty sock around your neck.
        (F, 20, R, 1961, + 14 F and 7 M)

1377   Wrap a cloth around a sore throat.
        (F, 19, 1956, + 1 F)

1378   Collect hog manure while it is still warm; wrap it in a cloth;
        and tie it around your neck.
        (F, 1961 [the contributor heard this from her grand-
        mother, who used this cure as late as 1925])

1379   Apply some Vicks Vaporub on a cloth bandage, and put the bandage around your neck.
   (F, 1961 [her grandmother])

1380   For a tickling in the throat, try putting a little bit of ground cloves on a spoon, gently swallowing it to relieve the condition.
   (M, 71, 1954)

1381   Heated lemon juice and bourbon will relieve a sore throat.
   (F, 1962)

1382   Remedy for a throat that tickles: suck a lemon to clear your throat.
   (F, 1962)

STIES ON THE EYELID

1383   If you urinate on the side of a road, you will get a sty on your eyelid.
   (F, 19, R, 1959 [her parents], + 3 F and 4 M)

1384   To rid yourself of a sty, rub a gold wedding band on it.
   (F, 20, R, 1958, + 7 F and 2 M)

1385   To cure a sty on your eyelid, rub it with a piece of solid silver, such as a ring, and repeat the following verse at the same time: "Sty, sty, go off my eye; / Go on the first person passing by."
   (F, 40, 1958 [her mother], + 1 F)

1386   If you have a sty on your eyelid, go to a crossroads and say: "Sty, sty, leave my eye, / And go to the next one passing by." The sty will leave, and you will never have another one.
   (M, 21, R, 1958, + 1 M)

1387   "Sty, sty, leave my eye. / Catch the next one passing by."
   (F, 30, R, 1962, + 1 F)

1388   Put a raw potato to a sty on the eyelid to bring the infection to a head and heal it more quickly.
   (F, 80, 1954)

1389   To cure a sty, soak a penny in vinegar, and put it on the eye.
   (F, 20, R, 1958)

1390   Pricking a sty with a rose thorn will cure it.
   (F, 60, R, 1957)

1391   Get rid of sty on the eyelid by touching it with a barley stem.
   (F, 50, 1961)

1392   A sty can be cured by cleaning it with one's very own urine.
   (F, 50, 1961)

WARTS

1393   If you touch a frog, you will get a wart.
        (F, 20, 1959 [her father], + 3 F and 2 M)

1394   Handling toads causes warts.
        (F, 19, R, 1962, + 30 F and 18 M)

1395   Place freshly cut raw potato on warts to get rid of them.
        (F, 40, R, 1966 [her mother], + 1 F and 2 M)

1396   To get rid of a wart, rub it with a potato peel every day for a
        while, and it will go away.
        (M, 70, 1959, + 1 F)

1397   Rub a potato on a wart; then bury the potato to get rid of the
        wart.
        (F, 19, 1959, + 14 F and 3 M)

1398   Bury a potato; tell no one where it is buried; and your warts
        will disappear.
        (F, 50, 1958)

1399   Rub a wart with a cut potato. Bury the potato. If the potato
        rots, the wart will disappear; if it grows, so will the wart. You
        must not tell anyone about it till the wart disappears.
        (F, 50, R)

1400   To get rid of a wart, rub it with a piece of potato peel. Bury
        the peel, and by the time this has rotted, the wart will have
        gone away. If someone digs up the peel, he will get the wart
        that you had.
        (F, 56, R, 1963)

1401   To get rid of a wart, bury half a potato in the full of the moon.
        (F, 1962)

1402   If you rub a wart with a raw potato and then throw the potato
        over your left shoulder without looking to see where it falls,
        the wart will disappear.
        (F, 40, R, 1963 [her mother], + 2 F)

1403   If someone rubs a piece of potato that has no eyes on it over
        your warts, then secretly buries it, your warts will disappear.
        (F, 1961)

1404   Cut a new potato in half; then rub half of it on your wart, and
        plant the other half.
        (F, 20, 1950)

1405   Pick a wart until it bleeds. Put a drop of blood from the wart on a potato, then bury the potato. When the potato rots, the wart will disappear.

(M, 40, R, 1957)

1406   Roll a small potato over a wart, close your eyes, and then throw the potato as hard as you can. If you cannot find the potato, the wart will go away.

(M, 20, R, 1961 [his aunt])

1407   To cure a wart, tie a horsehair tightly around it, and it will disappear permanently.

(F, 40, 1961 [the contributor heard this in about 1940 from her mother, who remembered having heard it from her mother around 1910], + 1 M)

1408   Tie a black hair from a horse's tail around a wart, bury the hair, and pay a penny. The wart will disappear.

(F, 30, 1960 [her mother])

1409   To get rid of a wart, tie a silk string around it.

(F, 19, 1959, + 7 F and 1 M)

1410   Tie a string in a knot over a wart, throw the string away, and the wart will go away.

(F, 20, R, 1960 [her father], + 3 F and 3 M)

1411   To cure a wart, tie a knot in a string; then rub the knot over the wart. Bury the string in the ground. When the string rots, the wart will be gone.

(M, 40, R, 1957, + 6 M and 11 F)

1412   To remove warts, take a hair from your head; wrap it around the wart; then throw the hair away.

(M, 60, R, 1959)

1413   To remove a wart, tie a string around it, and have the oldest brother in the family bury it.

(F, 60, R, 1957)

1414   When you have a wart, take a black thread, tie a knot in it, and bury the thread where the water drops from the eaves. By the time the thread rots, your wart will leave.

(F, R, 1959, + 1 M)

1415   Black silk thread used by one who knows the secret ritual will get rid of warts.

(M, 69, 1958)

1416   To get rid of warts, tie a knot in a piece of wool yarn for every wart that you have.

(F, 80, R, 1963)

1417   Put castor oil on a wart to get rid of it.

(F, 20, 1950, + 3 F and 2 M)

1418   Wash your hands in the water in an old stump to get rid of warts.

(F, 47, 1956, + 3M)

1419   If you let a grasshopper spit on a wart, the wart will disappear.

(F, 20, R, 1960, + 1 F)

1420   Rub onion juice on a wart; then put the onion in a sack, and bury it. This will make the wart go away.

(F, 20, R, 1959 [her father])

1421   Wart cure: cut an onion in two; rub each piece over the wart; put the halves back together; put them under the eaves; as the onion rots, the wart will disappear.

(F, 51, 1958)

1422   To get rid of warts, spit on them when you first get up in the morning.

(F, 20, R, 1959)

1423   If someone who isn't a relative of yours will spit on your wart, it will go away.

(M, 22, R, 1959 [his father])

1424   Spit on a wart; rub it real good with your thumb; then forget it. It will leave. The contributor who reported this said that the man who did this chewed cigars a lot, so perhaps it was the tobacco juice that did the trick.

(M, 17, R, 1962)

1425   The milk from milkweed will take off warts.

(M, 60, R, 1961, + 4 M and 2 F)

1426   Rub warts with a green pea, then wrap the pea neatly in a piece of paper, tie it with a string, and throw it away; the one who picks it up will get the wart.

(F, 50, R, 1959 [her parents])

1427   To remove warts, rub beans over them and say, "Hocus, pocus, presto change."

(M, 70, R, 1960 [his father])

1428   Take nine beans, and turn them around a wart. Throw them away in the pasture, and the wart will come off.

(M, 40, R, 1960 [his mother])

1429   Rub a bean on a wart; then take the bean out, and put it in a manure pile. When the bean rots, the wart will be gone.

(F, 60, R, 1960)

1430   One contributor said that the way one used to remove a wart was to cut a navy bean in two, rubbing one half on the wart.

Then one placed the two halves together, and planted or buried the bean in the ground. Within a week the wart would have disappeared.

(F, 50, R, 1958)

1431   If you want to get rid of a wart, rub it with a bean; spit on the bean twice; and then plant it in the ground. When the bean grows, the wart will be gone.

(M, 58, 1958)

1432   In order to cure warts, rub them with a navy bean; then throw the bean over your left shoulder, and don't look back.

(F, 50, 1961)

1433   For warts, apply mashed-up green-bean leaves; then bury them.

(M, 20, R, 1959, + 3 F and 2 M)

1434   To cure warts, kill a chicken, rub the warm heart on the warts; then bury the heart. When the heart rots, the warts will be gone. Or rub the warts with a dirty sour dishrag; then bury it.

(F, 80, R, 1960)

1435   Take the lining of a chicken gizzard, rub it on the warts, and then bury it in the ground. When the gizzard rots, the warts will go away.

(F, 70, R, 1962 [her mother])

1436   A wart will disappear if you put the blood from a chicken's head on it, and then bury the head. When the head rots, the wart will disappear.

(F, 55, 1959)

1437   Rub a wart with fresh meat, and get blood on the wart. Bury the meat, but don't tell anyone where you buried it, because if you do, the wart will come back.

(F, 20, R, 1958, + 1 M)

1438   If one gets a wart, he should take a piece of smoked bacon; rub it on the wart; then bury the bacon. When the bacon rots, the wart will drop off.

(M, 21, 1956, + 1 F)

1439   Take a piece of bacon, and rub it on a wart. Bury it under the eaves of the house for seven days. Then dig it up, and rub it again on the wart if it is still there. Then bury the bacon again, and the wart will disappear.

(F, 30, R, 1958 [her grandmother])

1440   Steal a piece of fat pork, and rub it on the wart; then take the
       pork out, and bury it. In time the wart will disappear.
           (F, 62, 1957, + 1 F)
1441   Rub a wart with fat meat; then bury the meat.
           (F, 60, 1960)
1442   After you have butchered, rub a piece of fresh hog rind on a
       wart. Bury the rind. The wart will drop off.
           (M, 20, R, 1961 [his father])
1443   Steal some of your mother's roast beef, and rub the warts
       well with the beef. Then bury the beef, and don't tell anyone.
       The warts will disappear.
           (M, 76, R, 1959)
1444   Pick a wart, put blood from it on a grain of corn, and feed the
       corn to a chicken. When the grain is digested, the wart will
       be gone.
           (F, 1963, + 2 M)
1445   Pick a wart until it bleeds, and put a drop of the blood on a
       grain of corn. Throw the grain of corn over your shoulder to
       some chickens, and if you don't look to see which chicken gets
       it, the wart will go away.
           (M, 65, R, 1963)
1446   To cure a wart, rub it with a grain of corn, then feed the corn
       to a rooster. The wart will go away.
           (M, 62, 1957, + 1 F)
1447   To cure a wart, cut it in four pieces, lay a grain of corn on it,
       and throw the corn to the chickens.
           (F, 60, R, 1961 [her mother])
1448   Rub a grain of blue corn on a wart, and then throw the corn
       over your left shoulder to get rid of the wart.
           (M, 50, R, 1959 [his uncle])
1449   To cure warts, take a lead pencil, and get a good point on it;
       then heat this pencil, and pick the skin around the base of the
       wart. The wart will fall out.
           (M, 70, R, 1959)
1450   Burn warts off with a magnifying glass.
           (F, 1962)
1451   One contributor reported that one of her cousins in Colorado
       had a pin stuck into a wart on her hand, and then a lighted
       match was held on the pin as long as she could stand the heat.
       That remedy removed the wart.
           (F, 70, R, 1962)

1452   If you have a wart, put a match head on it; then light the match. This will cure the wart.
        (M, 40, R, 1961, + 1 F and 1 M)

1453   To get rid of a wart, rub it with a match head. Light the match, blow it out, and rub the wart with the warm match head until the wart is hot.
        (M, 76, R, 1958)

1454   To get rid of warts, rub a match around the wart, and then bury the match.
        (F, 19, R, 1959)

1455   You can rub warts off with a penny.
        (F, 20, 1958, + 1 F and 1 M)

1456   Cut a wart until it bleeds; then rub a penny on the wart. Then throw the penny away, and do not look for it.
        (M, 21, 1957, + 1 M)

1457   Rub a penny on a wart; then throw the penny over your shoulder. The person who finds the penny will get the wart.
        (F, 60, R, 1961 [her mother])

1458   If you have a wart, take a copper penny, turn it three times on the afflicted area, and then throw the penny over your left shoulder into the back yard.
        (F, 32, R, 1958)

1459   To get rid of a wart, wish it off on someone else in the following manner: rub the wart with a penny; then have someone else rub the same part of his body with the penny. Your wart will disappear, and one will appear on him.
        (F, 20, 1958)

1460   Have someone give you a penny. Hide it, and forget where you put it. This method will remove your warts if you believe in it.
        (M, 20, 1957)

1461   Take an old piece of money, and rub it on a wart. This will get rid of the wart.
        (F, 20, R, 1963)

1462   Rub a wart with a bone, and throw the bone over your left shoulder. The wart will then leave.
        (F, 21, 1950, + 3 F)

1463   If you want to get rid of a wart, find an old bone, and rub it on the wart. Then drop the bone behind you, and don't look back.
        (F, 22, R, 1963, + 1 M)

1464   Burying a dead cat will get rid of warts.
        (F, 18, 1956, + 1 F and 2 M)

1465   If someone will buy your warts, you will lose them.
        (F, 30, R, 1962 [her parents], + 3 F and 2 M)

1466   If you can sell your warts, you will get rid of them.
(M, 24, 1956, + 1 F and 1 M)

1467   If someone will buy a wart from you and if you don't spend the money, the wart will go away.
(F, 20, R, 1963, + 1 F)

1468   If a person gives you a dime and says he is buying your wart, the wart will go away.
(M, 30, R, 1959)

1469   If someone buys a wart for a pin, and then leaves, your wart will leave.
(F, 14, 1959 [her mother], + 1 F)

1470   Remedy for warts: tie knots in a dishrag; then put it under a rock. When it rots, the warts will be gone.
(F, 1962)

1471   To get rid of warts, tie as many knots in a dishrag as you have warts; then bury the dishrag.
(F, 50, R, 1961, + 1 F)

1472   To get rid of warts, bury a dishrag under a rock, and leave it for a week. Then rub it on the warts, and they will go away.
(F, 20, R, 1959)

1473   To get rid of warts, touch each one with a dishrag; then bury the dishrag by the light of the moon.
(F, 1962)

1474   Hide a dishrag in the gutter of the house, and it will cure warts.
(M, 50, 1962)

1475   If you steal a dishrag and hide it in a tree stump, your warts will go away.
(F, 51, R, 1956)

1476   Put a stolen dishrag under your doorstep. This will remove all warts from your hands.
(F, 60, R, 1957)

1477   Steal a dishtowel from a neighbor, and bury it during the full of the moon. A wart will then go away.
(F, 19, R, 1956)

1478   Hide a dirty dishtowel on the west side of the house to rid yourself of warts.
(F, 80, 1955 [her parents])

1479   To remove warts, count the number of warts; then cut a dirty dishrag into the same number of pieces, and bury them. The warts will disappear.
(F, 30, 1957)

1480   To cure a wart, sneak the dishrag after the supper dishes are done. Tie the rag to cover the wart. This has to be left on during the night.
(F, 50, R, 1962)

1481   To get rid of a wart, hide your mother's dishrag.
(F, 60, R, 1959, + 1 M)

1482   To get rid of warts, stick a straight pin in the warts, and throw it over your shoulder. If you do not look back, the warts will disappear.
(F, 1972)

1483   To remove a wart, rub a small snail on the wart three times. Let the slime stay on all night.
(M, 40, R, 1958)

1484   Rub salt on a wart, throw the salt over your left shoulder, and you will get rid of the wart.
(F, 40, 1962)

1485   To get rid of a wart, a person must walk down the middle of a road, carrying salt in his hand. He must throw it over his shoulder and never look back. (The informant said that it worked, too! His wart went away.)
(M, 1962)

1486   If you rub a wart on an old tree stump, the wart will disappear.
(M, 21, 1955, + 1 M)

1487   Spit tobacco juice on a wart; this will remove it.
(F, 30, R, 1959)

1488   A sure cure for warts is to soak the warts in the blood of a toad and not wash it off. The warts will disappear in a few days.
(M, 70, R, 1958)

1489   If toads have made warts on your hands, play with frogs, and the warts will leave.
(F, 50, 1958)

1490   If you have a wart, pick it with a pin, get a little blood, and put it under the doorstep. The next person who walks across the doorstep will get the wart, and yours will be gone.
(F, 80, R, 1963 [her father])

1491   A good way to get rid of warts is to apply kerosene to them; they will fall out in a little while.
(M, 70, 1959)

1492   Apply fingernail polish to a wart to make it go away.
(F, 20, 1963)

1493   To get rid of a wart, cover it with a wad of spider web.
        (M, 46, 1973)

1494   Rub moss on a wart to make it go away.
        (M, 1961 [his grandmother])

1495   Take wax out of your ear, and rub it on your wart to get rid of
        it.
        (M, 30, 1967)

1496   You can put a piece of steel in boiling milk to get rid of warts.
        (F, 20, R, 1961)

1497   Prick a wart, extract a drop of blood, and put it in an
        envelope on the road so as to get rid of warts.
        (F, 21, 1950)

1498   To remove a wart, cut a small x on the wart and a small x on
        any tree when the sap is running upward.
        (M, 30, 1958)

1499   If a blind man rubs your warts, they will go away.
        (F, 1962)

1500   Talking to the moon will remove warts from your hand.
        (F, 20, 1958)

1501   Get an old pigskin; keep it on the wart; then bury the pigskin
        outside when no one is watching.
        (F, R, 1963)

1502   There is an Indian in Comanche, Oklahoma, who has the
        power to cure warts. He touches the warts, and they go
        away. This power will be taken away if he tells someone how
        he does it. Then the person whom he tells will have the
        power.
        (F, 30, R, 1961)

1503   Apply ink on a wart. Cut the top of the wart, and inject it with
        ink. This will remove the wart.
        (M, 1962)

1504   To get rid of a wart, put a bottle real tight against the skin.
        Heat it, so as to cause a lot of pressure. This will pull the wart
        off.
        (F, 19, R, 1959)

1505   To get rid of warts, put stock dip on them.
        (M, 50, 1960 [his aunt])

1506   To get rid of warts: someone should give you a small article
        (not money) in payment for your wart, then you and the per-
        son should bury the article, and you will get rid of the warts.
        But you're not supposed to tell anyone what the gift was or

where it was hidden. If you tell, then you will receive two warts.
(F, 1962)

MISCELLANEOUS

1507   A buckeye, carried in the pocket, will prevent certain types of disease.
(F, 21, 1956, + 1 M)

1508   If you carry a potato in your pocket, it will prevent diseases. Germs will go into the potato and dry up.
(M, 70, R, 1957)

1509   Put asafetida in a bag, and tie it around your neck to keep contagious diseases away.
(M, 64, 1957, + 1 M)

1510   This helps to prevent all diseases: take a whole nutmeg; make a hole in it; then hang it around your neck.
(F, 70, 1957)

1511   If a fishbone gets stuck in your throat, eat a lemon as soon as possible.
(F, 50, 1963)

1512   Hold a finger tightly under your nose to stop a sneeze.
(F, 1962)

1513   A pain can be removed by spitting under a rock.
(F, 60, R, 1961 [her mother])

1514   Put a pan of water under the bed to cure a night sweat.
(F, 60, R, 1961)

1515   A remedy for strained abdominal muscles or displaced organs is to place a penny in the navel, drop some hot wax on the penny so that it will support a lighted candle, and put a container (usually a glass) over the candle. Wait until the candle goes out, and you will then be cured.
(F, 60, 1964)

1516   If, by lifting something heavy, you have pulled your organs out of place, simply put a candle over your navel, and put a glass over it. This will suck them back into place.
(M, 50, R, 1964)

1517   To cure pyorrhea, mix black gunpowder with water; then brush your teeth with it.
(M, 76, R, 1958)

1518   Cure an ingrown toenail by making a *v* in the middle of the nail.
(F, 1961)

1519   To heal a broken leg, wrap an innertube around the leg, fill the tube with manure, and let the leg set.
(M, 54, R, 1964 [his grandfather])

1520   When someone has trouble sleeping, he should eat a few small onions with a piece of bread. This will bring about a natural sleep.
(F, 70, R, 1960)

1521   Pierce the ears to improve the eyesight.
(F, 80, R, 1962 [her parents], + 1 F)

1522   Growing a moustache will improve one's eyesight.
(M, 40, 1962 [his father])

1523   One's hearing may be improved by eating oranges.
(F, 70, 1957 [a country nurse])

1524   A cure for deafness: take one large onion; make a hole in it that is large enough to hold some tobacco; roast the onion until it is soft; then squeeze out the juice. Mix the juice with a little sweet oil, and put a few drops in each ear.
(F, 50, 1953 [her grandmother])

1525   A medicine for the whole system can be made from camomile flowers. An adult dose is a wineglassful two or more times a day as required.
(F, 80, R, 1964 [her mother])

1526   Prevent blood poisoning by covering a wound with cow manure.
(F, 52, 1955)

1527   Use white gas to prevent blood poisoning.
(M, 81, R, 1958)

1528   If you have blood poisoning or are afraid you will get it, put the infected part in coal oil (kerosene). This will draw out the poison.
(F, 53, R, 1958 [her grandfather])

1529   Use sweet cream to make a person vomit after he has been poisoned.
(F, 58, 1958)

1530   To ensure fertility, lay the trousers of a fertile man across the foot of the bed.
(M, 60, R, 1961 [his father])

1531   A cure for impotency: take two teaspoonfuls of apple cider

vinegar with each meal. Also eat two teaspoonfuls of honey with each meal.
(F, 20, R, 1963)

1532   Broth made from the testicles of a mountain sheep will increase one's fertility.
(M, 40, 1964)

1533   Boil live mice, and give one teaspoonful per day to a patient to cure him of bed-wetting.
(F, 70, 1958)

1534   Pull the lining from a chicken gizzard. Roll it into a powder after it has been baked dry, and make tea of it. This will cure bed-wetting.
(F, 70, 1958 [her mother])

1535   Cleanse well, then boil in water the inner lining of a chicken gizzard; then drink the liquid as a cure for bed-wetting.
(F, 30, 1960 [her grandmother])

1536   One contributor reported that her father was a diabetic when gangrene set into his leg back in 1890. The only cure for this condition was to cut the leg off. Whiskey was used for the anesthetic. Dr. Jacobs used a wooden saw for the operation. Members of the family buried the stump in the grape arbor. Whenever the nerve endings began to bother her dad, they would go out and dig up the stump, because it wasn't comfortable in the grave.
(F, 57, 1957)

1537   If a limb is amputated, it must be buried before sundown to save the person from pain.
(F, 1962)

1538   After a heart attack, open the blood veins, and let out blood. (This, according to the informant, was an old Russian belief.)
(M, 40, R, 1957)

1539   The bitterer the medicine, the quicker the cure.
(F, 50, R, 1950 [her mother])

1540   Plenty of cooked garlic is good for hardening of the arteries.
(F, 82, R, 1957)

1541   Raw potatoes will soon cause hardening of the arteries.
(F, 47, R, 1961)

1542   Eat garlic to relieve high blood pressure.
(F, 21, 1950, + 1 F)

1543   For high blood pressure, steep an ounce of crushed watermelon seed in boiling water, and drink two or three cupfuls of the liquid every day.
(F, 82, R, 1957)

1544   Eat onions to relieve high blood pressure.
        (F, 21, 1950)

1545   For lumbago, mix two teaspoonfuls of cream of tartar with
        the juice of several oranges. Put this into a quart jar, and
        sweeten to taste.
        (F, 50, R, 1963)

1546   Eating a small clove of garlic morning and evening will cure
        gout.
        (F, 70, R, 1969 [one of her neighbors])

1547   Boil mule's hoofs, and give the broth to people who have
        epilepsy.
        (F, 73, R, 1959)

1548   Unsalted warm butter, poured in the eyes, will cure a
        cataract.
        (F, 78, R, 1959)

1549   To treat chilblains, mix two tablespoonfuls each of saltpeter
        and alum in one pint of boiled water. Rub your feet every
        night with this solution.
        (M, 60, R, 1964)

1550   Quinine was used for everything in early Kansas. Mrs.
        Barger, a midwife and nurse, used to mix flour and water to
        the consistency of pancake dough and drop it in lumps about
        the size of a quarter on a stove lid. The pancake was then
        rolled with the quinine inside, and the patient swallowed it
        with the ease of one of today's capsules.
        (F, 1962)

1551   If you sweep under the bed of the sick person while the sick
        person is in the bed, he will not get well.
        (F, 70, R, 1962)

1552   Scissors placed under the bed when you are ill will cause you
        to get well soon.
        (F, 21, 1950)

1553   Boil a mouse, and feed the broth to a sick child to cure an
        illness.
        (F, 30, R, 1957)

1554   Rabbit pills rolled in flour and sugar are a good general
        remedy.
        (M, 50, R, 1960 [his mother])

1555   When a person is sick, cut a lock of his hair, and put it in the
        keyhole of his door. This will help the sick person get better.
        (F, 80, R, 1963 [her father])

1556   A cure for general sickness: bleeding with live leeches.
        (M, 24, R, 1957)

1557   Use herb tea to cure all your ailments.
        (F, 77, R, 1961)

1558   A good shot of whiskey will cure almost everything.
        (F, 1958)

1559   Sassafras tea is a good spring tonic.
        (F, 1962)

1560   One contributor reported that when he was a child and hurt himself, his father would say the following in Low German: "Heal, heal, cat dirt, / Tomorrow it will be well."
        (M, 60, R, 1962 [his mother])

1561   Some people believe that castor oil can cure anything; it used to be given in large capsules.
        (M, 50, R, 1960 [his father])

1562   Put castor oil in orange juice and stir it; when it foams, it is easier to take.
        (F, 1962)

1563   String salt around a sick person. This will prevent his disease from becoming contagious.
        (M, 64, 1957)

1564   Honey and apple-cider vinegar is supposed to cure everything.
        (F, 1962)

1565   One tablespoonful of honey and one tablespoonful of vinegar will cure anything.
        (F, 40, 1962)

1566   Sulfur used to be sprinkled on the top of a wood-burning stove to disinfect a cabin after a disease or a death.
        (F, 1962)

1567   The following methods used in hospitals to help patients are based on common beliefs: (1) putting cold compresses on wrists and (2) running tap water.
        (F, 1962)

1568   Take a baby by the heels and shake him once in a while, or he will get livergrown.
        (F, 1959)

1569   When a baby has thrush, have a child who has never seen his daddy blow into the baby's mouth, and it will cure the thrush.
        (F, 1962)

1570   A seventh son can cure a baby's thrush by blowing into the child's mouth.
        (F, 1961)

1571   To cure prickly heat, use cornstarch and fuller's earth.
        (F, 50, R, 1957)

1572   Gall-bladder trouble can be cured by eating a cup of diced cooked beets daily for a month.
        (F, 57, R, 1957)

1573   When you feel tired, drink dandelion tea.
        (M, 64, 1957)

1574   If you have a sharp, sudden pain, pick up a stone and throw it, and the pain will go away.
        (F, 60, R, 1958)

1575   To cure sinus troubles, throw nine small pebbles of the same size and color into the sun early in the morning.
        (M, 1963)

1576   One contributor reported that her Aunt Lizzie used to dampen moles and apply Lewis Lye to them with a stiff wing feather from a chicken. She let the lye remain a very short time, then applied lard to stop the lye from eating deep. It worked.
        (F, 70, R, 1962 [her aunt])

1577   If the leaves of a prickly pear cactus are chopped in small pieces and kept in the water given to chickens, this will cure and prevent cholera in the flock of chickens.
        (M, 62, R, 1959)

1578   A cure for colic or cholera (vary according to age): heat one-half a teacupful of sugar; then add two wineglassfuls of whiskey or brandy, and give it to the patient as hot as he can drink it two times, two minutes apart. If this fails to cure the disease in a reasonable amount of time, repeat the treatment.
        (F, 50, 1963)

1579   Tobacco juice is good for treating a scratch from a fishhook.
        (M, 1962)

1580   Rub lard on a bruise. It will keep down the swelling.
        (F, 50, R, 1963 [her mother])

1581   To cure head lice, put coal oil on your hair at night, and wrap it with a towel. Wash your hair the next day.
        (F, 1962)

1582   To heal cracked lips, use the natural oil from behind your ears and along the hairline.
        (F, 58, 1954)

1583   Rum, poured on one's head, will ensure against baldness and even make one's hair curly.
        (F, 1962)

1584   Athlete's foot may be cured by applying Clorox.
      (F, 57, R, 1957)

1585   The best remedy for a baby who is slow in walking is to soak his legs in dishwater.
      (F, 55, 1965 [her mother])

1586   When your arm or leg goes to sleep, make crosses on it with your finger to make it wake up.
      (F, 1962)

1587   If an antiseptic doesn't burn, it isn't any good.
      (M, 50, R, 1957)

1588   One contributor reported that she had recently gone to the income-tax man, who expressed amazement because she didn't have any doctor's bills. She told him that when anything went wrong, she went to her garden and took one of her herbs.
      (F, 79, R, 1957)

1589   In the past, when a person had tuberculosis (called consumption then), he had to sleep in a tightly shut up room, where no drafts of night air, which was believed to be dangerous, could enter.
      (M, 62, R, 1959)

1590   People used to fix black-pepper tea for menstrual cramps. Sometimes sugar was added for taste.
      (F, 1962 [her grandmother])

1591   Drink hot ginger tea for dysmenorrhea or cramps.
      (F, 1962)

1592   If parts of the body such as feet or hands are frozen, put them in coal oil. It will draw out the frost, and you will not have chilblains.
      (F, 53, R, 1958 [one of her neighbors], + 1 M)

1593   Use skunk oil to treat frozen hands, ears, or toes.
      (M, 60, R, 1961)

1594   In the past, Gilead salve was used for frost bite. It was made from Gilead breads, fried down in mutton tallow, with just enough lard added to make it soft.
      (F, 71, 1958)

1595   For frosted feet, roast a round white turnip in the ashes of a fire. When the turnip is soft, split it open, and bind it on the feet at night. Let it remain until morning. If it does not cure in one night, repeat the treatment.
      (F, 70, 1960 [her mother])

1596   Rub frostbitten hands or feet with snow to help circulate the blood again.
    (F, 71, 1954)

1597   To prevent frostbite, dip your hands in vinegar before going out in freezing weather.
    (F, 91, 1954)

1598   Soak a sprained ankle in vinegar and salt to relieve soreness. (The author had always heard this as hot water, with vinegar and salt added.)
    (F, 60, R, 1962)

1599   For a sprained ankle or wrist, apply mullein leaves that have been soaked in vinegar.
    (F, 61, R, 1957)

1600   When you sprain your ankle, remove the stone doorstep from the door you use the most. Then take some of the dirt from under it, and bind your ankle with that dirt.
    (F, 60, R, 1958 [her mother])

1601   If you have a pain due to a sprain, wrap the sprained area with a salty cloth to keep down the swelling.
    (M, 65, R, 1962 [his mother])

1602   Tie a horsehair cord around your ankle to keep from getting a charley horse.
    (M, 81, 1958)

1603   For a bruise or swollen area of the body, place a raw piece of meat on the affected area to draw out the swelling and blood.
    (M, 1958 [his grandfather])

1604   Put a steak on a black eye to take out the soreness.
    (F, 21, 1950, + 4 F and 2 M)

1605   Put bacon on a black eye.
    (F, 20, 1959)

1606   If you put a used tea bag on a black eye, the swelling and bruise will go away.
    (F, 40, 1958)

1607   When a child has a bump, run a table knife over the bump, and it will not swell.
    (F, 1963)

1608   When anyone gets a bad bump, immediately hold a silver knife on the bump. The knife will keep the bump from swelling so much and getting discolored.
    (F, 40, R, 1958 [her mother])

1609   Rub your bumps with a silver spoon, and they will go away.
    (F, 20, R, 1956)

1610   When a child falls and gets a bump on his head, put an onion slice on the bump. This will take the bump away.
       (F, 1962)

1611   Unsalted butter is the best cure for bruises, burns, and what have you.
       (F, 55, 1959 [her husband])

1612   Use cow manure on bruises.
       (M, 81, 1958)

ADVICE ON HOW TO AVOID ILLNESS

1613   Washing hair or taking a bath immediately after a meal is forbidden, because it will cause illness to a person.
       (F, 1962 [her parents])

1614   Don't go swimming during the dog days in August.
       (F, 60, R, 1958)

1615   Taking too many baths will weaken you.
       (F, 70, R, 1961)

1616   A penny in the bathtub while you are bathing will put copper in your bones.
       (F, 50, R, 1961 [her grandmother])

1617   Water that has iron nails sitting in it is good to drink, because it gives you the iron that rusts from the nails. (The informant reported that she had gone to see an old granny, who must have been over one hundred years old. The water buckets were on a shelf at one side of the porch. The granny's water bowl was there, too, and it always included a handful of rusting nails. She drank the water to get the iron.)
       (F, 1962)

1618   Place salt in spring water to purify it and keep it from becoming contaminated.
       (F, 57, R, 1957)

1619   Kissing on the lips spreads germs.
       (F, 18, R, 1958)

1620   Never step on an ant hill, or you will become ill.
       (M, 24, 1959)

1621   Always wear long flannel underwear, and you will not get sick.
       (F, 77, R, 1961 [an old doctor])

1622   A person should not lie on his left side when he is sleeping.

This is bad for the heart, because the organs on the right will all put pressure on the heart.

(F, 25, R, 1961 [her mother])

1623   To ward off disease, put your tongue to turpentine before leaving the house.

(F, 30, R, 1961 [her mother])

1624   In the past, freshly distilled turpentine was used to dissolve sugar in a spoon. This was taken to ward off fevers in the spring.

(F, 1962)

1625   To ward off disease, wear an onion around your neck.

(F, 18, 1961)

1626   Wearing a spider in a walnut shell around your neck will ward off illness.

(F, 50, R, 1957)

1627   It is believed, and, in fact, is still practiced, in an area near Baltimore, that a good scrubbing of the front steps or stoop of the house each day will prevent any visitors from bringing evil or disease into the house.

(M, 1963)

1628   If someone in the household is ill and the plant called wandering Jew is growing in the house, the ill person will not recover until the plant is destroyed.

(F, 20, 1957)

1629   For good health, eat lots of onions.

(F, 40, R, 1961 [her father])

1630   People used to believe that if you ate three eggs that had been laid on Good Friday, you would have no serious illness during the year.

(F, 45, R, 1963 [her grandmother])

1631   Eat raw eggs for good health.

(F, 50, R, 1957)

1632   Never feed first a person who is ill.

(M, 24, 1959)

1633   It used to be thought that eating hot bread or rolls or cakes was inviting sickness or even death. Bread was always thoroughly cooled before anyone was allowed to eat it.

(F, 40, 1963 [her mother])

1634   It doesn't matter what you eat; if you drink grapefruit juice, you won't gain weight.

(F, 47, 1956)

1635   If you eat cranberries frequently, this will help you to live longer.
        (F, 20, R, 1959)

1636   Too much salt will give you bad blood.
        (M, 1961 [his wife])

1637   When someone sneezes, you must say some version of "your health" to avoid becoming ill.
        (F, 35, 1956, + 1 M)

1638   Never look into the sun when it is coming up, or you will have bad eyes.
        (M, 71, R, 1958)

1639   Carrots are good for one's eyesight.
        (F, 21, 1955)

1640   Toenails will become ingrown if they are not cut in the light of the moon.
        (M, 69, 1958)

1641   Never trim or cut fingernails or toenails when you are sick; otherwise you won't get well until they have grown out again.
        (F, 1962 [her mother])

1642   According to one informant, some people used to believe that you could put your bellybutton out of place by working too hard. Only Dr. Lang (now deceased) could cure this. There were two types of bellybuttons: those that pushed in and those that screwed in. Only those that pushed in could get out of place.
        (M, 50, 1958)

1643   People used to take sagebrush boiled with water as a tonic.
        (F, 1962)

1644   Pick spring tonics, lamb's-quarters, and murdock. Good for all kinds of ailments and sickness.
        (M, 53, R, 1964 [his uncle])

1645   To purify your blood in the spring, eat cream of tartar, molasses, and sulfur every morning during the spring.
        (F, 61, R, 1957)

1646   Mix sorghum and sulfur for a spring tonic.
        (F, 64, 1958 [her mother])

1647   In the springtime, to purify the blood, you used to have to drink lots of sassafras tea and eat a lot of molasses.
        (F, 45, R, 1958 [her grandmother])

1648   A mixture of sulfur and molasses is good for thickening of the blood.
        (M, 21, 1956)

1649   Drink sassafras tea in the spring to thin your blood.
          (F, 50, R, 1948, + 8 F and 3 M)

1650   Take sulfur and molasses in the spring to thin your blood.
          (F, 21, 1950, + 13 F)

1651   Sulfur and molasses will cure spring fever.
          (F, 22, R, 1957, + 1 F)

1652   An apple a day keeps the doctor away; a rosary a day keeps
          the Devil away; an onion a day keeps everybody away.
          (M, 20, R, 1961 [his friends])

1653   An apple a day will keep the doctor away.
          (M, 20, R, 1956 [his mother], + 27 F and 4 M)

1654   You'll lose your mind if a full moon shines on you while you're
          sleeping.
          (F, 20, 1959, + 7 F)

1655   A cowboy belief about sleeping in the open used to be that he
          should not sleep where a full moon would shine on his face,
          because it would pull his face out of its proper shape.
          (M, 50, R, 1959)

1656   Do not play on an oboe, or you will go crazy.
          (F, 40, 1960)

1657   People who play the bassoon have a tendency to lose their
          minds or go crazy.
          (F, 21, 1961)

1658   Don't ever sweep hair combings outside. Birds will make
          nests of them, and you will lose your mind.
          (F, 50, 1959 [her grandmother])

1659   Kids shouldn't play with matches; for if they do, they will wet
          their beds.
          (F, 50, 1959, + 1 F and 2 M)

1660   The burnt part of a wooden match is good for children to eat.
          It is used for vitamins.
          (F, 1962)

1661   Children shouldn't be allowed out in the night air, because
          they will get diseases.
          (F, 1962)

1662   Dutch people used to put bread crumbs in their baby's cradle
          to ward off diseases.
          (F, 1962)

1663   Tea made from watermelon seeds used to be given to children
          and babies to increase the flow of urine.
          (M, 62, R, 1959)

1664   Put a dime around a baby's neck to keep him from catching any diseases.
      (F, 1962)

1665   Put black silk bibs around babies' necks to prevent disease.
      (M, 81, R, 1958)

1666   Tie a string to a door knob if you have illness in the home. Light the end of the string. This will purify the air.
      (F, 55, 1959)

1667   A small pouch of asafetida tied around the neck will ward off any disease.
      (M, 20, 1958 [his grandfather], + 22 F and 9 M)

1668   Burning sulfur will rid a room of germs.
      (F, 44, R, 1957)

1669   Wear red yarn around your neck to keep quinsy away.
      (F, 50, R, 1958 [her grandmother])

4

Death and Funeral Customs and Beliefs

FOLK CUSTOMS AND BELIEFS ASSOCIATED WITH DEATH IN our "life cycle" have widely varying degrees of significance in different cultures. Some social scientists have observed that the less sophisticated the culture, the more significant are the old beliefs. In the case of our own culture, it may be said, in a broad context, that funerals now are commercially standardized; and death itself—well, as a citizen put it, "They're trying to educate us all about it these days."

Of the 345 items in this chapter, 30 percent deal with animal and bird signs of death, and 24 percent deal with various household signs. The howling of dogs at night was reported by 87 people to be an omen of death; 43 said specifically that this would mean a death in the family or household. As for birds as omens of death, of the 137 people reporting on this, 96 were concerned with birds flying into the house or against windows, and 62 of these said specifically that this signified a death in the family. Other death beliefs with high frequency involved the crowing of cocks or the hooting of owls at night. Also widely reported items were if it rains on an open grave or if you count the cars in a funeral procession, there will be a death in the family.

These reminders that death may be just around the corner and that the messengers of death are often animals or birds are firmly fixed in many people's minds. Dr. Wayland Hand has noted that "most superstitious people would not take lightly any such death warnings." In any event, probably one of the underlying intentions of death omens and beliefs is to show that death is grimly inevitable, that we must be ready for it, and that proclamations, from whatever sources, reveal this in a supernatural way.

139

ANIMALS AS SIGNS OF DEATH

Cats

1670   A sick person will die if a cat walks across his bed.
        (F, 20, 1957)

1671   If cats yowl much at night, it means death.
        (F, 71, 1961)

1672   Cats or dogs know when there has been a death in the family
        and become restless. (When the contributor's grandmother
        died, the family's small dog ran up and down stairs and was
        quite restless.)
        (F, 49, R, 1961)

1673   If you move a cat, someone in the family will die.
        (F, 52, 1957)

1674   A man who makes enemies of cats during his lifetime will be
        accompanied to his grave in the midst of a storm and rain.
        (M, 70, R, 1963 [his father])

1675   Keep cats away from a dead body. They will eat its nose.
        (F, 58, 1959)

1676   When someone dies, the black cat will run around in the
        hayloft.
        (F, 65, R, 1957)

Dogs

1677   If someone has died, the dog will howl.
        (F, 30, R, 1962 [her parents], + 2 F and 2 M)

1678   A dog's howling means that someone is going to die.
        (M, 21, R, 1957, + 9 F and 4 M)

1679   If a dog howls at night, there will be a death in the family.
        (M, 30, R, 1959, + 13 F and 3 M)

1680   If a dog howls at night, you will hear of a death in the family
        the next day.
        (F, 40, R, 1963)

1681   In the past, when a person was sick and a dog howled, it was
        considered to be a sign of death.
        (F, 50, 1958, + 1 F and 1 M)

1682   A dog howling at midnight means death.
        (F, 21, 1956, + 1 F and 1 M)

1683   If a dog sits on the porch steps and howls, there will be a death in the family.
    (F, 50, R, 1961, + 1 M)

1684   A dog howling near your home means death.
    (F, 60, R, 1958 [her mother])

1685   A dog howling in the front yard means that there will be a death in the house.
    (F, 23, R, 1958)

1686   A dog howling under a window means that there will be a death in that house.
    (F, 29, R, 1958, + 6 F and 4 M)

1687   If the master is sick and his dog howls in the night, it is a sign of approaching death.
    (M, 65, R, 1960 [his grandmother])

1688   If a dog starts howling when his master is away, some calamity either threatens or has befallen the master.
    (M, 62, R, 1959)

1689   If there is a death in the home, the neighbors know because of the dogs' howling.
    (F, 63, 1958)

1690   If you hear a howling dog at night, there has been a death in the neighborhood.
    (F, 40, 1959 [her parents], + 6 F)

1691   A dog will know about a death in the family without being told.
    (M, 21, 1950)

1692   When there has been a death in the family, the family dog will often times give out with a deathly howl.
    (F, 50, R, 1959, + 1 F)

1693   If a dog howls and it is hard to get it out of the house, there will be a death in the family.
    (F, 1962)

1694   When a dog sits outside and howls five times, this is a sign of a death.
    (F, 60, R, 1959)

1695   A dog's rolling over three times is a death omen.
    (M, 50, R, 1958)

1696   If a dog howls three times under your window, it is a death omen.
    (F, 42, 1958)

1697   If a dog howls at the death of one person, there will be another death.
    (F, 60, R, 1956)

1698   When a dog lies with its head going out the door, there is
going to be a death in the family.
(F, 50, 1962)

1699   When Mr. Husky's mother died, their dog dug a hole and
howled all night outside of his mother's window. He still be-
lieves that this dog knew that his mother was dying.
(F, 20, R, 1963)

1700   When a dog crawls to you, this is the sign of death. The
distance that it crawls is the height of the person who is to
die.
(F, 1962)

1701   If a dog howls at the moon, someone will die.
(F, 28, 1956, + 2 F and 2 M)

1702   When a dog howls at the moon, there will be a death in the
family.
(F, 20, 1961 [her grandmother], + 2 F)

1703   When a dog bays at a full moon, that means there will be a
death in the immediate family.
(F, 70, R, 1958 [her mother])

1704   If a strange dog comes to town and howls in the night, there
has been a death in the town.
(F, 19, 1957)

1705   A howling dog means that death is close to where he howls.
(M, 60, R, 1962)

1706   If you hear a dog howl, it will mean that someone is dying.
(F, 60, R, 1957)

Other Animals

1707   If a person hears a coyote howl after midnight when the moon
is full, there will soon be a death in the family.
(F, 20, 1961 [her aunt], + 1 F)

1708   When there is a corpse in the neighborhood, the wolves will
howl.
(M, 24, 1956)

1709   If a person sees a swarm of bees on a dead branch of a live
tree, a death will occur in his family within a year.
(F, 70, R, 1963 [her mother])

1710   If a cow moos after midnight, a death will occur in the family.
(F, 70, R, 1959 [her mother])

1711   A family should never get a pet that is the same age as a

young growing child; for when the pet dies, the child will also die.
(M, 50, R, 1957)

1712   When you hear termites in the wall, that is a death watch. It means that someone in the family will die.
(F, 52, 1957)

BIRDS AS SIGNS OF DEATH

1713   If a bird flutters around the window, there will be a death in the family.
(F, 30, 1961, + 4 F)

1714   When a bird flies against a window of a house, this means death.
(F, 1961 [her mother], + 3 F and 1 M)

1715   If a bird lights on the window screen, there will be a death in the family.
(F, 17, 1960 [her parents], + 2 F)

1716   If a bird pecks on the window, there will be a death in the family.
(F, 19, R, 1957, + 2 F)

1717   If a bird pecks on your windowpane, a death is going to happen.
(F, 20, R, 1959 [her mother])

1718   If a bird pecks three times on the windowpane, there will be a death.
(F, 54, 1955)

1719   If a bird tries to get in through a window, someone is going to die.
(F, 54, R, 1958)

1720   If a bird flies up against a window, there will be death. However, if it flies into the window and kills itself, there will be a catastrophe.
(F, 60, 1957)

1721   When two birds hang together on the screen, there will be a death.
(F, 30, R, 1958)

1722   If a bird flies in a house and flies over someone's head, that person will soon die.
(F, 54, 1958)

1723   If a bird flies around the room three times, there will be a death in the family.
(M, 66, R, 1959)

1724   Bird feathers in a sickroom can delay the death of a patient so that it will be possible for someone who is hurrying to see the dying person to make his visit.
(M, 50, 1962)

1725   If you see a bird in a public building, someone you know has died.
(F, 20, 1960 [her mother])

1726   If a bird drops a piece of white paper in front of you, it is a sign that you will hear by telegram about a death.
(F, 60, R, 1958)

1727   If a bird flies into the house, someone must bury the shovel in the ashes of the stove; otherwise there will be a death in the family.
(F, 60, R, 1960 [her sister])

1728   If a bird flies into a house, the person who puts the bird out will be the next in the family to die.
(F, 50, R, 1957)

1729   If a bird flies into the house and you let it out, there will be a death in the family. You must kill the bird while it is in the house.
(M, 40, R, 1962 [his mother])

1730   If a bird flies around in the house and then flies back out, there will be a death in the family.
(F, 70, R, 1961 [her parents])

1731   If a bird goes in one door and comes out another, there will be a death in the family.
(M, 50, R, 1960)

1732   If a bird flies in the window, there has been, or soon will be, a death in your family.
(F, 24, 1957, + 1 M)

1733   If a bird flies into a house, someone will die.
(F, 21, 1961, + 15 F and 2 M)

1734   A bird in the house means that death will soon come to a member of that household.
(F, 21, 1950, + 5 F)

1735   If a bird gets in the house, there'll be a death in the family.
(F, 24, 1959, + 16 F and 6 M)

1736   Don't let a wild bird in the house, or there will be a death in the family. (The informant's sister died under such a circumstance.)

(M, 30, 1958)

1737   If a bird flies (or tries to fly) through the windows into a house, someone in that home is going to die. This belief was renewed with interest when a bird tried to fly into a house in Atwood in 1951; several days later, word came to the parents of that home that their son had been killed in Korea.

(F, 20, 1958)

1738   Someone will die if a live bird gets into the house. (The informant claimed that she was not superstitious, but she noted that she got cold chills once when a starling got into the house.)

(F, 30, 1959)

1739   If a bird flies down a chimney in your home, there will be a death in the family within thirty days.

(F, 1962)

1740   If a mocking bird sings close to your house, a member of your household will soon die.

(F, 60, R, 1961 [her mother])

1741   A black bird on your chimney means death.

(F, 60, R, 1961)

1742   If a black bird perches on your window, there will be a death in the family; but if a white bird perches on your window, you will have good luck.

(F, 20, R, 1957)

1743   If a woodpecker pecks on the window, there will be a death in the family.

(F, 40, R, 1959 [her mother])

1744   There is a belief among southern Negroes that if a woodpecker knocks on your door in the morning, someone in the house will die. (One informant said that this had happened when her husband died.)

(F, 50, 1962)

1745   If buzzards circle your house, someone will die.

(F, 50, 1957)

1746   A buzzard on the window is a sign of death.

(F, 50, 1957)

1747   A buzzard flying overhead is a sign of death.

(M, 60, R, 1961, + 1 F)

1748   If a bird, particularly a sparrow, flies into a church, someone in that church will die soon.

(F, 60, R, 1957)

1749   A sparrow flying against the window screen means that there will be a death in the house soon.
   (F, 40, 1957)

1750   If a sparrow lights on your window, someone is going to die.
   (F, 14, 1959 [her mother])

1751   A sparrow's flying into the house is a sign of death.
   (F, 52, 1956)

1752   If a dove hovers at your window three or four times, there will be a death among your relatives.
   (F, 50, 1958 [her mother])

1753   If a dove lights on your window sill, there will be a death in your family.
   (F, 75, R, 1956)

1754   The direction in which the first dove coos is the direction in which the next person to die lives.
   (F, 50, R, 1963 [her mother])

1755   A dove in the house means that there will be a death.
   (F, 50, 1959)

1756   If a dove coos and coos, there will be a death in the family.
   (F, 50, 1959 [her grandmother])

1757   If a dove lights in your yard, it's a sign of death.
   (F, 40, R, 1961 [her mother])

1758   If a dove comes close to a person who is very sick, this is bad luck, and the person will die.
   (F, 1962)

1759   When a cock crows at night, it means that there will be a death in the family.
   (F, 40, R, 1957, + 3 F and 1 M)

1760   If a cock crows three times, there will be a death in the family.
   (F, 20, 1955)

1761   It is bad for a rooster to crow in the doorway if someone is ill inside. It may mean death.
   (F, 65, R, 1962)

1762   If a hen crows, there will soon be a death in the family.
   (M, 50, R, 1958, + 1 F and 1 M)

1763   When you hear an owl hoot at night, it means that someone has just died.
   (M, 21, 1956, + 4 F and 1 M)

1764   If an owl hoots in the night, there is to be a death in the family. (A mournful hoot on a very still night.)
   (F, 21, 1959, + 5 F)

1765   If an owl hoots at night, someone in the neighborhood will die.
         (F, 31, 1956, + 2 F)

1766   If an owl lands on the roof, there will be a death in that house.
         (M, 50, R, 1960, + 1 F and 1 M)

1767   If an owl flies up to and sits upon a window sill, there will be
         a death in the family soon.
         (M, 60, 1961)

1768   If an owl hoots three times in the dark of the moon, there will
         be a death in the neighborhood.
         (F, 20, R, 1958)

1769   If a hoot owl hoots three times at a bedroom window, there
         will be a death.
         (F, 40, R, 1959 [her mother])

1770   If a hoot owl sits on a tree outside your house, there will be a
         death in the family.
         (F, 20, 1961 [her mother])

1771   A white owl that flies over your house means death.
         (M, 20, 1957)

HOUSEHOLD SIGNS OF DEATH

1772   Opening an umbrella in the house is a sign of death.
         (F, 19, R, 1962, + 8 F and 1 M)

1773   Don't raise an umbrella in the house, or there will be a death
         in the family.
         (F, 20, R, 1961, + 11 F and 1 M)

1774   Do not open an umbrella in the house, for it may bring a death
         in less than a year.
         (F, 50, R, 1958 [her mother], + 1 F and 1 M)

1775   If one sweeps or carries out any dirt on New Year's Day,
         there will be a death in the family before the end of the year.
         (F, 50, R, 1960)

1776   If a broom falls down across the door, it's a sign of death.
         (F, 50, R, 1957)

1777   When moving from one house to another, never take the
         broom along, because it is a sign of a death in the family.
         (M, 40, R, 1958, + 3 F)

1778   Don't sweep any dirt out of the house after dark, or there will
         be a death in the family.
         (F, 50, R, 1957, + 3 F)

1779   Don't sweep dirt out the back door after dark, or there will be a death in the family.
(M, 19, 1958)

1780   There will be a death in the family if you sweep after supper.
(F, 57, 1957)

1781   If the dust that you are sweeping out of the house blows back into the room (if you put your dustpan down to pick it up, and it blows back into the room), you're going to receive a message about a serious illness or death.
(F, 47, 1958)

1782   If you drop a knife or a pair of scissors and they stick in the floor, there will be a death in the family.
(M, 19, R, 1959 [his parents])

1783   Crossed silverware on the table will mean a death of one of your friends or a relative outside of the immediate family.
(M, 50, R, 1958 [his mother])

1784   If a knife lies with its sharp side up, there is sure to be a death in the family.
(M, 70, R, 1960 [his grandparents])

1785   If you set an extra plate at the table, someone will soon die.
(F, 20, R, 1956)

1786   Shaking the crumbs from the tablecloth out the door after dark will bring a death in the family.
(F, 44, R, 1957)

1787   If you ever throw a crumb of bread away, then someday you will starve to death.
(F, 50, 1957)

1788   Don't eat or drink out of a cracked dish at someone's house, or someone in the family will die soon.
(F, 20, 1959 [her mother])

1789   If a door opens and closes without visible means, there will be a death in the family.
(F, 50, 1958)

1790   A doctor should never put his hat on a patient's bed, for it might cause the patient to die.
(F, 50, R, 1956)

1791   Never throw a hat upon a bed; for if you do, there will be a death in the family.
(F, 40, 1958, + 1 F)

1792   After a person dies, if his pillow is cut open and a ring of feathers is found, the person went to heaven.
(F, 17, R, 1959 [her friends])

1793   If you find a pretty little ball of feathers in a pillow, it means that someone has died on that pillow.
(F, 60, R, 1961 [her mother])

1794   A crown of feathers formed in the pillow of a sick baby means that he's going to die.
(F, 26, 1956)

1795   If your feather pillow gets a crown in it, you are going to die.
(F, 1961 [her mother])

1796   A curled feather in your pillow means that there will be a death in a family.
(F, 60, 1958)

1797   If you take a feather bed off the bed when someone is sick, that person will die.
(F, 60, R, 1961)

1798   Always sleep with your feet pointing toward the west, since dead men sleep with their feet toward the east.
(F, 50, R, 1957, + 2 F)

1799   A person who sleeps in the bed that someone died in will be dead himself within a year.
(F, 50, 1961)

1800   Shoes set on a bed mean that there will be a death in the family.
(F, 1962)

1801   If a lamp chimney breaks without apparent cause, it is a sign that there will be a death.
(F, 70, R, 1958)

1802   If you break a clothespin while hanging clothes to dry, you will hear of a death within a day.
(F, 1961 [heard from someone whose ancestors came from Russia])

1803   When a window shade spontaneously rolls up, there will be a death.
(F, 40, R, 1958 [her mother-in-law])

1804   If you break a needle while sewing, you will not outlive the garment that you are making.
(F, 60, R, 1958)

1805   If you carry a hoe into the house, someone will die.
(F, 52, 1957)

1806   Bringing a garden hoe into the house will cause the death of someone in the family.
(M, 40, R, 1960 [his father], + 5 F and 2 M)

1807   If you bring a hoe into the house, a death will occur in the
        community within twenty-four hours.
            (M, 50, R, 1957)

1808   If you bring a garden hoe into the house, there will be death
        in the family within a year.
            (F, 68, 1954, + 1 F)

1809   Taking a garden hoe into the house means that there will be a
        death in the family within a short time.
            (M, 40, R, 1963 [his mother], + 1 F)

1810   If one were to carry a shovel through the house, there would
        be a death in the family.
            (M, 30, 1959 [his grandmother])

1811   If you bring a shovel in the house, you are digging your own
        grave.
            (F, 70, R, 1960 [her parents])

1812   Never carry garden tools through the house, or there will be
        a death in the family.
            (F, 75, 1961 [her mother])

1813   Carrying a rake through the house brings death.
            (F, 40, 1961)

1814   If you bring a pitchfork into the house, there will be a death in
        the family.
            (F, 40, R, 1961)

1815   If a spade is carried into a home without all the dirt being
        cleaned off it first, some member of the family will die.
            (M, 62, R, 1959)

1816   If you carry an ax into the house, one of your immediate
        family will die.
            (M, 1961)

1817   When something breaks for no reason, there has been a
        death.
            (F, 50, R, 1961)

1818   If a framed picture falls down and the glass breaks, there will
        be a death in the family.
            (F, 20, 1960 [her mother], + 1 F)

1819   If a picture falls from the wall, it is a sign of death.
            (F, 50, R, 1963 [her grandmother], + 5 F)

1820   If a picture falls off the wall for no reason, someone is going
        to die.
            (F, 30, 1960 [her grandmother], + 3 F)

1821   If a picture falls from the wall, a death will occur in the home
        where this happened within a year.
            (F, 60, R, 1962 [her grandmother])

1822   A picture's suddenly falling from the wall will result in a death in that house.
        (F, 57, R, 1962 [her mother])

1823   A picture's falling from the wall means that there will be a death or serious injury. If the picture is of a living person, that person will die.
        (F, 50, R, 1959)

1824   To stand a person's picture upside down is to wish death to that person.
        (F, 20, 1959)

1825   When someone dies, turn all the pictures so that they face the wall until after the funeral.
        (F, 70, R, 1958 [her family])

1826   If all members of the family are in one picture, one will die before the year is over.
        (F, 30, R, 1958)

1827   A picture that is hanging crookedly on a wall means death.
        (F, 22, 1956)

1828   If you break a mirror, there will be a death in your family.
        (F, 30, 1959 [her mother], + 2 F and 1 M)

1829   When a death occurs in the family, all mirrors and pictures in the home should be turned to the wall or covered up.
        (M, 65, 1959, + 1 F)

1830   When there has been a death in the family, cover all the mirrors.
        (M, 50, 1956)

1831   If the mirrors are not covered at the time of a death, another death will occur in the family within a year.
        (F, 45, R, 1961)

1832   Cover the looking-glass when a death occurs, because the next person to see himself in the mirror will be the next to die.
        (F, 1959)

1833   Never spin a chair on one leg, or someone will die.
        (F, 21, 1950, + 2 F)

1834   If you twirl a chair completely around in a house, someone will die.
        (F, 60, 1959)

1835   Never rock an empty rocking chair; for if you do so, the next person to sit in it will die.
        (F, 52, 1957)

1836   If you rock a rocking chair with your toe, you will die within a week.
(F, 20, 1958)

1837   To rock an empty rocking chair will mean a death in the family.
(F, 21, 1950, + 6 F and 2 M)

1838   If a rocking chair rocks with no one in it, there will be a death in the family.
(F, 19, R, 1959, + 2 F)

1839   If an empty rocking chair rocks, there will be a death in the family.
(F, 20, R, 1959)

1840   If you wake up at night and see a rocking chair rocking, someone near will soon die.
(M, 20, R, 1956)

1841   Never rock a rocking chair without anyone in it, or a death will occur.
(F, 30, R, 1958 [her family], + 1 F and 1 M)

1842   When a clock stops, there will be a death in the family.
(F, 21, R, 1959 [her mother])

1843   An old clock will ring just before death strikes.
(F, 60, R, 1957)

1844   If you cut a hole in a wall, this will cause a death in the family.
(M, 50, R, 1960 [his mother])

1845   If you make a door out of a window, in time you will carry a corpse through it.
(F, 44, 1961, + 1 F)

1846   If you cut out a window and put in a door, there will be a death in your family within the year.
(F, 70, 1958)

1847   When a loaf of bread cracks while baking or shortly thereafter, it means that a death is soon to come.
(F, 50, R, 1959, + 1 M)

1848   Never wash clothes between Christmas and New Year's Day, or you'll wash someone in the family into his grave.
(F, 60, R, 1958, + 3 F and 1 M)

1849   If a person washes on New Year's day, he will wash for a corpse before the year is over.
(F, 50, R, 1961 [her grandmother])

1850   If a person washes clothes between Christmas and New

Year's and hangs them up, that person will deck the graveyard during the following year.

(F, 75, R, 1960 [her mother])

1851   Clothing shouldn't be left on the clothesline overnight
between Christmas and New Year's; for this will cause a
death in the family.

(F, 44, 1960)

1852   A wash on the line between Christmas and New Year's signifies that there will be a death that year.

(F, 59, R, 1957)

THE MOON, THE STARS, AND PLANTS

1853   A falling star means that someone is dying.

(F, 18, 1956, + 6 F and 1 M)

1854   If you see a falling star, someone that you know will die.

(F, 19, R, 1956)

1855   Seeing a falling star indicates the death of a friend in the
near future.

(F, 49, R, 1956, + 2 F)

1856   If you see a falling star, it is a sign of the death of a friend.

(F, 60, R, 1961, + 1 F)

1857   A falling star means that there will be a death in the family in
the future.

(M, 68, R, 1958 [his mother])

1858   Whenever a star falls, a soul ascends to heaven.

(F, 21, 1950, + 1 F and 1 M)

1859   "Liebe Gutt geps sie avishe Ruh" ("Loving God, give them
everlasting peace"). People used to believe that if you could
say this rhyme before a star stopped falling, you would save
some soul from purgatory.

(F, 80, R, 1958 [her mother])

1860   When you see a falling star, say a prayer; for it represents a
soul on its way to heaven or hell.

(F, 54, 1959)

1861   A shooting star to the left indicates that a wicked person's
soul is entering the hot place.

(F, 66, 1955)

1862   When there's a ring around the moon, there will be a death in
the family.

(M, 20, 1957)

1863   If the moon goes under a cloud, someone has just died.
        (F, 20, 1958)

1864   If the moon is red, one of your friends is dying.
        (M, 1961)

1865   Blood on the moon signifies that there has been a death.
        (F, 1962, + 1 F)

1866   A reddish cast to the moon means death.
        (F, 21, 1956)

1867   Missing a row while planting a field of corn will cause a
        death in the family.
        (M, 50, R, 1957, + 1 M)

1868   If a cedar tree that you have planted in your yard dies, some-
        one in your family will die.
        (F, 58, 1958)

1869   When an evergreen tree in your yard grows high enough to
        cover a grave, someone in your family will die.
        (F, 1962)

1870   If fruit trees bear blossoms out of their regular season, it is a
        sign of the approaching death of some member of the com-
        munity.
        (F, 70, 1961)

1871   A shrub such as a lilac that is blooming out of season means
        that there will be a death.
        (F, 59, R, 1957)

1872   Count while you twist the stem of an apple; the number that
        you are saying when it pops off will be the age at which you
        will die.
        (F, 20, 1957)

1873   Don't burn flowers; for this will bring death.
        (F, 70, R, 1959)

1874   If a weeping willow branch touches the ground, it means
        death.
        (F, 19, 1956)

1875   Where there's a weeping willow, there's a weeping widow.
        (F, 60, 1959)

1876   If you take a pot of parsley in for the winter, someone in the
        family will die before the winter is over.
        (F, 50, 1958)

1877   If you have a lingering illness through the winter, you will die
        when the leaves start budding.
        (F, 60, R, 1961)

PREDICTING DEATH BY NUMBERS

1878   If three of the same things follow in succession, it is the sign
       of death.
          (F, 20, R, 1957)

1879   Deaths always come in threes.
          (F, 19, 1956, + 10 F and 5 M)

1880   Three deaths in a row always occur in the family.
          (F, 20, 1959 [her parents], + 2 F and 1 M)

1881   Whenever a person is killed by an accident, two other acci-
       dental deaths will occur in the same community.
          (F, 20, 1959)

1882   If there is one death in the family, there will be two more in
       the near future.
          (F, R, 1957, + 8 F)

1883   If there is one death in the community, there will be two more.
          (F, 20, R, 1959, + 8 F and 1 M)

1884   Death comes in cycles of three. If a woman dies in a town,
       there will be two other women who will die. If a man dies in a
       town, two other men will die in that town.
          (F, 60, 1962 [her parents])

1885   When death comes to one neighbor, there will always be two
       more deaths.
          (F, 70, R, 1957)

1886   Things come in threes. If there are two deaths among friends,
       they will be followed by a third. This also applies to wed-
       dings, births, and so forth.
          (M, 50, R, 1958 [his mother])

1887   One death in the community will bring two more before the
       change of the moon.
          (F, 37, R, 1961 [her grandmother])

1888   It never fails that if two old people die, a third old person will
       follow.
          (F, 20, 1958 [her parents])

1889   If there's one death in a family, two more will follow.
          (F, 50, R, 1959 [her relatives], + 2 F)

1890   Counting cars of a train will mean that someone in your
       family has died, or it will cause someone in your family to die.
          (F, 29, R, 1958, + 3 F)

1891   Never light three cigarettes on one match, or bad luck in the form of death will come to the third person.
(F, 20, 1961 [her friends], + 1 M)

1892   Three lights on in a room mean death.
(F, 22, 1956)

1893   If you go down three times (in water), you will never come up.
(M, 31, 1959 [his friends])

1894   Never turn a chair around three times before sitting on it, for this will cause a death in the family.
(M, 50, R, 1957)

1895   Don't sit at a table that is set for thirteen people. If you do, someone who is sitting at that table will die within the next year.
(M, 25, R, 1963, + 4 F and 4 M)

1896   If there is a death in the family, there will be a chain reaction of seven more deaths.
(F, 42, 1962 [her father])

1897   If four people shake hands with their arms crossed, one of them will die.
(F, 60, R, 1969)

1898   Never have an uneven number of people seated at your New Year's Day table, or death will come to one of the group.
(F, 52, R, 1958 [her mother])

FUNERALS, GRAVES, AND THE DEAD

1899   When a funeral procession goes by, touch a button on your dress; otherwise, someone dear to you will die.
(F, 19, 1956, + 2 F)

1900   If a funeral procession is stopped by accident on the way to the cemetery, another death will occur in the family within a short period of time.
(F, 44, 1961 [her mother-in-law], + 1 F)

1901   If a funeral is held on Friday, there will soon be another funeral in the family.
(F, 60, R, 1957, + 1 F)

1902   If you count the cars in a funeral procession, there will be a death in the family.
(F, 19, R, 1959 [her grandmother], + 8 F and 2 M)

1903   If you count the cars in a funeral procession, you will be the next person to die.
(F, 50, R, 1957, + 1 F and 1 M)

1904   Never count the cars at a funeral, because there will be a death in the family in the number of days that there were cars.

       (F, 40, R, 1961 [her father], + 1 M)

1905   If you rent a hearse, there will be a death in the family.

       (F, 1962)

1906   When you are at the rear of a funeral procession, there will be a death in your family soon.

       (F, 1959)

1907   Some people used to believe that if you met a funeral procession on some road, there would be a death in your family in a year.

       (M, 50, R, 1961 [his mother])

1908   People used to say that if the team of horses that was pulling the hearse was allowed to trot, the survivor "was anxious to get his mate in the grave so he could look for another"!

       (F, 80, R, 1962 [her mother])

1909   If you wear a new dress to a funeral, you will be the next to die.

       (F, 60, R, 1957)

1910   If you wear something new to a funeral, there will be a death in the family.

       (M, 60, R, 1959 [his relatives])

1911   If you go to a funeral and touch the deceased person, you will not dream about the deceased one.

       (M, 20, R, 1958)

1912   When you attend a funeral, you should always stop somewhere, such as a drugstore, before you return home. You should never go directly home.

       (M, 1962 [his mother])

1913   Looking into an open grave will bring death to a member of the immediate family.

       (F, 49, R, 1956)

1914   If a grave is left open overnight, another member of the family will die.

       (F, 60, R, 1962 [her parents])

1915   People should be buried with their heads to the west in order to face the rising sun.

       (M, 25, R, 1956, + 1 F and 1 M)

1916   If it rains on a casket, there will soon be another death in the family.

       (F, 40, R, 1960 [her parents], + 1 F)

1917   If it rains in an open grave, there will be another death in the
        family in three days.
             (F, 40, R, 1963 [her mother], + 1 F)
1918   If it rains or snows in an open grave, another death in the
        family will occur.
             (F, 40, 1960, + 2 F)
1919   If rain falls on an open grave, then death will come to some-
        one soon.
             (F, 50, R, 1960 [her mother], + 3 F)
1920   If it rains in an open grave, there will be three successive
        deaths in a community.
             (F, 40, R, 1960, + 1 M)
1921   Rain in an open grave means that there will be a death in the
        family in the next month.
             (F, 1962)
1922   If it rains in an open grave, some member of the family will
        die within six weeks.
             (M, 70, 1962)
1923   If rain falls in an open grave, there will be two more deaths in
        the immediate family.
             (M, 50, 1957)

1924   If it rains in an open grave, there will be three deaths in the family within a year.
(F, 40, R, 1960 [her parents])

1925   If it rains in an open grave, someone else in that family will die in the near future.
(F, 45, R, 1963, + 3 F and 1 M)

1926   If it rains or snows on an open grave before a burial, another relative will die within six months.
(F, 60, R, 1957)

1927   If it rains in an open grave, there will be a death in the family before a year is up.
(F, 20, R, 1959, + 17 F and 1 M)

1928   Happy is the corpse that the rain falls on.
(F, 40, R, 1962 [her mother], + 3 F and 1 M)

1929   If you happen to step across a grave, there will be a death in the family within a year.
(F, 60, R, 1962)

1930   Walking across a grave means death.
(F, 19, 1956)

1931   If there is a corpse on Sunday, there will be another one within three months.
(F, 31, 1956)

1932   Take a dead person out of a house feetfirst, or there will be another death in the family within a year.
(F, 70, R, 1961 [her father])

1933   A dead person must be carried from the room feetfirst.
(M, 64, 1957, + 1 F)

1934   Your hair and fingernails continue to grow after death.
(F, 50, R, 1960 [her parents])

1935   If you kiss a dead person, you will never fear death.
(F, 20, R, 1958)

1936   If one stays for one year and one day at a loved one's grave, the dead one will be restless and will talk to the visitor.
(M, 19, 1958)

1937   Hold your breath as you walk by a cemetery, or you'll be the next one in it.
(F, 1962)

1938   Hold your breath while going by a graveyard in order to prevent a death in the family.
(M, 1962)

1939   If you are cremated, you won't go to heaven.
(F, 60, R, 1961)

SPIRITS, SOULS, AND STRANGE SOUNDS

1940   As soon as somebody dies, open the window so that the soul
        can leave the body and get out of the room.
        (F, 55, 1958)

1941   If you sit in the same room as the corpse of a friend or
        relative with the lights off and the window open, there will be
        a breeze, which is supposed to be the person's spirit leaving.
        (M, 15, 1956)

1942   One contributor wouldn't go into the room with or touch dead
        persons for fear their ghosts would return to haunt her.
        (F, 90, R, 1961)

1943   Never speak ill of dead persons, or they will haunt you.
        (F, 20, 1959 [her friend])

1944   Never wear the shoes of a deceased person, because if you
        do, you will tread on the deceased person's soul.
        (M, 50, 1956)

1945   If a person dies (by some accident) before he would have died
        a natural death, his spirit will have to travel here until his
        natural death would have occurred.
        (M, 74, R, 1960)

1946   Bury married couples with their caskets touching so that they
        will be together throughout eternity. (The informant's par-
        ents were buried this way.)
        (F, 80, R, 1962 [her parents])

1947   If you answer when you think you hear someone call, there
        will be a death in the family.
        (M, 70, R, 1960 [his family])

1948   If you hear someone call your name when you know that they
        are away, don't answer; it's a sign of death if you do.
        (F, 50, R, 1958)

1949   If a dying person calls someone, that person will die before
        long.
        (F, 75, R, 1958 [her mother])

1950   If you hear three knocks on a door in the early morning, but
        no one is there, there will be a death in the family.
        (F, 20, R, 1959 [her mother])

1951   If you hear a knocking or stomping, like somebody is walking
        above or like the creaking in a house, it is a token of your
        death.
        (F, 80, R, 1961)

1952   If some far-away relative dies, you will hear a noise in the house as if a rafter were creaking or as if someone were pounding.
         (M, 70, R, 1962)

1953   A ringing in the ear is a sign of death.
         (F, 71, R, 1958)

1954   If you hear a bell ring in the night, it is a sign of a coming death in the family.
         (F, 20, R, 1960 [her grandmother])

1955   To hear a bell ringing in your ear is the sign of a death.
         (M, 70, R, 1960 [his father])

1956   If you hear ringing in your ears, it's death's bells. Knock on your chair to drive them away.
         (F, 50, R, 1958)

1957   If you hear a ringing in your ears, someone you know has just died.
         (F, 21, 1955, + 2 F)

1958   If a church bell gives an after toll, a member of the congregation will soon die.
         (F, 60, R, 1959)

1959   If you hear a pin drop, someone will die.
         (F, 21, R, 1957)

1960   If you hear a bunch of children singing on the street, you will hear of a death.
         (F, 75, R, 1958 [her mother])

DEATH, MISCELLANEOUS

1961   "Dance on Sunday. / Die on Monday." (Dances always should end by midnight on Saturday night.)
         (F, 20, R, 1963)

1962   "March will search, April will try, / And May will tell if you live or die."
         (F, 70, R, 1961)

1963   If there is a white Christmas, there will be a green graveyard (no deaths); a gray Christmas, a gray graveyard (a death).
         (F, 40, 1958)

1964   If there is a white Christmas, there will be a green Easter; a black Christmas, a full graveyard.
         (F, 70, R, 1962 [her parents])

1965   A green Christmas means a fat graveyard.
         (F, 40, R, 1963 [her mother], + 5 F)

1966   A black Christmas and a white Easter make a fat graveyard.
         (F, 60, R, 1962 [her parents])

1967   A black Christmas means a fat graveyard.
         (F, 20, R, 1957, + 1 F)

1968   A mild winter means a green graveyard. (People have more
         colds and sickness and there are more deaths during a mild
         winter.)
         (M, 20, 1958)

1969   A winter without snow means that there will be many deaths
         in the spring.
         (M, 62, 1958)

1970   If you hang up a new calendar before the New Year arrives,
         there will be a death in the family during that year.
         (F, 70, R, 1962 [her mother])

1971   If you climb through a window, someone in your family will
         die within a year.
         (F, 1961)

1972   If you walk around with your collar up, you'll have a widow.
         (M, 50, R, 1960 [his neighbors])

1973   If someone is very sick and unusually good on Sunday, it is a
         bad sign.
         (F, 95, R, 1958 [her mother])

1974   If you sneeze on Sunday morning before breakfast, you will
         hear of a death that week.
         (F, 77, R, 1961 [her mother])

1975   People never used to hang a bonnet or anything on the door
         knob, because that was a sign that there would be a death in
         the family within a year and that crepe would be hanging on
         the door.
         (F, 50, R, 1958)

1976   If a mother eats fish while her baby is little, the mother will
         die.
         (F, 59, R, 1959 [her mother])

1977   If a person eats at least one quail every day for a month, he
         will die.
         (M, 50, 1961)

1978   The order in which newlyweds get into bed on the first night
         of their marriage will indicate the order in which they will
         die. (The contributor learned this in 1907, when her daughter
         was getting married, from her great-aunt, who advised her

daughter to get into her husband's arms and for them to get into bed together.)
(F, 1961)

1979   If a sick person starts singing, then death is near.
(F, 1962)

1980   If a magician puts you to sleep and later on he dies, you will die that same week.
(F, 50, R, 1958)

1981   Every aspirin that you take will take six hours off your life.
(F, 21, 1961)

1982   There's a death rattle in the throat of a dying person.
(F, 20, 1959)

1983   A candle's going out signifies a death.
(F, 21, 1961)

1984   If you dig a hole and don't cover it up, someone will die.
(M, 50, 1959)

1985   If you lie down to eat, you will have to sit up to die.
(F, 63, R, 1959 [her parents])

1986   Never comb a sick woman's hair while she is in bed, or she won't get well.
(F, 70, R, 1961 [her father])

1987   A will-o'-the-wisp manifestation in summer—a moving ball of light, which is seldom seen except in heavy rainy spells—used to signify death (mostly by drowning). There is a phosphorescence that is similarly seen on the ground.
(F, 85, R, 1962 [her parents])

1988   If a wedding ring falls from the finger, it is a sign of a death in the family.
(F, 30, R, 1957)

1989   If you take off your wedding ring before seven years have elapsed, you will die young.
(F, 80, R, 1960 [her parents])

1990   During a wedding, if the candles on one side of the altar are brighter than on the other, the person on the side where the candles are brighter will live longer.
(M, 70, R, 1959)

1991   A flash of light in the window is a sign of death.
(F, 60, R, 1961 [her mother])

1992   Do not go swimming on Trinity Sunday, or you will surely drown.
(M, 74, R, 1960)

1993   If you step on a crack, death will come soon.
        (F, 21, R, 1963 [one of her cousins])

1994   If your gun goes off accidentally while you are hunting in the
        woods near home, someone in your family will die within a
        year.
        (M, 90, 1958)

1995   The ace of spades means death.
        (F, 18, 1955)

1996   The ace of spades is a bad-luck omen, usually meaning death.
        (M, 20, R, 1956)

1997   You should never inhale the first drag on a cigarette, or you
        will die before you are twenty-one.
        (M, 21, 1957)

1998   If you are walking and you and an automobile cross the rail-
        road tracks at the same time, someone in your family will die.
        (F, 21, R, 1958)

1999   If you get water on your wedding gown, you will die before
        the end of the year.
        (F, 70, R, 1957)

2000   Every time that you hear thunder, someone in the family will
        die within a year.
        (M, 22, R, 1958)

2001   If someone is dying and he hits you but you can't hit him back,
        you will be the next to die.
        (F, 50, 1962)

2002   If a mysterious light appears at night, it means a death in the
        family.
        (F, 80, R, 1959)

2003   If you see lightning and don't hear thunder, you are dead.
        (M, 60, R, 1962 [his father])

2004   In the past, if a widow took off her black mourning veil before
        a year was up after her husband's death, people would say,
        "She raised her veil early to look for another husband."
        (F, 80, R, 1962)

2005   Every time someone dies in a hospital, there will be a birth
        within the next twenty-four hours.
        (F, 50, 1958)

2006   When one person in a community dies, there will be another
        one born in his place.
        (F, 75, R, 1958)

2007   As a baby cries, an old man dies.
        (F, 14, 1959 [her mother])

2008   The position of a drowned man's body may be discovered by floating a loaf of bread.
        (M, 60, R, 1959 [his mother])

2009   If a child drowns, throw a loaf of bread in the water. It will float and stay on top of where the child's body is lying.
        (F, 1961)

2010   If you shiver, it is because a rabbit has run over your grave.
        (F, 1961)

2011   If chills run up your back, geese are walking on a grave.
        (F, 50, 1959 [her grandparents])

2012   If you suddenly get goose pimples or chills, someone is walking over the place where you are to be buried when you die.
        (F, 50, 1958, + 6 F and 1 M)

2013   Look through a looking-glass at the bottom of a well on a sunny New Year's Day, and you will see a casket.
        (F, 60, 1959)

2014   A silver bullet will kill a witch.
        (F, 21, 1957)

5

People

THIS CHAPTER WAS LABELED "PEOPLE" FOR TWO REASONS. First, these items of folklore seemed to be personally cogent, and second, they had been placed in a pile that served as a catchall for whatever didn't seem to fit conveniently into our other chapter designations. (It appeared later, however, that many would have.)

These 664 items concern a wide variation in subject matter and comprise 13 percent of our whole collection. Most deal with the common, local everyday realities, while a few are about the extraordinary or cosmic. Clothing concerns, general household, and "company coming" account for 31 percent of this chapter, with over 500 informants reporting on various ways to predict visitors. Ninety-seven people reported on dropped dishrags as an omen; dropped cutlery and an itching nose also were items with high frequency. Being guilty of lying is embarrassingly revealed by white flecks on fingernails or by having a sore tongue; while "If you start to say something and forget what it is you were going to say, it's a lie" is a specific of the lying stigma.

The 72 items that are classified broadly in the occult generally have the aura of evil or are concerned directly with evil. The significance of such objects as spirits, ghosts, witches, fairies, werewolves, and the devil is not to be overlooked. Two friends separating themselves by a tree or post as they are walking is strictly taboo; this will cause a quarrel between the two. However, if one incants "Bread and butter" or "Salt and pepper," the relationship will not be marred. In contrast, some signs and omens depict success or positive knowledge, the forked stick or branch for finding water, the long life line on one's palm, or "The third time is a charm," for example.

Red hair as a sign that someone has a bad temper has plagued people for centuries. Countless red-haired people have said that their lives have been influenced by this belief. As one girl put it, "I've found my red hair more trouble than a barrel of brunettes; I can't even get a job as a picker in an orange grove." Double crowns, heavy eyebrows, heavy hair on arms or chest, hair lines on foreheads all have various significances. The list goes on, with chins, ears, noses, dimples, the set and color of eyes, noses, and being thin or fat signifying various personality traits. While baldness is actually a genetic matter, the belief that tight hats cause baldness is still prevalent.

The proverbial "Whistling girls and crowing hens always come to some bad end" remains vigorous today; however, some people may not consider the saying to be broadly metaphorical in a social context.

COMPANY

2015   If a rooster crows in the morning, you are going to have company.
(F, 60, R, 1962 [her parents], + 1 F)

2016   A rooster crowing on your doorstep will bring company.
(F, 80, R, 1958)

2017   A rooster crowing in the dooryard signifies that the preacher is coming.
(F, 52, 1954)

2018   When a rooster crows three times, you are going to have company.
(F, 20, 1959 [her grandmother])

2019   If a rooster crows three times outside the back door, company is coming.
(F, 40, R, 1963 [her mother], + 1 M)

2020   If a rooster comes up to the back door and crows, that means company is coming.
(F, 50, R, 1958, + 2 F)

2021   A rooster that is looking toward your door and crowing will bring company.
(F, 48, R, 1961, + 2 F)

2022   If a rooster crows, you'll have company.
(M, 40, R, 1959 [his parents], + 2 F)

2023   If a rooster crows on your doorstep on Sunday, you'll have company that day.
(F, 20, R, 1963 [her mother], + 1 M)

2024   If a rooster crows in a doorway, it means that you will have company.
(F, 20, R, 1959, + 31 F and 8 M)

2025   If someone comes in the front door and goes out the back, you will have company.
(M, 14, 1959 [his grandmother], + 40 F and 3 M)

2026   If a broom falls in front of the door, you will have company.
        (F, 40, R, 1960 [her parents], + 7 F and 1 M)

2027   A fallen broom means that company is coming from the direction in which the handle points.
        (F, 1961)

2028   If you burn an old broom, you will get a lot of company.
        (M, 70, R, 1959)

2029   If a girl drops her mop while she is mopping, company will come from the direction in which the mop handle points.
        (F, 18, R, 1957)

2030   If you take two helpings of butter on your plate, company is coming.
        (M, 21, R, 1957)

2031   If you have some of a certain food and take more of the same, someone is coming who is hungry.
        (M, 62, R, 1957)

2032   If you take meat when you already have some, somebody who is hungry is coming.
        (F, 1961)

2033   If you take bread at the table when you already have some, somebody who is hungry is coming to see you.
        (M, 30, R, 1954, + 3 F and 2 M)

2034   If you drop food on the floor, someone is coming who is hungrier than you.
  (F, 21, 1951)

2035   If there is too much food on the table, the family is going to have a hungry guest.
  (F, 1961)

2036   If you clean out every dish on the table, someone who is hungry is coming.
  (F, 80, R, 1960 [her parents], + 1 F)

2037   When the cat washes itself, there will be company.
  (F, 21, R, 1957, + 7 F)

2038   When a cat is washing its face, whichever way its paw points over its ear means that you'll have company from that direction.
  (F, 19, 1956, + 1 M)

2039   If you drop a dishrag, you will have company.
  (F, 19, R, 1959, + 29 F and 4 M)

2040   If you drop a dishrag, someone is coming to visit that is sloppier than you are.
  (F, 23, R, 1958, + 6 F and 2 M)

2041   If you drop a dishrag, a poor housekeeper will come to visit you.
  (F, 20, R, 1957, + 6 F)

2042   If you drop your dishrag while you are washing dishes, that means there is a "slouch" coming.
  (M, 50, R, 1958, + 1 F and 1 M)

2043   If you drop a dishrag, someone who is dirtier than you is coming.
  (F, 19, R, 1959, + 37 F and 1 M)

2044   If you drop your dishcloth, someone is coming who is more ragged than you.
  (F, 60, R, 1963 [her mother])

2045   Dropping your dishrag is a sign that someone is coming. If the rag is warm, you will give them a warm welcome; if cold, you will give them a cold reception.
  (F, 1960)

2046   If a dishrag lands flat when you drop it, a lady is coming.
  (F, 50, R, 1958)

2047   Drop a dishrag, and someone hungry will come.
  (F, 21, 1950)

2048   If you drop a dishcloth, someone unpleasant is coming.
  (F, 21, R, 1961)

2049   A stem in your tea means that you will have company.
         (F, 77, 1961)
2050   Bubbles in a teacup foretell visitors.
         (F, 19, 1959, + 2 F)
2051   Foam on coffee indicates that company is coming.
         (F, 40, 1958)
2052   If the coffeepot rattles back and forth on the stove, company
         will come before nightfall.
         (F, 65, R, 1963)
2053   Offering salt to a guest indicates a spirit of friendly hos-
         pitality.
         (F, 40, R, 1957, + 1 F)
2054   If you spill sugar, company is coming.
         (F, 37, 1954)
2055   Dropping a dish means that company is coming.
         (M, 26, 1961)
2056   Spit in your hand, hit the spittle with your fist, and the
         direction in which the spittle goes will show which way com-
         pany is coming from.
         (F, 50, 1959 [her parents])
2057   Sneezing three times is a sign that company is coming.
         (F, 40, 1960 [her mother-in-law])
2058   If the hem of your dress is turned up in one place, company is
         coming.
         (F, 20, 1962)
2059   When you strike a match, the flame will point in the direction
         from which company is coming.
         (F, 20, R, 1963 [her parents])
2060   An itching skin means that you will have visitors.
         (F, 1959)
2061   If the palm of your hand itches, it's a sign that company is
         coming. The same is true if your nose itches.
         (F, 19, 1958)
2062   If your left hand itches, it's a sign of company; but if your
         right hand itches, it's a sign that you'll make some money.
         (F, 34, 1958)
2063   If your nose itches, someone will come to visit.
         (F, 19, 1958, + 57 F and 17 M)
2064   An itchy nose means that you will have inquisitive company.
         (M, 65, 1955)
2065   If your nose itches, a man is coming with a hole in his
         britches.
         (F, 20, R, 1961 [her mother], + 32 F and 1 M)

2066   If your nose itches three times, you will have company.
        (F, 60, R, 1962 [her parents])
2067   An itching thumb means that visitors are coming.
        (F, 23, 1957)
2068   A howling dog is a sign that company is coming.
        (F, 87, 1957)
2069   If you have two visitors, a third will appear.
        (F, 87, 1958)
2070   Make vast preparations for company or some event, and they
        won't come. Wait until you are sure, and they will come and
        you will not be ready.
        (F, 62, 1957)
2071   An invitation on the same day is an invitation to stay away.
        (F, 40, R, 1956)
2072   If you leave a dirty skillet, company is coming.
        (M, 55, R, 1957)
2073   When you catch yourself thinking of someone, he will be
        coming to visit soon.
        (F, 21, 1951)
2074   When a spider comes down in front of you, you will have
        guests for the next meal.
        (F, 14, R, 1959 [her grandmother])
2075   When the wind blows the door open, guests are coming.
        (M, 30, 1961)
2076   If two chairs have their backs together, company is coming.
        (F, 1961)
2077   If you see a redbird, you will have unexpected but pleasant
        company.
        (M, 50, 1958, + 1 F)
2078   If a bumblebee is buzzing at your door, company is coming.
        (F, 19, R, 1959 [her parents], + 2 F)
2079   If you have company on Monday, you will have company on
        every day of the week.
        (F, 20, R, 1957, + 10 F)
2080   If you set an extra place at the table, someone is sure to
        come.
        (F, 20, R, 1960 [her mother], + 1 F)
2081   If you have the spoon and fork in the wrong place when you
        set the table, you'll have company.
        (M, 20, 1957)
2082   If you unwittingly put two knives at a plate while you are
        setting a table, a woman is coming; if you put two forks at a

plate, a man is coming; if you put two spoons at a plate, a child is coming.

(F, 70, R, 1962 [her mother])

2083   If you drop all three eating utensils at one meal, a whole family is coming.

(F, 20, R, 1963 [her parents])

2084   If you drop tableware on the floor, you will be sure to have company.

(F, 20, 1959 [her friends], + 5 F and 2 M)

2085   If you drop a piece of silverware, someone will visit you from the direction in which it falls.

(F, 22, R, 1959 [her friends], + 5 F)

2086   If one drops a knife, he should expect company.

(M, 40, 1958, + 3 F)

2087   If you drop a table knife, a man is coming to visit.

(F, 20, R, 1962 [her parents], + 23 F and 2 M)

2088   If you drop a butcher knife, it is a sign that the preacher will come.

(F, 40, R, 1963 [her mother])

2089   If you drop a knife, company is coming from the direction in which the blade is pointing.

(F, 19, R, 1957, + 2 M and 3 F)

2090   If a knife falls and sticks in the floor, a guest will come.

(F, 1961)

2091   If you drop a fork, you are going to have a visitor.

(F, 18, 1955, + 3 F and 1 M)

2092   If your fork falls on the floor, you will have company that day, and they will come from the direction in which the fork is pointing.

(F, 15, 1958, + 7 F and 1 M)

2093   If you drop a fork and the tines turn toward you, it will bring you company.

(F, 60, 1958)

2094   If a fork is dropped while the dishes are being washed, someone is coming.

(M, 1962)

2095   If you drop a fork, hungry company is coming.

(F, 20, R, 1962 [her grandparents])

2096   If you drop a fork, a girl visitor will come from the west.

(F, 20, 1959)

2097   If you drop a fork, a woman is coming to visit.

(F, 20, 1963, + 15 F)

2098   If you drop a fork, a woman is coming to visit; if you drop a knife, a man is coming to visit; if you drop a spoon, a child is coming to visit.
(F, 19, 1955, + 22 F)

2099   If you drop a spoon, it means that company is coming.
(F, 19, 1960 [her mother], + 2 F and 1 M)

2100   If you drop a spoon on the floor, it means that in a very short time you will have company from the direction in which the spoon is pointing.
(F, 15, R, 1958, + 2 F and 1 M)

2101   If you drop a spoon, your visitor will be a little fool.
(F, 50, 1958)

2102   If you drop a spoon, you will be visited by a man.
(F, 38, 1958)

2103   If you drop a spoon, someone hungry will come.
(M, 21, 1950)

2104   If you drop a spoon while you are washing dishes, a fat woman will come to visit. The size of the spoon will tell you just how fat the woman will be. The spoon will also point in the direction from which the woman will come.
(M, 70, R, 1959)

2105   If you drop a spoon, you will have a child for company.
(F, 21, R, 1956, + 6 F)

2106   If someone leaves something behind when he visits you, it is a sure sign that he wants to come again.
(F, 60, 1959)

2107   When someone leaves, don't watch him go, as this means that he will have an accident.
(F, 29, 1959 [her grandmother])

THE SIGNIFICANCE OF
SINGING, CRYING, LAUGHING,
AND WHISTLING

2108   If you laugh before sunup, you will cry before sundown.
(F, 75, 1959)

2109   If you wake up laughing, you'll go to bed crying.
(F, 20, 1961 [her grandmother])

2110   If you laugh before seven, you'll be sad before eleven.
(F, 20, R, 1957, + 3 F)

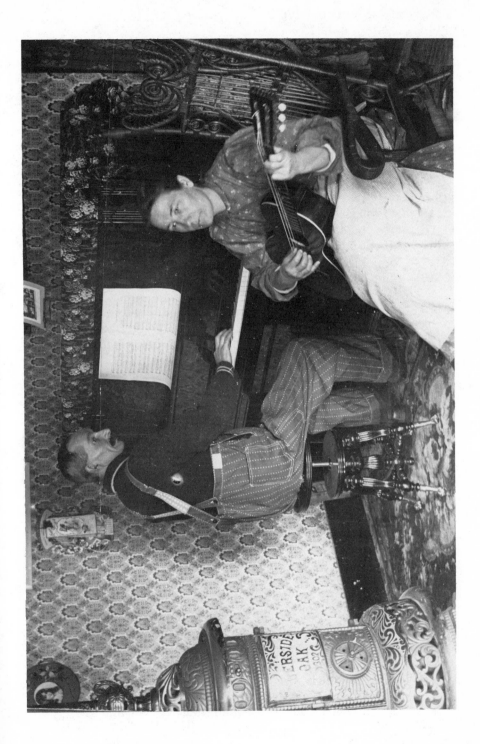

2111   If you laugh before breakfast, you will cry before lunch.
        (F, 54, 1955)

2112   If you laugh before breakfast, you'll cry before supper.
        (F, 42, R, 1958, + 2 F and 2 M)

2113   If you laugh before breakfast, you'll cry before night.
        (F, 18, 1956, + 3 F and 2 M)

2114   If you laugh in the morning, you will cry in the evening.
        (F, 35, 1954)

2115   If you sing before breakfast, you'll cry before you go to bed.
        (F, 18, 1956, + 13 F and 4 M)

2116   If you go to bed singing, you'll get up crying.
        (F, 45, R, 1963, + 1 F)

2117   If you sing at the table, you'll cry before nightfall.
        (F, 21, R, 1958, + 3 F)

2118   Sing in the morning; cry before evening.
        (M, 21, 1950, + 1 F)

2119   Don't sing before breakfast, or you'll cry before night.
        (F, 14, R, 1959 [her mother], + 23 F and 2 M)

2120   If you sing before breakfast, you'll cry before dinner.
        (F, 19, 1956, + 20 F and 2 M)

2121   Start the day smiling or singing, and you'll be happy all day. Wake up with a frown, and you'll be a grouch.
        (F, 50, 1958 [her grandmother])

2122   "Sing at the table; / Cry in the stable."
        (M, 60, R, 1959)

2123   If you sing after dark, it will bring sadness to your heart.
        (F, 60, R, 1961 [her mother])

2124   If you sing before sunup, you'll cry before sundown.
        (F, 1961)

2125   If you sing before breakfast, you'll cry all the day.
        (F, 50, 1954)

2126   A singing girl and a crowing hen will always come to some bad end.
        (F, 60, R, 1961 [her mother])

2127   If you sing on your pillow, you'll weep like a willow.
        (F, 62, R, 1962)

2128   If you spin a chair on its leg, you will cry before you go to bed.
        (M, 18, R, 1958)

2129   Cry before breakfast; sing before supper.
        (F, 55, 1957)

2130   Whistling girls and crowing hens always come to some bad end.
        (F, 21, R, 1958 [her grandfather], + 34 F and 5 M)

2131   A whistling woman and a crowing hen will always come to some bad end.
        (F, 30, R, 1958, + 1 F and 2 M)

2132   A whistling girl is supposed to come to a bad end.
        (M, 20, 1958)

2133   A whistling woman will come to a bad end.
        (M, 50, R, 1960 [his mother])

BODY SIGNS

2134   "Little head, little wit. / Big head, not a bit."
        (M, 80, R, 1957)

2135   A broad forehead denotes intelligence.
        (F, 27, 1956)

2136   People with low foreheads are dumb; those with high foreheads are smart.
        (F, 21, 1950)

2137   Red-headed people have bad tempers.
        (F, 19, R, 1959, + 9 F and 8 M)

2138   Red-headed women have hot tempers.
        (M, 20, R, 1959, + 1 F)

2139   Redheads are supposed to blush easily.
        (F, 40, 1963)

2140   If a strand of your hair is pulled out and it curls when stretched out by pulling it with your fingernail, you have a very bad temper.
        (F, 30, 1961)

2141   If you have two crowns on your head, it means that you will travel far.
        (M, 1962)

2142   If you have a double crown in your hair, you'll cross the sea.
        (F, 54, R, 1960)

2143   If you have a double crown, you'll live in a foreign land.
        (F, 60, R, 1969 [her parents])

2144   Heavy eyebrows signify that you will have a long life.
        (F, 1962)

2145   If your eyebrows grow close together, you will live a long time.
        (M, 1962)

2146   If a person's eyebrows grow together over his nose, he will be rich someday.
        (F, 29, 1961)

2147   An abundance of hair on the arms is considered to be a sign of impending wealth.
       (F, 1962)

2148   If a man has no hair on his chest, he'll never be bald.
       (F, 20, 1961)

2149   The higher up his hairline, the smarter the individual.
       (M, 20, 1961, + 3 F)

2150   White flecks on your fingernails represent lies that you have told.
       (F, 21, 1950, + 4 F and 4 M)

2151   The number of white spots that people have on their fingernails is the same as the number of big lies that they have told.
       (M, 22, 1961, + 2 F and 1 M)

2152   If you get a bruise on your fingernail it means that you have told a lie.
       (F, 1962)

2153   Broad fingernails show that a person is generous. Long fingernails reveal a lack of thrift.
       (F, 1962)

2154   A person with long fingers will make a good musician.
       (F, 21, 1950, + 1 F)

2155   People who have long fingers will play the piano well.
       (F, 20, 1965)

2156   A long, slender hand indicates an "artistic temperament."
       (M, 50, 1961)

2157   Long fingers; big stealer.
       (F, 1961)

2158   A weak chin indicates a weak character.
       (F, 21, 1950)

2159   If a girl's teeth are far apart, she is very passionate.
       (M, 28, R, 1958)

2160   Tall girls are the most graceful girls.
       (F, 20, 1957)

2161   A dimple in your cheek shows that you have been kissed by an angel.
       (M, 45, R, 1958 [his mother], + 2 F)

2162   A person with a dimple in his or her chin will never commit murder.
       (F, 22, 1962)

2163   A person who has a dimple on his chin is sure to be possessed by devils within.
       (F, 19, 1959 [her father], + 6 F)

2164   Small ears denote that a person is stingy.
        (F, 60, R, 1961, + 1 F)

2165   Big ears are a sign of generosity.
        (F, 24, R, 1961, + 3 F)

2166   The larger one's ears, the longer one will live.
        (F, 75, 1959, + 1 F)

2167   People who have ears that are low, the tops of which are even with their eyes, have criminal instincts.
        (F, 47, R, 1961)

2168   People who have bumps on the back of their heads are jealous.
        (F, 27, 1956)

2169   Eyes of blue mean one that's true.
        (F, 50, R, 1957, + 1 F)

2170   The eye is the mirror of the soul.
        (F, 19, R, 1959)

2171   Eyes that are spaced wide apart denote intelligence.
        (F, 40, R, 1957)

2172   Close-set eyes denote a criminal.
        (M, 21, 1956)

2173   Small eyes mean a shifty character.
        (F, 21, 1950)

2174   People with green eyes are usually jealous.
        (M, 52, 1954)

2175   Dark eyes mean a snappy temper.
        (F, 63, 1958)

2176   If a person has one blue eye and one brown eye, this is a sign of intelligence.
        (F, 42, 1961)

2177   Cold hands indicate a warm heart.
        (F, 19, 1955, + 16 F and 3 M)

2178   A cold nose means a warm heart.
        (M, 22, R, 1963 [one of his college classmates])

2179   If the toe next to it is longer than your big toe, you will be the boss of your family.
        (F, 19, R, 1959 [her family], + 2 F and 1 M)

2180   If you have a lot of moles on your body, you will be wealthy.
        (F, 1962)

2181   "Mole on the back; / Money by the sack."
        (F, 80, R, 1961 [her mother])

2182   "Mole on your neck; / Money by the peck."
        (F, 45, R, 1957, + 6 F)

2183   Fat people are good-natured.
        (F, 21, 1950, + 1 F)
2184   Fat people are jolly people.
        (F, 19, R, 1959 [her parents], + 2 F)
2185   If the lines in the palm of your hand form a perfect M, you will
        come into some money.
        (M, 25, R, 1961, + 2 F)
2186   Long lines in your hand denote a long, successful life.
        (F, 1959)
2187   A sore on your tongue means that you have told a lie.
        (F, 20, R, 1963 [her mother], + 16 F and 3 M)

THINGS THAT AFFECT THE BODY

2188   If you cut your hair on Thursday, it won't grow again.
        (F, 1961)
2189   If you cut your hair or trim your beard in the dark of the
        moon, it will grow thicker, stronger, and more beautiful.
        (F, 40, R, 1961)
2190   Anyone who fails to hold the top of his head while passing
        under an overpass will grow bald.
        (F, 22, R, 1963 [her sister])
2191   Wearing your hat in the house will cause you to become bald.
        (F, 50, 1960)
2192   If you twist your hair, you will become bald.
        (F, 22, R, 1959)
2193   A man is bald because his hats are too tight or because he
        doesn't brush his hair. A woman doesn't get bald, because
        she combs her long hair, thus stimulating her scalp.
        (F, 50, 1961)
2194   If you eat ice cream that you have refrozen in the same
        freezer after it has thawed, you will become bald.
        (F, 20, R, 1958)
2195   A boy who drinks coffee will have hair on his chest.
        (M, 20, 1957)
2196   A chew of snuff will make hair grow on your chest.
        (M, 20, R, 1961)
2197   Boys should eat bread crusts; it will make hair grow on their
        chests.
        (M, 53, 1963 [his mother])

2198   Coffee will turn your hair white; milk will make it black.
      (F, 30, R, 1961)

2199   Red-haired persons can turn their hair brown by shampooing it frequently in sage tea.
      (M, 62, R, 1959)

2200   Drinking tea made from senna leaves will darken a person's hair.
      (M, 62, R, 1959)

2201   A bad fright can make your hair turn white overnight.
      (F, 44, 1958)

2202   If you want your hair to turn darker, cut it in the light of the moon. If you want it to get lighter, cut it in the dark of the moon.
      (F, 30, R, 1962)

2203   Put kerosene on your hair to keep it dark.
      (F, 1960)

2204   For every gray hair you pull out, two will come in its place.
      (F, 20, R, 1958)

2205   Never pull out a gray hair, because seven gray ones will come in where you pulled out the one.
      (F, 53, 1963, + 2 F)

2206   If you pull out one gray hair, nine more will grow in the place that you pulled it from.
      (F, 40, R, 1960)

2207   Never pull out a gray hair; for ten will come in its place.
      (F, 50, R, 1960)

2208   Eat carrots so that your hair will curl.
      (F, 21, 1956, + 5 F)

2209   To have curly hair, eat burnt toast.
      (F, 20, 1958, + 3 F and 1 M)

2210   Eating the crust of bread will make your hair curly.
      (F, 20, 1961, + 9 F)

2211   Girls used to cut wild grape vines partly in two and catch the juice. This was used on the hair in the belief that it would make the hair curly. Also, it was thought that eating bread crusts and chicken gizzards would make the hair grow curly.
      (F, 40, R, 1959)

2212   If you want to have curly hair, shave your head, then place slices of onion on the bare skin. After that you will grow curly hair.
      (F, 21, 1957)

2213   To make a beard grow on a small boy, use chicken manure for fertilizer.
(M, 75, R, 1958)

2214   If you walk through the woods on Halloween, you'll lose all your hair.
(F, 44, 1958)

2215   If you put cream on your face and let the cat lick it off, your whiskers will grow.
(F, 18, R, 1962 [her father])

2216   If you pull out an eyelash, two curly eyelashes will grow in to take its place.
(F, 21, 1957)

2217   Do not step over a person who is lying on the ground, for this will stop his growth.
(F, 40, R, 1958)

2218   Crawling through a window will stunt your growth.
(F, 19, 1961, + 1 F)

2219   If you swallow a prune seed, a tree will grow in your stomach.
(F, 60, R, 1961)

2220   If you swallow orange seeds, orange trees will grow out of your ears.
(F, 22, 1966)

2221   If you swallow a watermelon seed, a watermelon will grow out of your ear.
(F, 21, 1956)

2222   Eat toast to make your cheeks rosy.
(F, 20, R, 1963, + 2 F)

2223   If you drink coffee, you'll turn black.
(F, 21, 1958, + 3 F)

2224   If you drink coffee, your knees will turn black.
(F, 1960, + 1 F)

2225   If you drink too much coffee, your toes will turn black.
(F, 50, R, 1961)

2226   People used to think that if raindrops were allowed to fall on a baby's face before it was a year old, the baby would have freckles.
(F, 50, R, 1960 [her mother], + 1 M)

2227   One contributor's grandfather always told her that she got her freckles by standing behind the old cow when it was eating bran.
(F, 20, 1961)

2228   May flowers gathered before sunrise will keep freckles away.
(F, 1955)

2229   If you put lemon juice on your freckles, they will disappear.
(F, 20, R, 1957, + 2 F)

2230   To remove freckles, cut a lemon in half, and rub the lemon over your face.
(F, 20, R, 1961)

2231   Washing in stump water (rain water collected in a hollow stump) will cause freckles to disappear.
(F, 50, R, 1963, + 1 F)

2232   Dew drops on the first day of May will wash the freckles away.
(F, 60, R, 1957, + 2 F)

2233   To get rid of freckles, wash your face for three successive mornings in May dew.
(F, 50, R, 1961, + 1 F)

2234   To get rid of freckles, rub them with dew from the grass before the sun comes up.
(F, 19, R, 1962)

2235   Wash your face with dew from the grass in the month of June to get rid of freckles.
(F, 60, R, 1959)

2236   If you place buttermilk on freckles, they will disappear.
(F, 20, R, 1957, + 1 F)

2237   To get rid of freckles, fresh green mint leaves crushed up in buttermilk should be applied to one's face.
(F, 1962)

2238   Washing one's face with the juice of milkweeds will clear it of freckles.
(F, 50, 1961)

2239   To remove freckles, apply a mixture of vinegar and kerosene.
(F, 20, 1961)

2240   In the past, a poultice of fresh thin cow manure was used to remove freckles from one's face.
(M, 62, R, 1959)

2241   Freckles may be removed by applying cow dung, which will bleach the skin. Apply it once a week.
(M, 86, 1957)

2242   Your freckles will go away if (1) you steal somebody's dish-rag, (2) go out in a full moon, (3) make a wish that your freckles will go away, (4) wash your body where you want the freckles to leave, and (5) bury the dishrag.

(F, 50, 1959)

2243   Washing your face with dew every morning in the summer will make you beautiful.

(F, 54, 1959)

2244   Washing your face in dew gathered on May Day morning will make you beautiful.

(F, 50, 1958, + 2 F)

2245   If a boy were to eat nine persimmons in a row, he would turn into a girl.

(F, 28, 1958)

2246   If you can kiss your elbow, you can change your sex.

(F, 18, 1955, + 2 F)

2247   If you make a face too often, your face will freeze that way.

(F, 21, R, 1956)

2248   If you sleep in a north-south alignment, you'll grow taller.

(F, 20, R, 1958)

2249   If you chew too much tobacco, your ears will grow big, and your legs will become bowed.

(M, 65, R, 1957)

2250   If you tell a lie, your nose will grow long.

(F, 1962)

2251   Eating burnt toast will make your eyes bright.

(F, 50, 1959)

2252   You can change light-colored eyes from their color to brown by burning olive oil in a pan and peering into it.

(F, 58, R, 1958)

2253   If a chicken gets your tooth, you'll never get a new one.

(M, 20, 1959 [his mother], + 1 F)

2254   When a little boy loses a tooth, if he says his prayers that night, the fairy will bring him a gift.

(F, 50, R, 1957)

2255   Put a tooth under a glass, and the next morning it will have been replaced by a dime.

(M, 20, R, 1962)

2256   When a child's tooth comes out, put it in a dish of salt water. Check later, and the tooth will have been replaced by a coin.

(F, 20, 1960)

2257   If a child puts his tooth under the rug and stamps on it three times, the fairy will leave money in place of the tooth.

(F, 70, R, 1958)

2258   Put a tooth under your pillow, and there will be a coin in its place in the morning.
(M, 12, R, 1957, + 10 F and 2 M)

2259   If you don't touch the opening where you have lost a tooth, a gold one will take its place.
(F, 42, R, 1962, + 10 F and 3 M)

ADVICE REGARDING CLOTHING, THE HOUSEHOLD, AND FOOD

2260   Women should never can tomatoes or any kind of meats when they are menstruating, as this will cause the things to spoil.
(F, 1962)

2261   If a woman cans fruit during her menstrual period, the fruit will spoil.
(M, 20, 1961, + 1 F)

2262   If butter will not come in winter, it's because of a witch in the cream. If you put a hot iron in the churn, it will burn the witch, and the butter will come.
(F, 77, R, 1961 [her mother])

2263   If butter will not come when you are churning, stick a hot poker in it to kill the witch, and the butter will come.
(F, 60, R, 1961)

2264   When butter is slow in coming, heat a poker and put it in the cream for a few minutes. This will burn the Devil out, and the butter will come very quickly.
(F, 1961)

2265   If cream will not turn to butter, place a fine-toothed comb under the churn.
(F, 75, R, 1958 [her mother])

2266   Cake will not get stale if it is left in a bright-colored box in the children's room.
(F, 35, 1962 [her mother])

2267   If you jar the floor while you have a cake in the oven, the cake will fall.
(F, 60, R, 1961)

2268   Batter should be stirred or mixed in only one direction.
(F, 40, R, 1963, + 1 F)

2269   Beating cake batter with your left hand will unbeat it, and your cake will be a failure.
(M, 1959)

2270   Using aluminum paint inside a cake or bread box will keep
the bread moist.
(F, 82, R, 1957)

2271   A cake will fall in the middle if the oven door is opened before
the cake is finished.
(F, 53, R, 1958)

2272   When cooling freshly baked bread, it is a sure sign that there
will be a fight in the family if the bread is turned upside
down.
(F, R, 1959)

2273   Bread won't rise if water is dipped downstream.
(M, 84, R, 1956)

2274   If you take more bread when you already have some, someone
is going to be hungry.
(F, 60, R, 1962 [her parents])

2275   Put a match in your mouth while peeling onions so that you
won't cry.
(F, 82, R, 1957)

2276   When peeling onions, put a slice of bread in your mouth to
keep from weeping.
(F, 50, 1963)

2277   Boil beans for five minutes before you taste them.
(F, 40, R, 1961 [her mother])

2278   Put baking soda in beans to keep them from forming so much
gas.
(F, 20, R, 1961 [her mother])

2279   Gravy won't thicken on a cloudy day.
(F, 60, R, 1961 [her mother])

2280   Don't make jelly on a cloudy day; it won't jell.
(F, 53, R, 1960 [her mother])

2281   Things cooked on cloudy days will not be as successful as
those cooked on sunny days.
(F, 45, R, 1957)

2282   Don't bake bread on a rainy day.
(F, 20, R, 1958)

2283   If your bread dough makes a squeaking sound when you are
kneading it, your baking will be a success.
(F, 50, 1958, + 1 F)

2284   Fat girls make the best cooks.
(F, 47, R, 1956)

2285   Fish is brainfood.
(F, 23, 1957)

2286   Hold a dandelion under your chin. If it reflects yellow, you like butter.
        (F, 20, 1964 [her father], + 3 F)

2287   People who eat spinach will be big and strong.
        (F, 21, R, 1958, + 1 F)

2288   Children should not drink coffee; it will stunt their growth.
        (F, 50, R, 1957, + 1 M)

2289   People used to think that tomatoes were love apples and that they were poisonous.
        (F, 50, R, 1962, + 1 F)

2290   It breaks up a friendship to borrow salt.
        (F, 20, R, 1958 [her mother])

2291   If two persons cross hands while reaching for food, they will quarrel.
        (M, 1962)

2292   When food is burned, burn a cord string to take away the odor.
        (F, 53, R, 1958)

2293   If you drop a dishrag on the floor, a dirtier cook will finish preparing the meal.
        (M, 48, R, 1958)

2294   Better is a dinner with herbs, where love is, than a stalled ox and hatred therewith.
        (F, 50, R, 1962)

2295   Lamb's-quarters boiled in hot water and salt taste a lot like spinach.
        (M, 20, R, 1963 [his mother])

2296   If you drink tomato juice, you can jump over the house.
        (F, 60, R, 1957)

2297   If you can eat the last things on the table to clear it, you can kiss the cook.
        (F, 60, R, 1960 [her mother])

2298   People who eat raw carrots can see like cats at night.
        (F, 21, R, 1958)

2299   People who eat liver will have especially red blood.
        (F, 21, R, 1958)

2300   Indians won't eat meat from an animal that has been killed by lightning, but they will eat pork from a pig that died from cholera.
        (M, 55, 1959)

2301   When you make mincemeat, don't eat it for two weeks, because the longer it sits, the better it is.
        (F, 78, R, 1959)

2302   Put an English shilling in the milk pail to keep the milk from souring.
　　　　(F, 70, R, 1963 [her mother])

2303   A teaspoonful of vinegar in the dough for one pie will make it crisper.
　　　　(F, R, 1958)

2304   Don't catch rain water in the months without an r, or it will sour in the cistern.
　　　　(M, 1962)

2305   Putting salt on a watermelon will make it sweeter.
　　　　(M, 50, R, 1959)

2306   If a pregnant woman puts up pickles, the pickles will spoil.
　　　　(F, 1962)

2307   Years ago, people considered Grape Nuts a brain food and allowed one person to have no more than two tablespoonfuls at one time—carefully measured out.
　　　　(F, 1960)

2308   All water that is clear blue is good to drink.
　　　　(F, 65, R, 1962)

2309   If you go to a restaurant where the cook is fat, the food will be good.
　　　　(F, 60, R, 1957)

2310   If a person is crabby, take him a jar of crab-apple jam.
　　　　(F, 20, R, 1962)

2311   Your animal instincts will be highly developed if you eat too much meat.
　　　　(F, 75, R, 1958 [her mother])

2312   If you crumple your napkin while you are dining, you won't eat there again.
　　　　(M, 1963)

2313   If a person bakes a ham in the dark of the moon, it will shrink. If a person bakes a ham in the full of the moon, it will expand.
　　　　(F, 60, 1957)

2314   Rabbits are not any good to eat after March.
　　　　(M, 50, R, 1959 [his father])

2315   Put lettuce leaves in sugar to keep it moist.
　　　　(F, 49, R, 1956)

2316   Put apples in brown sugar to keep it moist.
　　　　(F, 49, R, 1956)

2317   Never use a knife in a jar while you are canning; it will cause the jar to break.
　　　　(M, 60, R, 1959)

2318   To keep eggs until the hen is ready to set, you should wrap them in newspaper and keep them at room temperature.
(F, 1962)

2319   Cheese in the morning is golden; at noon, silver; and in the evening, lead.
(F, 50, R, 1959 [her mother])

2320   A watched pot will never boil.
(F, 70, R, 1961)

2321   Never make sauerkraut in the light of the moon.
(F, 20, R, 1961)

2322   Foods grown below the ground should be started to cook in cold water; those above the ground, in hot.
(F, 1961)

2323   If the sun shines upon cooked eggs, they will soon become poisonous; if the sun never shines upon them, they will never be poisonous.
(F, 40, R, 1958)

2324   If you are English, you hold your fork in your left hand both when cutting your meat and when eating it.
(F, 72, 1957)

2325   If a woman cuts thick slices of bread, she will make a good stepmother.
(F, 48, R, 1957)

2326   For every stitch that you sew on a garment that someone is wearing, you will tell a lie about that person.
(F, 20, 1950)

2327   "Sew your clothes upon your back, / And poverty you'll never lack."
(F, 1960)

2328   If you mend a garment while you are wearing it, there will be as many stories told about you as the number of stitches that you take.
(F, 59, R, 1959)

2329   If you or someone else sews clothes while you are wearing them, you will be caught in a war.
(F, 21, R, 1957)

2330   Don't mend a garment while you are wearing it, because every stitch will represent an enemy.
(F, 61, R, 1957)

2331   If you wash and wipe together, you will scrap and fight together.
(F, 40, R, 1961)

2332   You will quarrel if you wash with another person.
        (F, 1961)
2333   "Wash and wipe; / Quarrel and fight."
        (F, 1959)
2334   If you wash your hands in the same bowl with another person, you will be friends forever.
        (F, 42, R, 1958)
2335   If you wash and dry together, you will weep and cry together.
        (F, 65, R, 1962)
2336   Do not wipe on the same towel with anyone else, because this means that you will fight.
        (F, 62, R, 1960)
2337   If two people wipe their hands on the same towel at the same time, they will have a fight.
        (F, 54, R, 1960)
2338   If two people dry on one towel, they will have a fight before night.
        (F, 46, R, 1958)
2339   If you wash and dry together, you'll be friends forever.
        (F, 32, 1958, + 1 F)
2340   If you see a measuring worm on a dress or garment, you will get a new one.
        (F, 32, 1959, + 3 F and 1 M)
2341   Never sweep after supper.
        (F, 60, R, 1962 [her mother])
2342   Sweeping the floor after dark will bring sorrow to your heart.
        (F, 50, R, 1957)
2343   Never sweep after dark, or you will sweep out a member of your family.
        (F, 45, 1957)
2344   To keep flies away, put in each room a rag that has been soaked in oil of lavender.
        (F, 50, 1963 [her mother])
2345   Several small bunches of cotton tied to the screen door will keep flies out of the house.
        (F, 40, 1957)
2346   When your shoes squeak, they haven't been paid for.
        (F, 20, R, 1962, + 2 F)
2347   If you break one dish, you will have broken three before you are through.
        (F, 26, R, 1959, + 2 F)

2348   Woolly dresses and suits are fine for removing dog and cat hairs from chairs and sofas.
        (F, 1961)

2349   If you put peach-tree leaves in a bag and boil them with white clothes, it will bleach the clothes.
        (F, 82, R, 1957)

2350   In the winter, heat from a stove or a furnace produces cobwebs.
        (F, 50, R, 1960 [her mother])

2351   The color of the first butterfly that a girl sees in the spring will be the color of her new spring dress.
        (F, 21, R, 1958)

2352   If your hair squeaks after it has been washed, it is a sign that it is clean.
        (F, 1961)

2353   Don't go barefoot, or your feet will spread, and you will not be able to wear shoes at all.
        (F, 40, R, 1962)

2354   Soapwort (yucca) roots can be used as shampoo.
        (F, 50, R, 1961)

2355   If the clasp of a girl's necklace is in the front, the person who gave her the necklace is thinking about her.
        (F, 20, R, 1962 [her parents])

2356   If the hem of your dress is turned up when you put it on, you will get a new dress soon.
        (F, 1961)

2357   If the hem of your dress is turned up, you are going to take a ride.
        (F, 50, R, 1963)

2358   If you wear your shoes out at the heel, you spend a good deal. If you wear them out at the toe, you spend as you get. If you wear them out on the ball, you spend all.
        (F, 81, 1959)

2359   A hole in the toe of your sock means that you will have a long life. A hole in the end of your heel means that you will have a short life.
        (F, 67, R, 1961)

2360   People's ring size and shoe size are almost always the same or nearly the same.
        (F, 20, R, 1961)

2361   Putting straight pins in one's clothing or carrying them will help one to remember something.
        (F, 21, 1956)

2362   If you wear an article of clothing that has a broken button, you'll be a tramp.
        (F, 21, 1956)

2363   Always wear a black tie with a dinner coat.
        (F, 53, 1963)

2364   A person who steps over a broom or mop handle instead of picking it up is lazy.
        (F, 52, 1954)

2365   Wearing white is a sign of purity.
        (F, 23, 1954)

2366   If you drop a dishrag, you are a dirty housekeeper.
        (F, 50, R, 1963)

2367   Patch beside patch is neighborly; patch upon patch is beggarly. So never sew one patch on top of another.
        (F, 40, R, 1961)

2368   Burning the peel of an orange on the stove will make a pleasant scent through the house.
        (F, 50, R, 1957)

2369   Rub a clothesline with a salty rag during freezing weather so that the clothes won't freeze to it.
        (F, 50, R, 1958)

2370   If you sew a quilt top with black thread, you will never sleep under it with your husband-to-be.
        (F, 1963)

2371   When you have a garment on backwards, it means that you dressed in the dark.
        (F, 20, R, 1959)

2372   Never put a new pair of shoes on the table before you wear them, or they will never fit.
        (F, 30, R, 1963 [her grandmother])

2373   When fingers have worn off old gloves, sew the gloves together. They make unusual table covers.
        (F, 53, R, 1964)

                            THE OCCULT

2374   One contributor's mother believed that if you would go to the cemetery on mornings when there was a ground mist, you could see forms in the mist. These forms were signs from the dead and could be interpreted in order to forecast the future.
        (F, 50, 1959)

2375   When you find toadstools, make a circle around them with rocks, and fairies will dance there at midnight.
    (F, 21, R, 1963)

2376   People used to think that towards evening, the ghosts in white would appear in the pastures, and no one dared to go near because the ghosts would start after you.
    (F, 52, 1960)

2377   People used to think that women whose eyebrows had grown together over the nose had witchcraft powers.
    (M, 60, 1961)

2378   When you are cleaning the house or after you have finished, lay the broom down on the front step and run around the house three times to keep the witches away.
    (F, 20, R, 1963)

2379   If you are afraid of a witch and you know who is bewitching you, take a piece of wool cloth, give it the name of the witch, and throw it into the fire. As it burns, beat it with a stick, and you will beat the witch away.
    (F, 90, 1958)

2380   If you are afraid of a witch, cross a stream of running water. A witch can't cross running water.
    (F, 81, 1959)

2381   Witches fly on broomsticks on Halloween.
    (M, 20, 1956)

2382   To kill a werewolf, you must shoot him with a silver bullet.
    (M, 20, 1961)

2383   A crucifix held in front of a person will frighten away vampires.
    (M, 20, 1961 [his grandmother])

2384   Cover a yawn in order to keep out evil spirits.
    (F, 27, 1957)

2385   Carry a rabbit's foot in your hip pocket to ward off evil.
    (F, 1961)

2386   If the severed head of a criminal who has been hung is put outside a door, it will scare away evil spirits.
    (M, 20, 1961)

2387   If you hang an onion around your neck, you will scare away all evil spirits.
    (M, 20, 1955)

2388   Evil spirits leave the body when you sneeze.
    (M, 68, R, 1958 [his mother])

2389   Burn sulfur on the stove to drive away evil spirits.
        (F, 1959 [her grandparents])

2390   Always have a screen on the door to screen out the evil
        spirits.
        (F, 1961)

2391   The owl used to be considered to be the agent of an evil spirit
        or enemy, and it had been sent to call rats to the farm or
        barns of a neighbor. Whenever one heard an owl near the
        farm home, the family chased it away at any hour of the
        night.
        (F, 40, R, 1963)

2392   If the life line on your palm does not run down below the base
        of your thumb, the length of the line approximates the time
        that you will live. Crosses on it foretell serious illnesses or ac-
        cidents.
        (F, 60, 1959)

2393   If the life line on your palm runs down below the base of your
        thumb without any breaks, you will live to be very old.
        (F, 60, 1959)

2394   Carry a forked branch of a peach tree, with the fork pointed
        up, and balance it in the palm of your hand; then walk a
        straight line until the fork points down. At that spot there is
        water underground, and it is safe to dig for a well.
        (M, 19, R, 1958, + 3 F and 4 M)

2395   When a willow stick draws downward, it is the sign that
        there is water.
        (F, 50, R, 1960)

2396   Push a forked stick along the ground. If it begins to quiver,
        you will find oil directly below that spot.
        (F, 19, 1958)

2397   The seventh son of a seventh son can always find water.
        (F, 60, 1961 [her father])

2398   When witching for water, use a branch from a tree that
        bears fruit with a pit in it, and it will turn down when you
        reach water.
        (M, 80, R, 1958)

2399   The stars control your fate.
        (F, 1961)

2400   A person's destiny is influenced by the position of the stars
        and the time of his birth.
        (M, 50, R, 1957)

2401   If you're born under certain star formations, this will form your personality.
(F, 21, 1950)

2402   If you're walking with a friend, never let an object such as a tree, a post, or the like pass between you and the person you're walking with, or you'll have a fight.
(F, 20, 1963, + 9 F)

2403   Friends will part if a tree or post comes between them unless they say "Bread and butter."
(F, 20, R, 1957, + 10 F)

2404   If two persons walking together should pass on opposite sides of an object, they will quarrel unless they both say "Salt and pepper" before they say anything else.
(F, 20, R, 1958 [her grandmother])

2405   If a boy and a girl go on opposite sides of a lamppost or tree, they should go back and both go around it on the same side. If they don't, they'll have a fight.
(F, 18, 1961)

2406   If two people walk on opposite sides of a pole, they should say "Bread and butter" seven times so that they won't have a fight.
(F, 40, R, 1960)

2407   If you lose something, throw a stick into the air, and when it lands, it will point toward the lost article.
(M, 1959)

2408   To locate a lost article, spit in the palm of your left hand and slap the spittle with the first finger of your right hand. The greater part of the spittle will fly in the direction of the lost article. By repeating this process as you progress toward the object, you will eventually be able to find it.
(M, 65, R, 1961)

2409   The first image that you see when you look into stump water will tell you what will happen to you one year from that day.
(M, 22, R, 1958)

2410   Two hens' fighting is a sign that two women will soon fight.
(F, 1962)

2411   Don't put beads on a boy; it's a sign that he'll be hung.
(F, 80, 1959)

2412   Thump on a banana; cut off the end; yes or no will appear in seeds.
(F, 21, 1950)

2413   If you drink sow's milk, you can see the wind.
        (F, 1961)
2414   If two table knives become crossed, there is going to be an
        argument in the family.
        (F, 20, 1960 [her mother])
2415   If the northern lights are a bright red, it means that there will
        be a war.
        (F, 72, R, 1958)
2416   During a war, every time that the sky is blood-red at sunset,
        you will hear of a big battle.
        (F, 70, R, 1959 [her father])
2417   Read tea leaves to tell your fortune.
        (F, 1961)
2418   Every man's fate is predetermined with regard to every move
        that he will make and the goals that he will achieve in life.
        (M, 20, 1957)
2419   All signs fail in Kansas.
        (M, 76, R, 1957)
2420   If you drop a spoon, it will point toward someone who is
        talking about you.
        (F, 20, 1958)
2421   After making a bragging statement, knock on wood to prevent
        reverses.
        (F, 42, R, 1958)
2422   A long scratch or cut means that you're going to take a trip.
        (F, 59, R, 1957)
2423   If your right shoe comes untied, a man is thinking about you;
        if the left one, a lady.
        (F, 50, R, 1957)
2424   To have a pleasant day, you must get out of bed on the same
        side on which you entered.
        (M, 70, R, 1956)
2425   If you wish to harm someone, make an image of him, and then
        stick something sharp through the image.
        (F, 60, 1959)
2426   When people place their fingers on the planchette of a Ouija
        board, it will spell out forecasts of things to come or events in
        the past if they concentrate on the questions that they ask.
        (F, 60, 1959)
2427   If two people look in the mirror at the same time, they will
        soon fight.
        (F, 60, R, 1958)

2428   If you stick yourself, you will soon receive a pin cushion as a gift.
           (F, 18, 1959)

2429   When a house burns, another should not be built on the same spot. If it is, this one will burn too.
           (F, 1962)

2430   Forty-nine pounds is a witch's weight.
           (F, 35, 1956)

2431   If you sing at the table, the Devil will get you before night.
           (F, 30, R, 1958)

2432   If you cut your fingernails on Sunday, the Devil will rule you all week.
           (M, 50, R, 1957)

2433   Put a knife by the door so that the spooks won't come in.
           (M, 33, 1958)

2434   Throw salt over your shoulder to chase the Devil away.
           (M, 33, 1958)

2435   If you hang a pair of scissors in your window, they will cut the Devil's tail off when he comes in.
           (M, 20, 1957)

2436   What will happen twice shall happen thrice.
           (F, 40, R, 1963 [her mother])

2437   The third time that anything happens will be the last time.
           (F, 90, 1959)

2438   Most hospital nurses believe that deaths, births, accidents, and so forth, come in threes.
           (F, 60, 1959)

2439   The third time is a charm.
           (F, 1959)

2440   If you knock a salt shaker over, the person that it points to will be your enemy.
           (F, 20, 1959)

2441   If you spill salt, throw some over your left shoulder, or else you will have a fight.
           (F, 30, R, 1960 [her mother], + 3 F)

2442   When salt is spilled, be sure to sprinkle a pinch on the stove.
           (F, 75, R, 1961, + 1 F)

2443   When you spill the salt, you're going to fight with someone.
           (F, 18, 1956, + 7 F and 1 M)

2444   If you see a dove, you will have peace.
           (F, 21, 1950)

2445   If you see a bluebird, it will bring you happiness.
(F, 21, 1950, + 2 F)

PREDICTIONS REGARDING MAIL

2446   If you see a spider coming down a web, you will get a letter.
(F, 32, 1959 [her aunt], + 5 F)

2447   If you accidentally walk into a spider's web, you will receive
a letter.
(F, 62)

2448   If you drop a spoon, you will receive a package: a small
spoon, a small package; a large spoon, a large package.
(F, 21, 1950 [her mother], + 3 F)

2449   When eating a piece of pie, if you leave the point of the piece
till last, you will receive a letter.
(F, 60, R, 1961, + 1 F)

2450   If you pick a loose thread from your skirt, you will receive a
letter the length of the thread.
(F, 24, 1957, + 1 F)

2451   When the hem of your skirt is turned up, you have a letter in the mailbox.
        (F, 20, 1958 [her mother], + 1 F)
2452   Count the tea leaves in your cup of tea; this will indicate the number of letters that you will receive during the next week.
        (F, 21, R, 1959, + 1 F)
2453   A flea on the head is a sign that a letter is coming.
        (F, 1962)
2454   If a rooster crows at your doorstep, you will receive a letter containing good news.
        (F, 1962)
2455   Do not answer a letter if the stamp is upside down.
        (F, 40, 1960 [her father])
2456   If you find a pin, you will get a letter from the direction in which the point is facing.
        (F, 1961)
2457   Chains of letters will bring a fortune if the text of the letter says that it will and if one makes and mails as many copies of the letter as required by the text.
        (F, 21, 1957)
2458   Catch a ladybug, and you will get a letter from the direction in which it flies away.
        (F, 21, R, 1957)
2459   When a sparrow flies onto a window screen, you are going to get a letter.
        (F, 50, 1958)

PREDICTIONS RELATED TO ECONOMIC MATTERS

2460   You are supposed to eat fish at twelve o'clock midnight on New Year's Eve in order to have a prosperous New Year.
        (F, 20, 1963)
2461   Sweeping a floor after dark will sweep away your riches.
        (M, 40, R, 1960 [his mother])
2462   If you see a beggar going down the street with his hands in his pocket, money is going to be tight.
        (M, 80, R, 1960 [his father])
2463   If you drop your pocketbook, you will get some money.
        (F, 40, 1960 [her mother])
2464   If you always break your bread over your plate, you will never go hungry.
        (F, 47, R, 1956)

2465   A fool and his money will soon part.
    (F, 21, R, 1956)

2466   If you throw your pocketbook in first when you move into a new house, you will always have money in the house.
    (F, 75, 1957)

2467   When you move to a new house, take in a new broom first if you wish to be prosperous.
    (F, 50, R, 1957)

2468   If tea leaves float to the top of a cup of tea, they will bring you money.
    (F, 50, R, 1957)

2469   "Stamp" fifty white mules, and you will find some money. (To "stamp" a mule, first put the forefinger of the right hand on the tongue; pat the palm of your left hand with it; then hit your left palm with your right fist.)
    (F, 60, R, 1957)

2470   If you go to the end of a rainbow, you will find a great treasure.
    (F, 60, 1959)

2471   There is a pot of gold at the end of the rainbow.
    (F, 35, 1956, + 7 F and 1 M)

2472   If your initials spell out a name, you'll be rich.
    (F, 18, 1955, + 2 F and 1 M)

2473   A gift of money will be yours if you swallow a bubble while eating soup.
    (M, 70, R, 1956)

2474   You will be rich if your glass of milk comes with bubbles on it.
    (F, 1961)

2475   Bubbles on the surface of coffee will bring you money if you spoon them out without touching the side of the cup. If they touch the side, you will get kisses.
    (F, 50, 1959)

2476   The bubbles that rise in your coffee represent the amount of money that you will have in the near future.
    (M, 1962)

2477   If the bubbles in your coffee come toward you, you'll get some money; if they go away from you, you'll spend some.
    (M, 30, R, 1959)

2478   When rich cream poured into a cup of coffee forms small bubbles on the top of the coffee, gather all the bubbles into your teaspoon at one time, and sip this first. If you are successful in leaving not one bubble, you will be rich.
    (M, 1959)

2479   When bubbles form in the top of a cup as you are pouring coffee into it, if you say "Money, money" and can get the bubbles in a spoon before they disappear, you will surely receive some money.
(M, 1962)

2480   If you have bubbles in your coffee, you will receive money.
(F, 26, 1955 [her grandmother])

2481   If you spoon up the bubbles on your coffee, money will come to you.
(F, 44, 1958, + 10 F)

2482   If you can count to three before a falling star disappears, you will become rich.
(F, 60, R, 1961 [her parents])

2483   When you see a star falling, count to three, and you will inherit great wealth.
(F, 1961)

2484   When you see a falling star, if you can finish saying "Money" seven times before the star is out of sight, you will come into some money.
(F, 20, 1961)

2485   Say "Money" as many times as you can before a falling star vanishes from sight. The more times, the more wealth you will acquire.
(M, 1961)

2486   If you wish on a falling star, you will get rich.
(M, 20, R, 1959)

2487   If you see a falling star, say "Money, before the week's out." If you finish saying this before the light of the star goes out, you will get money before the week ends.
(M, 25, R, 1959, + 3 F)

2488   If you say "Money, money, money" on the first star you see at night, you will get a lot of money.
(F, 19, 1956, + 20 F and 3 M)

THE SIGNIFICANCE OF
ITCHES, SNEEZES, AND TICKLES

2489   If your ears burn, someone is talking about you.
(F, 18, 1961, + 16 F and 5 M)

2490   If your ear burns, someone is talking about you, and the things that they are saying are not nice.
(F, 18, 1955, + 1 F)

2491   If your left ear burns, someone is saying bad things about you. If your right ear burns, someone is saying good things about you.
     (M, 20, R, 1959, + 11 F)

2492   When your ears burn, right is for spite; left is for love.
     (F, 60, R, 1962)

2493   If your ear burns, someone is talking about you. If your left ear burns, someone is telling a lie. If you spit on your finger and touch it to your ear, the storyteller will bite his tongue.
     (F, 40, R, 1960)

2494   If your ear itches, someone is talking about you.
     (F, 22, 1964 [her grandparents], + 8 F)

2495   If your ear itches, someone is thinking about you.
     (F, 70, 1958)

2496   If your ear itches, someone is speaking well of you.
     (F, 1962)

2497   If your ears itch, someone is talking about you. If your right ear itches, what they are saying is good; and if your left ear itches, it is bad.
     (F, 20, R, 1959, + 4 F)

2498   If both ears itch, people are having an argument over you.
     (F, 21, 1950)

2499   If your left ear itches, someone is saying bad things about you.
     (F, 40, 1959, + 3 F)

2500   If your right ear itches, you will hear good news. If the left one itches, you will hear bad news.
     (F, 60, R, 1962, + 1 F)

2501   If your ears ring, someone is talking about you.
     (F, 19, R, 1957, + 19 F and 5 M)

2502   If your ears ring, it means that someone is talking about you. If you can guess who it is, your ears will stop ringing.
     (F, 22, R, 1957, + 1 F and 1 M)

2503   When your ears ring, someone is saying something bad about you.
     (F, 40, R, 1958 [her parents], + 1 F)

2504   Ringing in the right ear means that someone is saying something good about you. Ringing in the left ear means that someone is saying something bad about you.
     (F, 21, R, 1951, + 4 F)

2505   If your ears turn red, someone is talking about you.
     (F, 40, R, 1961 [her mother])

2506   When your hand itches, you are going to meet someone.
   (F, 19, R, 1962, + 8 F and 2 M)

2507   If the palm of your hand itches, you are certain to become rich.
   (F, 20, R, 1958, + 18 F and 7 M)

2508   If the palm of your hand itches, you will receive a letter.
   (F, 50, R, 1961 [her mother])

2509   If your left hand itches, you are going to get some money.
   (F, 15, 1958, + 14 F and 2 M)

2510   If your left palm itches, you are going to receive some money.
   (F, 21, 1956, + 6 F)

2511   If your left eye itches, you are going to be happy.
   (M, 1961, + 1 F and 1 M)

2512   If your foot itches, you are going to walk on strange ground.
   (F, 22, 1959, + 14 F and 2 M)

2513   If your left foot itches when you are entering a strange place, you are not wanted.
   (F, 1962)

2514   If your toe itches, you are about to take a trip.
   (M, 19, 1956, + 7 F and 3 M)

2515   If your nose itches, some one is thinking of you—probably in a nice way.
   (F, 20, R, 1963, + 7 F and 1 M)

2516   If your nose itches, someone is talking about you.
   (F, 19, 1957, + 9 F and 1 M)

2517   If your nose itches, you will hear some news.
   (M, 30, 1960 [his father], + 6 F and 3 M)

2518   If your nose itches, you are going to get a letter.
   (F, 21, 1950, + 1 F)

2519   If your nose itches, you've got a hole in your britches.
   (M, 20, R, 1960 [his father], + 1 M)

2520   An itchy nose is a sign of fright.
   (F, 1962)

2521   "Scratch your nose, and your mouth is in danger, / Kiss a fool or meet a stranger."
   (F, 60, 1958, + 1 F)

2522   Sneeze on Monday, sneeze for health;
   Sneeze on Tuesday, sneeze for wealth;
   Sneeze on Wednesday, sneeze for a letter;
   Sneeze on Thursday, sneeze for something better;
   Sneeze on Friday, sneeze for sorrow;
   Sneeze on Saturday, you'll see your beaux tomorrow.
   (M, 54, 1959, + 2 F)

2523   If you sneeze on Sunday, the Devil will have you the rest of the week.
(F, 1961)

2524   Sneezing is good for dusting out the brain and making a person think more clearly.
(F, 40, R, 1959 [her grandparents])

2525   If you are ticklish on the knee, then you steal sugar.
(F, 50, R, 1960 [her mother])

THE MEANINGS OF DAYS AND SEASONS

2526   If you sing on your birthday, you will cry every day afterward.
(F, 21, 1957)

2527   If you cry on your birthday, you will cry every day for the next year.
(F, 20, R, 1959, + 1 F)

2528   If you sew on Sunday, on Monday you will rip out what you sewed.
(F, 42, R, 1958, + 2 F)

2529   Every stitch sewn on Sunday you will have to rip out with your nose.
(F, 21, 1958, + 9 F)

2530   If you sew on Sunday, you will have to rip out every stitch with your nose when you die.
(F, 54, 1959, + 1 F)

2531   Every stitch that you sew on Sunday you will have to pick out with your nose when you get to heaven.
(F, 20, 1961, + 4 F)

2532   What you sew on Sunday you will rip out with your nose on Judgment Day.
(F, 40, R, 1959, + 2 F)

2533   If you cut your fingernails on Sunday, you'll act like the Devil all week long.
(F, 60, 1962)

2534   Cutting the fingernails or toenails on Sunday will result in a person's telling a lie that day.
(F, 60, R, 1960 [her father])

2535   If you work all day Sunday, you'll be broken down all day Monday.
(M, 50, R, 1963 [his uncle], + 1 F)

2536   What you work for on Sunday the Devil gets on Monday.
        (F, 56, 1954)

2537   If you move to a new house on Sunday, you will never leave it.
        (F, 50, R, 1959 [her parents])

2538   If you go somewhere on Monday, you'll be gone every night of
        the week.
        (F, 30, R, 1959 [her grandmother], + 2 F)

2539   Good girls don't wear pink on Mondays.
        (F, 20, R, 1960 ["the girls"])

2540   If you move from one place to another (to live) on Friday, you
        won't live there long.
        (M, 50, 1958)

2541   If you move on Monday, the house will burn down.
        (F, 80, 1961 [her father])

2542   A woman who washes after Monday isn't a good wife.
        (F, 20, R, 1957)

2543   Tuesday is presided over by Mars; therefore, it is the best
        day for undertaking new projects.
        (F, 40, R, 1961 [her parents])

2544   Thursday is queer's day. If you wear any green on Thursday,
        you are queer.
        (F, 20, R, 1962, + 1 F and 1 M)

2545   In high school, it was taboo to wear green on Thursday,
        because if one did, one was considered to be a queer.
        (F, 22, R, 1969)

2546   It's not advisable to wear green on Thursday.
        (F, 20, R, 1960 ["the girls"])

2547   Do not wear green and yellow on Thursday—this connotes
        bad character. (The informant said: "This is practiced here
        at K-State.")
        (F, 20, 1969)

2548   Never start a new task on Friday.
        (F, 20, R, 1957, + 3 F and 2 M)

2549   One contributor said that he never starts a new job on a
        Friday. It may mean that he has to work until midnight the
        night before starting the job that he had planned to do on Fri-
        day.
        (M, 40, 1962)

2550   Never start a task on Friday. If you do, you'll never live to
        complete it.
        (F, 50, R, 1961, + 1 F)

2551   Do not start a new task on Friday; if you do, you will fail to finish it.
(M, 21, 1957, + 15 F and 2 M)

2552   Never start a new job on Friday that cannot be finished on that day.
(M, 40, R, 1958, + 10 F and 1 M)

2553   "Friday flit (a move), short sit, / Saturday flit, shorter yet."
(F, 40, R, 1957, + 1 F and 1 M)

2554   Don't start a journey on Friday.
(F, 1961)

2555   If you leave on a Friday to take a trip, you won't stay long.
(F, 44, 1958, + 1 F)

2556   Never begin making a garment on Friday. You'll never live to wear it out.
(F, 44, R, 1957, + 1 F)

2557   Don't cut out a dress on Friday. You won't wear it out.
(F, 40, R, 1954, + 2 F)

2558   Don't start cutting out a dress on Friday unless you can finish it by evening.
(F, 46, R, 1948)

2559   Don't cut out a garment on Friday, because "Friday begun / Nothing done."
(F, 61, R, 1957)

2560   If you start making a dress on Friday and you don't finish it the same day, you will not live long enough to wear the dress out.
(F, 1962 [her mother])

2561   Never start sewing anything on Friday, because you will never finish it.
(F, 14, R, 1959 [her grandmother], + 6 F)

2562   A housewife seldom begins to sew on a new garment on Friday, because if she does, she will never finish it.
(M, 80, 1959)

2563   Never start to make a new garment on Friday unless you can finish it by Saturday night.
(F, 79, R, 1959)

2564   If you start to sew something on Friday and don't finish it that week, you will never live to wear it out.
(F, 70, 1954)

2565   If you start a new project on Friday, you won't finish it for a week.
(M, 70, R, 1961 [his father])

2566   Never start a new project on Friday; it will be a long tedious task.
        (F, 50, 1959 [her grandparents])

2567   Never begin a piece of work on Friday. If you do, some disaster will strike.
        (F, 52, R, 1958 [her husband])

2568   Don't start anything on Friday, for it won't turn out right.
        (F, 50, R, 1961 [her father])

2569   Never attempt a new undertaking on Friday. It will not succeed.
        (F, 70, 1958 [her mother])

2570   Don't start business transactions on Friday that cannot be immediately completed.
        (F, 30, 1958)

2571   Never start a job on Friday unless it can be completed before Sunday. The result will be "bad luck."
        (F, 85, R, 1962)

2572   Friday is always the fairest or the foulest.
        (F, 50, 1960 [her grandfather])

2573   Don't start any work on Friday the thirteenth.
        (F, 79, R, 1959)

2574   If you are born on Friday, you will do everything backward.
        (F, 50, R, 1958)

2575   If you clean mattresses on Good Friday, you won't have bedbugs.
        (F, 50, 1961)

2576   A Saturday flit (move) is not a very long sit.
        (F, 50, R, 1959 [her parents])

2577   It is bad luck to start a journey on Saturday.
        (M, 80, R, 1950)

2578   Never commence new work on Saturday.
        (M, 80, 1956)

2579   Whatever you do on New Year's Day you will do every day of the year.
        (F, 60, R, 1958 [her mother], + 1 F)

2580   What you do on New Year's Day determines your year—that is, whether it will be lazy or ambitious.
        (F, 50, 1957 [her grandparents])

2581   If you cry on New Year's Day, you will be sorry throughout the year.
        (F, 70, 1961)

2582   If you travel on New Year's Day, you will travel the whole year through.
    (M, 20, 1961)

2583   If you eat well on New Year's Day, you will eat well all year.
    (F, 50, R, 1959 [her family])

2584   Don't have any dirt in your house on New Year's Day, or it will be dirty all year long.
    (F, 20, 1961 [one of her friends])

2585   If you leave a washing hanging on the line on New Year's Day, you will be washing all year long.
    (F, 20, 1959 [her grandmother])

2586   If you don't clean your house, yard, and self on New Year's Day, you, the house, etc., will be dirty all year.
    (F, 60, 1959)

2587   Women shouldn't go visiting on New Year's.
    (F, 79, 1957)

2588   If you see the new moon when you have your hands full, your work will double that month.
    (F, 69, R, 1959 [her mother], + 1 F)

2589   If you make lye soap in the new of the moon in May, the bugs won't bother it, and it won't dry up; but no one except the one who started it can stir it, or else it will go stringy.
    (F, 60, 1953)

2590   Make soap in the dark of the moon.
    (F, 60, R, 1958)

2591   If soap is made in the dark of the moon instead of in the light of the moon, it will turn dark and boil over.
    (F, 78, R, 1959 [her grandmother])

2592   If you cut your hair in the light of the moon, it will grow faster.
    (F, 50, 1963, + 1 M)

2593   If you cut your hair when the moon is decreasing, it won't grow so fast.
    (M, 19, R, 1958 [his grandmother])

2594   If you cut your hair in the light of moon, it won't grow so fast; or, in the dark of the moon, it will grow faster.
    (F, 70, R, 1962)

2595   Home permanents should be given when the moon is full.
    (F, 20, R, 1959)

2596   For best results, you should get a permanent in the light of the moon.
    (F, 50, 1959 [an almanac])

2597   If you are weaning a baby or young animal, dehorning cattle, starting a journey or business, or having an operation, you should always consult the almanac and select a date when the signs of the zodiac are recommended as being favorable for each undertaking.
(M, 62, R, 1959)

2598   Ears should be pierced for earrings when the peach trees are in bloom.
(F, 65, R, 1962 [her family])

MISCELLANEOUS ADVICE AND OBSERVATIONS

2599   There is no man so far to market as he who has nothing to sell.
(F, 70, R, 1958)

2600   Sweep your own doorstep first.
(F, 40, R, 1962 [her mother])

2601   You can take the boy off the farm, but you can't take the farm out of the boy.
(F, 50, R, 1962)

2602   One girl, all girl; two girls, half girl; three girls, no girl at all.
(F, 1960)

2603   Fools walk in where angels fear to tread.
(M, 29, 1958)

2604   People used to say that if a young girl used a swear word in the presence of her grandmother or elderly aunt, all of the girl's future babies would be born without a caul.
(F, 62, R, 1959)

2605   Kill two birds with one stone.
(F, 60, R, 1961)

2606   Don't count your chickens before they are hatched.
(F, 60, R, 1962)

2607   "I never had a piece of bread exceeding broad and wide; / But when it fell upon the floor, it lit upon the butter side."
(F, 68, 1954)

2608   Gentlemen prefer blondes.
(M, 23, 1957)

2609   "Early to bed, / Lay as long as you can, / Eat ham and eggs / And you'll soon be a man."
(F, 55, R, 1959)

2610   No news is good news.
        (F, 1959)
2611   Uneasy lies the head that wears a crown.
        (F, 54, 1959)
2612   Don't worry about troubles until they come.
        (F, 68, R, 1958)
2613   "A man who snores / His wife adores."
        (M, 80, R, 1960 [his father])
2614   Speak of the Devil, and you'll soon hear the clatter of his horns.
        (F, 49, R, 1959)
2615   Speak of an angel, and you'll soon hear the flutter of the wings.
        (F, 49, R, 1959)
2616   A woman should never remove her wedding ring. If she does so, she will lose her husband by death or otherwise.
        (F, 60, 1959)
2617   Hearing an owl hoot is a sign of disaster.
        (F, 60, 1959)
2618   If a tree is struck by lightning, there is a treasure under the tree.
        (F, 60, 1959)
2619   Don't sing in a bathtub.
        (F, 1961)
2620   Have the head of the bed to the north, because the earth's axis runs north and south.
        (F, 1961)
2621   You'd better not spend the penny that weights the eye of the deceased, or you'll go blind in less than a year.
        (M, 56, 1958)
2622   I'd rather see the Devil than a January robin.
        (F, 43, R, 1961)
2623   If you see a white horse, something spectacular will happen.
        (F, 21, 1959)
2624   Never hand money over the threshold of a door; either go out to pay the collector, or have him come in.
        (F, 50, R, 1958)
2625   If you kill a spider, you will lose some of your sins.
        (F, 50, R, 1952)
2626   If a hairpin starts to fall out, push it back in. If it falls to the ground, it means that you are going to lose a friend.
        (F, 60, R, 1959)

2627   Don't cook turnips on cloudy days.
       (F, 20, R, 1961)
2628   Never eat rice on Monday.
       (F, 20, 1957)
2629   If you steal something from someone, you will lose twice as much.
       (F, 1962)
2630   Cobwebs on the ceiling indicate that there is no kissing in that house.
       (F, 81, 1959)
2631   When a person sneezes, it is customary to say, "God Bless You."
       (F, 21, R, 1958, + 1 F and 1 M)
2632   People who live in glass houses should not throw stones.
       (M, 20, 1959, + 1 F)
2633   If you shingle a house in the wrong sign, the shingles will curl up.
       (F, 50, R, 1961 + 1 F and 1 M)
2634   If you shingle a house in the dark of the moon, the shingles will always lie flat; in the light of the moon, the shingles will curl up and cause the roof to leak.
       (F, 50, R, 1962, + 1 F)
2635   Lumber cut in the light of the moon will warp, or the ends will turn up.
       (M, 65, 1958)
2636   A baseball bat has just so many "hits" in it, and when they've been used up, you have to change bats in order to get more hits. (The informant said that this was a very common belief among old-time ballplayers and that he had heard it said also by some recent players.)
       (M, 1962)
2637   If you have a bad rehearsal, you will have a good performance.
       (F, 20, 1955, + 2 M)
2638   Never give a friend a sharp or pointed gift; it will cut your friendship.
       (F, 40, R, 1957, + 9 F and 1 M)
2639   If you say someone's name unexpectedly, they are thinking about you.
       (F, 1959, + 1 F)
2640   If two persons say the same word or group of words together, they will be friends for another year.
       (F, 50, R, 1958)

2641   If two persons begin to speak at the same time, the first one to pinch the other will receive a reward of his choosing.
(M, 20, R, 1958)

2642   When two people say the same thing at the same time in the same place, it means that they will meet at that place a year later.
(F, 20, 1957, + 1 F)

2643   If you start to say something but forget what it is, it is a lie.
(F, 19, R, 1956, + 3 F and 2 M)

2644   If you forget what you started to say, it was of no importance.
(M, 21, 1950, + 2 F)

2645   If you forget what you were about to say, it means that you are thinking of something that is not nice.
(F, 60, R, 1964)

2646   If you forget what you were going to say, people probably wouldn't believe it anyway.
(F, 60, R, 1957)

2647   If you step on a crack in the sidewalk, you will break your mother's back. If you step in a hole, you'll break your mother's sugar bowl.
(F, 18, 1959, + 13 F and 3 M)

2648   Step on a crack; break your mother's back.
(F, 19, R, 1956, + 49 F and 7 M)

2649   Step on a crack, or you will break the Devil's back.
(F, 60, R, 1973)

2650   Step on a nail, and put your dad in jail.
(M, 84, R, 1956)

2651   Step on dirt, and tear your dad's shirt.
(F, 10, R, 1958)

2652   If you step on dirt, you'll tear your father's undershirt.
(M, 14, 1958)

2653   If you step on glass, your daddy will run out of gas.
(F, 20, 1960)

2654   Tear a flower apart, and break your mother's heart.
(F, 20, 1958)

2655   If you get out of bed on the wrong side in the morning, you will be cross for the rest of the day.
(F, 19, 1956)

2656   If a person reads something before he goes to sleep, he is supposed to remember it.
(F, 21, R, 1958)

2657   A child who is continually picking his nose in school is a slow learner.
(F, 50, 1960)

2658   If there is a small house and a large barn, the man is boss; but if there is a large house and a small barn, the wife is boss.
(F, 40, R, 1957)

2659   If a woman gets a permanent during her menstrual period, the permanent will not take.
(M, 20, R, 1958)

2660   "Whiskey on beer, / Never fear; / But beer on whiskey / Is pretty risky."
(M, 24, 1958)

2661   When you come in out of the cold, back into the room so that your glasses won't fog over.
(F, 27, 1957)

2662   The entire composition of the body changes every seven years.
(F, 60, R, 1961)

2663   If you hit a man with a broom, he'll go to jail.
(F, 57, R, 1958)

2664   When you are angry, count to ten before you speak.
(F, 80, R, 1957)

2665   If a person's initials spell a word, he will be famous.
(M, 30, R, 1958)

2666   If a person gets up from the left side of his bed, he will have a bad disposition.
(F, 1961)

2667   If one's fingers are crossed when one is telling a lie, the lie doesn't count.
(F, 35, 1956)

2668   A curled up rug means that someone will soon take a trip.
(F, 21, 1950)

2669   If someone comes in through the back door and leaves through the front door, he will never come back.
(F, 1962)

2670   Every hour of sleep that you get before midnight is worth two hours after midnight.
(F, 20, R, 1961)

2671   A person who walks in his sleep leads a lonely life and is searching for love.
(F, 20, R, 1961)

2672   One contributor's father insisted that the children make their beds so that their heads would not be toward the west, because all dead people were placed that way, and he thought that his family would have to lie that way long enough.

(F, 40, R, 1962)

2673　If you tell a lie, the Good Lord will punish you by driving a nail in your head.

(F, 60, R, 1963)

2674　A person whose handwriting slants to the left is pessimistic.

(F, 60, R, 1957)

2675　If you put your tongue on a very cold iron, you will learn to speak German.

(F, 88, R, 1961 [her mother])

2676　If you sleep on your textbook the night before a test, you will make a good grade on the test.

(F, 20, R, 1963, + 4 F)

2677　If you want to remember something, tie a string around your finger.

(F, 60, 1959, + 4 F)

2678　When two people are conversing and they say the same thing simultaneously, the first person to say "Jinx, you owe me a coke" gets a free coke from the other person.

(F, 20, R, 1957)

Making Wishes

COUNTING THE TIMES WE USE THE WORD "WISH" EACH DAY either in conversation or in thoughts would be an interesting activity. However, these daily utterances are spurious compared to real wishing. For instance, making a wish for one's own benefit or other fulfillment often imposes a condition or some manipulation by the wishmaker. This may be almost sacred in character. When wishing on a falling star, the wish must be made before the star goes out.

When wishing on the first star seen at night, the tender rhyme

> Starlight, star bright,
> First star I see tonight,
> Wish I may, wish I might,
> Have the wish I wish tonight

must be recited aloud and accurately before one makes a wish. Furthermore, one must not look at another star that might pop out before the rhyme is finished and the wish made. Wishing on the "wishbone" of a chicken or trying to blow out all the candles on your birthday cake with one breath depends on fulfilling an act that is not quite so simple. These wishing practices—plus many more, such as wishing on a load of hay, white horses, or even cars with only one light—are popular today, as revealed by a high frequency in our collection. Over one hundred people reported on falling stars; sixty on wishbones and candles on birthday cakes; and sixty or more on hay, horses, and cars with one light.

Is there mock seriousness on the part of adults when they tell children about wishes such as those above, or does the adult want to instill some sort of faith in the desire to succeed, or whatever, despite the child's lack of scientific knowledge? These are questions that arise. In any event, these beliefs, whether verbal or behavorial, do function because they convey an inherent and intended seriousness. There is more to wishing than wishing is the implication of the old adage "If wishes were horses, beggars would ride."

CARS AND HIGHWAYS

2679   When you see a car with only one light, make a wish.
          (M, 20, R, 1957, + 4 F)

2680   When you see a car with only one headlight, make a wish and
        don't look at the car again.
          (F, 20, 1957 [one of her friends], + 1 M)

2681   If you see a car with one light, yell "Cockeye," and make a
        wish.
          (M, 21, 1950, + 1 F)

2682   If you see three cockeyes on the same night, make a wish, and
        it will come true.
          (F, 21, 1950, + 2 F)

2683   When you see three cockeyed cars, spit in your hand, rub it,
        and your wish will come true.
          (M, 20, 1957)

2684   If you see a car with one light, pinch someone, say "Pike's
        Beaver," and make a wish.
          (M, 39, R, 1959 [his grandmother])

2685   When you see a car with one light, say "Hawkeye," hit one
        hand with your other, and your wish will come true.
          (F, 20, 1959)

2686   When you see a car with one light, lick your thumb, and
        stamp it in the palm of your opposite hand; then hit your palm
        with your fist, and make a wish. If you see three cars with one
        light before midnight, your wish will come true.
          (F, 21, 1950)

2687   When you see a car with only one headlight at night, kiss the
        palm of your left hand, hit it with your right fist, and you will
        have good luck.
          (M, 20, R, 1957)

2688   If you see a "cat-eyes car" (A '57 or '58 Mercury from the
        rear) and you make a wish and turn around three times be-
        fore the car is out of sight, your wish will come true. (This
        makes for *much* confusion in the back seat of a car.)
          (M, 20, 1958)

2689   If a person sees a cat-eyes car, he should look over his left
        shoulder and make a wish. His wish will come true.
          (M, 20, R, 1962)

2690 Honk the horn and make a wish before you go under a bridge.
 (F, 21, 1950)

2691 If you make a wish when you go under a bridge, your wish will come true.
 (M, 21, 1950)

2692 When you go under a bridge, if you wet your finger, make a wish, and then put your finger on the roof of a car, your wish will come true.
 (F, 19, 1959 [her friends], + 1 F)

2693 If you make a wish the first time you cross a bridge, it will come true.
 (F, 60, R, 1957, + 1 F)

2694 Hold your breath while going over a bridge, and make a wish.
 (M, 30, 1961)

2695 When you go under a viaduct, you should put your hand on the ceiling of the car, honk the horn three times, and make a wish.
 (F, 46, R, 1958)

2696 While you are in a car, drive through an underpass, honk the horn, and hang on to something green; then close your eyes and make a wish.
 (F, 18, 1956)

2697 When you drive under an overpass, say the word "Pedella," and make a wish. You may honk while going through the underpass to ensure that the wish will come true, but you must not honk on the return trip through the underpass.
 (F, 25, 1958)

2698 When going through an underpass in an automobile, make a wish, lick your finger, touch the roof, and honk the horn to make it come true.
 (M, 26, 1958)

2699 A wish made while you are driving across railroad tracks with both feet off the floor will come true.
 (F, 19, R, 1958, + 1 F)

2700 Honk the car horn three times while going through a tunnel, and make a wish.
 (M, 22, R, 1963 [his sister-in-law])

2701 Raise your feet, put your hands on the roof of the car, and make a wish while you are going through a tunnel.
 (F, 15, R, 1958)

2702 If you touch a moving car, shake hands with someone, and make a wish. Then your wish will come true.
 (F, 21, 1950)

2703   Touch a moving car, have someone slap your hand, and then your wish will come true.
        (F, 1958)

2704   If you go over a county or state line while traveling in a car, lift your feet off the floor, and make a wish.
        (F, 20, R, 1956, + 1 F)

2705   Pick out a car, and turn the ring on your finger every time that you see the car. When you have turned your ring thirty-two times, make a wish.
        (F, 21, 1950)

2706   Wish on a red truck or car.
        (F, 23, 1956)

THE MOON AND THE STARS

2707   If you make a wish while looking at the moon each night of the full moon, the wish will come true.
        (F, 20, R, 1958, + 4 F)

2708   Make a wish when you see a full moon over your left shoulder.
        (F, 21, R, 1961 [her grandfather], + 7 F)

2709   Look at the new moon over your shoulder, and make a wish.
        (F, 21, 1950, + 1 F)

2710   If you see a new moon over your right shoulder, make a wish, and it will come true.
        (F, 53, 1954, + 2 F and 1 M)

2711   Wish on the first star you see at night.
        (M, 20, 1954, + 38 F and 5 M)

2712   If you wish on the first star you see and don't look back, your wish will come true.
        (F, 21, 1950, + 5 F and 1 M)

2713   Wish on the first star, and then do not look at it again for five minutes.
        (F, 21, 1950)

2714   Do not look at the stars until after you have made your wish, or it will not come true.
        (F, 60, 1961 [her family])

2715   When you see a lone star in the sky, make a wish; then don't look at it again until another one appears, and your wish will come true.
        (F, 18, 1958)

2716　　When you wish on the first star of evening, you must never take your eyes from the star while making the wish; otherwise the wish will not come true.

(M, 22, R, 1963)

2717　　A wish made on the brightest star will come true.

(F, 18, 1956)

2718　　"Star light, star bright, / First star I see tonight, / I wish I may, I wish I might, / Have the wish I wish tonight."

(F, 21, 1950, + 32 F and 7 M)

2719　　When you see the first star at night, turn around three times and say: "Star light, star bright, / First star I see tonight, / I wish I may, I wish I might, / Have the wish I wish tonight," and you will get your wish.

(F, 21, 1957)

2720　　When you see the first star at night, kiss your hand three times on the back and say, "Star light, star bright, / Give me the wish I wish tonight"; then throw your kiss toward the star.

(F, 60, R, 1957)

2721　　To make a wish come true, wish on the first star of the evening, and throw a kiss at or count each of three other stars before again looking at the first star.

(F, 35, 1956)

2722　　Make a wish on the first star you see, blow three kisses, and your wish will come true.

(F, 21, R, 1956)

2723　　Never repeat a wish that you have made on a star.

(F, 53, 1955)

2724　　Make wishes when you see falling stars.

(F, 21, 1950, + 31 F and 3 M)

2725　　When you see a falling star, if you make a wish on it before the star goes out of sight, your wish will come true.

(F, 19, R, 1959, + 3 F and 1 M)

2726　　When you see a falling star, count to ten, and make a wish before the star goes out of sight.

(F, 20, R, 1959 [her grandparents], + 2 F)

2727　　If you can say, while a star is falling, "Star light, star bright, / First star I've seen tonight, / I wish I may, I wish I might, / Have this wish I wish tonight," your wish will come true. However, you must finish saying this before the light is extinguished.

(F, 60, R, 1958, + 1 F)

2728   Say this under a falling star, and your wish will come true: "I wish I may, I wish I might, / Have the wish I wish tonight."
        (M, 30, R, 1962 [his parents])

2729   When you see a falling star, make a wish, and start counting. The higher you count, the better are your chances that the wish will come true.
        (F, 60, R, 1961)

2730   If you can repeat a wish three times before a falling star fades, your wish will come true.
        (F, 20, 1959)

2731   When you see a falling star, make a wish, and it will come true unless you tell what the wish is.
        (M, 26, 1955, + 1 M)

FOOD

2732   Make a wish before you try to blow the candles out on your birthday cake. If you blow them all out in one breath, you will have good luck, and your wish will come true.
        (F, 20, 1951, + 11 F and 1 M)

2733   If you don't blow out all the candles on a birthday cake, each remaining one represents a year until your wish will come true.
        (F, 21, 1950, + 4 F)

2734   If you put your ring on a birthday candle and make a wish, it will come true if all the candles are blown out.
        (F, 21, 1962, + 2 F)

2735   When eating your own birthday cake, you must not talk from the time you take your first bite till your piece is gone, or the wish that you have made won't come true.
        (M, 50, R, 1958)

2736   At birthday celebrations, each person should drop his ring over a candle before the candles are blown out. If the candle that your ring is over is blown out, your wish will come true. (A practice at college.)
        (F, 19, 1958)

2737   If there is a full moon on your birthday, make a wish, and it will come true.
        (F, 20, R, 1961 [her father])

2738   If you put a piece of bride's cake under your pillow, your wish will come true.
        (F, 57, 1957)

2739   Take a small hen's egg, throw it over a building, and your wish will come true.

           (F, 20, R, 1961 [her mother])

2740   Make a wish when you see a curl in your coffee. Try to pick it up without breaking the bubbles and say "Money, money."

           (M, 81, R, 1961)

2741   If you spill some salt, throw a pinch of it over your right shoulder, make a wish, and the wish will be sure to come true.

           (F, 50, 1953 [her mother])

2742　A wish made on the first olive taken from a jar will come true.
　　　　(F, 20, R, 1957)

2743　At the dinner table, if you pass a dish to a person who is passing one to you, make a wish.
　　　　(F, 35, 1956)

2744　If you take the middle stick of gum from a package, your wish will come true.
　　　　(F, 20, R, 1958)

2745　Throw a potato peeling three times around your head. Then make a wish, and that wish will come true.
　　　　(F, 65, R, 1957)

2746　Make a wish on the wishbone of a chicken.
　　　　(F, 21, 1950, + 5 F and 2 M)

2747　Wish on the short end of a wishbone.
　　　　(F, 19, 1956, + 2 F)

2748　If two people make a wish while breaking a wishbone, the person who gets the longer end will get his wish.
　　　　(F, 19, R, 1962, + 20 F and 8 M)

2749　If two people make a wish when pulling on a wishbone, the one with the shorter piece will get his wish. If the one who has the longer piece hangs it over the door, he will marry the first person to come through the door.
　　　　(F, 60, R, 1961)

2750　If you get the hook of the wishbone, you must hang it over the door and kiss the first person who enters the door. This will break the spell.
　　　　(F, 80, R, 1961)

2751　Put a wishbone over your door, walk under it, and your wish will come true.
　　　　(F, 60, 1958)

CLOTHING

2752　If you have put an article of clothing on wrong side out, make a wish as you change it.
　　　　(F, 20, 1957, + 3 F)

2753　If you have put your dress on backwards, make a wish, and take your dress off. Your wish will come true.
　　　　(F, 60, R, 1961 [her parents])

2754　Make a wish when you put a garment on wrong side out.

Wear the garment wrong side out all day to make the wish come true.

(F, 70, 1961)

2755   If you have put a garment on wrong side out, stand behind the door, and make a wish.

(F, 70, R, 1962 [her parents])

2756   If a girl's skirt hem is turned up, she should make a wish before turning it down.

(F, 20, R, 1963 [her parents], + 12 F and 2 M)

2757   If your dress gets a hitch in the hem, make a wish, kiss the hitch, and your wish will come true.

(F, 20, R, 1960, + 13 F)

2758   A girl may make a wish when her hem is turned up unless it shakes down first.

(F, 50, R, 1958)

2759   If the hem turns up while you are putting on a dress and if you can turn around three times before it falls down, make a wish, and your wish will come true.

(F, 80, R, 1958)

2760   If the hem turns up while you are putting on a skirt, make a wish, and it will come true within three days.

(F, 20, R, 1958)

2761   When the clasp of a necklace is alongside another ornament, the person who is wearing the necklace and ornament is given a wish. Another person takes the clasp and the ornament, one in each hand, and, after the wish has been made, places the clasp at the back of the neck.

(F, 30, 1961)

2762   If the clasp of a girl's necklace is in front, she should ask someone else to turn it around to the back; then she should make a wish, which is supposed to come true.

(F, 20, 1963 [her high-school friends])

2763   If you make a wish, let someone else put your ring on your finger. The wish will come true if you do not remove the ring.

(F, 20, R, 1957, + 1 F)

2764   Turn another person's ring three times, and make a wish.

(F, 70, 1961)

2765   If you want to be sure that a wish will come true, have your best friend make a wish to herself as she puts a ring on your finger. She must not tell you the wish, but when it comes true, she may take the ring off.

(F, 90, 1958)

2766   If you make a wish while putting on a ring, never take the ring off, or you will break the wish.
(F, 20, 1959)

MISCELLANEOUS

2767   Eat a wedge of pie backwards, making a wish when you eat the point. If you don't say anything until you leave the room, your wish will come true.
(F, 40, 1958)

2768   Make a wish before you eat the last corner of your pie, the point end, and then don't say another word until you have left the dining room.
(F, 21, 1950)

2769   Leave the corner of a piece of pie on your plate, make a wish, eat the corner, and then walk out of the room backwards, holding your hands.
(F, 21, 1950)

2770   If you save the first bite of a piece of pie until the last and then eat it, your wish will come true.
(F, 19, 1956, + 1 F)

2771   Save the point of your piece of pie until the last bite. While eating it, make a wish. Do not drink any water, and walk backwards out of the room.
(F, 21, 1950)

2772   Cut the point of your pie off, and save it until the last bite. If you don't eat it until the last bite, your wish will come true.
(F, 20, 1950, + 6 F and 2 M)

2773   Cut the point off a piece of pie, place it at the back of your plate, turn the plate around, and your wish will come true.
(F, 1958)

2774   Make a wish when you see a load of hay.
(F, 21, 1957, + 3 F and 2 M)

2775   When a person passes a hay truck, he should make a wish, saying: "Load of hay, load of hay, / Make a wish, and turn away." If he looks at the truck after wishing, the wish will not come true.
(F, 25, 1958, + 11 F and 1 M)

2776   When you see a load of hay, make a wish, and turn away.
(F, 20, 1958, + 14 F)

2777   If you see a load of hay, wet your finger, stamp your other
        hand, clench your fist, and close your eyes in order to have a
        wish come true.
            (F, 20, R, 1957)

2778   If you see a load of hay going down the street, turn around
        three times, and make a wish; the wish will come true.
            (F, 84, 1955)

2779   At the first sight of a load of hay, wish without moving your
        eyes until you have finished making the wish; then shut your
        eyes, and do not look again at the load of hay.
            (F, 87, 1958)

2780   Stamp white horses for a wish. This is done by licking your
        thumb, pressing it into the palm of your other hand, and then
        hitting the palm with your clenched fist.
            (F, 1962, + 1 F)

2781   Stamp the palm of your hand with a wet finger for each white
        horse you see; then make a wish.
            (F, 22, 1956, + 5 F and 1 M)

2782   When you see a white horse, lick your thumb, hit it in the
        palm of your hand three times, and make a wish. Your wish
        will come true.
            (F, 40, R, 1951)

2783   If you see six white horses, make a wish.
            (F, 21, 1956)

2784   Make a wish when you see a white horse. Don't look at the
        horse again.
            (F, 21, 1950)

2785   If you see a white horse, make a wish.
            (F, 20, 1959 [heard as a child], + 11 F and 3 M)

2786   Count one hundred white horses, and you will get a wish.
        (When you see a white horse, count it by licking three fingers
        of your right hand, slapping the palm of your left hand with
        them, and then hitting the palm of your left hand with your
        right fist.)
            (M, 47, 1958)

2787   While traveling, count all the white horses that you see.
        When you reach one hundred, make a wish, and it will come
        true.
            (F, 60, R, 1960 [heard as a child])

2788   If you see a white mule while you are riding along the road,
        make a wish, and it will come true.
            (F, 50, R, 1960 [her friends], + 1 F)

2789   If you lick your thumb and stamp it in the palm of your other
        hand when you see a white mule, your wish will come true.
            (M, 61, 1957)

2790   Put a four-leaf clover in your shoe, and make a wish.
            (F, 71, 1961)

2791   Scotch-tape a four-leaf clover onto a small square of paper;
        write a wish on the paper; then throw the paper away. Your
        wish will come true.
            (F, 15, R, 1958)

2792   When you find a penny, hold it, and make a wish. Then give it
        away; you must not save it. Your wish will not come true
        unless the penny is kept going.
            (F, 25, 1958)

2793   Throw a penny in a wishing well, and make a wish.
            (F, 21, 1950)

2794   "Penny in your shoe, / Your wish will come true."
            (F, 42, 1955)

2795   If an eyelash falls on your cheek, pick it up with your
        forefinger and thumb, make a wish, and drop the eyelash; if it
        sticks to your finger, your wish will not come true.
            (F, 21, 1958, + 4 F)

2796   If an eyelash comes off on your finger, press your finger to
        someone else's, and make a wish. The one whose finger the
        lash remains on when the fingers are separated will get his
        wish.
            (F, 20, R, 1950, + 1 F)

2797   If you make a wish on and blow an eyelash from your first
        finger, your wish will come true.
            (F, 18, 1959)

2798   If you tell a wish to anyone, it won't come true.
            (M, 21, 1950, + 3 F and 2 M)

2799   It is lucky when an ace, two, three, and four are played on
        one trick in a bridge hand. When this occurs, every player
        should put his hands on the trick and make a wish.
            (F, 23, 1957, + 4 F)

2800   Step on a Lucky Strike package, and make a wish.
            (F, 21, 1950, + 1 F and 1 M)

2801   Cross your fingers when making a wish. This will help to
        make the wish come true.
            (F, 23, 1957, + 2 F)

2802   Make a wish when you find a pin.
            (F, 21, 1950)

2803 If you're walking and find a straight pin pointing toward you, pick it up, make a wish, and stick the pin on your left shoulder. When you lose the pin, your wish will come true.
(F, 57, 1958)

2804 If you find a straight pin facing you, pick it up, stick it in the wall, and make a wish. Your wish will come true.
(F, 70, R, 1959)

2805 If you make a wish when a white mark appears on one of your fingernails, the wish will come true when the mark grows out.
(F, 50, 1958)

2806 If you will count the white spots on your fingernails, your wish will come true.
(F, 18, 1955)

2807 Make a wish as you enter a new home.
(F, 21, R, 1957, + 1 F)

2808 If you make a wish when a redbird crosses your path, your wish will come true.
(F, 21, 1950)

2809 If you see a redbird, you should make a wish.
(F, 30, 1959)

2810 When you see a redbird, make a wish before he flies away, and your wish will come true.
(F, 22, 1961, + 4 F)

2811 When you see a redbird, pinch someone, and make a wish.
(M, 30, R, 1959)

2812 If you make a wish when you see the first robin in the spring, your wish will come true.
(F, 81, 1959)

2813 Make a wish when you see a bluebird.
(F, 71, 1961)

2814 When you hear the first whippoorwill in the spring, lie down, and make a wish. If you roll over three times, your wish will come true.
(M, 52, R, 1958)

2815 When one of your teeth comes out, put it under your pillow, and make a wish.
(F, 21, 1950, + 1 F and 1 M)

2816 If two people say the same thing at the same time and each of them makes a wish, it will come true.
(F, 40, R, 1960 [her parents], + 3 F)

2817 If two people say the same word or words simultaneously and link each of their little fingers together before they speak, whatever they wish will come true.

(F, 20, R, 1957, + 2 F and 3 M)

2818   When two people say the same thing at the same time, they should hook their little fingers together and say these phrases alternately: (1—first person) "Needles"; (2—second person) "Pins"; (1) "Triplets"; (2) "Twins"; (1) "When a man marries"; (2) "His trouble begins"; (1) "When a man dies"; (2) "His trouble ends." Then each one should make a wish, and they should pull their fingers apart.

(F, 19, 1957)

2819   Make a wish on a horseshoe when you find one.

(M, 1961)

2820   After making a wish of any kind, close your right hand into a fist, kiss your fingers (folded), and hit the palm of your left hand with your fist. The harder you hit, the more likely it is that the wish will come true.

(F, 90, 1958)

2821   After making a hopeful prediction, knock on wood three times to be sure that it will come true.

(M, 50, 1958)

2822   If you put a written wish under your pillow, it will come true.

(F, 63, 1958)

2823   Cross your fingers when you want something to happen.

(F, 20, 1958)

2824   A wish will never come true unless you are firmly sincere.

(F, 50, R, 1960 [her mother])

2825   Pinch a straw crisscross with your finger and thumb. Start at the middle with both hands, and pull towards both ends of the straw. If both hands reach the ends at the same time, the wish that you made will come true.

(F, 20, 1959 [her family])

2826   If you blow off all the seeds of a dandelion, you will get your wish.

(F, 21, 1950)

2827   If you and a friend see a piece of unpainted wood while you are walking along, you should both touch it and make a wish at the same time. Your wish will be fulfilled.

(F, 21, 1957)

2828   If you make a wish as you throw coins in a well, your wish will come true.

(F, 21, 1959 [her friends])

2829   When a funeral procession passes by, one should hold on to a button on his clothing and make a wish; one's wish will come true.
(F, 20, 1958, + 1 F)

2830   Make a wish, turn around in a circle three times with your eyes closed, and your wish will come true.
(F, 19, 1959)

2831   Make a wish as you step into a strange church.
(F, 60, R, 1957)

2832   Wish when you sleep in a strange bed. Put your mind on your wish as you go to sleep, and it will come true.
(F, 71, 1961)

2833   If you spit on a flat rock and then throw it over your shoulder, you can make a wish.
(F, 20, 1963 [her father])

2834   Make a wish on a piece of small, clear sandstone.
(F, 21, 1950)

2835   If in your conversation you unintentionally say a rhyme, make a wish, and your wish will come true.
(F, 77, R, 1961)

2836   If a person blows a smoke ring, then runs his finger through the center of the ring, he will be granted one wish.
(M, 20, 1963)

2837   Make a wish; then open the Bible; if a verse begins with "And it came to pass," your wish will come true.
(F, 71, 1961)

2838   Make a wish when you look into a well for the first time.
(F, 71, 1961)

2839   If you make a wish and then step on a water main, your wish will come true.
(F, 21, 1950)

7

The Significance of Dreams

HOW TO REGARD DREAMS HAS BEEN A SERIOUS QUESTION
for a long time; it has also been the subject of much study, especially
since the time of Freud. One researcher catalogued over six hundred
dream subjects. Today, people are generally content to leave the in-
terpretation of dreams to psychologists and psychoanalysts. But for
centuries, millions have stood in awe of dreams and have generally believed them to be a revelation of the future or of the will of the gods.
Egyptian pharaohs sometimes attributed their success to instructions
received in dreams. Also, there was the belief that the soul was able to
leave the body and travel to distant places and even converse with
God.

Likewise, rank-and-file folk have their beliefs in dream reality,
many of which remain today. That dreams may be interpreted in several ways, however, is accepted by everyone—ancients, our rank-and-
file people, and the experts. The items here from the present-day nonacademic folk reveal this.

Although this chapter comprises only 2 percent of our collection, it
is interesting to note the subject matter of items that have high frequencies. Over one hundred people reported on the matter of telling dreams
before breakfast, while over sixty reported on dreams about death having a connection with marriage. To dream of snakes points up in various ways that the dreamer has enemies, while eating before going to
bed is a sure way to have bad dreams. All of us have had dreams of falling—one interpreter said that this indicates that our aims are too high.

Since dream folklore in this collection was reported in short, terse
statements, classification by subject matter was convenient; but it
should be added that many could be classified as precognitive, that is,
as "content which anticipates future events in a way which could not
be inferred rationally from information available to the dreamer in a
waking state."

ANIMALS

2840   It is good luck to dream about chickens.
(F, 35, R, 1962)

2841   To dream about deer means that you will have quarrels.
(F, 70, 1954)

2842   One contributor reported that her Grandma Bearley had a terror of dreaming about white geese, because she was sure that it meant there would be a death in the family. Death had coincided with a dream of this type so many times that it was impossible for her to shake this belief.
(F, 30, R, 1960)

2843   If you dream about rats fighting, there will be a death.
(F, 19, R, 1956)

2844   If you dream about fish, you will come into money.
(F, 30, 1962)

2845   A woman who dreams about a fish is going to have a baby.
(F, 66, 1955)

2846   If you dream about cattle, you will soon be in a crowd.
(F, 70, R, 1957)

2847   If you dream about horses, you'll get a letter.
(F, 48, R, 1957)

2848   If you dream about horses, you will hear of a fire.
(M, 65, 1954)

2849   Dreaming about a brown horse is good luck. If you ride the horse, you'll be a success. If you dream about a white horse, you'll have bad luck.
(F, 50, R, 1959 [her mother])

2850   If one dreams that a member of his family is riding a white horse, the person dreamed about will die.
(M, 30, 1959 [his grandmother])

2851   A dream about white horses foretells a death in your family.
(F, 30, 1961 [her grandmother])

2852   If you dream about gray horses, there will be a death in the family.
(F, 30, 1960)

2853   A dream about a cat refers to an enemy; a dog signifies a friend.
(F, 60, R, 1958)

2854   If you dream about cats, someone is telling bad things about you.
        (F, 70, R, 1962)

2855   A dream about a sleeping cat is a sign of contentment in your family.
        (F, 45, 1954)

2856   If you dream about snakes, it means that you have enemies.
        (F, 20, 1956 [her mother], + 7 F)

2857   If you dream about snakes, you must kill them in your dream, or you will have an enemy.
        (F, 50, R, 1959 [one of her neighbors], + 1 F)

2858   Dreaming about snakes is a sign of trouble. The number of snakes indicates the number of people involved.
        (F, 50, 1960 [her father], + 1 F)

2859   If you dream about snakes and if you kill them in the dream, you will conquer your enemies. If you do not dream that you kill them, they will conquer you.
        (F, 45, 1958, + 4 F and 1 M)

2860   If you dream about a snake, you have a secret enemy.
        (F, 27, 1954, + 2 F)

2861   If you kill a snake in your dreams, it means that an enemy will become your friend.
        (M, 21, 1954)

2862   If you dream about snakes, someone is critically ill in the family.
        (F, 20, R, 1960 [her mother])

2863   If you dream about a snake, beware of the Devil when you awaken.
        (F, 60, R, 1962)

BIRTHS AND WEDDINGS

2864   If you dream about a birth, you'll hear about a death.
        (F, 21, 1950, + 2 F)

2865   If you dream about a birth, there will be a death in the family.
        (F, 50, 1962)

2866   If you dream about a birth, you are going to hear about a marriage.
        (F, 70, 1954)

2867   Dreaming about a wedding, is a sign of a birth.
        (F, 21, 1950, + 1 F)

2868   If you dream about a wedding, there will be a death.
        (F, 20, R, 1957, + 18 F)
2869   If you dream about a wedding, there will soon be a funeral; if
        you dream about a funeral, there will soon be a wedding.
        (F, 19, R, 1957, + 2 F)
2870   If you dream about a wedding, there will be a death in the
        family.
        (F, 20, R, 1957, + 7 F and 1 M)
2871   If you dream about marriage and brides, it means sickness or
        death.
        (F, 74, 1955)
2872   If you dream about marriage, you'll have bad luck.
        (M, 79, R, 1962)

DEATH

2873   If you dream about talking with someone who is dead, you'll
        get a letter from someone who is living.
        (F, 40, R, 1958)
2874   Dream about the dead, and you will hear from the living.
        (M, 21, 1950, + 23 F and 4 M)
2875   If you dream about the dead, you will see someone of the
        living whom you haven't seen for a long time.
        (F, 52, 1957)
2876   Dream about a person who has passed away, and you will
        soon have news about a living person.
        (F, 60, 1954)
2877   To dream about a death means that there will soon be a
        wedding.
        (F, 21, 1950, + 7 F and 2 M)
2878   If you dream about a funeral, you'll hear about a wedding.
        (F, 40, R, 1958, + 4 F)
2879   If you dream about a death, there will be a marriage in the
        family within a year.
        (F, 30, R, 1959 [her mother])
2880   If you dream about death, there will be a wedding in your
        family.
        (F, 21, 1950, + 4 F)
2881   If you dream about a funeral, there will be a wedding.
        (F, 21, 1950, + 4 F)

2882   If you dream about the dead, you'll hear about a birth.
        (F, 75, R, 1956)

2883   If you dream about a death in the family, there will be a birth.
        (F, 20, 1957, + 2 F)

2884   If you dream about death, there will be a birth.
        (F, 30, R, 1962, + 5 F)

2885   When you dream about a dead person, it is a sign that he
        needs your prayers for help.
        (M, 1959, + 1 F and 1 M)

2886   To dream about death is a sign of the approaching sickness of
        some member of one's family.
        (F, 50, R, 1957)

2887   If you dream of the dead, the weather will get worse within
        twenty-four hours.
        (F, 70, R, 1961 [her parents])

2888   It is a good sign to dream about death.
        (M, 79, R, 1962 [his parents])

2889   If you finish a dream about your own death, you'll die.
        (F, 40, 1958)

2890   If you dream about the dead, there will be a death among
        your relatives.
        (F, 40, 1958 [her aunt])

HOW TO MAKE DREAMS COME TRUE

2891   One contributor said that on Friday night, when she went to bed, she used to put her petticoat under her head and say: "Dream of the living and not the dead, / Dream of the one I shall wed."
(F, 40, R, 1962)

2892   If you put a piece of your wedding cake under the pillow, your dreams will come true.
(M, 60, R, 1957, + 1 F)

2893   Eat three unwashed fish tails, and all the dreams that you have will come true.
(F, 42, R, 1958 [told to her by a lady who was born in Sweden])

2894   After you have finished making a new quilt, the first time that you sleep under it, whatever you dream will come true.
(F, 50, 1962 [her mother], + 1 F)

2895   One contributor's grandmother used to say: "Saturday night dreamt, Sunday morning told, / Come to pass before a week old."
(F, 60, + 2 F)

2896   "Friday's dreams on Saturday told / Are sure to come true before they grow old."
(F, 20, 1958, + 5 F)

2897   If you tell a dream before you eat breakfast, it will not come true.
(F, 20, 1963 [her family], + 7 F and 5 M)

2898   If you tell a bad dream before breakfast, it will come true.
(F, 19, R, 1959, + 7 F and 2 M)

2899   If you want a dream to come true, don't tell it before breakfast.
(M, 20, R, 1958, + 6 F)

2900   If you have a dream and tell it after sunrise, it won't come true.
(F, 1962)

2901   If you tell your dreams after breakfast, they will not come true.
(F, 50, R, 1960)

2902   Never tell a dream before breakfast; it's a sign of bad luck.
(F, 42, R, 1960)

2903   If you tell a dream before breakfast, it will come true before dinner.
        (F, 21, 1956, + 1 F)

2904   If you tell your dream before breakfast, it will come true before dark.
        (F, 47, 1958)

2905   If you tell your dreams before breakfast, they will come true.
        (F, 20, 1959, + 51 F and 5 M)

MISCELLANEOUS

2906   A dream about losing a tooth means that someone in your family will pass away. If the tooth is big, it will be an adult. If the tooth is small, it will be a child.
        (F, 50, 1962)

2907   If you dream that you are losing a tooth, there will be a death in the family.
        (F, 60, R, 1958)

2908   To have sweet dreams, eat sweet pickles before you go to bed.
        (F, 1961 [her mother])

2909   If you sleep with perfume on, you'll have sweeter dreams.
        (F, 1962 [her mother])

2910   If you eat cherry pie for supper, you will have a dream during the night.
        (M, 30, R, 1958 [his mother])

2911   If you eat something sweet before you go to bed, you will have bad dreams.
        (F, 25, R, 1962)

2912   If you eat before you go to bed, you will have bad dreams.
        (F, 22, 1959)

2913   If you eat meat before you go to bed, you will have bad dreams.
        (F, 20, 1950, 1950, + 1 F)

2914   If you have often been troubled with bad dreams, sleep with a Bible under your pillow, and you will never be bothered again.
        (F, 50, R, 1957)

2915   If the moon shines on you, it will make you have bad dreams.
        (F, 17, R, 1955)

2916   A dream about crystal-clear water foretells a pleasant happening.
(F, 58, 1954, + 1 F)

2917   If you dream about going through H_2O that is clear, you will overcome some difficulties.
(F, 21, 1950)

2918   Dream about clear water for good fortune.
(M, 21, 1950, + 2 F)

2919   To dream about water means death.
(M, 60, R, 1958)

2920   You'll have bad luck if you dream about walking in clear water.
(F, 50, R, 1959)

2921   If you dream about muddy water, you'll have bad luck.
(F, 21, 1950, + 2 F and 1 M)

2922   If you dream about muddy water, there will be a death in your family.
(F, 20, R, 1959, + 1 F and 1 M)

2923   A dream about muddy water is a sign of illness or death to come.
(F, 56, 1954)

2924   If you dream about muddy water, you will die within three days.
(M, 22, R, 1956)

2925   A dream involving muddy water means that you will have trouble.
(F, 50, 1958, + 1 F and 1 M)

2926   To be in or around muddy water in your dreams is a sign of sickness in the family.
(F, 67, 1954)

2927   A dream about muddy water is a sign that a person who is close to you is ill.
(F, 45, 1954, + 2 F)

2928   If you dream about mud, a relative will die.
(F, 25, 1961)

2929   If you dream that you are falling and that you land before you wake up, you'll die.
(F, 20, R, 1956, + 7 F and 4 M)

2930   If you dream that you are falling, your aims are too high.
(F, 21, 1950)

2931   A dream about falling foretells a loss.
(F, 40, 1955)

2932   If you dream the same dream for three nights, it will come true.
      (F, 20, R, 1957, + 5 F and 1 M)

2933   Reality is just the opposite of what you dream. For example, if you dream about the birth of a brown-eyed boy, you will have a blue-eyed girl.
      (F, 30, R, 1959 [her parents], + 1 F)

2934   If you dream that you are sad and are crying, you will be glad and happy about something. If you dream that you are glad and happy about something, you'll be sad about something.
      (F, 27, 1954)

2935   Dreams go by opposites. For example, if you dream about getting money, you will lose some; if you dream about something good, something bad will happen to you.
      (F, 27, 1954)

2936   Believe the opposite of what you dream.
      (M, 42, 1955, + 1 F and 1 M)

2937   You will have good news if you dream about letter-writing.
      (F, 71, 1961)

2938   If you dream about receiving a letter, on the following day you will receive one in the mail.
      (F, 60, R, 1961)

2939   If you dream about a girl and the dream is vivid enough to wake you up, you will sleep with her the next night.
      (F, 20, R, 1958)

2940   If you dream about someone during the night, you will hear from him in the near future.
      (F, 50, R, 1963)

2941   Dreaming about bright flowers is an indication of death.
      (F, 56, R, 1953)

2942   If you dream about flowers, it means that there is love and happiness ahead.
      (F, 1962)

2943   It is bad luck to dream about flowers out of season. It is good luck to dream about flowers in season.
      (F, 70, R, 1962 [her grandmother])

2944   To dream about going up steps is good luck. To dream about going down steps is bad luck.
      (F, 35, 1962)

2945   It is bad luck to eat and drink in your dreams.
      (F, 21, R, 1957)

2946   Dreams foretell the future.
          (F, 21, 1950)
2947   People used to think that having a mixed-up dream meant
          that a storm was coming.
          (F, 40, 1961)
2948   If you dream about trains, you are going to take a long trip.
          (F, 40, 1961)
2949   If you dream about feet, there is going to be an illness in the
          near future.
          (F, 1962)
2950   If you dream about harvesting grain, there will be a death in
          the family.
          (M, 63, R, 1961 [learned in Ohio])
2951   A dream about a rolling snake is the sign of a death.
          (F, 50, R, 1963 [her parents])
2952   If you see a light in your sleep, it is a sign that there will be a
          death in your family.
          (F, 46, R, 1958)

8

Luck

THE SURVIVAL OF AGE-OLD BELIEFS AND SUPERSTITIONS, however the individual considers them, is surprising, especially when it comes to the subject of luck. The background idea that fate is controlled by unseen powers seems, in the light of our scientific world, to be quite out of place. Nevertheless, the thought that there is magical power for good luck or bad luck in objects or in our actions remains a part of our unquestioned folk heritage. The long-standing evil significance of taboos and how to counteract them, either verbally or by action, occupies the attention of countless people. Although much scholarship has been devoted to the historical circumstances or other reasons to explain why and how these "luck" factors have arisen, much remains clouded. But one thing is certain: there is hardly anything in man's environment about which some belief or superstition has not arisen in order to help him equalize the positive and negative aspects of life that he continues to meet.

Luck, good and bad, accounts for 14 percent of the total number of items in our collection. The subject matter, which is arranged in 32 categories, is broad. Of the 710 numbered items listed, some have a very high frequency. It should be noted that most collections of folk beliefs and superstitions do not treat luck in a separate chapter.

The force of the older American belief that it is bad luck to carry a two-dollar bill was felt recently when the attempt to popularize the two-dollar bill failed (the bad luck could be avoided by tearing off a corner, however). Merchants felt that this failure was justified, not because of the luck condition, but because "you can't break a five with two-dollar bills; customers don't count that way; and there's no place in the cash register with a two-dollar designation." Among modern bad-luck beliefs that have a high frequency is "It's bad luck to light three cigarettes from one match," which reportedly arose from nighttime combat conditions.

Of the current bad-luck beliefs reported to us, the ones that have the highest frequencies concern breaking mirrors, black cats, walking under ladders, spilling salt, and finding pins. Others that have high frequencies deal with putting on clothing backwards or wrong side out, finding four-leaf clovers, starting trips or new tasks on Friday, stepping over brooms or taking old brooms to new houses, hanging or finding horseshoes here and there, umbrellas, lighting three cigarettes on one match, and thirteen as a bad-luck number.

The variety of possibilities to help ensure good luck or to ward off bad luck is of course almost endless. Practicing some or many of these belief customs depends a good deal on the individual's point of view, which is generally kept secret, in spite of the fact that performing them suggests belief in them.

ACTORS AND ACTING

2953   A good-luck sign for an opening performance is to have a cat backstage.
      (M, 24, 1959)

2954   Having a black cat backstage brings good luck.
      (M, 20, 1959)

2955   A bad dress rehearsal means a good show.
      (M, 65, R, 1955)

2956   Say to an actor, "Give 'em hell, old chap," before a performance for good luck.
      (F, 20, 1959)

2957   Telling a person who is going on stage to break a leg means good luck.
      (F, 20, 1961)

2958   It is bad luck for actors to whistle in the dressing room on opening night.
      (F, 21, 1955, + 5 F and 2 M)

2959   It's bad luck to whistle in a theater.
      (F, 35, 1956)

2960   Among theater folk, peacock feathers are thought to bring bad luck; they are not used in costumes or sets.
      (F, 50, 1958)

2961   It is bad luck for actors to peek through the stage curtain before the first curtain goes up.
      (F, 21, 1956)

2962   An actor never travels with a humpbacked trunk. It is a sign of bad luck.
      (F, 1962, + 1 F)

2963   It is bad luck to wish an actor "Good luck."
       (F, 20, 1960, + 1 F and 1 M)

ANIMALS

2964   If a spider comes down in front of you on a web, you'll have
       good luck if you do not kill it.
       (F, 45, 1958, + 2 F)

2965   If there is a spider beneath the bed, the person who is
       sleeping in it will have good luck.
       (F, 50, 1957)

2966   If a spider crawls on you, you will have good luck. It's
       supposed to be a sign of money.
       (F, 1956)

2967   Do not kill spiders, as they will bring you money.
       (M, 60, R, 1957)

2968   If a spider is seen on the ceiling, it is better luck than if one is
       seen on the floor.
       (F, 59, R, 1957)

2969   It is a sign of good luck if a spider drops down from the ceiling
       and then goes back up.
       (F, 60, R, 1961)

2970   Yellow spiders bring good luck.
       (M, 24, R, 1955)

2971   Never kill a spider in the house. It brings bad luck.
       (F, 60, R, 1963, + 1 F and 1 M)

2972   If a spider tumbles from the ceiling down over your nose, it is
       a sign of impending evil.
       (M, 80, 1959)

2973   It is good luck to have a cricket in the house.
       (F, 60, 1959, + 3 F)

2974   A cricket singing upon your hearth will bring good luck.
       (F, 60, 1958, + 3 F)

2975   If you hear a cricket chirp, you will have good luck.
       (F, 26, R, 1957, + 2 F)

2976   A cricket chirping early in the morning brings bad luck to the
       family.
       (F, 45, R, 1958)

2977   If you kill a cricket, you will have bad luck.
       (F, 20, 1959, + 9 F and 1 M)

2978   It is bad luck to kill a cricket in the house.
          (M, 22, R, 1958, + 7 F and 1 M)
2979   If you kill a cricket, you will have seven years of bad luck.
          (M, 60, 1957)
2980   A yellow bee buzzing around you brings bad luck.
          (F, 50, 1959)
2981   If you have a fly in the house at Christmas, it will bring you good luck.
          (F, 72, R, 1958, + 1 F)
2982   When you see a tiny red bug, if you throw it three kisses, you will have good luck.
          (F, 46, R, 1958)
2983   Catch a lucky bug (water bug); it will bring you good luck.
          (F, 20, R, 1956)
2984   Ladybugs bring good luck.
          (M, 50, 1956)
2985   It is bad luck to find a ladybug.
          (F, 20, 1959)
2986   If you kill a snake, hang it up in a tree, and it will bring you good luck.
          (F, 35, 1958)
2987   If you kill a rattlesnake, you will live a long time.
          (M, 14, R, 1958)
2988   For luck, get some hair from a dog that has bitten you.
          (M, 24, R, 1967)
2989   It is good luck to have a strange dog or cat come to your home.
          (F, 60, 1959)
2990   It is bad luck to kill a cat or a dog.
          (M, 80, R, 1958)
2991   If a dog howls all night, something serious will happen to the family within a short time.
          (M, 40, R, 1963)
2992   It is a sign of good luck if you see a white horse.
          (F, 45, 1957, + 1 F and 1 M)
2993   "If you see a white horse upon a ridge, / Wait till tomorrow to cross the bridge."
          (F, 50, R, 1959 [her grandparents])
2994   When you see a white horse, "stamp" him for good luck.
          (F, 21, 1956, + 3 F and 1 M)
2995   If you see two white horses in a field, something good will happen to you before the day is done.
          (F, 20, R, 1958)

2996   A grey mare brings good luck.
            (M, 20, 1961)

2997   If you see two gray horses standing together in a field, you
        will have good luck.
            (F, 30, 1958)

2998   When you see a gray horse, spit on your finger, put that
        finger in the palm of your other hand, and stamp; this will
        bring you good luck.
            (F, 50, 1959)

2999   If you find a horsehair under a stone, you find good luck.
            (F, 30, R, 1958)

3000   It used to be considered bad luck to work the little horse on
        the right side of a team; one should always work it on the left.
            (M, 53, R, 1959)

3001   It is extremely bad luck to ride a palomino horse.
            (M, 50, 1958)

3002   If you see a white mule, lick your thumb, and stamp it in your
        palm for good luck.
            (F, 35, 1958)

3003   One cow brings sorrow; two cows bring joy; three cows mean
        that you will get a letter.
            (F, 1963)

3004   The left hind leg of a rabbit that has been shot in the dark of
        the moon in a graveyard is a lucky omen. Carry it with you for
        luck.
            (M, 70, 1960)

3005   The left hind foot of a rabbit will bring good luck, especially if
        it (the rabbit) was found in a graveyard at midnight.
            (F, 11, 1956, + 1 F and 1 M)

3006   If you wear a rabbit's foot around your neck, you will have
        good luck.
            (F, 60, R, 1961)

3007   For good luck, carry a rabbit's foot with you.
            (M, 19, 1958, + 37 F and 6 M)

3008   If a bird is seen flying overhead while you are about to make
        a decision, it is a symbol of success. In case of a battle, it is
        the symbol of victory.
            (F, 18, 1955)

3009   Put salt on a bird's tail for luck.
            (F, 1961)

3010   If a bird looks in your window, you will have good luck.
            (F, 40, R, 1960)

3011   Having a stork on your rooftop means good luck.
        (F, 20, R, 1958)
3012   Storks will bring good luck.
        (F, 30, R, 1957)
3013   If when you are going up a hill, you hear the first meadowlark
        in the summer, your luck will improve. If you are going down
        hill when you hear the first meadowlark, then your luck will
        decrease.
        (F, 1960)
3014   For luck, wet your thumb, touch your palm, and hit the place
        with your fist when you see the first robin of spring.
        (F, 40, 1957)
3015   Redbirds bring good luck.
        (F, 1961)
3016   When you see a redbird in the yard or around your place, it is
        a sign of good luck.
        (F, 46, R, 1958)
3017   Swallows bring good luck.
        (M, 62, R, 1959)
3018   It's good luck to see a bluebird.
        (F, 21, 1950, + 2 F and 1 M)
3019   A crane in your chimney brings good luck.
        (F, 21, 1956)
3020   You will have good luck if you're the first to hear the cuckoo
        sing in the spring.
        (F, 21, 1950)
3021   It is unlucky to have a peacock feather in your possession.
        (M, 60, 1957)
3022   It is bad luck to have a bird fly into your house.
        (F, 20, 1963, + 8 F and 3 M)
3023   If you hear a catbird call at night, you will have bad luck.
        (M, 66, R, 1959)
3024   If an owl hoots or a dog howls for any length of time near your
        home, it is a sign of bad luck or death.
        (F, 40, 1958)
3025   If you hear an owl hooting at night, it is a bad-luck omen.
        (F, 57, 1958, + 1 F)
3026   Never kill a sea gull at sea—it is bad luck.
        (F, 21, 1950)
3027   If you hear the cry of a mourning dove, sorrow will come.
        (F, 21, 1950)

3028   For good luck, set your hen on the first of the month.
        (F, 47, R, 1959)
3029   It's bad luck to kill a setting hen.
        (F, 21, 1950)
3030   Put a couple of black chicks into a new batch to bring good
        luck.
        (M, 20, 1958)
3031   A black chicken will bring good luck.
        (F, 21, 1950)
3032   He who gets up with the chickens will have good luck.
        (F, 21, 1950)
3033   Fried young chicken's feet are given for good luck to a newly
        married couple when they leave on their honeymoon.
        (F, 1957)
3034   If a hen crows like a rooster, it means severe bad fortune.
        (M, 20, R, 1963)
3035   If a rooster crows before four o'clock in the morning, sad
        news will follow.
        (F, 1962)
3036   After a Thanksgiving dinner, hang the turkey's carcass over
        the front door, and all who enter it will have good luck.
        (F, 80, R, 1958)
3037   Catch horned toads for good luck.
        (F, 20, 1960)
3038   If a squirrel crosses your path, it means good luck.
        (F, 50, R, 1959)
3039   If a bat gets into your house and flies around, it is a bad
        omen.
        (F, 30, R, 1962)

BROOMS AND SWEEPING

3040   Always carry a broom into a new house first for good luck.
        (M, 60, R, 1959)
3041   You shouldn't take an old broom to a new house; it is bad
        luck.
        (F, 21, 1965, + 31 F and 3 M)
3042   When you buy a new broom, throw the old one away.
        (M, 17, R, 1960)
3043   Don't sweep the kitchen after dark, or you'll have bad luck.
        (F, 23, 1957, + 2 F)

3044   Don't sweep the house after dark, or you'll have bad luck.
        (M, 23, 1957, + 15 F and 3 M)

3045   Don't sweep dirt out the door after dark, or it will bring bad
        luck.
        (M, 20, R, 1963, + 15 F)

3046   Never sweep dirt out the back door, as it will bring you bad
        luck.
        (M, 1962)

3047   Never sweep under anyone's feet; this will bring you bad
        luck.
        (F, 40, 1959)

3048   It is bad luck to sweep beneath the bed in which a baby has
        recently been born. To do so may mean the death of the
        mother and the infant.
        (F, 22, 1958)

3049   Don't step on a broom, or you will have bad luck.
        (M, 1961)

3050   Stepping over a broom in a doorway brings bad luck.
        (F, 22, R, 1956, + 8 F)

3051   It is bad luck to turn a broom upside down in a corner.
        (F, 22, 1958)

3052   It is bad luck for a broom to fall across a doorway. Kick it
        across the room before picking it up.
        (M, 1962)

3053   If a broom falls across the door, bad luck will follow.
        (F, 1962)

3054   It is bad luck to carry a broom through the house.
        (F, 60, 1958)

3055   Riding a broom in the house brings bad luck.
        (F, 30, 1962)

3056   It is bad luck to buy a broom in August.
        (F, 20, 1958)

3057   It is bad luck to sweep after dark or to begin any piece of
        work on Friday.
        (F, 50, R, 1961)

CARDS AND GAMBLING

3058   It brings good luck to sit next to the big winner at a poker
        game.
        (M, 28, 1958)

3059   Some people believe that one can change one's luck by cutting cards.
         (F, 1962, + 1 F)

3060   "Cut the cards thin, / Sure to win."
         (F, 40, 1958)

3061   When a card game is going badly for everyone, the players should move to the right to bring luck and better hands.
         (F, 40, 1958)

3062   If you sit the same way as a bathtub when you are playing cards, you will have good luck.
         (F, 19, 1961, + 5 F and 1 M)

3063   Walk around your chair to change your luck while playing cards.
         (F, 19, R, 1959 [her parents], + 7 F and 2 M)

3064   If you are having bad luck while playing cards, run around the table three times to change your luck.
         (F, 70, 1958)

3065   If you are having bad luck while playing cards, get up and walk around your chair three times for luck.
         (F, 40, R, 1960 [her parents], + 1 F and 1 M)

3066   Sitting on a handkerchief will change your luck at cards.
         (M, 80, 1950, + 2 F)

3067   If you want to change your luck at cards, put a handkerchief (white) on your head, and roll your stockings down.
        (F, 35, 1955, + 1 F)

3068   Lucky at cards; unlucky at love.
        (F, 30, R, 1958, + 1 M)

3069   It is unlucky to win the first deal at poker.
        (M, 28, 1958)

3070   It changes your luck to change the deck at a poker game.
        (M, 28, 1958)

3071   If you give away money that you won at gambling, you are giving away your luck.
        (M, 50, R, 1957)

3072   Some gamblers say that it is bad luck to take another player's last dollar, as it will break his streak of luck.
        (M, 1961)

3073   If the winner in a card game lends money to an unlucky person in the same game, his winning streak will be broken.
        (M, 1961)

CARS, TRAINS, PLANES, AND ROADS

3074   For luck, lift up your feet while you are crossing over a railroad track or county line.
        (F, 20, 1961, + 1 F)

3075   For good luck, raise your feet up when crossing a county line or bridge.
        (F, 20, 1958, + 1 F)

3076   It is good luck to kiss your girlfriend or boyfriend when you see a one-eyed car.
        (F, 21, 1961)

3077   For good luck, always have your shoes on when you cross a bridge.
        (F, 20, R, 1957)

3078   If you can count boxcars on a passing train, it will bring bad luck.
        (F, 20, 1955, + 1 F)

3079   A green car at a race track will bring bad luck.
        (M, 40, R, 1959)

3080   Professional race-car drivers will never paint or drive a blue

car in a race. Nor will they drive a car numbered thirteen.
(M, 1962)

3081   If you have a friend in a plane, never watch the plane take
off, as it is bad luck. Always turn your back.
(F, 22, 1961)

CATS IN GENERAL

3082   A Siamese cat brings good luck.
(F, 19, R, 1959)

3083   A white cat brings good luck.
(F, 20, 1958)

3084   If a white cat crosses your path, you will have good luck.
(F, 50, R, 1957, + 1 M)

3085   If a yellow cat crosses your path, you will get some money
soon.
(F, 24, R, 1955)

3086   If a stray white cat comes to your house to live, you will have
good luck.
(F, 60, R, 1958)

3087   Never move a cat; it brings bad luck.
(M, 60, R, 1959 [his parents], + 1 M)

3088   When moving to a new house, it is bad luck to move a cat.
(F, 50, R, 1960 [her mother])

3089   Taking a cat with you when you move will bring bad luck.
(F, 30, 1956)

3090   Never move a cat or an old broom to a new place, or you will
have bad luck.
(F, 78, 1960 [her friends])

3091   Never let a cat follow you into your house; let it go in first, or
you will have bad luck.
(F, 60, R, 1958)

3092   It is bad luck to kill a cat.
(M, 50, R, 1958, + 2 F and 2 M)

3093   It is bad luck to kill a cat in a cruel manner.
(M, 50, R, 1957)

3094   If you kill a cat, you will have seven years of bad luck.
(F, 30, 1960 [her grandmother], + 5 F and 2 M)

3095   Killing a cat that is two years old will mean seven years of
bad luck for you, since a cat has nine lives.
(F, 76, 1957)

3096   Never burn a dead cat.
         (F, 49, R, 1959, + 1 F)

3097   Never burn a dead cat, for if you do, you will have bad luck
         for nine years.
         (M, 73, R, 1957)

3098   It is bad luck not to bury a dead cat.
         (F, 50, R, 1958)

3099   Never let a cat in where there is a dead body, as this surely
         will bring bad luck.
         (F, 72, R, 1958)

3100   If a calico cat comes to your door, it is bad luck.
         (M, 74, 1959)

3101   If a meowing cat follows you at night, you will have bad luck
         before morning.
         (M, 50, R, 1957)

3102   It is bad luck for a cat to cross your path.
         (F, 50, R, 1958 [her parents])

BLACK CATS

3103   A black cat brings good luck to his owner.
         (F, 30, 1958)

3104   If a black cat comes to your home, it will bring you good luck.
         (F, 47, R, 1956)

3105   It is good luck for someone to give you a black cat.
         (M, 30, R, 1962, + 1 F)

3106   A stray black cat that comes to stay at your house will bring
         good luck.
         (F, 35, 1956)

3107   If a black cat comes towards you, it is good luck.
         (F, 45, R, 1957)

3108   Good luck is yours if a black cat comes near you.
         (F, 60, R, 1957)

3109   If a black cat catches a white mouse, it is good luck.
         (M, 74, 1959)

3110   If you can hold a black cat in your arms while on a trip, it will
         make your trip a success.
         (F, 1959 [heard from an Englishwoman])

3111   Black cats mean good luck in Scotland.
         (F, 50, 1957)

3112   In England, a black cat is good luck.
        (M, 76, R, 1959)

3113   If a black cat has any white markings, it is not bad luck.
        (F, 50, R, 1958)

3114   When a black cat crosses your path going left, it brings good luck.
        (F, 90, 1961 [her mother])

3115   If a black cat crosses the path in front of you, turn back home for luck.
        (F, 1960)

3116   Giving a black cat for Christmas is bad luck.
        (F, 1960)

3117   It is bad luck to kill a black cat.
        (F, 50, R, 1958)

3118   It is bad luck to stroke a black cat.
        (F, 58, R, 1958)

3119   Black cats bring bad luck.
        (F, 19, R, 1962, + 2 F and 1 M)

3120   Don't let a black cat cross your path.
        (F, 40, R, 1959 [her father], + 3 F and 2 M)

3121   If a black cat crosses your path, you will have an accident.
        (F, 75, R, 1956)

3122   If a sign of bad luck has happened—for example, if a black cat has crossed your path—you can break the bad luck by turning around three times.
        (F, 50, R, 1960)

3123   A black cat crossing your path is a sign of bad luck.
        (M, 17, 1959 [his grandparents], + 110 F and 39 M)

3124   If a black cat walks across your path, you'll have bad luck all day.
        (F, 40, R, 1959 [her father], + 2 F and 1 M)

3125   Don't cross a black cat's path, or you will have bad luck.
        (M, 22, 1958, + 1 F and 2 M)

3126   Not only a black cat, but any cat crossing in front of you, means bad luck.
        (M, 60, R, 1959)

3127   If a black cat crosses your path, turn around and go the other way.
        (F, 20, 1957, + 5 F and 1 M)

3128   If a black cat crosses your path, it will cause bad luck unless you turn around and go away from it.
        (M, 17, R, 1960 [his father], + 3 F)

3129   If a black cat crosses your path, turn around and walk backwards twenty steps.
(F, 70, R, 1961)

3130   If a black cat crosses your path, it will bring bad luck unless you turn around and walk across his path backwards.
(F, 20, R, 1960)

3131   In the past, a man would go home and start on his travels again if a black cat crossed his path before he reached his destination.
(M, 90, 1960)

3132   If a black cat crosses your path, you'll have bad luck. But if you back up and take another route, not crossing the path of the cat, this will keep you from having bad luck.
(M, 18, R, 1963 [his aunt])

3133   If you cross your fingers while a black cat is crossing your path, this will prevent bad luck.
(F, 50, R, 1958 [her aunt])

3134   To take away the bad luck when a black cat crosses your path, stop, and split a weed.
(M, 47, 1958)

3135   If a black cat crosses your path, you will have bad luck unless you toss your hat over your shoulder.
(F, 1960)

3136   "See a black cat; / Spit in your hat."
(F, 50, 1958 [her mother])

3137   If a black cat crosses your path, spit in your hat or hand before the cat gets out of sight.
(M, 80, R, 1958 [his father])

3138   If a black cat crosses the road going to your right, you are all right. But if it crosses to your left, it is bad luck.
(M, 53, R, 1959 [his grandfather])

3139   If a black cat crosses your path, it brings bad luck; you can of course avoid this by turning around and going in the other direction, which might bring you the bad luck that you are trying to avoid—for instance, an argument with the traffic cop.
(M, 10, 1958)

3140   Beware if a black cat crosses the route you intend to take. You'd better change your course.
(F, 55, 1959)

3141   If a black cat crosses your path, turn in another direction; otherwise, bad luck will come to you.
(M, 74, 1958)

3142   Don't let a black cat cross your path, or you will have seven
        years of bad luck.
        (F, 70, R, 1959)

3143   If a black cat walks across your path, go nine steps back, and
        spit over your left shoulder to prevent bad luck.
        (F, 50, 1958)

3144   If you turn around three times after a black cat crosses your
        path, you will break the bad-luck spell.
        (F, 34, 1958)

3145   If a black cat crosses your path while you are in your car,
        drive around the block to get rid of the spell. If you don't,
        you'll have bad luck.
        (F, 30, R, 1959 [her mother])

3146   If a black cat crosses your path, do not proceed, or bad luck
        will follow.
        (F, 62, 1957)

3147   If a black cat crosses your path, don't go on—it will bring you
        bad luck.
        (F, 40, R, 1962 [her grandmother], + 1 F)

3148   A black cat crossing the road in front of you means bad luck.
        Black cats are associated with witches; therefore they are
        bad luck.
        (F, 21, 1957)

3149   If a black cat crosses your path, you will have bad luck unless
        you turn around and go back.
        (F, 40, R, 1960 [her parents])

3150   If a black cat crosses your path, turn back.
        (F, 70, R, 1962 [her mother])

CHRISTMAS AND NEW YEAR'S

3151   To ensure yourself of a prosperous forthcoming year, don't
        take down your Christmas tree before New Year's Day.
        (F, 72, R, 1958)

3152   Put mistletoe on Christmas packages; this will bring you good
        luck.
        (F, 40, R, 1961 [her parents])

3153   It is a good omen when a spider crawls on a Christmas tree
        and spins a web on Christmas day.
        (F, 19, R, 1959)

3154   Take the Christmas tree down twelve days after Christmas.
(F, 50, R, 1963)

3155   If you hold money in your hand on New Year's Eve till the old year goes out, you'll have money all year.
(F, 50, R, 1958)

3156   To ensure having money in your pocket for the coming year, always place a coin under your plate at the table on New Year's Eve.
(F, 52, R, 1958)

3157   Eat black-eyed peas on New Year's Day so that your year will be prosperous.
(F, 20, 1963 [her father], + 3 F and 2 M)

3158   Drinking sauerkraut juice on New Year's Day will bring you money the following year.
(F, 50, R, 1963)

3159   It is a German tradition to eat fresh pork and sauerkraut on New Year's Day in order to have a prosperous forthcoming year.
(F, 75, R, 1958)

3160   Put your purse out on New Year's, and you'll have money coming in all year.
(F, 60, R, 1959 [her parents])

3161   When the New Year comes in, always let a man enter your house first; this will ensure you of prosperity for the coming year.
(F, 1957)

3162   When returning home on New Year's Eve, the man must cross the threshold first in order for a couple to have good luck in the New Year.
(F, 50, R, 1958)

3163   One contributor reported that her sister always makes a new pair of pillowslips on New Year's Day to bring good luck for the coming year.
(F, 1960)

3164   If you stay up to watch the sun come up on New Year's Day, it will start the year off right.
(F, 21, 1950)

3165   The eating of goose eggs on New Year's Day will bring health and wealth.
(F, 50, 1961)

3166   On each New Year's day you should be extra careful, as any bad luck occurring on that day will keep recurring through-out the year.

(F, 62, R, 1959)

3167 Never throw out anything on New Year's, or you will throw away your luck.

(M, 60, R, 1959 [his parents])

3168 Don't sweep the floor on New Year's, because you'll sweep out your luck for the year.

(M, 60, R, 1959 [his parents])

3169 Thoroughly clean your house before the New Year, or bad luck will come to you.

(F, 50, R, 1959)

3170 You are supposed to burn Christmas mistletoe on Twelfth-night (January 6); otherwise the goblins and elves will come and play in your house.

(F, 40, R, 1961 [her parents])

3171 It is bad luck to cut your fingernails or your hair from Christmas till January the sixth, and any dreams that you have during these twelve nights will come true.

(F, 50, R, 1961)

3172 Take your Christmas tree down before New Year's Day, or you will have bad luck.

(F, 40, R, 1963)

3173 To avoid bad luck, the oldest daughter of the household should burn the Christmas tree by New Year's Day.

(F, 35, 1956)

CLOTHING AND JEWELRY

3174 If you wear your clothes wrong side out, you will have good luck.

(F, 19, 1955, + 3 F)

3175 If you put your shoes and socks on before you put your pants on, you will have good luck.

(M, 20, R, 1963)

3176 If the hem of your dress is turned up, and you leave it up, it's good luck.

(F, 20, R, 1960, + 1 F)

3177 If your dress tail is turned up, kiss it, turn around three times, and then put it down. This will bring good luck.

(F, 30, R, 1960, + 2 F and 1 M)

3178   Spitting on new shoes will bring luck.
(M, 50, R, 1958, + 1 F and 1 M)

3179   If you accidentally put your underwear on wrong side out, and then you change it around, you will have bad luck all day long.
(F, 26, R, 1957, + 3 F)

3180   One woman contributed this rhyme: "I don't know how it came about; / I put my vest on wrong side out. / I could not change it back all day; / For that would drive my luck away."
(F, 1960)

3181   If you happen to put some article of clothing on backwards or wrong side out, you should not change it; for if you do so, you will have bad luck.
(F, 20, R, 1957, + 41 F and 10 M)

3182   If you put your clothes on wrong side out, spit on them before you put them on again, in order to ward off bad luck.
(F, 19, 1956, + 5 F and 1 M)

3183   It is bad luck to put the left shoe on before the right one.
(F, 60, R, 1958, + 1 F and 1 M)

3184   If you walk across the floor with one shoe off and one shoe on, you will have bad luck.
(F, 20, R, 1963, + 5 F and 2 M)

3185   If a person puts his new shoes on the table, he will have bad luck.
(F, 20, 1964, + 1 F and 3 M)

3186   If you break a shoestring in the morning, you will have bad luck all day.
(F, 1961)

3187   Never wear a boot that has been bitten by a rattlesnake.
(M, 20, 1959)

3188   Giving gloves as a gift is bad luck.
(F, 70, R, 1963)

3189   It is bad luck to sew on a button or to mend your clothes while you are wearing them.
(F, 48, R, 1957, + 1 F)

3190   It is bad luck to wear the clothes of the dead.
(F, 1961)

3191   It is bad luck to let someone else try on your wedding ring.
(F, 40, R, 1957)

3192   Opals bring bad luck to the wearer.
(F, 44, R, 1957, + 3 F)

CROSSING FINGERS

3193   If you cross your fingers, you will have good luck.
(F, 18, 1955, + 5 F)

3194   Crossing the fingers of both hands is bad luck.
(F, 1961)

3195   If you cross two fingers of your right hand, you will have good luck.
(F, 1961)

3196   Cross your fingers for good luck in sports.
(F, 21, R, 1957)

3197   Always cross your fingers when taking off or landing in an airplane.
(M, 40, R, 1959 [his parents])

3198   Crossing the first two fingers of one hand will either bring good luck or avoid a jinx, but crossing the fingers on both hands is bad luck.
(F, 20, R, 1957, + 1 F)

3199   Crossing your fingers will prevent a threatened incident from happening.
(F, 60, 1959)

3200   If you think that something bad is about to happen, it will be avoided if you make a cross on your forehead or breast.
(F, 60, 1959)

DREAMS

3201   Dreaming about clear water is good luck.
(F, 1959)

3202   If you dream about climbing, that is an omen of good luck.
(M, 44, 1959)

3203   If you dream about something green such as money or grass, you will have good luck. But if you dream about silver, you will have bad luck.
(F, 1962)

3204   If you dream about dances, you'll have good luck.
(F, 74, 1955)

3205   Dreaming about babies will bring you good luck.
(F, 47, R, 1956)

3206   It is bad luck to dream about a newborn baby.
        (F, 70, 1961)

3207   Dreaming about a white horse will bring you good luck.
        (F, 47, R, 1956)

3208   It is bad luck to dream about a white horse.
        (F, 1962)

3209   Telling a dream before breakfast will bring bad luck.
        (F, 21, R, 1958, + 5 F)

3210   Dreaming about water means that bad luck is to come.
        (F, 40, 1957)

3211   If you dream about muddy water, you will surely have bad
        luck.
        (M, 57, R, 1956, + 4 F)

3212   If you dream that you are falling, that is an omen of bad luck.
        (M, 49, 1959)

3213   If you dream about money, you will have bad luck.
        (F, 70, R, 1957)

3214   Dreaming about a cat means that you will have bad luck.
        (F, 65, 1954)

3215   If you dream about snakes, you will have bad luck.
        (F, 45, 1956, + 1 F)

3216   It is bad luck to dream about teeth.
        (F, 70, 1961)

3217   If you dream about pulling teeth or getting stuck in a mud-
        hole, this is a sign that bad luck will follow.
        (F, 60, R, 1957)

FOUR-LEAF CLOVERS

3218   A three-leaf clover means luck; a four-leaf clover, better luck;
        a five-leaf clover, still better luck.
        (F, 30, R, 1957)

3219   A four-leaf clover is a sign of luck.
        (F, 19, R, 1962)

3220   Four-leaf clovers bring good luck to their possessors.
        (F, 21, R, 1957, + 7 F and 3 M)

3221   Finding a four-leaf clover in the grass will bring you good
        luck.
        (F, 20, R, 1959, + 29 F and 10 M)

3222   Pick a four-leaf clover for good luck.
        (F, 45, R, 1960)

3223   It's good luck to find and keep a four-leaf clover.
        (F, 21, 1950)

3224   A four-leaf clover, if you find one and pick it, will bring you
        luck.
        (F, 19, 1958)

3225   Four-leaf clovers and rabbit's feet bring good luck.
        (F, 40, R, 1959)

3226   A four-leaf clover carried in your pocketbook will bring you
        good luck.
        (F, 35, 1956)

3227   Don't step over a four-leaf clover, or you will have bad luck.
        (F, 80, 1958)

3228   Carry a four-leaf clover found by a friend for good luck.
        (F, 20, R, 1957)

3229   If you find a four-leaf clover, put it in your shoe for good luck.
        (F, 40, 1960 [her mother], + 1 F)

3230   Carrying a four-leaf clover brings good luck.
        (M, 26, R, 1957, + 2 F)

3231   If you don't pick a four-leaf clover, you will have bad luck. If
        you do pick a five-leaf clover, you will have bad luck.
        (F, 20, R, 1959 [her mother])

3232   Finding a four-leaf clover means good luck. Finding a five-leaf
        clover means bad luck.
        (F, 35, 1956)

3233   A four-leaf clover brings good luck, but a five-leaf one brings
        bad.
        (F, 1960)

3234   If you pick a five-leaf clover, mistaking it for a four-leaf
        clover, you will have bad luck.
        (F, 21, 1951 [her grandmother])

3235   It's bad luck to find a five-leaf clover.
        (F, 20, 1958, + 1 F)

3236   Finding a five-leaf clover will bring you bad luck unless you
        give it to someone else. It will then be lucky for both of you.
        (F, 60, 1959)

FRIDAYS, SATURDAYS, AND SUNDAYS

3237   Friday is an unlucky day.
        (F, 21, 1957, + 2 F)

3238   Fridays are unlucky, as are days numbered thirteen.
        (M, 40, 1963)

3239   It's bad luck to sneeze on Friday.
          (F, 54, 1959)
3240   Never start a job on Friday, as it's bad luck. (The informant's uncle used to take a machine to the field on Thursday evening, or he would wait until Saturday.)
          (M, 50, R, 1963, + 3 F and 2 M)
3241   Never start anything new on Friday; it brings bad luck.
          (F, 19, R, 1956, + 4 F and 4 M)
3242   If you start something on Friday that you can't finish, you will have bad luck.
          (M, 50, R, 1963, + 5 F and 5 M)
3243   It is bad luck to move from one house to another on Friday.
          (F, 40, 1958, + 2 F)
3244   It is bad luck to start a trip on Friday.
          (F, 35, 1956, + 7 F and 2 M)
3245   It is bad luck to cut one's toenails on Friday.
          (F, 1955)
3246   Bad luck will come to you if you work on Good Friday.
          (F, 70, 1963)
3247   A child born on a Saturday will have bad luck.
          (F, 60, R, 1959)
3248   It used to be thought that you would have bad luck if you were weaned on Sunday.
          (F, 20, R, 1962)
3249   To work on Sunday brings bad luck.
          (F, 56, R, 1963, + 1 F)
3250   Don't do unnecessary work on Sunday, or you'll have bad luck until Monday.
          (F, 20, R, 1960)
3251   Never sew on Sunday; it brings bad luck.
          (F, 21, R, 1959, + 2 F)
3252   It is bad luck to fish or hunt on Sunday.
          (F, 50, R, 1958)
3253   Never go any place on the first Sunday after you move into a new home.
          (F, 50, 1963)
3254   Never set a hen on Sunday, or it will bring bad luck.
          (F, 40, R, 1963)
3255   It's bad luck to cut your fingernails on Sunday. Always cut them on Friday.
          (F, 42, R, 1958, + 4 F and 1 M)

FUNERALS AND THE DEAD

3256   When passing a cemetery, if you will lick your right thumb, then touch it on something blue, then touch it on your left palm, and then hit the spot that you just touched in your left palm, you will have good luck.
(F, 21, R, 1961, + 1 F)

3257   If it rains in an open grave, good luck will come to the bereaved family.
(F, 55, R, 1958 [one of her friends])

3258   Never say that a funeral is pretty, as it is bad luck to do so.
(F, 1962)

3259   If you ever hear someone call you and you know that he is dead, don't answer. It's bad luck.
(F, 1962)

3260   It is bad luck for a woman who has been a widow for two years not to remove her wedding ring.
(F, 1962)

3261   If you see a cross of light through a widow's mourning veil, it is a sign of bad luck.
(F, 55, 1957)

3262   If a pregnant woman views a corpse, she will have bad luck.
(F, 80, 1955)

3263   It is bad luck to take a picture of a casket.
(F, 26, 1959 [her mother])

3264   Never sleep with your head to the west, as that's the way the dead are buried. It's bad luck.
(F, 37, R, 1961)

3265   It is bad luck not to start a funeral on time.
(F, 60, R, 1961)

3266   Never point at a hearse; it is bad luck. It is said that a loved one will soon die.
(F, 1962)

3267   It is bad luck to pass through a funeral procession.
(F, 70, R, 1960 [her parents])

3268   It is bad luck to count the cars in a funeral procession.
(F, 40, R, 1958 [her grandfather], + 6 F)

3269   It is bad luck to whistle in a graveyard.
(F, 1961)

3270   It is bad luck to walk on anyone's grave.
            (F, 60, R, 1960)
3271   It is bad luck to read the names on gravestones.
            (F, 1961)

HATS ON THE BED

3272   It is bad luck to put your hat on a bed.
            (F, 21, 1959, + 10 F and 6 M)
3273   An actor never puts his hat on a bed. It is a sign of bad luck.
            (F, 1962)
3274   A ballplayer never throws his hat on a bed before a ball
            game. It is considered to be a jinx.
            (F, 27, 1957)
3275   It is bad luck for a cowboy to lay his hat on a bed.
            (M, 30, 1972)
3276   If you put a hat on a bed, you will have no end of bad luck.
            There is no way that you can break your bad luck.
            (F, 60, 1957)
3277   A hat lying on a bed is considered very bad luck.
            (F, 23, 1959 [her grandmother])
3278   It is a sign of bad luck if, while visiting a star in her dressing
            room, you throw your hat on the bed.
            (F, 50, R, 1960 [her father])
3279   Bad luck will come if there are three hats on a bed at the
            same time.
            (F, 21, 1950)
3280   Never lay a hat on a bed with the brim down, or its owner will
            have bad luck.
            (F, 35, 1958)

HORSESHOES

3281   Horseshoes are a sign of luck.
            (F, 19, R, 1962, + 3 F and 3M)
3282   Keep a horseshoe outside any building for good luck.
            (M, 50, R, 1959)
3283   If you hang a horseshoe over a gate, you will have good luck
            when you walk through that gate.
            (F, 60, R, 1961)

3284   Hang a horseshoe on your door or in your room for good luck.
        (M, 19, 1958)

3285   Nail a horseshoe over the door for good luck.
        (F, 18, 1956, + 18 F and 10 M)

3286   If you nail a horseshoe over the door with its ends down, everyone who passes through the door will have good luck. If the ends are up, the luck gathers at the bottom and falls on only one person.
        (M, 70, R, 1956)

3287   A horseshoe nailed with the opening up brings good luck.
        (F, 19, R, 1959)

3288   A horseshoe hung with both ends up brings good luck; with the ends down, all the luck runs out.
        (F, 35, 1956, + 4 F and 3 M)

3289   Finding a horseshoe with the open space toward you means that your troubles are over.
        (F, 1955, + 1 M)

3290   Finding an old horseshoe will bring good luck.
        (F, 18, 1955, + 6 F and 4 M)

3291   If you find a horseshoe, the number of nails in the horseshoe will indicate the number of years of good luck you will have; the spaces will indicate the number of years of bad luck.
        (F, 18, 1955, + 1 M)

3292   To ensure good luck, or to shatter bad luck, throw a horseshoe over your left shoulder when the moon is full.
        (F, 1961)

3293   If you find a horseshoe, spit on it, and throw it over your right
       shoulder. This will bring good luck.
           (M, 40, 1957)

3294   Spit on a horseshoe, and throw it over your shoulder; this will
       bring good luck.
           (M, 22, 1961, + 1 F and 2 M)

3295   If you find a horseshoe, pick it up with your right hand, and
       throw it over your left shoulder for good luck.
           (M, 25, R, 1959)

3296   Toss a horseshoe over your left shoulder, and it will bring you
       good luck.
           (M, 20, 1959, + 4 F and 2 M)

3297   Hang a horseshoe over the barn to keep bad spirits away
       from the animals.
           (F, 21, R, 1963)

3298   A horseshoe nailed over a door keeps away evil spirits.
           (F, 19, 1959 [her father], + 1 F)

3299   It is bad luck to hang a horseshoe with the points down over a
       door; your luck will all run out.
           (F, 21, 1950)

3300   All the luck runs out of a horseshoe if it is hung upside down.
           (F, 1961)

3301   Don't pick up a horseshoe unless it is facing you, or you will
       have bad luck.
           (F, 60, 1961 [her mother])

3302   It is bad luck to lose a horseshoe.
           (M, 50, R, 1958)

HOUSEHOLD ITEMS

3303   Get up on the right side of the bed for luck.
           (F, 1961)

3304   If you get out of bed on the wrong side, you will have bad luck
       for the rest of the day.
           (F, 18, 1955, + 2 F and 1 M)

3305   It is a sign of good luck for the coming day if all the bowls are
       cleaned up at supper time.
           (F, 70, R, 1961)

3306   Bubbles in a coffee cup mean money or good luck.
           (F, 1959)

3307   If you have a ring on your coffee in the cup, it means that you will have good fortune, usually meaning money.
        (F, 68, R, 1958)

3308   People used to think that if tea leaves floated in your cup, you would have good luck.
        (M, 44, 1959)

3309   A broom and a piece of bacon should be taken into one's new house and left overnight for good luck.
        (F, 50, R, 1957)

3310   When you move into a new house or apartment, have a housewarming party to ensure good luck.
        (F, 23, 1957)

3311   If you burn eight fresh bread crusts, you will wind up in the poorhouse.
        (F, 70, R, 1961)

3312   It's bad luck to burn bread in a trash fire.
        (F, 44, 1960)

3313   Good luck will come if you can blow out all the candles on your birthday cake with one breath.
        (F, 1961)

3314   "A bayberry candle, / Burned to the socket, / Brings joy to the heart / And wealth to the pocket."
        (F, 1961)

3315   It is bad luck to burn sassafras in the house.
        (M, 90, 1958, + 1 F)

3316   If you find a needle that has white thread in it, you will have good luck.
        (F, 50, R, 1957)

3317   If you find a needle with black thread in it, you will have bad luck.
        (F, 50, R, 1957)

3318   It's bad luck to start sewing on Friday.
        (F, 50, R, 1958)

3319   Never sit on a table, because this brings bad luck.
        (M, 21, 1956, + 2 F)

3320   Singing at the table brings bad luck.
        (F, 40, R, 1962, + 7 F)

3321   To tip over a chair is bad luck.
        (M, 1961)

3322   Twirling a chair on one leg is an omen of bad luck.
        (F, 49, R, 1956, + 3 F)

3323   If you rock a rocking chair when no one is sitting in it, it will bring bad luck.
(F, 20, R, 1958, + 13 F and 4 M)

3324   Always stir batter in the same direction, or you will have bad luck.
(F, 40, R, 1957, + 3 F)

3325   If you eat the tip of a piece of pie, it will bring good luck.
(F, 21, R, 1959, + 3 F)

3326   It is bad luck for two people to use the same dish towel at the same time.
(F, 20, R, 1956, + 3 F)

3327   Never hang anything on a doorknob, or something will happen that will be bad luck.
(F, 30, 1960, + 3 F)

3328   Whistling in the house is bad luck.
(F, 60, 1963)

3329   It is considered bad luck to whistle in your bedroom.
(F, 23, 1959, + 1 F)

3330   You will have bad luck if you sing in bed.
(F, 19, R, 1959, + 3 F)

3331   If you sing before breakfast, you'll have bad luck.
(F, 20, 1955, + 8 F and 3 M)

3332   If you get out of bed on the same side that you got in, you will have bad luck.
(F, 18, 1955, + 2 F)

3333   It is bad luck to get out on the left side of the bed.
(F, 19, 1956, + 2 F and 1 M)

3334   Combing one's hair after dark will comb sorrow into your heart.
(F, 50, R, 1961, + 4 F and 1 M)

3335   Dropping a comb while combing your hair will bring bad luck.
(F, 56, 1954, + 2 F)

3336   If you step on a dropped comb, you will have bad luck.
(F, 21, 1950)

3337   If you drop a comb, it will bring bad luck unless you step on it.
(F, 60, R, 1961, + 1 F)

3338   It is bad luck to shake a tablecloth after sundown.
(F, 20, 1961, + 7 F)

3339   Don't carry a hoe or ax through the house. It's bad luck.
(M, 20, 1957, + 28 F and 6 M)

3340   It is unlucky to carry a hoe, rake, or any other gardening tool into a house. If you do so, you must carry it back out the same way.

(F, 48, R, 1958, + 1 F and 1 M)

3341   Breaking a sugar bowl is bad luck.

(M, 67, 1959)

3342   Never return a dish empty; this brings bad luck.

(F, 28, 1956)

3343   Sleeping at the foot of the bed brings bad luck to one's family.

(F, 45, 1958)

3344   If a picture falls from the wall, there will be bad luck.

(M, 30, 1960)

3345   It is bad luck to put the head of the bed to the north.

(M, 80, 1958)

3346   To give a person your handkerchief is bad luck.

(F, 50, R, 1958)

3347   For good luck, throw an egg over the house backwards. The person on the other side of the house has to catch the egg without letting it break.

(F, 1961)

3348   If you drop a piece of silverware, let someone else pick it up so that you won't have bad luck.

(F, 60, R, 1959)

3349   It is bad luck to burn the wood of a fruit tree.

(F, 1962)

3350   It is bad luck for two people to break bread from the same loaf at the same time.

(F, 50, R, 1958)

3351   It's bad luck for two people to make a bed.

(F, 1961)

3352   If you look out into the yard from the house and think you see a white object that isn't there, you will have bad luck.

(F, 40, R, 1962)

3353   It is bad luck to hand a person something that is pointed, such as scissors, knives, ice picks, and so forth.

(F, 50, R, 1958, + 2 F)

3354   If you find a pair of scissors and pick them up, it's bad luck.

(F, 70, R, 1962 [her father])

3355   If scissors stick in the ground when you drop them, you'll have good fortune.

(F, 50, R, 1958)

3356   It's bad luck to give scissors or a knife unless the receiver gives you a penny in return.

(F, 40, R, 1961)

3357   To give a knife as a gift is bad luck.
         (M, 50, R, 1958)
3358   Never take a knife with its blade open, for this brings bad luck.
         (M, 20, R, 1956)
3359   If you close a knife that someone else has opened, it will bring you bad luck.
         (F, 13, R, 1959)

GOING IN AND OUT OF HOUSES

3360   Always start off on a walk, and so forth, with your right foot in order to be "going right" all day long.
         (F, 20, 1961 [her friends])
3361   Never go back to get something that you have forgotten, or you will have bad luck.
         (M, 21, R, 1961, + 12 F and 2 M)
3362   If you return to the house after forgetting something, sit down for luck.
         (F, 53, 1955)
3363   If you forget something and go back into a house for it, sit down for a while, or you will have bad luck.
         (F, 20, R, 1956, + 17 F and 3 M)
3364   When leaving home, if you forget something and have to return for it, you'll have bad luck if you don't sit down on a chair before you leave. (The contributor's grandfather used to say that you should spit three times before you leave.)
         (F, 54, R, 1960)
3365   For good luck, always go back and sit down in a chair before you leave someone.
         (F, 59, R, 1957)
3366   If you forget something and have to go back to the house to get it, you must sit down for a minute as soon as you go in.
         (F, 50, R, 1958)
3367   If you forget something and go back after it, sit down, and count one, two, three before going on.
         (F, 60, 1969)
3368   If you leave home and you forget something, return home to get the article; then sit on the front steps, and count to three.
         (F, 21, 1957)
3369   If something is forgotten when you start out from home and

you return for it, you should sit down and count to five before starting out again. This will ward off bad luck.

(F, 50, 1959)

3370   If you return to the house after starting on a trip, you will have bad luck unless you sit down for five minutes.

(M, 70, R, 1956)

3371   If you start to go someplace and have to return, you must then sit down and count to ten. Then make a cross on the floor, and spit on it. If you do this, you can be sure of good luck when you start out again.

(F, 42, R, 1936)

3372   Bidding a person good luck before he leaves on a trip foretokens disaster.

(M, 24, 1959)

3373   If, while you are packing your bags for a trip, you have already locked them before you discover that you have left out something, do not open them. If you do, you will have bad luck.

(F, 1962)

3374   If you get two or three miles from home and have to turn back for something that you forgot, you will have bad luck.

(F, 27, 1959, + 6 F and 2 M)

3375   It is bad luck to knock on your own door.

(M, 22, 1958, + 1 F)

3376   If you are going on a trip and you forget something and go back for it, you must sit on a chair for three minutes before starting out again.

(F, 19, 1960)

3377   If you leave the house and have to return, count to eleven before leaving again.

(F, 61, R, 1957)

3378   Never enter a house on your left foot. This is considered to bring bad luck.

(F, 1962)

3379   It's bad luck to leave by the same door that you entered.

(F, 70, 1957)

3380   It is bad luck for a visitor to go out a different door from the one that he came in.

(F, 20, R, 1956, + 16 F and 10 M)

3381   If you leave through one door to fetch a pail of water, you must then return through the same door; otherwise you will have bad luck.

(F, 1962)

3382   It is bad luck to go into a house and then leave again without first sitting down. (The informant recalled that her mother always saw to it that all members of the family observed the practice of "sitting down" to avoid bad luck.)
(F, 90, 1963)

KNOCKING ON WOOD

3383   Knock on wood for good luck.
(F, 18, 1956, + 3 F and 2 M)

3384   Knock on wood to prevent a change of luck.
(F, 19, 1959)

3385   A person should knock on wood after making an optimistic statement to make sure that he has good luck and that his remark will come true.
(F, 21, R, 1958)

3386   If something happens to a person that hasn't happened to him before, he should knock on wood for luck.
(M, 26, R, 1958)

3387   Knock on wood to ensure that what you say will or will not happen.
(F, 23, 1957)

3388   A person mentioning a misfortune that has never happened to him should touch or knock on wood to prevent the mere mentioning of the misfortune from bringing it on.
(F, 19, 1959)

3389   Knock on wood so that something you are saying won't come true.
(M, 20, R, 1959)

3390   Knock on wood to prevent bad luck.
(F, 20, R, 1959, + 3 F and 1 M)

3391   After commenting on good fortune, knock on wood three times in order to prevent bad luck.
(F, 28, 1956)

3392   If you speak of some good fortune that has come your way, be sure to knock on wood so as to avoid breaking it.
(F, 54, 1959)

3393   Knock on wood after making a bragging statement, or it will never come true.
(F, 20, 1950)

3394   After boasting, knock on wood to keep from having bad luck.
(F, 20, 1950)

3395   If you brag, knock on wood to prevent a disaster.
(F, 20, R, 1956, + 2 F)

3396   After you make a bragging statement, knock on wood to prevent reverses.
(F, 44, R, 1957, + 2 F)

3397   Knocking on wood will keep away bad luck, because spirits live in trees.
(M, 50, R, 1957)

LADDERS

3398   It brings bad luck to walk under a ladder.
(F, 18, 1956, + 109 F and 37 M)

3399   Walking under a ladder that has a rung missing will bring good luck.
(M, 20, 1957)

3400   It is very unlucky to pass under an upright ladder.
(F, 75, 1959)

3401   Don't walk under a ladder.
(M, 20, R, 1958, + 7 F and 3 M)

MIRRORS

3402   It is unlucky to break a mirror.
(M, 20, R, 1958, + 4 F and 3 M)

3403   You will have seven years of bad luck if you break a mirror.
(F, 18, 1956, + 125 F and 39 M)

3404   If you break a mirror, you'll have seven years of bad luck or a death in the family.
(F, 60, R, 1961, + 1 M)

3405   It is bad luck to break a mirror, unless you break it on a Thursday; then it is good luck.
(F, 1962)

3406   If you break a mirror, in seven years you'll be rich.
(F, 48, 1958)

3407   "Break a mirror, large or small, / Seven years bad luck for all."
(M, 55, R, 1957)

3408   Breaking a mirror will bring seven weeks of bad luck.
   (F, 60, R, 1963)

3409   If you break a mirror, you'll have seven years of bad luck; but
  if you count all the pieces, you will take away the bad luck.
   (F, 49, R, 1959)

3410   If someone looks over your shoulder while you are looking in a
  mirror, it will bring bad luck to you.
   (M, 70, 1956)

MONEY

3411   It is considered good luck to carry a pocketful of coins.
   (F, 23, 1959 [her grandmother], + 1 M)

3412   If you find a penny, you will have good luck all day.
   (M, 26, 1955, + 1 F)

3413   If you find a penny, keep it; it will bring good luck to you.
   (F, 20, R, 1957, + 2 F)

3414   A penny in the shoe brings good luck.
   (F, 21, R, 1958, + 7 F and 2 M)

3415   Put a penny in your right shoe for good luck.
   (F, 21, 1950)

3416   "Find a penny; pick it up; / All day you'll have good luck."
   (F, 19, R, 1959, + 14 F and 4 M)

3417   Put a penny in a billfold before giving it as a present so that
  the person who receives it will not be unlucky.
   (F, 21, R, 1957, + 5 F)

3418   Keep a lucky penny in your pocketbook, and you'll always
  have money.
   (F, 35, 1956)

3419   Carry a silver dollar, and you'll have good luck.
   (F, 23, 1957, + 2 M)

3420   A silver dollar, kept as a cherished pocket piece, will bring
  you wealth, health, and friends galore.
   (M, 80, R, 1958)

3421   A good many farmers carry a silver dollar; they wouldn't be
  caught without one.
   (M, 20, R, 1963)

3422   Silver in one's pocket brings luck.
   (F, 1961)

3423   Silver coins bring good luck.
   (F, 62, R, 1959)

3424 A dollar in your shoe will bring good luck.
       (F, 22, 1954)

3425 If you save a coin that you have found, it will bring you good
       luck.
       (F, 20, 1959, + 1 M)

3426 It is a good-luck sign to find money.
       (M, 50, R, 1958)

3427 If you find money and then give it away, you'll have good luck.
       (F, 59, R, 1957, + 1 M)

3428 If you drop a piece of silver while you are eating, you will lose
       your day's wages.
       (F, 55, 1959)

3429 It is bad luck to throw a half-dollar on a bed.
       (F, 1963)

3430 Never put a two-dollar bill in your cash register.
       (M, 19, 1958)

3431 A two-dollar bill brings good luck.
       (M, 22, R, 1963, + 1 M)

3432 Carrying a two-dollar bill brings bad luck.
       (M, 22, 1958, + 4 F and 1 M)

3433 It is bad luck to carry a two-dollar bill unless you tear one
       corner off of it.
       (F, 30, 1958, + 4 F and 2 M)

3434 Money that a person gets by cheating will bring him bad luck.
       (M, 1961)

3435 If you find a coin, you should never spend it; if you do, you will
       have bad luck.
       (M, 38, R, 1958)

3436 When you find money, you must give it to the first person you
       see; otherwise you will have bad luck.
       (F, 60, 1961)

3437 Never give something sharp to anyone without giving him a
       penny, or he will cut your luck.
       (F, 21, 1955, + 2 F and 3 M)

THE MOON AND THE STARS

3438 If you turn your money over in your pocket when you see a
       new moon, you will double your total assets.
       (M, 1961)

3439　Look over your right shoulder at the new moon, shake the money in your pocket, and you will have good luck.
(F, 67, R, 1962 [her father])

3440　In order to have good luck, one must look at the moon over one's left shoulder and turn the silver in one's pocket.
(M, 40, 1958)

3441　Seeing a new moon over one's right shoulder is good luck.
(F, 35, 1956, + 6 F and 6 M)

3442　It is a sign of good luck if the moon draws a rainbow to it.
(F, 60, 1961)

3443　If you look at a new moon over your left shoulder, you will have good luck.
(F, 23, 1957, + 10 F)

3444　If you look at a full moon over your left shoulder, you will have good luck.
(M, 15, R, 1958, + 1 F)

3445　If you first see the new moon over your right shoulder, you will have bad luck; if over your left shoulder, good luck; if straight ahead, six weeks of hard labor. (The left side is lucky because that is the side the heart is in.)
(F, 68, R, 1962)

3446　To see the new moon over your right shoulder is bad luck.
(F, 50, R, 1960 [her parents])

3447　It is bad luck to look over your left shoulder at the moon.
(F, 17, R, 1963 [her mother], + 15 F and 5 M)

3448　If the moon shines over your left shoulder, it means bad luck.
(F, 60, 1959)

3449　A new moon in the old moon's arms is a bad sign.
(F, 1961)

3450　If you see the new moon through a tree limb or through a window, you will have bad luck.
(F, 72, R, 1962 [her mother])

3451　It is bad luck to look at the moon through the branches of a tree.
(F, 23, R, 1958, + 1 F)

3452　During the First World War, it was considered a bad sign if one saw a cross in the moon.
(F, 60, R, 1962)

3453　Don't look at the moon through a glass.
(F, 21, 1956, + 1 F and 1 M)

3454　It is bad luck to point a finger at the moon.
(F, 82, R, 1957)

3455   It is bad luck to sleep with the moon shining on you.
        (F, 21, 1960)
3456   A ring around the moon means bad luck.
        (F, 21, R, 1957)
3457   People who are born in the dark of the moon have bad breaks
        during their lifetimes.
        (F, 80, 1955)
3458   It's unlucky to start on a trip in the dark of the moon.
        (F, 1959)
3459   Wishing on a falling star brings good luck.
        (F, 20, R, 1957, + 1 F)
3460   Shooting stars are lucky for lovers.
        (F, 23, 1956)
3461   It's bad luck to point at a star.
        (F, 21, 1950)
3462   Never point out a shooting star to anyone.
        (F, 53, 1963 [her mother])
3463   It's bad luck to see a falling star.
        (F, 22, 1958)
3464   If you talk about a star that is falling, you'll have bad luck.
        (F, 21, 1950)

                              PEOPLE

3465   Put a pulled tooth under your pillow for luck.
        (F, 1961)
3466   A vacancy caused by a pulled tooth should not be touched by
        the tongue. It is a promise of gold sometime during one's life.
        (M, 80, R, 1958)
3467   If you sneeze at the beginning of an argument, you will have
        good luck.
        (F, 18, 1955)
3468   Hold your thumbs up for luck.
        (M, 21, R, 1961)
3469   Stamp your right foot for good luck.
        (F, 1962)
3470   When a splinter is removed, rub it in your hair for good luck.
        (M, 50, R, 1957)
3471   "If your hand itches, scratch it on wood; / And all things will
        turn out good."
        (F, 45, R, 1958 [her father])

3472   It is good luck to rub the hump of a hunchback.
(M, 60, 1958)

3473   Rubbing his hand over a baldheaded man will aid a student in remembering what is needed in an examination.
(M, 1962)

3474   If the right side of your nose itches, you will have good luck; but if the left side of your nose itches, you will have bad luck.
(F, 21, R, 1956)

3475   If you meet a Chinaman, you'll have good luck.
(F, 21, 1956)

3476   To stumble going upstairs means that you will stumble to good luck.
(F, 50, R, 1958)

3477   A chimney cleaner brings good luck.
(F, 21, 1957)

3478   You will have bad luck if you watch somebody until he goes out of sight.
(F, 70, R, 1960 [her parents])

3479   If your initials spell a name, you will have good luck.
(F, 21, R, 1961)

3480   If a baby is baldheaded, he will always have good luck.
(F, 21, 1950)

3481   If a boy is born looking like his mother, he'll have good luck.
(F, 50, R, 1958)

3482   Being born with a caul is supposed to be lucky.
(F, 21, 1950)

3483   If a baby is born with placenta over his face, there will be good luck.
(F, 21, 1956)

3484   It is better luck for a baby to look like his father than like his mother.
(M, 50, 1958)

3485   The first-born in a family is the lucky one.
(F, 42, 1955)

3486   Kiss a newborn baby for good luck.
(F, 42, 1955)

3487   Good luck comes to a seventh child.
(F, 1961)

3488   A golden-haired child brings good luck to your home.
(F, 60, 1959)

3489   If you stub your toe on the sidewalk, kiss it to keep from having bad luck.
(F, 1961)

3490   When you stub your toe, you must kiss your thumb, or you will have bad luck.
        (M, 17, R, 1960, + 1 F)

3491   Sneezing is considered to be an omen almost everywhere. English people say "God bless you." Germans say "Gesundheit" ("your health").
        (F, 1959)

3492   If you sneeze, say "Bless me," or you will have bad luck.
        (F, 80, R, 1958)

3493   It is bad luck to step over a person who is lying on the floor.
        (M, 72, 1958, + 3 F)

3494   Don't compare your fingers with someone else's fingers; for doing this will bring bad luck.
        (M, 26, 1958)

3495   It's bad luck to stamp your left foot.
        (F, 1962)

3496   A cross-eyed person brings bad luck when he looks at you.
        (F, 21, 1950)

3497   Always turn back home when you meet a cross-eyed person, lest bad luck overtake you before you turn the next corner.
        (F, 60, R, 1961)

3498   Meeting with a hunchback brings bad luck.
        (F, 19, R, 1958)

3499   If you see a priest or a minister while you are going along the street, you must get home before he goes into your place, or you will have bad luck. In other words, if he enters the same door before you do, you will have bad luck.
        (F, 1963)

3500   Meeting someone on the stairs will bring you bad luck.
        (M, 70, 1956)

3501   If a person or a family is continually encountering accidents or misfortunes, never take either one into a partnership. If you do, the venture is fated to be a failure.
        (F, 60, 1959)

3502   Bad luck will come if a girl returns your wink.
        (F, 1961)

3503   If an old lady crosses your path, you should turn around, and go in the other direction. It is bad luck to continue going in the same direction.
        (F, 50, R, 1961 [her mother])

3504   When two people said the same thing at the same time, they used to count to ten as rapidly as possible, saying "You owe me a coke." In this way they would avoid bad luck.

(F, 20, 1963)

3505   If the first person to come into your place of business doesn't buy anything, you will have bad luck all day.

(M, 42, R, 1957)

3506   Always beware if you are around a redhead when she takes off her bonnet in the sunshine. Something frightful may happen.

(F, 20, R, 1961)

3507   If a red-headed woman comes into your place of business and you fail to get a hair from her head, you will have bad luck all day.

(M, 42, R, 1951)

3508   Never go into a coal mine after a woman has gone into it, or you will have bad luck.

(F, 50, R, 1957)

3509   It used to be that when men would depart on a trip for business and would meet a woman before entering their carriage, they would postpone their trip, because women were considered to be bad luck.

(F, 1961)

3510   If a man starts to go some place and a woman gets in his way, he will have bad luck.

(F, 50, R, 1957)

3511   It is bad luck to have a ship with a woman on board.

(M, 20, 1961, + 1 M)

3512   There will be bad luck if two or more persons in one family get married within a year.

(F, 70, R, 1962)

3513   If two couples are married at the same ceremony, bad luck will follow them.

(F, 80, R, 1962 [her mother])

3514   Double weddings are bad luck for the ones who get married last.

(F, 60, 1961 [her father])

3515   If you cut a baby's hair before he is a year old, something bad will happen to him.

(F, 50, R, 1960, + 1 F)

3516   It is a bad omen if a child doesn't cry at its baptism.

(M, 20, 1959)

3517   It is bad luck to kiss a baby.
       (F, 21, 1950)
3518   It is bad luck to change a baby's name.
       (F, 1961)
3519   It is bad luck to cut a baby's fingernails with scissors. You
       should bite them off.
       (F, 50, R, 1959)
3520   When little children put their arms above their heads while
       sleeping, the mother must put them down at once; for the
       children are calling down misfortunes upon themselves.
       (F, 50, R, 1959 [her parents])

PINS

3521   It is good luck to find a pin.
       (M, 54, R, 1957)
3522   Pick up a pin for good luck.
       (F, 75, 1957)
3523   You will have good luck if you see a pin and pick it up.
       (F, 50, R, 1960)
3524   If you pick up a straight pin, you will have good luck.
       (F, 32, 1959 [her aunt], + 2 F and 1 M)
3525   To find a pin is good luck; also horseshoes and four-leaf
       clovers.
       (F, 1959)
3526   "See a pin, pick it up; / All the day you'll have good
       luck. / Heads, a miss; / Tails, a kiss."
       (M, 60, R, 1959)
3527   It brings luck to say: "Pin! Pin! Bring me luck because I
       stopped to pick you up."
       (F, 50, R, 1961)
3528   "Drop a pin, and pick it up. / All the day you'll have good
       luck."
       (F, 40, R, 1962)
3529   "See a pin, let it lie, / And everything will go awry."
       (M, 70, R, 1956)
3530   "See a pin and let it lay. / You'll have bad luck all that day."
       (M, 15, 1959 [his grandmother], + 7 F)
3531   "See a pin and pick it up, / All day you will have good luck."
       (F, 19, 1955, + 41 F and 2 M)
3532   "See a pin and pick it up, / All the day you'll have good

luck. / See a pin and let it lay, / Bad luck will follow all the
day."
    (F, 20, R, 1958 [her grandmother], + 22 F and 3 M)

3533   "You see a pin and pick it up, / All the day you'll have good
luck. / But see a pin and let it lie, / You'll come to want before
you die."
    (M, 57, R, 1956, + 1 F and 1 M)

3534   "Find a pin—pick it up, / All that day you'll have good
luck. / Find a pin, let it lay, / Have bad luck all that day."
    (F, 30, 1960, + 4 F and 1 M)

3535   "See a pin and pick it up, / The rest of the day you'll have
good luck. / See a pin and leave it lie, / The rest of the day
you'll have to cry."
    (F, 50, 1960, + 1 F)

3536   "If you see a pin and leave it lay, / You will have bad luck the
rest of the day. / If you see a pin and pick it up, / All day long
you will have good luck."
    (F, 50, R, 1958 [her mother], + 1 F)

3537   When you see a pin on the floor, if you pick it up, you will
have good luck; if you let it lay, you will have bad luck all day.
    (F, 20, 1959 [her grandmother])

3538   If you find a pin that is pointing toward you, you will have
good luck.
    (F, 18, 1958, + 6 F and 1 M)

3539   If you see a straight pin on the floor, you should walk around
to where the pin point is facing you and pick it up. This will
bring you good luck.
    (F, 30, 1959 [her parents])

3540   If you find a pin on the ground, pick it up if it is pointing
toward you; otherwise let it lie.
    (F, 60, R, 1958))

3541   It's bad luck to pick up a pin that's pointing toward you.
    (M, 30, R, 1958)

3542   If you see a pin, pick it up. If the point is toward you, you are
going to have good luck. If the head is pointing toward you,
you are going to take a trip.
    (F, 60, 1959 [her mother])

3543   Never pick up a pin that is pointing toward you.
    (M, 47, R, 1962 [his family])

3544   If you find a pin that is pointing toward you, you will have
good luck. If it points away, you will have bad luck. And if it is
broadside, you will have broad luck.
    (M, 50, R, 1957, + 1 F)

3545   A pin that is pointing toward you brings good luck; if its head is toward you, it will bring bad luck.
    (F, 40, R, 1961, + 1 F)

3546   If you find a pin whose point is pointing toward you, you will have good luck. If its head is toward you, you will have bad luck. If it is lying sideways, you will take a buggy ride.
    (F, 59, 1959, + 1 F)

3547   If you find a pin on the floor that is pointing away from you, you will have bad luck. If the pin is pointing toward you, good luck will come your way.
    (F, 48, R, 1957)

3548   It is good luck to pick up a pin. If the point is toward you, you will have "sharp" luck.
    (F, 74, R, 1959 [heard from old-timers])

3549   If you find a crooked pin, you will have bad luck.
    (F, 70, R, 1961)

3550   Don't pick up a pin if the head is toward you, as it will bring "dull" luck.
    (F, 60, R, 1959)

3551   When you see an open safety pin, picking it up will bring good luck.
    (F, 45, 1958 [one of her friends])

3552   If you see a hairpin, pick it up, as it will bring you good luck.
    (F, 21, 1950, + 1 F)

3553   If you find a bobby pin, you find good luck.
    (F, 40, R, 1960 [her mother])

PLANTS

3554   Carry a buckeye for good luck.
    (M, 20, R, 1958, + 4 F and 2 M)

3555   Find a red ear of corn; it is good luck.
    (F, 35, 1956)

3556   A corncob behind the ear brings good luck. (The informant said: "I've often heard my dad tell about the coach who always had a corncob behind his ear at ball games because he felt he couldn't win unless it was there.)
    (M, 1961)

3557   Parsley takes a long time to germinate. It is said that it goes down to the Devil nine times to make peace with him before it comes up; and therefore it is a good-luck charm.
    (F, 50, 1958)

3558   Finding a pod with seven peas in it brings good luck.
       (F, 49, 1958)
3559   Seeing a load of hay on the road will bring you good luck.
       (F, 29, 1959 [her grandmother])
3560   A lilac flower with five petals brings good luck if you eat it.
       (F, 21, 1961)
3561   If you plant daffodils on a windy day, all your bad luck will
       blow away.
       (F, 50, 1963)
3562   A hawthorn branch, suspended over a doorway like a horse-
       shoe, will bring good luck.
       (F, 1962 [her mother])
3563   Mistletoe brings good luck at Christmas time.
       (F, 21, 1950)
3564   A mustard seed will bring good luck.
       (F, 21, 1950, + 1 M)
3565   Eating black-eyed peas on New Year's Day will bring good
       luck.
       (M, 22, R, 1955)
3566   A dogwood tree in the yard brings good luck.
       (M, 74, R, 1959)
3567   It is bad luck to have an oleander plant in the house.
       (F, 50, R, 1961)
3568   It used to be considered bad luck to plant an evergreen tree.
       People thought that the planter would die before the tree
       could make a shadow as large as the planter.
       (F, 60, 1959)
3569   It is bad luck for fruit trees to bloom twice a year.
       (F, 1961)
3570   Growing a rubber plant in the house is supposed to be bad
       luck.
       (F, 40, R, 1963)
3571   Never bring may into the house; for it is bad luck. (May is a
       bush that blooms in England.)
       (F, 20, 1960 [her mother])
3572   Scattering the petals of the red rose on the ground is a
       bad-luck omen.
       (F, 84, 1955)
3573   It is bad luck to plant a weeping willow tree.
       (M, 50, R, 1958, + 1 F)

SALT

3574   If you spill salt, you should throw a pinch of it over your left shoulder so that you will not have bad luck.
    (F, 19, 1960, + 61 F and 10 M)

3575   If salt is spilled, pick up some of the spilled salt, and throw it over your left shoulder to offset bad luck.
    (F, 21, 1956, + 9 F and 1 M)

3576   Throw salt over your right shoulder; it will bring you good luck.
    (F, 21, R, 1959, + 3 F and 1 M)

3577   If you spill salt, pick some up, and throw it over your shoulder for good luck.
    (M, 20, R, 1960, + 9 F and 3 M)

3578   It is good luck to throw salt over your shoulder.
    (F, 19, R, 1956, + 9 F and 6 M)

3579   If salt is spilled, throw some over your shoulder three times.
    (F, 23, R, 1958, + 1 F and 3 M)

3580   It is bad luck to spill salt.
    (M, 19, 1959, + 8 F and 3 M)

3581   Never hand anyone the salt shaker; set it down, so that he can pick it up himself, or he will have bad luck.
    (F, 30, 1960, + 10 F)

3582   If you borrow salt from a neighbor, never return it, as this will bring you bad luck.
    (F, 47, R, 1956, + 10 F)

3583   Never borrow salt; always pay a penny for it in order to have good luck.
    (F, 1963)

3584   It is bad luck to loan or borrow salt; always consider it a gift.
    (F, 51, 1958, + 1 M)

SPORTS

3585   Always touch first (or second or third) base for luck when going to and from your position.
    (M, 24, 1957, + 1 M)

3586   For luck, a first baseman should run down the first-base line and kick the base before taking his position in the outfield.
    (M, 20, 1960, + 2 M)

3587   For luck, many baseball players make the sign of the cross over home plate with their bats before assuming their batting stances.
(M, 28, 1958)

3588   A ballplayer should never allow his suit to be washed as long as the team is winning. Washing the suit might break the lucky winning streak.
(F, 1960)

3589   If you win a game when playing basketball, you should wear the same socks at the next game for luck.
(M, 21, 1959 [his brother])

3590   One should always wear the same color for a basketball game or a solo performance of some kind for good luck. Some coaches wear the same tie to each game.
(M, 20, 1957)

3591   A good basketball player wants to have the same number on his uniform throughout his career for good luck.
(F, 21, 1961)

3592   For luck, athletes should eat the same thing before every game.
(M, 18, 1959)

3593   After the fifth inning, it is unlucky to mention the possibility that a game might be a no-hitter.
(M, 18, 1958)

3594   Knock the dust off your cleats after a bean ball, or you will be unlucky enough for the next one to get you (in baseball).
(M, 20, 1957)

3595   It is bad luck if you ever cross baseball bats.
(M, 22, 1957)

3596   If a baseball pitcher has a shutout going (that is, if the opposing team has no runs), it is bad luck to talk about the shutout.
(M, 1962)

3597   When playing baseball, one should not wash his socks until one loses a game. It is unlucky to wash socks after winning.
(M, 22, 1961)

3598   It is bad luck for a pitcher in baseball to strike out the first batter.
(M, 40, 1963)

3599   It is bad luck for a woman to be in a boxer's dressing room before a fight.
(M, 28, 1958)

3600   It is bad luck to play golf when it is lightning.
        (M, 55, 1958)
3601   To mention the word "shank" before a golf match is con-
        sidered bad luck.
        (M, 30, 1957)

THREES, SEVENS, AND THIRTEENS

3602   Three is a lucky number.
        (M, 20, R, 1958)
3603   The third time is a charm.
        (F, 19, R, 1959 [one of her parents], + 5 F)
3604   If you have an accident, you will have two more during the
        next few days.
        (F, 1960)
3605   Bad luck comes in threes.
        (F, 18, 1961, + 2 F)
3606   If you see three white horses, it is a sign of good luck.
        (F, 60, R, 1959 [her mother])
3607   Tragedies happen in threes.
        (F, 21, R, 1956)
3608   Accidents come in threes.
        (F, 19, R, 1956)
3609   A lilac flower that has three petals brings bad luck.
        (F, 21, R, 1957)
3610   Trouble always comes in threes.
        (F, 50, R, 1957, + 2 F)
3611   If you break one dish, you will break two more within a short
        time.
        (F, 60, R, 1957, + 2 F)
3612   If you break a dish, you will break three more before you'll
        have good luck.
        (F, 40, R, 1958, + 1 F and 1 M)
3613   It's bad luck to light three cigarettes on the same match.
        (F, 18, 1956, + 33 F and 16 M)
3614   The third man to light his cigarette on a match will have bad
        luck.
        (F, 20, 1955)
3615   Three on a match is bad luck, unless the second person blows
        it out.
        (F, 45, R, 1957)

3616   Seven is the lucky number.
         (F, 21, R, 1957, + 1 F)

3617   Thirteen is an unlucky number.
         (F, 19, 1959, + 16 F)

3618   Friday the thirteenth is a day of bad luck.
         (F, 17, R, 1960 [her mother], + 22 F and 6 M)

3619   Don't start anything new on Friday the thirteenth, or you will
         have bad luck.
         (F, 50, 1963, + 3 F and 2 M)

3620   It is unlucky to have a child born on Friday the thirteenth.
         (F, 19, R, 1962, + 1 F)

3621   Do not go to town on Friday the thirteenth, because it is
         unlucky.
         (F, 23, R, 1958)

3622   To walk under a ladder on Friday the thirteenth brings bad
         luck.
         (F, 20, R, 1959)

3623   Do not get married on Friday the thirteenth.
         (F, 19, R, 1959, + 1 F)

3624   Thirteen is the Devil's dozen; therefore it is unlucky.
         (F, 21, 1957)

3625   The reason for thirteen's being unlucky is because thirteen
         sat at the Last Supper.
         (F, 78, R, 1958 [her father])

3626   The number thirteen is regarded as an unlucky number.
         Tradition says that Christ and his disciples made thirteen
         and that he was betrayed by one of them.
         (F, 40, 1960 [her mother])

3627   It is bad luck to seat thirteen people at the same table.
         (M, 20, R, 1958, + 5 F and 1 M)

3628   If one has to give $13.00 to anyone, one should give an extra
         penny for luck.
         (F, 23, R, 1958)

3629   If there are thirteen pigs in a litter or chicks in a hatch, kill
         one to avoid bad luck.
         (M, 62, R, 1959)

                              UMBRELLAS

3630   Opening an umbrella in the house brings bad luck.
         (F, 18, 1959, + 65 F and 20 M)

3631   It is a taboo to open up an umbrella inside the house, because
then the roof will leak.
(F, 22, R, 1960)

3632   The person who opens an umbrella in a house will have bad
luck.
(M, 60, R, 1962)

3633   Leaving an umbrella open inside a house is bad luck.
(M, 67, 1959)

3634   It is bad luck to open an umbrella inside a house or to put a
hat on one's head.
(F, 20, 1950)

3635   It means bad luck if you put an umbrella on the bed.
(F, 69, R, 1958)

3636   A raised umbrella in the house will bring bad luck.
(F, 20, 1960, + 16 F and 5 M)

3637   To raise an umbrella in a doorway means hard luck.
(F, 60, R, 1960)

WALKING TOGETHER

3638   Two people who are walking down the street should never
separate to go around a post; it is bad luck to do so.
(M, 60, R, 1959, + 2 F)

3639   Don't split a post (that is, walk on either side of an object), or
it will bring bad luck.
(M, 56, R, 1956)

3640   When a couple is walking down the street, it is bad luck to
separate for a post or tree.
(F, 60, 1960)

3641   Parting in order to go around a tree is bad luck.
(F, 1959)

3642   When couples walk along the street and someone parts them,
this means bad luck.
(F, 60, R, 1957)

3643   If two people are walking along and one passes on one side of
an object (post, pole, tree, or the like), the other should pass
on the opposite side, always saying "Bread and butter," or it
will mean bad luck.
(F, R, 1960)

MISCELLANEOUS

3644   Spit on something for good luck.
    (F, 20, 1959)

3645   If you see a white stone, spit on it, and throw it over your left shoulder for luck.
    (F, 30, 1957)

3646   A rock with a hole in it is supposed to be lucky.
    (F, 20, R, 1958)

3647   Spit on a baby, and both you and the baby will have good luck.
    (M, 29, 1956)

3648   Spit on a person for luck.
    (M, 55, 1955)

3649   If two people say a word at the same time, it is good luck for them to lock little fingers and say "Salt and pepper."
    (F, 60, R, 1957)

3650   The large half of a wishbone will bring good luck, and if you get it, your wish will come true.
    (F, 21, 1950)

3651   If you are carrying a small bone from a fish's head and you lose it, you will have good luck.
    (F, 40, R, 1959)

3652   Being born or dying during a storm is a sign of a good person or of good luck.
    (F, 40, R, 1963 [her grandmother])

3653   To bring good luck, a child should be named after the first thing that the mother sees when the baby is born.
    (F, 21, 1950)

3654   On your birthday, you should get your nose buttered for good luck.
    (M, 30, 1957)

3655   Receiving a spanking on a birthday is good luck.
    (F, 20, R, 1956)

3656   If you turn the page of a calendar before the first of the month, you will have bad luck.
    (F, 40, 1959)

3657   It's bad luck to say good-by.
    (M, 50, R, 1958)

3658   Never write your own name, and then erase it or cross it out. You will have bad luck if you do.

(F, 19, 1958)

3659   Circus performers consider it bad luck to mention rain on the day of a performance for fear it will rain.

(F, 1961)

3660   When a baby rolls itself up in a blanket, bad luck will follow.

(F, 85, 1958)

3661   It is bad luck to ''measure'' (compare) hands.

(F, 22, 1959)

3662   Never step in or on a crack in the sidewalk, for this will bring bad luck.

(F, 20, R, 1959, + 2 F and 2 M)

The Weather

THE FOLKLORE OF WEATHER ACCOUNTS FOR 14 PERCENT OF our whole collection, which indicates an extensive knowledge of this lore. The over seven hundred items fall into ten general categories, centering mainly around the flora, the fauna, and the cosmos.

That animals of many kinds have served the unique purpose of aiding knowledge about the weather is not unusual in the sense that man has traditionally been close to and dependent upon animals. In this chapter, 44 percent of the lore involves animals. In addition to domestic animals, our list includes snakes, birds, coyotes, prairie dogs, rabbits, muskrats, turtles, mice, worms, toads, frogs, and rats. About 25 percent concern nature in general, such as cloud formations, rainbows, and even dew on the grass. More specifically, the sun, the moon, the stars, and plants give their individual prognostications.

Rain, snow, and fog also speak to man; a few items with high frequency are "Rain on Easter Sunday means rain for seven Sundays" and "The date of the first snow represents the number of snows for the winter."

Weather is everyone's favorite topic, and it certainly has tremendous power over human life and well-being. But we are approaching the time when the "Old Farmer's Almanacs" and oral weather lore, as dispensed by our people, may be a lost legacy, because today's reading and listening public is kept fully informed by scientific meteorologists from all parts of the world. If the local media do not satisfy one's curiosity, one has only to pick up the telephone, and a National Weather Service Office will give the latest quite reliable scientific prognostication.

As many have observed, folk weather lore may complement scientific knowledge or contradict it. In the meantime, there is still considerable folk weather knowledge or "beliefs" for which there is no contradictory evidence; therefore, it may be considered valid and trustworthy, even knowledge in its own right.

DATES AND SEASONS

3663   If it rains on Sunday, it will rain three days that week.
        (F, 19, 1957, + 1 M)

3664   If it rains on Sunday, it will rain for the entire week.
        (M, 30, 1955, + 1 M)

3665   If it rains on Sunday, it will rain the next four days in a row.
        (F, 21, 1950)

3666   If the sun sets behind a cloud on Sunday, it will rain before
        Wednesday night.
        (F, 82, R, 1958 [her parents])

3667   When rain falls on the first Sunday of the month, most
        old-timers expect showers on the three following Sundays.
        (F, 60, R, 1963 [her father])

3668   If there is rain on Monday, there will be rain on three days
        that week.
        (F, 14, 1959, + 6 F and 3 M)

3669   If it rains on Monday, it will rain all week.
        (F, 22, 1954, + 1 F and 2 M)

3670   If it rains on Monday, it will rain twice more that week.
        (F, 40, R, 1958, + 1 F and 1 M)

3671   Rain on Monday means that there will be rain on four days
        that week.
        (F, 1958)

3672   Friday is usually considered to be either the fairest or the
        foulest.
        (F, 20, R, 1958, + 1 F and 1 M)

3673   If it is clear on Friday evening, it will be clear on Sunday
        morning.
        (F, 40, 1959)

3674   "If on Friday it rains, / 'Twill on Sunday, again."
        (F, 81, R, 1958)

3675   The sun will always shine on Saturday, regardless of how
        bad a day it is.
        (F, 75, R, 1958, + 1 M)

3676   The first three days of December rule the first three months
        of winter.
        (M, 55, R, 1957, + 1 F and 2 M)

3677   If there is a green Christmas, there will be a white Easter.
        (F, 1958)

3678   The weather on the last six days of the old year predicts what the weather will be like for the first six months of the new year; and the weather on the first six days of the new year predicts the weather for the last six months of that year. (If it is cloudy on December 26, January will be a cloudy month, and so forth.)

        (M, 60, R, 1957, + 2 F and 3 M)

3679   Watch the wind on the first day of January; for it will tell you what kind of weather you will have for the next forty days.

        (F, 30, R, 1957)

3680   If it is dry on New Year's Day, it will be dry all year.

        (M, 21, R, 1961)

3681   If the wind blows all day from the southwest on January the first, the year will be dry.

        (F, 40, R, 1960)

3682   The first day of the year will determine the weather for the summer.

        (F, 65, R, 1956)

3683   If the first three days in January are cloudy, there will be a frost in May.

        (F, 70, R, 1960 [her parents])

3684   The weather during the first three days of the year will determine the weather for the next three months.

        (F, 60, 1958, + 3 F and 3 M)

3685   The first twelve days of January will rule the twelve months of the year (with regard to weather).

        (F, 25, 1958, + 3 F and 2 M)

3686   If there is fog in January, there will be frost in May.

        (F, 60, R, 1961, + 1 F)

3687   The weather on the first three days of February determines the weather for June, July, and August. Many say that they can tell by those three days whether or not there will be a good corn crop.
(F, 55, 1954)

3688   If there is thunder in February, it means that there will be severe storms.
(F, 1961)

3689   If there is a thunderstorm in February, there will be a severe frost in May.
(F, 60, R, 1959, + 3 F and 1 M)

3690   If March comes in like a lion, it will go out like a lamb; if it comes in like a lamb, it will go out like a lion.
(F, 19, 1954, + 17 F and 5 M)

3691   The prevailing winds on March 19, 20, and 21 will be the prevailing winds on those days of the following months.
(F, 60, 1959)

3692   One should always look forward to some kind of storm at the equinox (March 20, 21, and 22).
(F, 70, R, 1957)

3693   The first three days after the sun crosses the line (March 30) rule the first three months of spring.
(M, 55, R, 1957)

3694   If rain doesn't fall at the time of the equinox, you can expect the following three months to be eeicient i moisture.
(F, 52, 1954)

3695   If it is dusty and windy on March 21, it will be a dry, dusty summer.
(F, 66, R, 1958)

3696   At the spring equinox if the wind is from the north, the spring will be cold; if from the east, it will be rainy; if from the west, clear and breezy; and if from the south, warm.
(F, 72, R, 1957)

3697   If the wind blows from the southwest during the equinox, the weather will be wet.
(M, 81, 1958)

3698   April showers bring May flowers.
(F, 47, R, 1959, + 2 F and 1 M)

3699   If it rains on Good Friday, it will rain every weekend for six weeks.
(M, 80, R, 1957)

3700   If it thunders before Easter, the frogs will look through the ice.
         (F, 1962)

3701   If Easter falls on an early date, there will be an early spring.
         (F, 1958)

3702   The weather on Easter Sunday will be the same as that for the next seven Sundays.
         (F, 20, R, 1959 [her father], + 1 F)

3703   If it rains on Easter, it will rain for the next five Sundays.
         (F, 40, R, 1960 [her parents])

3704   If it rains on Easter, it will rain on the next six Sundays.
         (F, 21, R, 1958, + 2 F)

3705   Rain on Easter Sunday means rain each Sunday thereafter for seven Sundays.
         (F, 12, 1957, + 36 F and 22 M)

3706   If it rains on Easter Sunday, there will be thirteen Sundays of rain thereafter.
         (F, 19, R, 1957, + 1 F)

3707   If it rains on Easter, there will be seven weeks of bad weather.
         (M, 22, R, 1958)

3708   The date of the first snow represents the number of snows for the winter.
         (F, 14, 1959, + 70 F and 20 M)

3709   If when the first snow of autumn falls, you count how many days old the moon is, that number will be how many snows will fall during the winter.
         (F, 62, R, 1959)

3710   If fruit trees bloom in March, it will freeze in April.
         (F, 20, R, 1959)

3711   If there is no rain in March, the summer will be hot and windy.
         (F, 55, R, 1958)

3712   As the days grow longer, the cold waxes stronger.
         (F, 45, 1955)

3713   Every year, on May 30 there is a tornado in Harper County.
         (F, 19, R, 1959)

3714   If you wash on Monday, then you will be sure to have at least one good day for drying your clothes.
         (F, 50, R, 1960 [her mother])

LIGHTNING AND THUNDER

3715   Thunder is caused by clouds bumping their heads.
         (F, 21, 1958)

3716   Thunder is the sound made by a giant.
         (F, 20, 1958)

3717   Thunder is caused by the roll of immigrant wagons on the Santa Fe Trail.
         (M, 24, 1957)

3718   If you point at lightning, it will strike near you.
         (M, 50, R, 1957)

3719   Take white clothes off a clothesline when it lightnings and thunders, or you will be struck.
         (F, 80, 1958)

3720   If you keep a leftover hard-boiled colored Easter egg in your house all year, lightning will never strike your house.
         (F, 50, R, 1959)

3721   You should always wear a hat or some covering while in a storm to keep from being hit by lightning.
         (M, R, 1961)

3722   Don't pet animals during a thunderstorm, as they attract lightning.
         (F, 50, R, 1959)

3723   If you hang a china cup on a string around your neck when it is lightning, it will keep the lightning from striking you.
         (F, 45, R, 1958)

3724   Never stand in an open doorway during an electrical storm.
         (M, 70, R, 1959, + 1 F)

3725   If a man has his suspenders crossed, he will not be struck by lightning.
         (M, 53, 1958, + 1 M)

3726   A man who wears his suspenders crossed is afraid of lightning.
         (M, 20, R, 1961, + 3 F and 3 M)

3727   Sit on a feather bed in an electrical storm to keep lightning from hitting you.
         (F, 60, R, 1958, + 1 F and 1 M)

3728   During a storm, run or crawl under or into the middle of a feather bed.
         (F, 53, R, 1958, + 2 F)

3729   If you sleep on a feather pillow, lightning won't strike you.
        (F, 30, 1960)

3730   To be safe from lightning, never stand under a tree or run in an open field.
        (M, 80, R, 1958, + 1 M)

3731   An electrical storm will cause milk to sour.
        (F, 21, R, 1961, + 5 F and 1 M)

3732   Thunder will turn milk sour.
        (M, 24, R, 1957, + 9 F and 3 M)

3733   If there is lightning at night, the milk will be sour before morning.
        (F, 80, R, 1961)

3734   If milk sours quickly, it is a sign that there will be an electrical storm soon.
        (F, 59, 1958)

3735   If the lightning is straight in the north, there will be rain within twenty-four hours.
        (F, 50, 1958)

3736   When there is lightning in the north, it will rain within three days.
        (F, 70, 1962)

3737   If there is lightning straight north in the evening, it will rain before morning.
        (M, 50, R, 1963)

3738   Lightning means a change to cooler weather.
        (F, 24, R, 1957)

3739   Thunder in the morning means rain before night.
        (F, 20, R, 1963)

3740   If there is lightning in the northeast, it will rain within three days or three weeks.
        (F, 60, R, 1957)

3741   Lightning from the west or the northwest is from a storm that will strike.
        (F, 70, R, 1962)

3742   Lightning from the east or south is from a storm that will usually miss you.
        (F, 70, R, 1962)

3743   Since sound travels at about one thousand feet per second, the lightning is about a thousand feet away for every second between the lightning and the sound of the thunder.
        (F, 26, 1977)

3744   Count one, and pick up a match; count two, and pick up a match; and so forth, after lightning until you hear the thunder. That will tell how many miles the lightning is from you.

(M, 50, R, 1957)

3745   By counting the number of seconds between the lightning and thunder, you will know how many miles away they are.

(F, 50, R, 1961)

3746   A storm is only as far away as the time between the thunder and the lightning.

(M, 20, R, 1963)

3747   Lightning never strikes in the same place twice.

(M, 20, R, 1958, + 13 F and 7 M)

3748   Lightning always strikes in the same place.

(M, 40, R, 1960)

MOON SIGNS

3749   A ring around the moon means bad weather.

(F, 20, R, 1960, + 7 F and 4 M)

3750   A ring around the moon means that it will rain in three days.

(F, 56, R, 1963)

3751   A haze around the moon means that it will storm within three days. It will never storm in the face of a full moon.

(M, 70, R, 1960)

3752   If there is a ring around the moon, it means that the moon is holding water. As the moon turns up, it will rain.

(M, 16, 1958, + 1 F)

3753   A ring around the moon indicates an approaching storm. The number of stars within the circle indicates the duration of the storm.

(F, 65, R, 1958, + 1 F)

3754   When there is a ring around the moon, the number of days until a storm will be the same as the number of stars in the ring.

(M, 14, 1959, + 35 F and 22 M)

3755   The number of stars in the ring around the moon denotes the number of days until the weather will change.

(F, 21, 1950, + 5 F and 6 M)

3756   A large ring around the moon means that there will be a storm within forty-eight hours.

(F, 55, 1957, + 1 F)

3757   If there is a ring around the moon, there will be rain soon.
       (F, 60, R, 1959, + 30 F and 14 M)

3758   A ring around the moon means that there will be rain tomorrow.
       (F, 17, 1959, + 4 F)

3759   A ring around the moon means that there will be some sort of precipitation.
       (M, 20, R, 1963, + 3 F)

3760   A ring around the moon foretells a change in the weather.
       (F, 19, R, 1957, + 1 F and 13 M)

3761   A ring around the moon means that wind is coming.
       (M, 70, R, 1959)

3762   A ring around the moon means that you'll have windy weather the next day.
       (M, 60, R, 1959, + 1 F)

3763   If the moon is tipped up, the weather is going to be dry.
       (F, 20, 1950, + 10 F and 5 M)

3764   When the crescent moon is tipped downward, rain will follow, because the rain will pour out of the crescent.
       (M, 20, R, 1959, + 5 M)

3765   If the moon is tipped forward, the water will spill out, and there will be rain.
       (M, 24, 1956, + 6 F and 6 M)

3766   When the moon is like a boat, the world will float.
       (F, 61, R, 1957)

3767   When the tip of the moon is downward, there will be dry weather.
       (M, 21, 1950, + 10 F and 5 M)

3768   If you can hang a powder horn on the tip of a new moon, it will be a dry moon.
       (M, 50, 1956, + 7 F and 4 M)

3769   When there is a change in the moon, there will be a change in the atmosphere.
       (M, 94, 1957)

3770   In a time of drought, it won't rain until the new moon comes.
       (F, 40, 1959 [her father])

3771   It is said that the moon holds water.
       (M, 22, R, 1958)

3772   The position of the moon in the sky will sometimes determine the moisture in the atmosphere.
       (F, 1959)

3773   If a moon changes after midnight, it is a sign that there will be moisture.
   (F, 40, R, 1960)

SUN SIGNS

3774   If it rains while the sun is shining, the Devil is dancing.
   (F, 40, R, 1963)

3775   If it rains while the sun is shining, the Devil is beating his wife.
   (F, 50, R, 1956, + 1 F and 2 M)

3776   If the sun shines while it is raining, it will keep on raining.
   (F, 1961)

3777   If it rains when the sun is shining, the next day will be clear.
   (F, 65, R, 1956)

3778   If the sun shines while it is raining, it will rain all the following day.
   (M, 66, 1955)

3779   If it rains while the sun is shining, it will rain again tomorrow.
   (F, 16, R, 1962, + 46 F and 18 M)

3780   If the sun shines while it is raining, there will be more rain within the next twenty-four hours.
   (F, 50, R, 1963)

3781   If it rains on Monday while the sun is shining, it will rain three days out of the week.
   (M, 69, R, 1961)

3782   "Sunshine and shower; / Rain again in an hour."
   (F, 20, R, 1963)

3783   "A sunshining shower / Won't last half an hour."
   (F, 39, R, 1956, + 2 M)

3784   A clear sunset means a clear night.
   (F, 20, 1959 [her father])

3785   If the sun goes down clear, the morrow will be a good day.
   (M, 21, 1950, + 6 F and 6 M)

3786   If the sun goes down clear on Thursday night and then on Friday night the sun goes down behind the clouds and the wind is from the south, it will rain before Monday night.
   (M, 22, R, 1963)

3787   A red sunset foretells rain.
   (M, 20, R, 1959, + 1 F)

3788   If you see a red sunset, it's going to be windy the next day.
　　　　(F, 50, R, 1958, + 2 F and 4 M)

3789   If there is a red sunset in the evening, it will be clear the next day.
　　　　(F, 20, R, 1956, + 5 F and 1 M)

3790   Red sunsets bring bright tomorrows.
　　　　(M, 60, R, 1961)

3791   A red sunset indicates dry weather.
        (M, 15, 1958, + 1 F)

3792   A red sun in the evening means that it will be windy on the morrow.
        (M, 20, R, 1961 [his father], + 3 F and 1 M)

3793   If there is a lot of red and purple in the sunset, there will be a storm that night.
        (F, 20, 1961)

3794   When the sun sets in pink and gold, it will be fair the next day.
        (F, 68, R, 1958)

3795   A cloudy sunset means a rainy day on the morrow.
        (M, 18, 1957, + 7 F and 1 M)

3796   If the sun goes down behind some clouds, it is going to rain within the next few days.
        (M, 1961)

3797   If the sun goes down behind a cloud, there will be a storm before morning.
        (F, 50, R, 1961)

3798   If the sun goes down behind a cloud on Friday, it will rain before Monday.
        (F, 14, 1959, + 14 F and 13 M)

3799   If the sun goes down behind a cloud on Friday, it will rain before Tuesday.
        (F, 40, R, 1960, + 3 F and 2 M)

3800   If the sun sets behind a cloud on Friday, it will storm before Sunday.
        (F, 30, R, 1960, + 2 F and 3 M)

3801   Clouds crossing the sunset mean a clear morning the next day.
        (F, 69, R, 1958)

3802   "If the sun comes up bright / And goes to bed soon, / It will rain before night / If not before noon."
        (F, 50, R, 1959, + 1 F)

3803   A ring around the sun brings water by the ton.
        (M, 20, R, 1959, + 2 F)

3804   A ring around the sun means that a storm is coming.
        (M, 20, 1959, + 1 F and 1 M)

3805   The wind goes down with the sun.
        (F, 48, 1958)

SUNDOGS

3806   A ring around the sun is called a sundog.
        (M, 25, R, 1959)

3807   A sundog is a really bright spot near the sun.
        (F, 70, 1958)

3808   A sundog is formed when the sun is behind the clouds and a reflection of the sun is seen on another cloud.
        (F, 57, 1957)

3809   If you see a sundog, there is going to be a storm.
        (F, 19, 1955, + 17 F and 3 M)

3810   When there are sundogs around the sun, there will be three days before a storm.
        (F, 56, R, 1963 [her father], + 1 M)

3811   If there is a sundog on each side of the sun, there will be a change in the weather.
        (F, 50, R, 1961)

3812   Two sundogs mean that there will be a change in the weather.
        (M, 20, R, 1962 [his father])

3813   If there is a sundog on each side of the sun, there will be a storm within twenty-four hours.
        (M, 80, R, 1959)

3814   If there are two sundogs, there will be two days before a rain; three sundogs, three days; and so forth.
        (M, 60, R, 1958)

3815   "Sundog at night, / Sailor's delight. / Sundog in morning, / Sailor's warning."
        (F, 20, R, 1959, + 3 M)

3816   Sundogs mean that cold weather is coming.
        (F, 43, R, 1961)

3817   Sundogs before sundown are a sign of cold weather.
        (F, 70, 1958)

3818   A sundog in winter means that you will have a bad cold spell in three days.
        (F, 40, R, 1958)

3819   Sundogs in the evening during the winter will be followed in three days by a storm and colder weather.
        (M, 69, R, 1956)

3820   Sundogs are a sign of foul weather.
        (M, 65, R, 1958, + 1 M)
3821   A sundog means that there will be a change of weather.
        (M, 50, R, 1958 [his father], + 8 F and 10 M)
3822   Sundogs on the north side of the sun mean that there will be a
        change in the weather from that direction in a few days.
        (F, 27, 1957)
3823   A sundog indicates that there will be a change of weather in
        three days.
        (F, 60, R, 1964)
3824   When the sundogs are out, it will rain for three days.
        (F, 65, R, 1957)
3825   Sundogs, or rays, draw water from the earth.
        (M, 20, R, 1959)
3826   A sundog after a snowstorm means that the weather will be
        clear for five days.
        (M, 20, 1959 [his father])
3827   Many people used to foretell the weather by sundogs.
        Sundogs in the morning meant that there would be rain; sun-
        dogs at night meant that there would be dry weather.
        (F, 27, R, 1961)
3828   If you see sundogs when the sun sets in the summer, there
        will be a long, dry, and hot spell.
        (F, 40, R, 1963)
3829   A sundog in the west means that there will be a dry spell.
        (M, 40, R, 1957)
3830   If there is a sundog north of the sun, the weather will be
        stormy. If it is south of the sun, there will be nice weather.
        (F, 70, R, 1960 [her parents], + 2 F and 1 M)
3831   A sundog north of the sun means that there will be cold
        weather; a sundog south of the sun means that there will be
        warmer weather.
        (M, 53, R, 1959 [his grandfather], + 14 F and 5 M)

                            STAR SIGNS

3832   The direction of the Milky Way at night indicates that the
        wind will blow parallel to it the next day.
        (F, 55, R, 1954, + 5 F)
3833   The direction in which the Milky Way points is the direction
        in which the wind will blow.
        (M, 60, R, 1960)

3834   When the Big Dipper is tipped down, it is going to rain.
       (F, 45, R, 1961)

3835   When the Big Dipper is upside down, it is going to rain.
       (M, 50, 1958, + 1 M and 1 F)

3836   "When the stars begin to huddle, / The earth will soon
       become a puddle."
       (F, 21, R, 1958 [her grandmother])

3837   At night, when the stars are all bright, it's a sign of good
       weather. When you can't see many stars, it's a sign of bad
       weather.
       (M, 70, R, 1962 [his uncle])

3838   A sky full of stars at night means that it will be windy the next
       day.
       (M, 66, R, 1959 [his relatives])

3839   If the stars are all out, it will not rain.
       (M, 21, 1950)

3840   Unusual brightness of the atmosphere and stars indicates
       that there will be rain.
       (F, 21, 1950)

3841   If the stars are not shining, it will rain.
       (M, 20, R, 1956)

3842   When a star falls, the wind will blow from the direction in
       which it falls.
       (F, 81, 1955)

3843   Many people used to foretell the weather by the stars. A
       clear night that was loaded with stars meant that there
       would be a nice day ahead; a hazy sky and not so many stars
       meant that a change of weather was coming.
       (F, 70, R, 1961)

3844   When stars are close, there will be rain; when stars are far
       away, no rain.
       (F, 23, 1957)

                              PLANTS

3845   If the ears of the corn crop have many shucks on them, there
       will be a hard winter.
       (M, 40, R, 1948 [his father], + 1 F and 1 M)

3846   Heavy husks on the corn indicate that there will be a hard
       winter.
       (F, 20, 1959, + 12 F and 9 M)

3847   A lot of silk on the corn means that there is going to be a hard winter.
   (F, 20, R, 1956)

3848   Tight corn shucks signify that there will be a cold winter.
   (M, 24, R, 1956, + 1 F and 4 M)

3849   If the crops are good and grow rapidly, you can look forward to a hard winter.
   (F, 40, R, 1962, + 2 F)

3850   If the leaves turn upward, there is going to be a storm.
   (F, 20, R, 1950, + 4 F and 2 M)

3851   When oak leaves turn over, there is going to be rain.
   (F, 23, 1957, + 3 M)

3852   If a lot of leaves stay on the trees late into the fall, there will be a bad winter.
   (F, 54, R, 1961 [her mother], + 1 F)

3853   If moss in a water tank comes to the surface, a rain will follow.
   (M, 55, 1954, + 4 M)

3854   Frost will come in six weeks after the goldenrod blooms.
   (F, 30, R, 1960)

3855   When the shells on the walnuts are thick, there will be a cold winter.
   (M, 21, 1950, + 2 F)

3856   After the first of the year, wrap an onion securely with a cloth. If the onion is still moist after a few weeks, the new year will be wet. If the onion is dry, the year will be dry.
   (F, 40, 1958)

3857   "Onion skin mighty thin, / Easy winter comin' in."
   (F, 65, R, 1962)

3858   If there is moss on the north side of the trees, there will be a late spring.
   (M, 50, 1957)

3859   A new crop of weeds late in July or August means that there will be a long, beautiful fall. They will not start growing unless they have time to set on seed.
   (F, 30, R, 1961)

3860   When grass grows between the cracks, it's going to be a hard winter.
   (F, 20, R, 1959)

3861   Flowers in bloom in late autumn denote a bad winter.
   (F, 50, R, 1957)

NATURE IN GENERAL

Sky Color

3862 "Evening red and morning gray, / Helps the traveler on his way; / Evening gray and morning red, / Brings down rain upon his head."
  (F, 18, 1956, + 41 F and 14 M)

3863 "Morning red and evening gray, / Will set the traveler on his way; / Evening gray and morning red, / Will bring down rain upon his head.
  (F, 18, 1955, + 6 F and 3 M)

3864 "Evening red and morning gray, / Sure sign of a fair day; / Evening gray and morning red, / Might as well go to bed."
  (M, 80, R, 1958 [his father])

3865 "Evening red, morning gray, / Sure to have a very fine day."
  (F, 40, R, 1961)

3866 "Evening red, morning gray, / Sets the traveler on his way. / Morning red, / Wet bread."
  (F, 90, R, 1957)

3867 A buff-colored sky is never dry.
  (F, 60, R, 1964 [her mother])

3868 If there is a freckled sky, there will not be twenty-four hours dry.
  (M, 50, R, 1957)

3869 A grey dawn brings good weather; a pink dawn brings bad weather.
  (F, 20, R, 1959)

3870 There will be stormy weather if it is red toward sunrise in the morning.
  (F, 70, R, 1960 [her parents])

3871 "Red in the east, / Sailor's grief."
  (F, 1959 [her grandparents])

3872 If it is red in the west, the next day will be clear.
  (F, 1959 [her grandparents])

3873 A red sky in the west at night indicates that there will be wind the next day.
  (F, 61, R, 1961)

3874 A red sky has water in its eye.
  (F, 21, R, 1958 [her grandmother])

3875   "Red sky at night, / Sailor's delight. / Red sky in the morning, /
        Sailors take warning."
            (M, 19, 1959 [his grandparents], + 52 F and 1 M)
3876   "Red sky at night is a shepherd's delight. / Red sky in the
        morning is a shepherd's warning."
            (F, 72, 1957)
3877   "Red sun at dawning, / Sailors take warning."
            (F, 21, 1950)
3878   If it is red before dawn, sailors should be warned.
            (F, 21, 1950)
3879   If there is a red sky at dawn, sailors will mourn.
            (F, 21, 1950)
3880   If the sky is red by day, it's a sailor's dismay.
            (F, 20, 1957)

Fog

3881   When the fog comes down, you can expect a clear day.
            (F, 50, 1955, + 1 F)
3882   If the fog rises up, it will rain.
            (F, 21, R, 1957, + 2 F and 1 M)
3883   One hundred days after a fog, it will cloud up and rain.
            (F, 50, R, 1958, + 1 F and 3 M)
3884   It will rain ninety days after a fog.
            (M, 50, R, 1958 [his father], + 2 F and 4 M)
3885   Thirty days after a fog there will be a rain.
            (F, 60, R, 1960 [her father])
3886   If snow or rain doesn't come three days after a fog, it will
        come back in ninety days.
            (F, 47, R, 1961 [her father])
3887   Three foggy days indicate that there will be rain or snow in
        ninety days.
            (F, 60, R, 1960 [her father])
3888   "Fog in the hollow, / Nice weather will follow."
            (F, 40, R, 1962 [her father])
3889   "Fog on the hill, / Water for the mill."
            (F, 40, R, 1962)
3890   A summer fog means that there will be fair weather; a winter
        fog, rain.
            (M, 60, R, 1962 [one of his neighbors])
3891   A fog in the winter will freeze a dog before morning.
            (F, 60, R, 1959)

3892   If a fog rains itself out, expect fair weather; if it rises, expect it to return as rain within three days.
        (M, 1961)

3893   If a fog does not come completely down to the ground, it will rain thirty days later. (The calendar used to be marked so that a person could take advantage of this information.)
        (F, 60, 1964)

3894   If a fog lifts before 10:00 A.M., it will be clear all day.
        (F, 45, R, 1961)

3895   If it's foggy in the morning and the fog goes up, it will come down as rain. If the fog just drifts away, it will be a clear day.
        (F, 71, 1955)

Rain Bubbles

3896   If bubbles form on the water when it rains, there will be rain the next day also.
        (F, 75, R, 1958 [her mother])

3897   Bubbles on the water when it's raining indicate that there will be three more days of rain.
        (F, 21, 1956)

3898   If rain causes water in a stream or pond to bubble, there will be fair weather.
        (M, 65, R, 1957)

Frost, Snow, and Ice

3899   The first and last frosts are usually preceded by temperatures that are very much above the mean.
        (F, 21, 1950)

3900   There will be three days of rain after the first frost.
        (F, 53, R, 1956)

3901   If there is a frost on the ground and the weather clears up before the frost melts, it will rain in three days.
        (M, 50, 1958)

3902   Three heavy frosts signify that there will be rain or snow.
        (M, 94, 1957)

3903   When fine snow is falling, it will snow a long time; but if big flakes are falling, it will quit snowing soon.
        (F, 30, R, 1962, + 1 M)

3904   It has to warm up in order to snow in the winter.
        (M, 22, R, 1959)

3905 For every day that the snow remains on the trees after a snow, it will stay on the ground for a week.
(F, 47, R, 1961)

3906 When snow-on-the-mountain blooms thick in the pasture, there will be lots of snow on the ground the next winter.
(F, 80, R, 1968 [her father])

3907 If little patches of snow are left when the snow melts, it will snow again before they melt completely.
(M, 50, R, 1957)

3908 If ice freezes hard enough to carry a goose in early fall, the backbone of the winter is broken (that is, it will not be a hard winter).
(F, 47, R, 1956)

Dew

3909 "When the dew is on the grass, / Rain will never come to pass."
(F, 21, R, 1958, + 3 F)

3910 "When grass is dry at morning's light, / Look for rain before the night."
(F, 21, R, 1958, + 1 F)

3911 Rain will follow a heavy dew.
(F, 21, 1950)

3912 "When the morn is dry, / No rain is nigh; / When the morn is wet, / Rain you'll get."
(M, 65, R, 1960 [his grandmother])

3913 The absence of dew on the grass is an indication of ill tidings.
(F, 21, 1956)

3914 "When the morn is dry (no dew on grass), / The rain is nigh. / When the morn is wet (dew on grass), / No rain you get."
(M, 50, R, 1962 [his father])

3915 If the dew falls before 9:00 P.M., there will be no rain during the night, no matter how much it thunders and lightnings.
(M, 50, R, 1960 [his father])

3916 Three good dews in hot weather constitute a sign of rain.
(M, 94, 1957)

Rain

3917 If an area doesn't get any rain, it will blow away all winter.
(F, 16, R, 1962)

3918   "Rain in the morning, / Sailors take warning, / Rain at night, /
Sailors' delight."
(F, 34, 1958, + 1 M)

3919   After the rain comes the fair weather.
(F, 21, 1950)

3920   If the rain splashes up and down as it lands, there will be rain
for three days out of the next seven.
(F, 58, 1958)

3921   While it is raining, if the raindrops cause the water to splash
up high, it will not rain for long.
(F, 77, R, 1961)

3922   The direction from which the first spring rain comes shows
the direction from which most of the summer rains will come.
(M, 65, R, 1960 [his father])

3923   "A storm in the southwest / Never breeds best."
(F, 21, 1957, + 1 F)

3924   A hard rain means a short rain.
(F, 21, 1954, + 1 F)

3925   If the raindrops are small, it will be a long rain. If the
raindrops are big, it will be a short rain.
(F, 20, R, 1958, + 1 F and 1 M)

Wind

3926   A wind from the east will bring rain.
(M, 20, R, 1958, + 1 F and 5 M)

3927   Three days of east wind will bring rain.
(M, 20, R, 1959 [his parents], + 2 F and 1 M)

3928   If the wind blows from the east, you can pray for rain. If it
doesn't blow from the east, there's no use in praying.
(F, 80, R, 1961)

3929   If an east wind blows for thirty-six hours, it will bring rain.
(M, 60, R, 1961)

3930   There will be rain if the wind blows from the east for five
days.
(F, 45, 1959 [her parents])

3931   It never rains when the wind is from the southwest.
(F, 53, 1958, + 1 M)

3932   It is sure to rain if the wind blows strong and steady for three
days and three nights from the southwest.
(M, 30, R, 1957, + 1 F)

3933   A northwest wind brings clear weather.
(F, 40, R, 1960, + 1 M)

3934   When the wind changes to the northwest, it will rain.
       (M, 21, 1950, + 1 F)
3935   A wind that blows from the south steadily for thirty-six hours
       will bring rain.
       (F, 40, 1959 [her father])
3936   Wind from the south brings a drought.
       (M, 80, R, 1961)
3937   A prevailing wind from the south for three days will bring
       rain.
       (M, 21, 1950, + 2 F and 3 M)
3938   If the wind comes from the southwest, there is sure to be rain.
       (M, 20, R, 1958, + 1 M)
3939   As long as the wind stays in the southeast, it will not rain. If
       the wind shifts to the southwest, it will rain.
       (M, 70, R, 1957)
3940   When the wind blows for three days from the southeast, you
       can look for at least one foot of snow.
       (M, 49, R, 1963 [his parents])
3941   If the wind shifts counterclockwise, there will be a storm.
       (M, 49, R, 1963, + 1 M)
3942   If the wind shifts clockwise, there will be dry weather.
       (M, 49, R, 1963 [his parents])
3943   If the wind makes a complete circle during the day, there will
       be rain within twenty-four hours.
       (F, 43, R, 1960 [her father])
3944   When the wind turns against the sun, rain is coming.
       (M, 70, R, 1959)
3945   Never look for rain when the wind turns with the sun.
       (M, 70, R, 1959)
3946   If the wind is from the northeast, it will soon rain.
       (F, 40, R, 1958, + 3 F)
3947   If a north wind is blowing, you won't have rain.
       (F, 20, R, 1963 [her mother])
3948   Fair weather comes from the north.
       (F, 21, 1950)
3949   When the wind changes from the south to the north, it is going
       to rain.
       (F, 20, R, 1961 [her grandmother], + 1 M)
3950   When the wind blows from one direction for three days, there
       will be rain.
       (F, 60, 1958, + 5 F and 3 M)
3951   "Wind in the east, / Famine for man and beast. / Wind in the

west, / Fruits of the earth will be blest. / Wind in the south, / Wind and drouth.''
   (F, 75, R, 1958 [her mother])

3952   Several windy days on the Kansas prairie foretell the coming of a severe storm—usually rain, cold, or snow.
   (F, 40, R, 1959 [her parents])

3953   A change in the direction of the wind means that there will be a storm.
   (F, 21, 1950)

3954   Wind from the west during the summer months always means that there will be warm humid air.
   (M, 24, R, 1957)

3955   When the wind backs and the weather glass falls, be on your guard against winds and gales.
   (M, 50, 1956)

3956   If the wind blows from the east on the first day of spring, there will be a good crop; if from the southwest, the crop will be a failure.
   (M, 40, R, 1962)

Clouds

3957   If the sun comes up and heads west, and then a cloud comes from the west and moves east and covers the sun, there will be moisture before night.
   (M, 40, 1962)

3958   If it's cloudy at sunset, it won't freeze that night.
   (F, 21, 1954)

3959   When you see a lot of little clouds, moisture is on the way.
   (M, 70, R, 1959)

3960   Red clouds in the sunset foretell fine weather, especially if there is a tint of purple in them.
   (F, 70, 1958)

3961   Long lingering clouds mean that there will be rain.
   (F, 23, 1957)

3962   If thunderheads in the northwest come up against a southeast wind, there will be rain.
   (F, 47, R, 1959 [her father])

3963   If the clouds come up against the wind, there will be rain.
   (F, 50, 1958)

3964   Fast-rising thunderheads on a hot sultry day indicate that hail and windstorms are in the clouds.
   (F, 60, R, 1957)

3965   A cloudless sky will bring a storm.
     (F, 50, R, 1959)

3966   If it is cloudy all day and the sun sets "rosy," the next day will be a nice one.
     (F, 71, 1955)

3967   If it is cloudy and then "fairs off" at night, the weather won't stay fair; but if it "fairs off" during the day, the weather will continue to be fair.
     (M, 50, 1958)

3968   The higher the clouds, the finer the weather.
     (F, 21, R, 1958)

3969   The higher the clouds, the drier the air.
     (F, 70, R, 1962)

3970   If the clouds are egg shaped or look like "eggs in a basket," there will be rainy weather.
     (F, 76, 1957)

3971   If a winter sky is cloudy, there will be no frost.
     (F, 1961)

3972   "When the clouds appear like rocks and towers, / The earth's refreshed by frequent showers."
     (F, 18, 1956)

3973   A cloud with a silvery lining means that it will rain before Monday.
     (F, 57, R, 1957)

3974   If clouds come up in the west, there will be a cyclone.
     (F, 70, R, 1960 [her mother])

3975   If the clouds are red and rolling, there will be foul weather.
     (F, 70, R, 1960)

3976   Red clouds at night indicate fair weather for the next day. Red clouds in the morning indicate that there will be foul weather.
     (M, 75, R, 1961)

3977   Mares' tails in the sky indicate that the weather will continue to be dry.
     (F, 1961)

3978   If there are "fish scales" in the sky, it's going to rain by and by.
     (F, 55, R, 1965 [her grandmother])

3979   A "mackerel sky" (when clouds are scaly like fish) never leaves the ground dry.
     (M, 55, R, 1957)

3980   "Mackerel skies and mares' tails, / Lofty ships carry lower sails."

   (M, 80, R, 1963 [his parents])

3981   A mackerel sky will be more wet than dry.

   (F, 70, R, 1963)

3982   If there is a mackerel sky, there will not be twenty-four hours dry.

   (M, 30, 1958)

3983   "Mackerel sky, / Soon wet or long dry."

   (F, 70, R, 1962)

3984   If the sky is cloudy all around and the rain is pouring down in the middle, this is a sure sign of rain.

   (M, 20, R, 1959, + 5 M)

3985   On a cloudy day, if you can see a patch of blue in the sky large
        enough to repair a pair of overalls, the weather will clear off.
            (M, 42, 1958 [his mother])
3986   When the rain stops, if you can see a piece of blue sky that is
        large enough to make a pair of man's pants from, the sky will
        clear off.
            (F, 82, R, 1957)
3987   If you can see enough blue sky in the northwest to make a
        Scotchman a shirttail, the sky will clear.
            (F, 40, R, 1960)
3988   When the sky is full of clouds, if you can see enough blue sky
        to make a pair of Dutchman's Breeches, the sky will clear up,
        and it will be safe to do a washing.
            (F, 40, 1959 [her mother], + 2 F and 1 M)

Clear Sky

3989   If it clears off during the night, it will be cloudy the next day.
            (M, 27, 1958, + 2 F)
3990   If the sky clears during the night, it will rain again.
            (F, 60, R, 1958, + 1 F)
3991   If the sky is clear at night, the weather will be dry.
            (F, 60, 1959)
3992   A clear day, without a cloud to be seen, is a sure sign that
        there will be a change in the weather in the next three days.
            (F, 40, R, 1963)
3993   A light-blue sky indicates foul weather ahead.
            (F, 21, 1950)
3994   A deep-blue sky indicates fair weather ahead.
            (F, 21, 1950)
3995   A clear winter sky means that there will be frost.
            (F, 1961)

Whirlwinds

3996   Whirlwinds of dust mean that there will be dry, windy
        weather.
            (F, 48, R, 1963 [her father], + 1 F and 2 M)
3997   Whirlwinds mean that the summer will be dry.
            (F, 58, R, 1958)
3998   A small whirlwind foretells dry weather.
            (F, 40, R, 1962)

3999   Lots of whirlwinds are the sign of dry weather.
       (F, 1959)

4000   A whirlwind is a sign of hot, dry weather.
       (F, 46, R, 1958, + 1 M)

4001   If the wind blows dust into a clockwise whirlwind, rain is
       sure to follow.
       (M, 20, R, 1958, + 1 M)

4002   Whirlwinds are a sign of rain.
       (F, 45, 1957, + 1 F and 1 M)

4003   If you see a whirlwind going towards the sun, there will be
       rain in the near future.
       (M, 50, R, 1957, + 1 M)

4004   Little whirlwinds signify a change in the weather.
       (F, 54, R, 1958)

4005   Little whirlwinds in the road or on fields are regarded by
       many as sure signs of rain.
       (F, 60, R, 1963 [her mother], + 1 F)

4006   Whirlwinds are a sign of bad weather.
       (F, 50, 1959 [her mother])

4007   If a whirlwind turns in the opposite direction from the sun,
       there will be rain; but if a whirlwind turns with the sun, there
       will be dry weather.
       (M, 19, R, 1958)

4008   It is a sign of good weather if a whirlwind moves in the same
       direction as the sun; it is a sign of bad weather if it moves
       against the sun.
       (F, 71, R, 1958)

4009   If there is an early frost, there will be an early spring.
       (F, 21, 1950)

4010   A cold winter brings a hot summer.
       (M, 21, 1950)

4011   A comfortable summer precedes a harsh winter.
       (F, 21, 1950)

4012   If it starts being cold rather early, there will be a hard
       winter.
       (F, 19, R, 1962)

4013   A late spring means that there will be a late fall.
       (F, 60, R, 1957)

4014   A storm that approaches from the east will inevitably be a
       bad one.
       (M, 37, 1959)

4015   The way it winters is the way it summers.
        (M, 74, R, 1960)
4016   Dust storms are signs of dry weather.
        (F, 1961)
4017   A halo after fine weather indicates that a storm is coming.
        (F, 21, 1950)
4018   In dry weather, all signs fail.
        (F, 20, R, 1959 [her parents], + 1 M)

Time

4019   If it rains before seven, it will quit before eleven.
        (F, 20, R, 1957, + 40 F and 17 M)
4020   If there is sunshine before seven, there will be rain before
        eleven.
        (F, 21, 1955)
4021   If it rains before seven but quits before eleven, it will rain
        again the same day.
        (F, 82, R, 1957)
4022   If there is fog before seven, rain will come down before
        eleven.
        (F, 78, R, 1961 [her mother])
4023   Rain before seven means that there will be more rain before
        eleven.
        (M, 20, 1956)
4024   If the wind comes up before seven, it will go down before
        eleven.
        (M, 47, R, 1963 [his father])
4025   If it rains after seven, it will be over by eleven.
        (F, 53, 1958)
4026   If you sing before seven, it will rain before eleven.
        (F, 21, 1950)
4027   If it thunders before seven, it will rain before eleven.
        (F, 81, 1955)
4028   If there is thunder before seven, the weather will be clear by
        eleven.
        (F, 23, R, 1958 [her grandmother])
4029   If it clears before 7:00 P.M., it will rain before 11:00 A.M.
        (F, 70, R, 1958)
4030   A clear night is a sailor's delight. A storm in the morning is a
        sailor's warning.
        (F, 80, R, 1961)

4031   "Clear in the morning, / Sailor's warning."
            (F, 1959)

Rainbows

4032   "A rainbow in the morning is a sailor's warning. / A rainbow
            at night is a sailor's delight."
            (F, 18, 1956, + 98 F and 37 M)

4033   "Rainbow at night, / Shepherd's delight. / Rainbow at morn-
            ing, /Shepherds take warning."
            (M, 40, R, 1962 [his mother], + 1 F and 1 M)

4034   When a rainbow appears after a storm, the storm is over.
            (M, 26, R, 1958, + 3 F)

4035   If you see a rainbow in the morning, it will rain; if you see one
            at night, it will not rain.
            (F, 40, R, 1960, + 8 F and 3 M)

4036   If there's a rainbow before sundown, it will rain before
            morning.
            (F, 21, 1950)

4037   One rainbow is a sign of clear weather; two rainbows mean
            that there is bad weather ahead.
            (F, 60, 1959 [her parents])

4038   Half a rainbow means that there will be another storm soon.
            (F, 21, 1956)

4039   If you see a rainbow while it's still raining, there'll be
            another rain within three days.
            (F, 21, R, 1959 [her parents])

4040   If the sun shines while it is raining, there always will be a
            rainbow.
            (F, 21, R, 1958)

4041   If there is a rainbow while the sun is shining, it will rain at
            the same time the next day.
            (F, 20, R, 1957)

4042   A rainbow assures a person that there will not be a flood.
            (M, 50, 1955)

4043   If there is a rainbow in the west in the early morning, it will
            rain within seven days.
            (M, 30, R, 1957)

4044   One contributor said that rain prediction was easy in the
            early days. If there was a rainbow in the west when the sun

came up in the morning, it was a sure sign that there would be rain before sunset that evening.
(M, 72, R, 1962)

4045   A rainbow in the west or northeast indicates that there will be a storm.
(F, 61, R, 1960)

4046   If you see a rainbow in the east, there will be rain before the next night.
(F, 80, R, 1961 [her parents])

4047   A Saturday rainbow is sure to bring a week of rainy weather.
(M, 40, 1955)

General Portents

4048   If there is a late fall, there will be a late spring.
(F, 80, R, 1960 [her mother])

4049   If there is a cool, rainy summer, there will be a cold, snowy winter.
(F, 20, 1961, + 1 F)

4050   There is a calm before a storm.
(F, 50, R, 1957, + 1 F)

ANIMAL SIGNS

Ants

4051   The higher the anthills, the harder the winter will be.
(M, 20, 1959, + 1 M)

4052   When ants build their hills up high, it is a sign of rain.
(F, 60, R, 1957, + 1 F)

4053   If the ants crawl into their holes, it is going to storm.
(F, 20, 1961)

4054   When ants build their hills in the shape of a cone, there will be wet weather. When they build their hills flat, it is going to be dry.
(M, 40, R, 1958 [his parents])

4055   When ants build their homes (hills) on high ground, a rainy season is ahead.
(F, 30, 1960 [her grandmother])

4056   When ants travel in lines or are unusually active, look for rain.
(M, 50, R, 1962 [his parents])

Birds and Fowl

4057   The early flight of birds in the spring or the fall means that
there will be an early summer or an early winter.
(F, 16, R, 1962)

4058   When the birds are singing in the rain, the rain will soon stop.
(F, 1961)

4059   A bird's flying high in the sky is a sign of rain.
(F, 50, R, 1961)

4060   If the birds are quiet, it will storm.
(F, 60, R, 1956)

4061   When birds are noisy all morning, you can expect a bad
storm that day.
(F, 60, R, 1962 [her family])

4062   A flock of birds means an early fall.
(M, 68, 1957, + 1 F)

4063   If birds fly close to the ground, there will be rain.
(F, 21, R, 1957, + 1 F)

4064   When one sees birds flocking together, it is usually the sign of
a storm.
(F, 47, R, 1959 [her grandmother], + 4 F and 2 M)

4065   It is a sign of rain if birds fly a yard or two apart. If someone
tries to catch one of these birds, it is a sign of death.
(M, 20, 1961)

4066   When birds fly low, fast, and in big groups, a storm is
brewing.
(F, 30, R, 1961)

4067   In late fall, birds will fly south ahead of an approaching
storm.
(M, 60, R, 1958)

4068   When woodpeckers are especially noisy, they are preparing
to shelter themselves from coming rain.
(M, 60, R, 1962)

4069   When a woodpecker pecks on a tin roof, it's a sign that wet
weather is coming.
(M, 75, 1958)

4070   When you see the first robin, spring is near.
(M, 20, R, 1959, + 5 F and 5 M)

4071   If a robin enters the house, there will be severe snows and
frosts.
(F, 70, R, 1959 [her mother])

4072   If the robin sings on the bush, the weather will be rough. If
        the robin sings on the barn, the weather will be warm.
            (F, 18, 1955)

4073   When turkeys that usually roost outside go inside, you can
        almost be sure that a bad storm is coming.
            (M, 60, R, 1962)

4074   If turkeys make nests near water along the creeks, there will
        be no floods that season. If turkeys make nests high up on the
        creek banks, there will be high water.
            (F, 77, R, 1957)

4075   When turkeys roost unusually high, a storm is brewing.
            (F, 77, R, 1957)

4076   A turkey will fly up on the roof or chimney when a storm is
        coming.
            (M, 71, R, 1958)

4077   When turkeys and chickens stand with their backs to the
        wind, a storm is coming.
            (F, 65, R, 1962)

4078   The cooing of doves is a sign of rain.
            (F, 74, R, 1958, + 1 F)

4079   If two doves are sitting facing in the same direction, it will
        rain.
            (F, 80, R, 1958)

4080   Rain will come from the direction of the first turtledove that
        you hear.
            (F, 70, R, 1960 [her parents])

4081   If a turtledove coos repeatedly, it will soon rain.
            (M, 50, R, 1958)

4082   If you hear a mourning dove, it will rain that day.
            (F, 40, R, 1957)

4083   When snowbirds assemble in flocks, a storm is approaching.
            (M, 60, R, 1962, + 1 F and 1 M)

4084   If you see snowbirds hopping around, it is going to snow.
            (F, 20, R, 1959 [her mother])

4085   When you hear an owl hoot, there is going to be rain.
            (M, 1961)

4086   When you hear an owl hoot before 4 P.M., there is sure to be
        rain.
            (M, 15, R, 1958)

4087   If you hear an owl hoot at night, it is a sign of rain.
            (M, 15, R, 1958)

4088 When an owl hoots, the weather will change soon; but if it shrieks, you will soon hear ill tidings.
(M, 60, R, 1957)

4089 If an owl hoots in the daytime, it is a sign of rain.
(M, 60, R, 1963 [his father])

4090 When cranes fly up the creek, it is going to flood.
(M, 80, R, 1957)

4091 If you see a bunch of cranes flying north, you will have warm weather. If you see them flying south, it is going to get cold.
(F, 40, R, 1962)

4092 If the birds commonly called killdeers cry a great deal (making a whining cry that sounds like "more rain"), rain is surely near.
(M, 50, R, 1958, + 1 F)

4093 There is always one late winter storm after the killdeers show up.
(M, 70, R, 1958)

4094 If, over a space of time, two or three killdeers fly over a herd of cattle while you are bringing them in, it will rain before morning.
(M, 50, R, 1959 [his father])

4095 A killdeer's cry in the evening means that it will rain before the next evening.
(M, 53, R, 1959 [his grandfather])

4096 Whenever sea gulls fly inland, rain may be expected.
(M, 50, R, 1962 [his father], + 1 M)

4097 Sea gulls over a plowed field foretell rain.
(M, 20, R, 1959 [his father])

4098 If sea gulls follow the plow, there will be rain inside of three days.
(M, 60, R, 1958)

4099 When the geese go north, spring is near. When they go south, winter is approaching.
(F, 60, R, 1961, + 4 F and 1 M)

4100 If the wishbone of a goose is thick, this is a sure sign of a long winter.
(F, 60, R, 1961 [her parents])

4101 When the breastbone of a goose is dark, there will be a lot of rain.
(F, 1961 [her grandmother])

4102 If the breastbone of a fowl is thick, it will be a cold winter.
(M, 60, R, 1957)

4103   If the breastbone of a fowl is cloudy all the way, the winter will be long and cold.
         (M, 50, R, 1962 [his mother])

4104   One can predict the severity of the weather by a goose's wishbone.
         (F, 35, 1956)

4105   You can tell when there is going to be a cold snap by the flying geese.
         (M, 24, 1956)

4106   When ducks and geese build their nests close to the creek, the season is going to be dry. When they build them on high points, the season is going to be a wet one.
         (M, 60, R, 1960 [his mother])

4107   When a goose's neck is long, it will be a long, hard winter.
         (F, 40, 1961)

4108   If geese are heavily feathered out, it's a sign that a hard winter is coming.
         (M, 50, R, 1963)

4109   If the geese have lots of feathers, a bad winter is coming.
         (F, 50, R, 1959)

4110   If there is heavy down on a duck, expect a hard winter.
         (F, 70, R, 1959, + 2 F)

4111   Heavy feathers on fowl foretell a severe winter.
         (F, 60, R, 1961)

4112   If you hear the call of the "rain crow," it is going to rain.
         (F, 19, R, 1959, + 4 F and 6 M)

4113   Loud and continued cawing by crows is an indication that it is going to rain.
         (F, 40, R, 1962 [her grandmother], + 1 F)

4114   When crows flock together, a storm is approaching.
         (F, 56, R, 1963 [her grandfather], + 2 F and 1 M)

4115   It is a storm warning if you see a lone crow flying.
         (F, 40, R, 1960, + 1 F and 3 M)

4116   If you see a crow flying alone, it is a sign of a storm; but a flock of crows means fair weather.
         (M, 26, R, 1957)

4117   "Crow on the fence, / Rain will go hence. / Crow on the ground, / Rain will come down."
         (F, 19, 1955)

4118   If a crow lands in a tree, the weather will get cooler.
         (F, 20, R, 1958)

4119   If a crow flies low, there will be cold weather.
       (M, 65, R, 1958)

4120   If crows fly low, you're sure to have rain.
       (F, 40, R, 1957)

4121   Large numbers of crows foretoken a bad harvest or a hot, dry summer.
       (F, 21, 1950)

4122   If a cock crows when he goes to bed, he'll get up with a wet head.
       (F, 50, 1962 [her mother], + 7 F and 2 M)

4123   If a rooster crows before midnight, there will be rain before morning.
       (F, 50, R, 1957)

4124   If a rooster crows between 6 P.M. and midnight, it will rain within twelve hours.
       (F, 60, 1958 [her parents])

4125   A rooster's crowing after dark means that bad weather is coming that night.
       (M, 21, 1950, + 3 F)

4126   If a rooster crows at night, the weather will soon change.
       (M, 21, 1950, + 2 F and 4 M)

4127   If a rooster crows at sundown, the next day will be fair.
       (F, 21, R, 1961)

4128   If the roosters crow around 10 P.M., it will rain.
       (F, 54, R, 1958)

4129   When a cock crows at seven, there will be rain by eleven.
       (F, 22, 1954)

4130   If the roosters crow at midnight, there will be a change in the weather.
       (F, 40, R, 1963 [her grandfather])

4131   If a rooster crows while standing on a manure pile, it will rain.
       (F, 40, 1962)

4132   If the chickens have lots of feathers, it will be a bad winter.
       (F, 59, R, 1958, + 1 M)

4133   If the chickens stay out while it's raining, it is going to rain all day.
       (F, 19, 1959, + 6 F and 6 M)

4134   If the chickens go into their house when it starts to rain, it means that it will be a long storm; but if they stay out, a short one.
       (M, 50, R, 1958, + 1 F)

4135 A little chicken on a hen's back means rain.
      (F, 60, 1959)
4136 When chickens crow or they go to roost, it's a sign of rain.
      (F, 80, 1958)
4137 If chickens stay out in the rain, it means that the rain will last
      for three days.
      (F, 60, R, 1964)
4138 A tough lining in a chicken's gizzard indicates that there will
      be a mild winter.
      (F, 44, R, 1956)
4139 If a chicken cackles loudly, the next day will be fair.
      (F, 1961 [her mother])
4140 When the chickens made a different sound, it used to be con-
      sidered a sign that there would be a storm.
      (M, 70, R, 1962)
4141 Watch the actions of chickens for weather signs.
      (M, 20, 1955)
4142 When the chickens keep strolling out in the rain, it will
      continue until the chickens stop doing so.
      (M, 50, 1955)
4143 If chickens go to roost late in the evening, there will be bad
      weather the next day.
      (F, 60, R, 1957)
4144 Chickens will go to roost early if a rainstorm is coming.
      (F, 30, R, 1958)
4145 When a redbird sings, there will be a change in the weather.
      (F, 40, 1959)
4146 When a quail is sitting on a post saying "Bob white," there is
      sure to be rain.
      (F, 61, R, 1957)
4147 Pheasants' roosting in the trees is a sign that there is going to
      be a storm.
      (F, 30, R, 1960 [her mother])
4148 If a hawk circles in front of a storm, look out for a cyclone.
      (M, 50, R, 1959)
4149 Hummingbirds are most active before a rain.
      (M, 21, 1950)
4150 When kingfishers and swallows nest in holes near water, a
      dry season is coming.
      (F, 65, R, 1962)
4151 Water never freezes after the buzzards come in the spring.
      (M, 80, 1957)

4152   Whenever pigeons return slowly to roost, anticipate rain.
       (M, 60, R, 1962)
4153   When the phoebe bird starts calling to its mate, spring is just
       around the corner.
       (F, 73, 1956)
4154   When prairie larks flock together and fly low to the ground, a
       storm is surely on the way.
       (F, 55, R, 1958)
4155   If you destroy a barn swallow's nest, lightning will strike your
       barn.
       (F, 16, R, 1961)
4156   If a swallow flies low, swooping close to the ground, there is
       going to be rain.
       (F, 1958)
4157   If sparrows fly low, it is going to rain.
       (F, 16, R, 1962)

Caterpillars and Worms

4158   If the caterpillars are furry, the winter will be hard.
       (F, 30, 1968, + 1 F and 1 M)
4159   If the front part of a caterpillar worm is longer than the rest
       of the body, there will be an early winter. If the back part is
       longer, there will be a late winter.
       (F, 70, R, 1962)
4160   If you count the rings on an inchworm (caterpillar), you can
       tell by the number whether the winter will be severe (lots of
       rings mean a severe winter).
       (M, 1961)
4161   If the caterpillar has more black on the head of its trunk, the
       first part of winter will be more severe. If more black ap-
       pears at the tail of the trunk, the last part of winter will be
       the harder.
       (F, 50, R, 1957)
4162   If a caterpillar is black on its head and tail, but brown in the
       middle, this means that there will be an early and a late cold
       spell, with a mild winter in between.
       (F, 54, R, 1958)
4163   If the caterpillars are all black, then it is going to be a long
       hard winter.
       (F, 54, R, 1958)
4164   Caterpillars that are all one color foretell a long winter. If
       they are light-colored on each end, there will be a late fall

and early spring. If they are light in the middle, there will be a good winter, a bad fall, and a late spring.

(F, 70, 1962 [her parents])

4165   When earthworms come out of the ground, it's a sign of rain.

(F, 50, R, 1958 [her father], + 2 F)

4166   Fishworms stay close to the surface of the ground if it is going to be a mild winter.

(M, 50, R, 1959, + 1 F)

4167   When the worms work in the ground, it is a sign that there will be rain.

(M, 52, 1958, + 1 M)

4168   If woolly worms in the fall are black, it will be a bad winter; if they are light brown, it will be a mild winter.

(M, 70, R, 1958)

4169   If the woolly worms have narrow bands, it will be a short winter.

(M, 23, R, 1959)

Cats

4170   It is going to turn cold when a cat lies with its back to the fire.

(F, 1961)

4171   When cats sit with their backs to the fire, snow is on its way.

(F, 18, 1959)

4172   If the cats want to play, there will be a storm the next day.

(F, 60, R, 1962 [her mother])

4173   If barn cats come to the house at the approach of winter, this is a sign of a long, cold, hard winter ahead.

(F, 60, R, 1960)

4174   When a cat sleeps or sits with its head under its paws, it is a sign of cold weather.

(M, 60, R, 1957)

4175   When a cat lies down with the back of its head down, so that both ears touch what it is lying on, look for rain within twenty-four hours. (The contributor had seen this happen often.)

(M, 80, R, 1958)

4176   When cats curl up and sleep on their backs, cold weather is coming.

(F, 50, R, 1956)

4177   If the cat lies in a coil, bad weather is coming; if it yawns and stretches, good weather is on its way.

(F, 65, R, 1962)

4178   When cats go along chewing wheat, it's going to storm.
        (F, 50, R, 1958 [her father])
4179   When a cat eats grass, it is going to rain.
        (F, 20, 1961, + 3 F and 3 M)
4180   When a cat washes its ears, it is a sign of rain.
        (M, 50, R, 1963, + 2 F)
4181   If a cat washes itself all over, it is going to rain.
        (F, 20, 1956, + 1 F)
4182   If a cat sleeps with its nose in the air, there is going to be rain.
        (M, 21, R, 1956, + 1 F)

Cattle and Horses

4183   If horses and cattle run, there is going to be bad weather.
        (M, 20, 1959, + 2 F and 3 M)
4184   If it's going to storm, horses will play.
        (M, 23, 1957, + 4 F and 1 M)
4185   When a horse prances, a storm is drawing near.
        (F, 20, R, 1961 [her father])
4186   When horses and cattle are frisky, there is going to be a
        change in the weather.
        (F, 40, R, 1960 [her mother])
4187   When a horse is skittish, it's going to rain.
        (F, 63, 1958)
4188   If a horse rolls clear over, it is going to storm.
        (F, 20, R, 1961 [her mother])
4189   A horse won't drink during a storm unless the storm is going
        to last a long time.
        (F, 50, 1961 [her parents])
4190   If the horses have a lot of hair in the autumn, the winter will
        be a cold one.
        (M, 60, R, 1957)
4191   When horses or cows hug south fences, a storm is coming
        from the north.
        (F, 52, 1956)
4192   When the cows kick up their heels, there will be rain within
        the next twenty-four hours.
        (F, 20, R, 1958)
4193   When a cow rolls and a horse runs, there will be rain.
        (M, 22, 1964)
4194   If the cows are restless, then it is going to rain.
        (F, 20, R, 1956, + 6 F and 5 M)

4195   If the cows are frisky, there will be a storm.
(F, 20, 1959, + 2 F and 2 M)

4196   If the cows run around in the lot, it is going to rain.
(F, 20, R, 1961, + 10 F and 4 M)

4197   If cattle gather in a corner of a field, it is going to rain.
(F, 60, R, 1960 [her father])

4198   If cattle crowd up at the farthest end of the lot, a storm is coming.
(F, 30, R, 1957)

4199   Cows will go to the part of the pasture that is in the direction from which the wind is blowing.
(M, 62, R, 1962)

4200   If it is going to storm, the cattle will go to high ground.
(M, 54, R, 1959)

4201   If you see the cattle eating in the morning, there will be a storm before night. If the cattle are resting, the weather will be clear.
(F, 50, R, 1958)

4202   On New Year's Eve at midnight, visit a cattle lot to see which way the cattle are lying. If their heads are facing north, good weather is in store for the coming year. If their heads face south, bad weather is ahead.
(F, 60, R, 1957)

4203   When the cows form a straight line, it is a sign of a storm.
(M, 70, R, 1963 [his father])

4204   If an old cow sneezes, there is going to be rain.
(F, 50, R, 1962)

4205   If you do not succeed when you try to drive livestock, it is a sign of bad weather.
(M, 59, R, 1959)

4206   If cattle are huddled against the fence, a storm is coming.
(F, 21, 1960, + 1 M)

4207   Cows gather together in a sheltered spot before a thunderstorm.
(F, 40, 1959 [her father], + 2 F)

4208   If the cows bunch together, it is going to rain.
(F, 20, 1963, + 3 F and 3 M)

4209   When cattle grow heavier pelts, the winter will be very cold.
(M, 21, 1950, + 2 F)

4210   Livestock turn their heads away from the direction of an approaching storm.
(M, 70, 1958)

4211   A cow always puts her tail to the storm, but a horse puts its
        head to the storm.
        (M, 30, R, 1962, + 1 M)

4212   Cattle always face the wind if a storm is brewing.
        (M, 1961)

4213   When a cow "moos" with pain, there is going to be rain.
        (M, 50, 1958)

4214   When a cow bawls before midnight, there is going to be a
        change in the weather.
        (M, 70, 1956)

4215   If cows bawl a lot, there is going to be colder weather or a
        storm.
        (F, 56, R, 1963 [her uncle])

4216   It is a sure sign of rain when you see all the cows lying down
        in a field.
        (F, 20, 1958, + 5 F)

4217   When cattle graze at night, there is going to be a storm.
        (M, 20, R, 1957, + 2 M)

4218   When cattle sniff the wind, there is sure to be a storm.
        (M, 60, R, 1958 [his parents], + 1 M)

Crickets and Hornets

4219   If you hear a cricket chirp, it will rain.
        (M, 20, 1957, + 1 F)

4220   By counting the chirps of the black field cricket for fourteen
        seconds, and then adding forty, you will have the temper-
        ature reading.
        (M, 78, R, 1960)

4221   Count the number of times a cricket chirps during a period of
        fifteen seconds; then add thirty-two. This will tell you the
        temperature.
        (M, 20, 1963)

4222   It will frost six weeks after the first cricket chirps in the fall.
        (F, 70, 1961 [her grandmother])

4223   One indication of a coming severe winter is a low-hanging
        hornet's nest.
        (F, 40, 1958)

Dogs and Coyotes

4224   If a dog rolls on its back, rain is coming.
        (F, 19, 1954)

4225   When a dog rolls on its back and looks at the moon, it will rain.
       (M, 50, R, 1960)

4226   When a dog scorns meat and eats grass, there will be rain.
       (F, 19, 1959)

4227   Very seldom does a dog run out in the wheat and snap off heads of wheat. When this happens, it will soon rain.
       (M, 50, R, 1960 [his father])

4228   If a dog is found on its back, there will be wind the next day.
       (M, 70, R, 1959, + 1 M)

4229   If a dog sleeps on its back, it means that there will be rain.
       (F, 20, 1958, + 2 F and 2 M)

4230   When dogs eat grass, it means that it is going to rain.
       (F, 20, R, 1961, + 11 F and 8 M)

4231   If the coyotes howl in late August or early September, there will be an early winter.
       (M, 60, R, 1957)

4232   If a coyote howls while the sun is shining in the wintertime, there is bound to be a change in the weather.
       (M, 60, R, 1959)

4233   Howling coyotes at night foretell rain.
       (M, 20, R, 1958, + 2 F and 2 M)

Fish

4234   If fish swim upstream in spring, it will be a wet season. If they go downstream, it will be a dry one.
       (M, 59, R, 1957)

4235   When the fish go downstream, a drought is coming.
       (M, 63, R, 1961)

4236   When fish are swimming along the top of a pool, there will be unsettled weather.
       (F, 50, R, 1956)

Flies and Gnats

4237   If there are flies on the screen door, it is going to rain.
       (M, 20, R, 1963 [his mother], + 4 F and 3 M)

4238   If flies group around a door, on a porch, or in any enclosure, it is going to rain.
       (M, 50, R, 1960, + 1 F)

4239   If the flies are biting, it is a sign of rain.
       (F, 20, R, 1958, + 1 F and 1 M)

4240   The flies bite the hardest before it rains.
           (F, 21, 1954, + 4 F)

4241   If the flies are bothering the cows excessively, there is going to be rain.
           (F, 50, R, 1960 [her parents], + 2 F)

4242   If flies get bad in the house, it is going to rain.
           (M, 23, 1964, + 2 M)

4243   If the flies are thick, it is sure to rain.
           (F, 22, 1955)

4244   When flies are numerous and are biting, it is going to rain.
           (F, 50, 1962 [her mother])

4245   Houseflies become thick under porches before a rain.
           (F, 1961)

4246   A fly in the house in April or March is a sign that spring is approaching.
           (F, 50, R, 1961)

4247   When gnats swarm, it is going to rain.
           (F, 50, R, 1958, + 1 M)

Frogs and Toads

4248   Turn a frog over on its back; this will bring rain.
           (M, 1961)

4249   Many little frogs on the road signify that it is going to rain.
           (F, 64, 1958)

4250   When frogs begin to croak in early spring, there is no further danger of frost.
           (F, 60, R, 1957)

4251   If frogs are found on high ground, one can predict a wet season.
           (M, 23, R, 1959)

4252   In the spring when the frogs start croaking, they will see through three glass eyes (that is, there will be ice three more times).
           (M, 63, R, 1961, + 1 M)

4253   When the frogs croak, it's a sign of rain.
           (F, 61, R, 1960, + 2 F)

4254   When toads and tortoises move to high ground, it's a sign of wet weather.
           (M, 65, R, 1958, + 1 M)

4255   At night, if toads hop toward the hills (across a road), wet

weather is on its way. If they hop toward the river, a dry spell
is coming.
(M, 62, R, 1956)

4256   A certain way that a toad croaks is a sign of rain.
(M, 70, R, 1958)

4257   If a toad hops after sundown, it is going to rain.
(F, 70, R, 1961)

4258   If you see a toad first, it will be a good summer. If you see a
snake first, it'll be a bad summer.
(F, 21, R, 1959)

4259   If the tree toads are singing, a rain is coming.
(F, 70, R, 1958)

Hogs

4260   When butchering, one can tell from the milt (spleen) of a hog
what kind of winter is ahead.
(F, 77, R, 1960, + 1 F)

4261   The old people used to determine the severity of the winter by
the size of the milt in the hogs when they butchered. If it was
wider in front, the first part of the winter would be rougher;
if the back part was wider, the last part would be rougher. If
it was even, the winter would be normal.
(M, 50, R, 1960)

4262   In the past, when a hog was butchered in mid winter, the milt
was examined. If the big end of it was toward the head, the
big end of the winter was yet to come. If the big end of the milt
was toward the tail, most of the winter weather was past.
(The informant said that he had killed two hogs in one day:
the first had the big end one way; the second, the other way.)
(M, 62, 1959)

4263   If the large end of the tenderloin of a hog is on top, it will be a
hard winter.
(M, 20, R, 1961)

4264   If you see a hog carrying feed for a nest, look for a change in
the weather.
(F, 74, R, 1959)

4265   If pigs make beds, the winter will be bad.
(M, 50, R, 1960 [his father])

4266   If a sow makes the nest for her pigs deep, it's a sign of a
storm, usually cold.
(M, 65, R, 1960 [his father])

4267 Hogs will root out from under a fence if a bad electrical storm is coming.
      (M, 30, R, 1958)

4268 If you see a pig pick up a cornstalk in its mouth and run around and around, there will be change in the weather.
      (M, 53, R, 1959 [his father])

4269 When the pigpen starts to stink, it will soon rain.
      (F, 50, R, 1960)

4270 It's a sign of rain if hogs run around in their pens making a woofing noise.
      (F, 80, R, 1958 [her father])

4271 If a hog carries sticks to build a nest for protection, it is going to rain.
      (M, 22, R, 1953, + 1 F)

4272 When hogs make a bed in the winter, a big snowstorm is brewing.
      (M, 60, R, 1961, + 1 F and 4 M)

4273 Pigs will play in the pen when a storm is approaching.
      (M, 67, R, 1962, + 1 F and 1 M)

4274 When the hogs carry sticks in their mouths, it is going to rain.
      (M, 24, 1956, + 2 M)

Locusts

4275 The first frost will come ninety days after you hear the first locust.
      (F, 50, 1963, + 1 F)

4276 When the locusts sing, it's a sign of dry weather.
      (F, 21, 1950, + 1 F)

4277 Hearing a locust for the first time in the summer foretells that there will be six weeks until frost.
      (M, 20, R, 1959, + 8 F and 3 M)

4278 When cicadas are noisy, rain is coming.
      (M, 45, 1955)

4279 When locusts stop singing towards the end of summer, it means that there will be only six weeks until frost.
      (M, 80, R, 1958)

4280 Nine weeks after the first locust sings there will be frost.
      (F, 50, R, 1961)

4281 It will frost thirteen weeks after the first locust sings.
      (F, 43, R, 1963)

4282 When you hear the first locust, summer is half over.
      (F, 75, 1957)

Rodents

4283   When the squirrels build their nests high in the trees, the
       winter will be mild.
                (M, 85, R, 1958, + 1 M)

4284   When the squirrels bury nuts in the fall, there will be a hard
       winter.
                (F, 65, R, 1959 [her parents])

4285   When the squirrels start to gather nuts, winter is near.
                (F, 21, 1950)

4286   If the squirrels pack up lots of acorns, there will be a hard
       winter ahead.
                (F, 60, R, 1957)

4287   If squirrels gather an excess of nuts, a long winter will
       follow.
                (F, 21, 1950, + 2 F and 1 M)

4288   If the squirrels build their nests shallow, there will be a mild
       winter.
                (M, 20, R, 1959)

4289   When the squirrels are busy, there is going to be bad
       weather.
                (M, 21, 1950)

4290   If the squirrels build their nests in the hollow of a tree, there
       will be a cold winter.
                (M, 94, 1957)

4291   If it is hard to skin squirrels in the fall, you can predict a hard
       winter.
                (M, 23, R, 1959)

4292   Prairie dogs build higher mounds when it is going to be a very
       rainy season.
                (M, 50, 1959 [his father], + 3 M)

4293   If prairie dogs dig holes on top of the draws, the season will
       be wet, and the draws will run.
                (F, 60, R, 1961)

4294   If a rabbit shot in August is fatter than usual, it will be a
       hard, cold winter.
                (M, 55, R, 1958)

4295   If there are lots of cottontail rabbits, a dry spell is coming.
                (M, 20, R, 1958)

4296   You can tell when it's hot, because of all the jack rabbits sitting in the shade of the telephone poles, since the poles furnish the only shade around.

(M, 39, R, 1958)

4297   If the muskrats make big houses for the winter, you will have a hard winter.

(F, 65, R, 1957)

4298   If muskrats grow long hair, it will be a hard winter. (An Indian saying.)

(M, 50, R, 1960)

4299   If the field mice are plentiful and are trying to find cover in the fall of the year, it will be a bad winter.

(M, 54, R, 1959)

4300   When many (as compared to few) mice enter the house in the fall, a long, cold winter can be predicted.

(M, 68, R, 1956)

4301   When mice build their nests high in the fodder shocks, the winter will be a wet one.

(M, 65, R, 1960)

4302   When the groundhog begins to build his home on higher ground, you can look for a rainy season.

(F, 50, R, 1957)

4303   If a groundhog sees his shadow on February 2, there will be six more weeks of winter weather.

(F, 20, R, 1957, + 42 F and 15 M)

4304   If rats move into buildings, it is going to be a cold winter.

(F, 20, R, 1961 [her father])

4305   When the beavers go to high ground, there will be a flood.

(M, 20, R, 1959)

4306   When beavers pile large quantities of willow trees near their dens in the fall, there will be a cold winter; when they make very little or no preparation by late fall, the winter will be very mild.

(M, 61, 1964)

Snakes

4307   If you see snakes crossing the road, it is a sign of rain.

(F, 50, R, 1961 [her mother], + 2 F and 3 M)

4308   If a snake crawls across the road in front of you while you are walking or driving along the road in the morning, there will be rain before sundown.

(M, 72, R, 1962)

4309   If there are bullsnakes on the road between one and three in the afternoon, it will rain.
   (M, 49, R, 1963 [his mother])

4310   If you see a lot of snakes, it will rain soon.
   (F, 19, 1959, + 4 F and 2 M)

4311   When snakes leave the creek, there is going to be a flood.
   (F, 1961, + 1 F)

4312   When you kill a snake, hang the body over a fence, and it will bring rain.
   (F, 22, R, 1958, + 1 F and 5 M)

4313   If you kill a snake, hang it up on a fence. If it wiggles until sundown, there will be rain.
   (F, 20, 1958)

4314   Kill a snake, and hang it on a fence. It will wiggle until it rains.
   (F, 55, 1959)

4315   If you hang a rattlesnake on a fence, it will bring rain.
   (F, 20, R, 1958)

4316   When you kill a snake, hang it over the fence. It won't rain until the snake rots in two.
   (F, 50, 1958)

4317   If you hang a dead snake on a fence and it stays there till sundown, there will be rain the next day.
   (F, 49, R, 1961)

4318   Put a snake upside down over a fence, and it will rain.
   (F, 22, R, 1956, + 3 F and 1 M)

4319   If a snake turns over on its back when it dies, it will bring rain.
   (M, 20, 1959 [his grandparents], + 3 F and 5 M)

4320   When you kill a snake, throw it over your shoulder. If it lands on its back, it is going to rain.
   (F, 19, R, 1956, + 1 F and 1 M)

4321   Throw a dead snake into the air. If it lands with its stomach in the air, there will be rain within twenty-four hours.
   (M, 50, 1963, + 4 F and 3 M)

4322   If you turn a snake on its back when you kill it, there will be rain before night.
   (M, 20, R, 1957, + 2 F and 5 M)

4323   If a snake turns over on its back, it is going to rain.
   (M, 50, R, 1963, + 1 M)

4324   If you see a snake, pick it up and throw it; if it lights on its back, there will be rain.
   (F, 40, R, 1960)

4325   Snakes lying on their backs in the middle of the road are signs of rain.
        (M, 29, R. 1958)

4326   If you kill a snake and fasten it so it will remain belly side up, it will rain in a few days.
        (F, 1961)

4327   If a snake that you have tried to kill dies before sundown, there will be stormy weather.
        (M, 20, 1957)

4328   If snakes turn over on their backs before sundown after having been killed, it is going to rain.
        (M, 50, R, 1959)

4329   Kill a snake, and put it on its back. If it turns over before sunset, it will rain.
        (M, 30, R, 1961)

4330   If you leave a dead snake lying on its stomach, there will be rain.
        (F, 20, 1959)

4331   When snakes move uphill, a heavy rain will follow.
        (M, 22, R, 1957, + 3 F and 3 M)

4332   When snakes crawl to higher ground, it is a sign of rain or possibly a flood.
        (M, 40, 1962 [his father], + 1 F)

4333   If you see three snakes in one day, it is going to rain.
        (F, 40, R, 1962)

4334   It is generally believed that snakes, particularly rattlesnakes, become very active just before a rain.
        (M, 80, 1959)

4335   When the snakes are fat, it is going to be a hard winter.
        (M, 50, R, 1962 [his father])

4336   If you see a snake first in the spring, it will be a rainy year. If you see a frog first, it will be a dry one.
        (F, 19, R, 1957)

4337   If snakes are observed stretched out on roads or other barren spots sunning themselves, it is a sign of rain.
        (M, 60, R, 1957)

4338   Hang a snake in a tree to get rain.
        (F, 60, R, 1958)

Spiders

4339   If there are many spiders around, it will be a wet year.
        (M, 50, R, 1958)

4340   It is a sign of clear weather when cobwebs lie flat on the grass.
    (F, 85, R, 1962)

4341   If there are lots of cobwebs in the summer, the winter will be unusually cold.
    (F, 58, R, 1958)

4342   When spiders desert their webs, rain is coming.
    (M, 50, R, 1962 [his father])

4343   A spider in the sink (or bathtub) means that it will rain.
    (M, 60, R, 1959 [his parents])

4344   If a spider spins its web horizontally, it won't rain; but if the spider spins its web perpendicularly, it will rain. (The contributor said that she had heard her father repeat this many times when he would see a spider spinning a web; his father before him had told him this.)
    (F, 1961)

4345   If spider webs hang on power lines and fences in the early fall, it means that the fall will be warm.
    (M, 40, R, 1960)

4346   If you step on a daddy-longlegs, it is supposed to rain.
    (F, 1961)

4347   Fair weather may be expected if a spider spins a new web.
    (M, 40, R, 1959)

4348   If you kill a spider, it will cause rain.
    (F, 50, 1960, + 1 F)

4349   When tarantulas first appear in the fall, it will be six weeks until frost.
    (F, 60, R, 1957)

Turtles and Snails

4350   If turtles are seen crawling uphill, it is a sign that it will rain.
    (M, 18, 1957, + 11 F and 5 M)

4351   When you see the turtles coming out of the river headed for higher ground, there is going to be a flood.
    (F, 19, R, 1957, + 1 M)

4352   A turtle going uphill is a sign of high water.
    (F, 50, 1959)

4353   If turtles crawl towards higher ground, there is going to be a flood.
    (M, 1961 [his grandmother])

4354   When turtles come out on the road, there is going to be rain.
    (M, 19, R, 1958, + 1 M)

4355   When you see a turtle, it is a sign of rain.
        (M, 55, R, 1957)
4356   When land turtles crawl away from draws, there is going to
        be a rainstorm.
        (M, 20, R, 1961 [his grandfather])
4357   If turtles are found coming from the river, it's a sign of wet
        weather.
        (M, 40, R, 1959)
4358   When the turtles are going toward the river, there is going to
        be a dry spell.
        (F, 30, R, 1959)
4359   A furry snail foretells a hard winter.
        (M, 75, R, 1961)

General Indicators

4360   Heavy fur on animals is an indication that there will be cold
        weather.
        (F, 21, 1950, + 15 F and 8 M)
4361   When the farm animals are running around in the pasture,
        rain is coming.
        (M, 70, 1959, + 1 F and 1 M)
4362   Animals are restless before a storm.
        (F, 70, 1958, + 4 M)
4363   If animals in the farmyard are frisking about, there will be a
        change in the weather.
        (F, 26, R, 1957)
4364   If animals burrow deep, there will be cold weather.
        (M, 70, R, 1959)
4365   When animals build their winter homes high up, there is
        going to be a flood in the spring.
        (M, 74, 1959)
4366   If wild game sits tight, bad weather is in sight.
        (F, 50, R, 1957)
4367   Animals migrate to higher ground when a storm is impending.
        (M, 20, R, 1963)
4368   When the animals are hurrying to and fro during a nice day
        in the fall, a snow storm is on its way.
        (M, 20, R, 1959)
4369   The opossum burrows in the trees before a mild winter; if the
        winter is to be a hard one, it burrows into the ground.
        (F, 50, R, 1957)

4370   When old sheep lose their appetites, there is going to be a thaw.
        (M, 40, R, 1959)

MISCELLANEOUS INDICATORS

4371   When your rheumatism acts up, wet weather is coming.
        (F, 19, 1954, + 2 F and 1 M)
4372   If your joints ache, there is going to be a change in the weather—usually bad.
        (M, 23, 1964, + 2 F)
4373   Aching bones forecast a change in the weather.
        (M, 20, R, 1962, + 3 F)
4374   If your corns hurt, there will be a change in the weather.
        (F, 45, 1957, + 7 F and 2 M)
4375   Aching feet or arms foretell a change in the weather.
        (F, 20, 1959, + 2 F)
4376   If your feet itch or burn, rain is on the way.
        (F, 50, 1954, + 1 F)
4377   If glasses sweat in summer, a storm is coming.
        (F, 20, R, 1959 [her parents])
4378   When you see a water pitcher sweating, there will be rain within the next twenty-four hours.
        (F, 50, R, 1958, + 2 F)
4379   If you fill a bucket of water and it sweats, there will soon be rain.
        (M, 50, R, 1960, + 2 F)
4380   If the windmill pipe sweats, it will rain soon.
        (F, 50, R, 1960, + 1 F and 1 M)
4381   When a pump sweats while you are pumping water, rain is in the offing.
        (F, 40, 1963, + 1 F and 1 M)
4382   When a water pipe sweats, it is going to rain.
        (F, 20, R, 1961, + 4 F and 4 M)
4383   If the air is clear so that you can hear noises at great distances, a storm is coming.
        (F, 55, R, 1958, + 2 F and 1 M)
4384   If a train's smoke follows the train and does not rise, there will be a storm.
        (M, 1961)

4385   If train smoke settles to the ground, there is going to be a
       storm.
           (F, 20, R, 1959, + 9 F and 6 M)
4386   If the smoke from a chimney settles to the ground, there is
       going to be rain.
           (M, 76, R, 1956)
4387   If potatoes burn dry, it will rain the next day.
           (M, 20, R, 1958, + 1 F and 6 M)
4388   If you clean up all the food on the table, it will be nice the next
       day.
           (F, 20, R, 1959, + 23 F and 4 M)
4389   If there is a blue flame burning in the coal stove, expect snow
       soon.
           (F, 70, R, 1962)
4390   One contributor offered this fact about the atmosphere,
       which most weather bureaus disdain: whenever his suit has
       been newly pressed, it is virtually certain to rain.
           (F, 60, R, 1961)
4391   A sign of rain is when the water in the stock tank turns milky.
           (F, 61, R, 1961)
4392   When you start out in Kansas, take an overcoat, an umbrella,
       and a fan, for you'll need them all before you get back.
           (F, 83, R, 1961)
4393   A tornado will never hit a town that is located in the bend of a
       river.
           (F, 50, R, 1957, + 1 M)
4394   Tornadoes will never hit where two creeks or rivers meet.
           (M, 1959, + 4 F and 1 M)
4395   Only fools and strangers predict weather in Kansas.
           (M, 50, R, 1957, + 1 F and 2 M)
4396   All weather signs fail in Kansas.
           (M, 20, 1957, + 2 F and 3 M)

10

Plants and Planting

THE STUDY OF PLANTS IS MORE VIGOROUS TODAY THAN IT
has ever been. Plant shops, spurred by TV and radio programs, nur-
series, botanical gardens, horticultural societies, and community
lecture series, meet a wide range of interests. College courses in horticultural therapy are relatively new, but the practical knowledge of
this apparent therapeutical result from close contact with plants is
not. In England, over two centuries ago, prison wardens observed that
inmates who worked with plants were far happier than those who
were assigned to other details.

As did travelers in ancient times, our immigrants brought with
them plant seeds from their native lands, and as soon as native plants
could be utilized, they were. It is difficult today to realize that we are
so well supplied with plant food only because generation after generation experimented in one way or another. By trial and error, people
learned that nature has its own way of telling when or when not to
plant or harvest. The condition of the moon, the size of leaves on certain trees, or pelicans in the field seemed to aid people in making their
decisions. Thus, folk knowledge, aided sometimes by the almanacs,
guided our pioneer agriculturists.

Of the 245 items that follow, over 50 percent deal with when to
plant; 73 items are directly concerned with the moon. There are not
many people in America's heartland who have not had experience
with a potato crop, so it is not surprising that some 32 items are concerned with this staple crop, which, according to the folk, should be
planted either on Good Friday or St. Patrick's Day.

With the U.S. Department of Agriculture, the U.S. Weather Bureau, college agricultural departments, the states' extension services,
and other know-how organizations at quick hand, it is quite amazing
that so many traditional beliefs are still vigorous and ready on the lips
of so many of our people.

WHEN TO PLANT

4397   The moon influences the growth of crops.
        (M, 1959)

4398   Plant your garden according to the moon.
        (F, 70, R, 1963 [her mother])

4399   Crops should be planted according to the moon.
        (M, 20, R, 1962 [his grandparents], + 1 F and 4 M)

4400   Farmers should plow their ground in the new moon, because ground plowed at this time of the moon will not settle back and get hard; it will also produce twice as much.
        (F, 30, R, 1957)

4401   Crops that are planted under a full moon will have a large yield.
        (F, 21, R, 1958, + 1 F)

4402   Always plant your garden when the full moon is out, so that the plants will produce better.
        (F, 20, R, 1958 [her mother and grandmother], + 3 F)

4403   When you plant seed in the light of the moon, the seed will do better, and the ground won't rust.
        (M, 1959)

4404   A new moon means a good time for planting seeds.
        (F, 60, R, 1958 [her father])

4405   Plant things that grow under the ground by the light of the moon. Plant things that grow above the ground by the dark of the moon.
        (M, 22, R, 1959, + 2 F and 1 M)

4406   Plant according to the moon: in the dark for the root vege-tables, and in the light for the aboveground vegetables.
        (F, 30, 1957, + 25 F and 16 M)

4407   Everything that produces under the ground should be planted in the dark of the moon.
        (F, 21, 1950, + 8 F and 8 M)

4408   Plant root crops from the last quarter to the new moon.
        (M, 60, R, 1962 [his father])

4409   For nice root vegetables, plant when the moon is getting darker.
        (F, 1959 [her grandparents])

4410   You must plant root crops in the light of the moon.
        (F, 1962 [her grandparents])

4411   Anything that produces above the ground must be planted in the light of the moon.
        (M, 21, 1950 [his mother], + 8 F and 8 M)

4412   The time to plant things that grow on top of the ground is from the new moon until the full moon.
        (M, 94, 1957)

4413   When you plant crops other than root crops, plant them be-tween the first quarter and the new moon.
        (M, 60, R, 1962 [his father])

4414   Grain should be planted in the waxing moon, which is a fruit-ful sign.
        (M, 24, 1957)

4415   Planting by the light of the moon makes good bushes; when one plants by the dark of the moon, all the energy goes to the roots.
        (F, 20, R, 1963 [one of her friends])

4416   Indians say to plant when you can hang a powder horn on the. moon, which indicates that there will be rain.
        (M, 30, 1954)

4417   If you plant crops when the half-moon is tilted upward, no rain will fall.
        (M, 22, R, 1958)

4418   Dig vegetables that grow underground after the full moon, so that they will keep better.
(M, 70, R, 1960)

4419   Annual crops will freeze if planted while the moon is declining.
(F, 70, R, 1958 [her father])

4420   Never plant anything on the day that the moon changes, because it will not grow.
(M, 70, R, 1960)

4421   Always plant seeds in the morning; if you plant them in the evening, the crop will not grow.
(F, 1956 [her grandmother])

4422   Crops should be planted according to the almanac.
(M, 1961)

4423   Don't plant any flowering vegetables, such as peas, except when the "signs" are right.
(F, 60, R, 1959)

4424   Plant root crops under the sign of Cancer.
(M, 54, R, 1959)

4425   Seeds planted under the sign of the Ram will rot. (You need an almanac to observe this one.)
(F, R, 1958)

4426   Don't plant your garden until the middle of April.
(M, 80, R, 1959)

4427   If a garden is planted on Monday, Tuesday, or Wednesday, it will be successful.
(F, 70, 1958 [her mother])

4428   Do not plow the garden while the dew is still on the ground, or the garden will not grow.
(F, 1956 [her grandmother])

4429   Never plant, harvest, or plow on leased land before the landlord does.
(M, 28, R, 1958)

4430   Never plant anything on Friday, for it will take a long time to get through planting.
(F, 57, R, 1957)

4431   Do not plant seed on Friday unless the work was already started.
(F, 75, R, 1961)

4432   Never start plowing a field on Friday. If you do so, you will have a bad crop.
(M, 65, 1958)

4433   It is bad luck to begin to plant a crop on Friday unless you can finish it.
(M, 40, R, 1958 [his uncle])

4434   If you break ground on Good Friday, lightning will strike your field and burn up your crop.
(F, 50, R, 1959 [one of her parents])

4435   Always plant cabbage on Good Friday.
(F, 60, R, 1959 [her mother])

4436   If you plant peppers on Good Friday, they will all be hot.
(F, 50, 1958)

4437   Plant fruit trees by the light of the moon.
(M, 20, R, 1961)

4438   If you plant a cherry seed on the first day of the month, it will bear fruit the first year; if on the second day, the second year; and so forth.
(F, 1962 [her grandmother])

4439   Don't plant sugar beets except at the dark of the moon, or they'll grow aboveground and be "sunburned."
(F, 60, R, 1959)

4440   If you plant radishes in the dark of the moon, they will grow mostly into tops.
(F, 50, R, 1961 [her mother], + 1 M)

4441   Plant cucumbers and beans in the light of the moon.
(F, 60, R, 1958)

4442   If you plant cucumbers under the Twins sign of the zodiac, you will have twice as many cucumbers.
(F, 40, R, 1959 [her mother])

4443   Plant your cucumbers on the first of May, and you'll have some to give away.
(F, 1962)

4444   Beans are to be planted on the hundredth day of the year.
(F, 60, R, 1957)

4445   If you walk backwards to the melon patch before sunup to plant your melons, you'll have a good crop this year. You must do this on May the first.
(F, 60, R, 1961)

4446   Plant watermelons before sunup on the first of May in your shirttail.
(M, 32, R, 1959 [one of his friends])

4447   If you plant watermelon seeds on Easter Sunday before breakfast, rain or shine, you will be sure to raise melons.
(F, 50, R, 1958)

4448   Plant all your flower bulbs on Easter Sunday.
        (M, 1962)

4449   For nice flowers and leaf vegetables, plant when the moon is
        getting lighter.
        (F, 1959 [her grandparents])

4450   Plant flowers in the light of the moon.
        (F, 30, 1958)

4451   You should replant house plants in the light of the moon.
        (F, 67, R, 1958)

4452   If you slip geraniums in the new moon, the blooms and the
        plants will be large; if you slip them in the dark of the moon,
        they will grow tall and lanky.
        (F, 75, R, 1958 [her mother])

4453   A slip or leaf from a house plant that has been planted in July
        or August will positively take root and grow. Certainty of
        growth cannot be guaranteed in other months.
        (F, 40, R, 1957)

4454   Plant sweet peas at the time of the first thaw in February.
        (M, 58, 1958)

4455   For a good crop, plant sweet peas on St. Patrick's Day.
        (F, 50, 1959 [her mother])

4456   In order to germinate, sweet peas must be planted on March
        22.
        (F, 1962)

4457   Plant sweet peas after dark to ensure that they will bloom.
        (F, 1961)

4458   If you plant peas on Good Friday, you will have a good crop.
        (F, 80, R, 1961 [her mother])

4459   To assure a good crop, always plant peas in February.
        (F, 1959 [her parents])

4460   Plant peas in the dark of the moon.
        (F, 46, R, 1958)

4461   Plant your turnips, wet or dry, on the first day of July.
        (F, 47, R, 1956)

4462   Plant turnips on the seventeenth of July, whether it's wet or
        dry.
        (F, 70, R, 1961, + 1 M)

4463   Plant turnips on the twenty-fourth of July, wet or dry.
        (F, 75, R, 1958 [her mother])

4464   Plant turnips on the twenty-fifth of July, wet or dry.
        (F, 20, R, 1957, + 2 M and 6 F)

4465   Plant turnips on the twenty-sixth of July, wet or dry.
      (M, 51, 1960 [his father], + 1 M)

4466   Sow late turnips on the twenty-eighth of July, wet or dry.
      (M, 84, R, 1956)

4467   For best results, plant your corn in the dark of the moon.
      (F, 57, 1955)

4468   If corn is planted in the light of the moon, the ears will stand up next to the stalk. If planted in the dark of the moon, the ears will drop.
      (M, 78, R, 1958)

4469   To get a good crop, plant your corn under a full moon.
      (M, 24, R, 1956)

4470   It is time to plant corn when the leaves on the trees are as big as rats' ears.
      (M, 21, 1956)

4471   Plant corn when the buds on the trees are as big as a squirrel's ears.
      (F, 50, R, 1956)

4472   Plant corn when the leaves on the trees are as big as a squirrel's ears.
      (F, 60, R, 1961 [her father])

4473   When elm leaves are the size of squirrels' ears, it is time to plant corn.
      (M, 80, R, 1957)

4474   Plant corn when maple leaves are the size of a squirrel's foot.
      (F, 20, R, 1963, + 1 M and 1 F)

4475   When oak leaves are the size of a squirrel's ears, it is the time to plant corn.
      (M, 24, R, 1957, + 1 F and 1 M)

4476   It is time to plant corn when the cottonwood trees leaf out.
      (F, 50, R, 1962 [her mother])

4477   Plant corn when the leaves on an Osage orange tree are the size of a squirrel's ear.
      (F, 21, R, 1956, + 4 F and 10 M)

4478   When the leaves on the hedge trees are as big as a rat's ear, it is time to plant corn.
      (M, 50, R, 1958, + 1 M)

4479   If you see a pelican in the field in the spring, it is time to plant corn.
      (M, 57, R, 1958)

4480   Always plant your wheat when the full moon is out.
      (M, 50, R, 1963 [his father], + 2 F)

4481   Plant wheat only in the light of the moon, never in the dark of the moon.
(F, 77, R, 1958)

4482   To get a good crop, plant wheat in the second quarter of the moon.
(M, 70, R, 1960)

4483   In the fall, if you see a jacksnipe in the field, it is time to plant wheat.
(M, 57, R, 1958)

4484   If it rains in September, plant wheat in October.
(M, 60, R, 1957)

4485   The time to plant crops is when a blue wheat flower blooms.
(F, 21, R, 1963 [her uncle])

4486   Plant oats when the moon is waning.
(F, 54, R, 1959 [her father])

4487   If you plant alfalfa on the first of April or the twentieth of August, rain or shine, you will get a good stand.
(M, 1961)

4488   When the dogwood is blooming in Arkansas, it is time to plant cotton.
(M, 1962)

4489   It is best to plant potatoes according to the moon.
(F, 21, 1950, + 1 F and 1 M)

4490   Plant potatoes when there is a new moon.
(F, 20, 1959, + 1 M)

4491   Potatoes planted in the waxing moon will not grow.
(M, 70, R, 1957)

4492   Plant potatoes when the moon is new; as the moon develops and gets fuller, the potatoes will grow in proportion with the moon.
(F, 1961 [her grandfather])

4493   Plant potatoes in the full of the moon.
(F, 21, 1950, + 6 F and 6 M)

4494   Plant potatoes in the light of the moon.
(F, 20, R, 1957, + 4 F and 3 M)

4495   Plant potatoes during the dark of the moon.
(M, 20, R, 1959, + 14 F and 11 M)

4496   Plant potatoes in dark of the moon; in light of the moon, plant things that bear aboveground.
(F, 50, R, 1959)

4497   If you do not plant potatoes in the dark of the moon, they will all turn to tops.
(F, 48, 1957, + 1 F)

4498   Plant potatoes in the dark of the moon so that there will be plenty of potatoes and few vines.
(M, 24, R, 1956, + 2 F and 1 M)

4499   Plant potatoes in the dark of the moon in March.
(F, 70, R, 1957)

4500   Don't plant potatoes in the dark of the moon.
(M, 56, R, 1956)

4501   Never plant potatoes by the dark of the moon; if you do so, they will freeze.
(M, 62, R, 1956)

4502   Potatoes should be planted in the light of the moon and before March the seventeenth.
(F, 40, R, 1960 [her father])

4503   Always plant potatoes before March the seventeenth.
(F, 78, R, 1959 [her grandmother])

4504   Plant potatoes on March the seventeenth.
(F, 20, R, 1957, + 5 F)

4505   The week in which St. Patrick's Day falls is the only time to plant potatoes.
(M, 70, 1959)

4506   Plant potatoes on the seventeenth day of March, because that is St. Patrick's Day.
(F, 19, R, 1959 [her parents], + 10 F and 7 M)

4507   You will have a good potato crop if the potatoes are planted on St. Patrick's Day.
(F, 19, R, 1959, + 2 F and 6 M)

4508   If you plant potatoes on St. Patrick's Day by moonlight, they will grow with little vine.
(F, 30, 1958)

4509   Unless potatoes are planted on St. Patrick's Day, they won't grow.
(F, 59, R, 1957)

4510   Plant potatoes on St. Patrick's Day; if not then, the next best chance is Good Friday.
(F, 21, 1950, + 3 F and 1 M)

4511   The ninetieth day of the new year is the day to plant potatoes.
(F, 50, R, 1957)

4512   In order to have a good crop, it used to be considered necessary always to plant potatoes on the hundredth day of the year.
(M, 70, R, 1960 [his father], + 1 F and 1 M)

4513   In order to have a good crop, plant potatoes on the tenth day
of April.
(F, 1961)

4514   Don't plant potatoes before Good Friday.
(F, 50, R, 1958)

4515   Don't plant potatoes on Good Friday.
(F, 50, R, 1963 [her father])

4516   Potatoes grow best when planted on Good Friday.
(F, 40, R, 1963, + 9 M and 10 F)

4517   People used to think that potatoes had to be planted no later
than Good Friday, if you wanted to have a good crop.
(F, 80, R, 1958 [her father], + 1 M)

4518   To ensure a good potato crop, plant the potatoes on Holy
Saturday.
(M, 1961)

4519   If potatoes are planted under the sign of the toes, there will
be a lot of them but they will be small.
(F, 65, R, 1958)

4520   Always plant potatoes in the morning if you want to have a
good crop.
(F, 60, R, 1957)

THE CARE OF PLANTS

4521   "Plant wheat in the dust, / And your granaries will bust."
(M, 19, R, 1957, + 1 F)

4522   "If you die in the dust, / The granary will bust."
(M, 50, R, 1963 [his father], + 1 F)

4523   As you broadcast seed, you should say: "Some for you and
some for I, / Some for the Devil and some for the fly."
(M, 70, R, 1957)

4524   When planting corn, put three seeds in each hill: one for the
Devil and one for the crow and one to grow.
(F, 50, R, 1958 [her father])

4525   How many kernels of corn you should plant to the hill: "One
for the blackbird, / One for the crow, / One for the cutworm, /
And two to grow."
(M, 70, R, 1957)

4526   Plant some for the worm, some for the crow, some to pull out,
and some to grow.
(F, 54, R, 1958)

4527   If you kill a jack rabbit and bury it in the field, you will have a good wheat crop.
(F, 44, R, 1958)

4528   Tie a wounded or captured crow to a fence post in order to keep other crows out of the corn or watermelons.
(F, 50, 1962 [one of her friends])

4529   If plants are transplanted when the moon is waxing, the plants will do better.
(F, 60, R, 1963 [her mother])

4530   Hoe the garden when the moon is dark, or you won't kill the weeds.
(M, 70, 1959)

4531   Plant trees in square holes so that the roots will not ball up.
(M, 1959)

4532   You have to be angry when you plant peppers, or they won't be hot.
(M, 54, 1954)

4533   Plant beans right side up.
(M, 20, R, 1959)

4534   When planting corn and beans together, put in an extra bean seed.
(F, 63, R, 1958)

4535   If you put an aspirin in a vase of roses, they will keep fresh-looking longer.
(F, 20, 1957)

4536   If anyone gives you a flower, name it after the donor, or it will die.
(F, 50, 1960)

4537   Put bits of tobacco in fern pots to make the ferns grow.
(F, 71, 1961)

4538   Soak tree seeds in hot water overnight if you expect them to grow.
(M, 91, R, 1963 [his father])

4539   Talk to plants as you work with them.
(F, 50, 1959)

4540   If you baby a plant, it will die.
(F, 21, 1950)

4541   Plant your potatoes in rows that run north and south, because they won't grow in east and west rows.
(M, 28, R, 1956)

4542   Indians plant fish at the end of each row of corn to ensure a good crop.
(F, 50, R, 1960)

4543   When you break a leaf off a plant or take a cutting from it, put mud on the opening to keep the plant from bleeding to death.
(F, 54, R, 1957)

4544   If you steal slips off a plant, they'll grow; but if you thank someone for them, they won't grow.
(F, 60, R, 1961 [her mother])

4545   Soak watermelon seeds in sweet milk overnight before planting them.
(F, 65, R, 1962 [her family])

4546   Where the apple trees bloom, plant watermelons.
(F, 80, R, 1960 [her parents])

4547   Put a blade of grass on a watermelon. If the blade turns of its own accord, the melon is ripe.
(M, 30, R, 1957)

4548   To check a watermelon to see if it is ripe, take a stem of crab grass that is four to five inches in length, dust off a spot on the melon, and place the stem of grass on this spot. If the stem turns, the melon is ripe.
(M, 20, R, 1959)

4549   Drive a nail in a tomato stalk to make the plant bear more.
(F, 58, R, 1958)

4550   If you pound nails into the ground surrounding a tomato plant, the worms will not eat the green tomatoes.
(M, 60, R, 1958 [one of his friends])

4551   If you wrap a tomato plant with paper to the root of the plant, cutworms won't bother it.
(F, 50, 1958 [one of her friends])

4552   If a fruit tree does not bear fruit, it will help if you drive a peg or a nail into the tree.
(M, 1962)

4553   It is good for a tree if you plant nails at the base of it.
(M, 60, R, 1957)

4554   If you lay a nail beside a young plant, cutworms will pass that plant by.
(F, 65, R, 1958)

4555   Never thank anyone for seeds or plants; if you do, they won't grow.
(F, 27, R, 1960 [her mother], + 24 F and 1 M)

4556   Don't thank a person who gives you a slip off a plant, or it won't grow.
(F, 20, R, 1961, + 5 F)

4557   Only mean people can grow ivy.
        (F, 21, 1950)
4558   People with mean dispositions will never be able to grow any
        ivy.
        (F, 50, 1959)

SIGNS OF SUCCESS OR FAILURE

4559   If the moon is out on Christmas Eve, there will be a good
        harvest.
        (M, 20, R, 1963 [his grandfather])
4560   If the sky is clear at midnight mass on Christmas, your bins
        will be full (that is, the next crop will be good).
        (M, 50, R, 1960 [his father])
4561   If the wind is in the northeast on New Year's Day, there will
        be a good crop. If it's in the northwest, there will be a poor
        crop.
        (F, 70, R, 1958 [her stepmother])
4562   If it rains on Easter, you will have a good crop.
        (F, 70, R, 1957)
4563   If there is rain on Easter, it will be a good year for corn.
        (F, 19, R, 1963)
4564   If it rains on the last day of April, there will be an abundant
        crop of wheat in the summer.
        (F, 66, R, 1958)
4565   A mild, wet May brings good harvests for the year.
        (F, 60, R, 1957)
4566   A wet May makes no hay.
        (F, 40, 1961 [her parents])
4567   Rains in May bring lots of corn and hay.
        (F, 49, 1957)
4568   May, cool and dry, makes wheat and rye.
        (M, 50, R, 1959)
4569   May, wet and warm, makes oats and corn.
        (M, 50, R, 1959)
4570   When cats are plentiful, there will be good crops.
        (M, 60, R, 1957)
4571   If the possum hangs by its tail in the moonlight, the
        persimmon tree won't bear fruit.
        (M, 56, 1958)

4572   If there is a lot of fog, there will be a good wheat crop.
        (F, 19, R, 1959 [her parents])

4573   If the wheat can cover a rabbit by Easter, the crop will be
        good.
        (M, 60, R, 1961 [his grandmother])

4574   Early ripe, early rotten.
        (F, 44, 1958)

4575   If it thunders and lightnings in November, the crops will be
        good the following year; but if it thunders and lightnings in
        January, the crops will be poor the following year.
        (F, 60, R, 1960 [her mother])

4576   "Wet and warm / For potatoes and corn. / Cool and dry / For
        wheat and rye."
        (F, 68, R, 1957)

4577   If a sow has a lot of pigs in the spring, a lot of grain will be
        grown that year.
        (M, 50, R, 1958)

4578   When there are lots of sunflowers in the summer, there will
        be a good wheat crop the next year.
        (M, 72, R, 1962)

4579   If there is a lot of snow in the winter, there is a good chance
        for a good wheat harvest the next year.
        (M, 72, R, 1962)

4580   People used to believe that for every live fly in the house at
        Thanksgiving time, there would be a thousand bushels of
        wheat in the bin the next year.
        (F, 50, R, 1962 [her grandmother])

4581   Icicles in February make the corn grow.
        (F, 60, R, 1957)

4582   If the wind blows from any direction but the south on the
        twenty-first of March, you will have a good corn crop.
        (M, 70, 1957)

4583   Corn should be as high as a horse's back by the fourth of July.
        (M, 62, 1958)

4584   Corn should be knee-high by the fourth of July.
        (M, 40, 1960)

4585   When the wild plums produce heavily, the corn crop will be
        light.
        (M, 50, R, 1958)

4586   If it rains during the week of the summer soltice, either
        before or after the soltice, one is sure of a corn crop.
        (F, 72, R, 1956)

4587   An abundance of tree seeds foretells a good corn crop.
        (F, 94, 1957)
4588   If the wind blows from the north on the second of March, it
        will be a good year for corn.
        (M, 69, R, 1956)
4589   Frost during the light of the moon doesn't do as much damage
        as frost during the dark of the moon.
        (F, 21, 1950)
4590   If a frost comes when the moon is shining, it won't kill plants.
        (F, 70, R, 1961)
4591   When you have a freeze during the light of the moon, the fruit
        on fruit trees does not freeze.
        (F, 77, R, 1961)

        HARVESTING, TRIMMING, AND KILLING

4592   Don't do any major plant-pruning except under the sign of the
        Twins (Gemini).
        (F, 21, 1973)
4593   Do not trim trees during any month of the year except August;
        for if you do, they will die.
        (M, 70, R, 1960)
4594   The time to prune a fruit tree is when you're in the orchard
        with a sharp knife.
        (M, 76, R, 1959)
4595   Don't trim trees in the new moon, or the sap will run out, and
        they will die.
        (F, 74, R, 1958 [her parents])
4596   You must cut trees for rails in the early part of the day and in
        the light of the moon.
        (F, 51, R, 1956)
4597   You can't transplant a tree.
        (F, 68, R, 1957)
4598   If you dig up a cedar tree and turn it halfway around, it will
        die.
        (F, 1963)
4599   You can kill a tree by driving a copper nail into it.
        (M, 60, 1963 [his father])
4600   To kill a stump of tree, cut its sprouts in the dark of the moon
        in July or August.
        (M, 84, R, 1956)

4601   If you mow, rake, or hoe crops in the dark of the moon, you will have poor crops.
        (M, 80, R, 1958)

4602   If you chop down your cockleburs and then turn them upside down, they won't sprout.
        (M, 70, R, 1959 [his neighbors])

4603   Grain should be harvested during the third quarter of the moon.
        (M, 24, 1957)

4604   When you think that wheat is ripe and ready to cut, wait three more days; then it will be ready.
        (F, 53, R, 1958 [her father])

4605   Taste a kernel of wheat; if it is hard, it is ready to harvest.
        (F, 80, R, 1958 [her father])

4606   Throw a hat into a wheat field, count the number of heads of wheat under the hat, and you'll know the number of bushels that the field will yield per acre.
        (M, 39, R, 1957)

4607   Count the number of shoots on one head of wheat: that will be the yield in bushels per acre.
        (M, 30, 1958 [his grandparents])

4608   The number of kernels of wheat in one head will tell you the number of bushels that your wheat will give per acre.
        (M, 80, R, 1957)

4609   You should pick apples and pears in the old moon; if you do, the bruised spots will dry up.
(F, 40, R, 1961 [her parents])

4610   If you lay a board on the grass in the dark of the moon, the grass will die. If you lay a board on the grass in the light of the moon, the grass will live.
(M, 93, R, 1959 [his wife], + 1 M)

4611   If you cut your feed by the light of the moon, the sweet juice will stay up in the stalk, and it will not seep out at the cut end.
(M, 40, R, 1963 [one of his friends])

4612   Cut feed in the light of the moon when the sap is up.
(M, 65, R, 1960 [his mother])

4613   Always cut feed in the light of the moon, for then it will make better hay or fodder.
(M, 50, R, 1958)

4614   Cut feed when the moon is going toward full. The sap will be coming up, and the stock will eat the feed better.
(M, 67, R, 1962)

4615   Cut crops while the moon is full, because the juice is in the stalk. During the dark of the moon the juice is in the roots.
(M, 70, R, 1961 [his father])

FLOWERS

4616   Keep a geranium in the window to keep flies out of the house.
(F, 1954)

4617   Flowers that have been stolen will always grow.
(M, 21, 1950)

4618   Lovers sometimes used to send a mixed bouquet of flowers, and certain flowers would symbolize jealousy and disappointments, as well as friendships, love, and passion.
(F, 60, 1961 [her mother])

4619   Starting slips of violets and transplanting should be done under the sign of Cancer.
(F, 54, R, 1958)

4620   If you bring a handful of violets into the house, your little chickens will die. If you will put a leaf in the bouquet, it will counteract the bad luck.
(F, 96, 1954)

4621   It is warm enough to go barefooted when the dandelions are in bloom.
(F, 50, 1958)

4622   If a dandelion reflects yellow when you hold it under a person's chin, that person likes butter.
   (F, 40, 1954)

4623   Take a silver-headed dandelion (one in seed); then blow, counting each blow until all the seeds are gone; and that will tell you the time of day.
   (F, 40, 1954)

4624   Peonies won't bloom unless there are ants on them.
   (F, 40, 1960 [her mother], + 1 F)

MISCELLANEOUS

4625   Wild onions that have white flowers are poisonous.
   (M, 1959 [his mother])

4626   Cucumbers are poisonous unless they have been soaked in salt water before they are eaten.
   (F, 52, R, 1962 [her mother])

4627   Cauliflower is poisonous if eaten raw.
   (F, 52, R, 1962 [her mother])

4628   To determine whether mushrooms are poisonous, cook them with a silver coin. If it turns black, they are poisonous.
   (F, 52, 1955)

4629   One way to tell a mushroom from a toadstool is to cut one open and put a nickle inside. If the nickel turns black, it is a toadstool; if not, it is a mushroom.
   (M, 50, R, 1959)

4630   If a field is plowed in the light of the moon, then the next plowing will be easy. If it is plowed in the dark of the moon, the next plowing will be difficult.
   (M, 1962)

4631   If you transplant an evergreen, you will die before it casts a shadow over you.
   (M, 70, R, 1962)

4632   Pigweed will always go to seed before frost.
   (F, 60, R, 1961)

4633   If there is a pine tree growing in your yard, your life will be long.
   (F, 60, R, 1957)

4634   If you listen real hard, you can hear corn growing on a warm, still night.
   (M, 50, R, 1961)

4635   Clover denotes rich soil. Its trefoil leaves are a sign of the Trinity. If the clover is quivering, there will be rain.
        (F, 96, 1954)

4636   The number of little threads left on the roots of a rock plant when it is pulled up indicate the number of lies that you have told during the day.
        (F, 40, 1958)

4637   Bark is thickest on one side of a tree.
        (F, 40, R, 1959 [her father])

4638   Moss grows on the north sides of trees.
        (M, 21, 1950)

4639   If one is lost in the woods, one can find one's way by looking for moss, which grows on the north sides of trees.
        (M, 19, 1958)

4640   You can tell the north side of a tree by the way the moss is growing.
        (M, 24, 1956)

4641   If you can make plants grow easily, you are said to have a green thumb.
        (F, 21, 1950, + 1 F)

11

Animals, Birds, and Insects

THE UNITED STATES IS BECOMING URBANIZED; THEREFORE, the folklore in this chapter does not play the functional role that it once did. Our westward movement of yesteryear, with its inevitable primitive living conditions, made it necessary for all people to be cautious about varmints of all kinds, some of which were poisonous. Parents had to urge their children to be cautious; thus, one must understand that the cautionary element is a serious factor, rather than the possible manifestation of the truth of some quite wild beliefs or admonitions.

Of the 268 items in this chapter, snake lore constitutes almost 20 percent, with cattle lore about the same. The hoop snake—pure Americana, about which there are many legends—simply is a reminder that one should be on the lookout for snakes. The belief that snakes do not die completely until sundown means that one should keep hands off them; likewise, the belief that snakes travel in pairs and that the mate is probably near. To those who have witnessed or suffered the agonies of a poisonous snake bite, any cautionary knowledge existing in snake folklore is beneficial. The belief that when you kill a snake, you conquer your enemy may be a metaphorical application of the scriptural snake.

Advice about when to dehorn cattle, when to wean and castrate calves, when to butcher, and the like, appears in various forms as it was handed down by generations whose living depended on nonacademic knowledge about animal life and its welfare. The item "If you grease a fence after a cow gets cut on it, the cow won't get an infection" is an extension of the ancient practice of sympathetic magic. In these modern times, however, this item was probably submitted tongue-in-cheek.

Information on the dominant nature and behavior of the dog and cat that has been preserved in oral tradition and in the many books about these animals is overwhelming. Recognition of their human or anthropomorphic traits appears in considerable lore from ancient Egypt to our present-day bomb-sniffing dogs or the nine-lived cats.

367

Beliefs that the howling of dogs at night portends death and that dogs smell fear in a person are still prevalent. The hunting power and the hunting characteristics of dogs are considerable; they are included in the chapter entitled "Hunting and Fishing."

Spiders, flys, bugs, and mice continue to plague the housewife. In Mid-America, where hedge apples are still available, rural housewives put them in basements to kill the bugs and to take away odors. The dire portents associated with rats' leaving ships are no doubt a remnant of immigrant lore. Our high frequency count on "Put salt on a bird's tail so that you can catch it" (or a rabbit) is interesting in the light of today's society, but who would take away this metaphoric advice from the image of the young child?

CATS

4642   Never let a cat near a baby's crib; for the cat will take the child's breath, thus suffocating him. (The cat will supposedly be after milk, which it smells on the baby's breath.)
(F, 30, 1960 [her grandmother], + 11 F and 2 M)

4643   Cats will suck babies' breath away.
(F, 55, 1957, + 1 F)

4644   Don't let a cat stay around a child, or the cat will draw the life out of the child.
(F, 20, R, 1958)

4645   When you move and take your cat with you, put butter on the bottom of its feet so that it won't run away.
(F, 50, R, 1955)

4646   No cat is all black. Every cat has some white hair somewhere.
(F, 55, 1959)

4647   Never take a picture of a cat. If you do, something will happen to the cat.
(F, 56, 1963)

4648   A tomcat will kill any kittens that it finds.
(M, 50, R, 1959)

4649   If you take a cat away, put it in a sack, and carry it away after dark so that it won't be able to find its way back.
(F, 50, R, 1960)

4650   Tomcats never have more than three colors.
(M, 19, R, 1958)

4651   A three-colored cat will be a good mouser and mother.
(F, 19, R, 1956)

4652   A cat has nine lives.
      (F, 17, R, 1959, + 6 F and 3 M)
4653   Rub a black cat's back in the dark of the night to get sparks to
see by.
      (M, 75, R, 1958)
4654   If you cut off a cat's whiskers, it won't be able to smell.
      (F, 50, R, 1957)
4655   If you cut off a cat's whiskers, it will die.
      (F, 48, R, 1957)

CATTLE

4656   If a cow loses her cud, she will become ill; but if you give her
a dishrag to chew, she will become well again.
      (F, 40, R, 1957, + 1 M)
4657   If a cow loses her cud, make her swallow a greasy dishrag.
      (F, 56, R, 1958)
4658   A red cloth will excite a bull.
      (F, 18, 1955, + 2 F and 1 M)
4659   Young bulls will give you more bull calves; old bulls, more
heifer calves.
      (M, 30, R, 1960 [one of his friends])
4660   Trim your (cows') horns on Monday, you trim for health; trim
your horns on Tuesday, you trim for wealth; trim your horns
on Wednesday, you trim for a new pair of shoes; trim your
horns on Thursday, you will travel far; trim your horns on Friday, that is the worst day of all, you will have bad luck; trim
your horns on Saturday, you will see your beau on Sunday.
But it would be better not to be born than that you should trim
your horns on Sunday.
      (F, 70, 1962)
4661   If you dehorn cattle when the signs of the zodiac are right, the
cattle won't bleed much; but if you dehorn them under the
wrong sign, they will bleed a lot.
      (M, 50, R, 1963 [his mother], + 1 F)
4662   When you dehorn cattle, put the horns in some dry place.
      (M, 63, R, 1961 [one of his Amish neighbors])
4663   To keep cattle from bleeding, dehorn them during the full
moon.
      (M, 19, R, 1958)

4664   If you dehorn cattle in the light of the moon, the horns will grow back.
      (F, 68, R, 1960)

4665   Calves won't bleed as much if you dehorn them when the moon is waning.
      (F, R, 1958 [her parents])

4666   Dehorn and castrate cattle in the dark of the moon, as the dark of the moon aids clotting.
      (M, 60, R, 1959 [his father])

4667   When dehorning cattle, you should wait until the sign of the zodiac is in the knees going down, never in the head or heart; otherwise they will bleed a lot more.
      (F, 47, R, 1960 [her mother], + 1 M)

4668   Cattle should be branded in the dark of the moon.
      (M, 60, R, 1959 [one of his neighbors])

4669   When branding and dehorning cattle, one should follow the zodiac. Never dehorn or brand when the sign of the zodiac is above the knees.
      (M, 50, R, 1959, + 1 M)

4670   If calves are branded in the light of the moon, the brand will stay the same size. If they are branded in the dark of the moon, the brand will grow as the calves grow.
      (M, 70, R, 1957)

4671   When a cow has twins, one male and one female, the female will not be fertile.
      (M, 22, R, 1958, + 1 M)

4672   If you wean calves three days before a new moon, they will wean in three days.
      (M, 50, R, 1958)

4673   If you wean calves in the full moon, they won't bawl.
      (F, 45, R, 1961)

4674   You should wean calves in the dark of the moon when the sign of the zodiac is going down.
      (F, 40, R, 1961 [her parents], + 1 F and 1 M)

4675   You should wean calves after the sign of the zodiac leaves the heart on the way down.
      (F, 70, R, 1959 [her father-in-law])

4676   If you wean a calf under the right sign, it won't bawl.
      (M, 32, R, 1959, + 1 F)

4677   Calves won't shrink if you wean them in the dark of the moon.
      (M, 40, R, 1964)

4678   If you wean a calf on Friday night, the next calf will come during the day.
(M, 60, R, 1963 [his mother])

4679   If you kill a toad, the cows will give bloody milk.
(F, 40, R, 1962 [her grandparents], + 6 F and 4 M)

4680   If you find birds' nests and steal the eggs, the cows will give bloody milk.
(F, 50, R, 1957)

4681   If you kill a barn swallow, the cow will give blood.
(M, 75, R, 1960 [his grandfather])

4682   Always castrate cattle in the full of the moon.
(M, 30, R, 1961)

4683   Calves that are castrated under the wrong sign of the zodiac won't heal.
(F, 20, R, 1959, + 1 M)

4684   If you cut a calf when the moon is turned up, it will bleed badly.
(M, 55, R, 1961)

4685   Cattle used to be driven to the local market. Often cattle shied away from narrow wooden bridges, because they could see the witch on the bridge chasing them back, although their drover couldn't see it. To get rid of the witch, the drover would stop and would change his socks from one foot to the other.
(F, 40, R, 1963)

4686   If a cow's hair becomes curly when she licks herself, she will have a heifer calf.
(M, 52, R, 1958)

4687   Don't let the cows near the chicken yard when it rains, or the cows will become wild.
(F, 80, 1958)

4688   Some man declared that he could cure pinkeye in cattle by putting a copper ring in the ear opposite to the eye with the pinkeye.
(M, 30, R, 1962)

4689   If you grease a fence after a cow gets cut on it, the cow won't get an infection.
(M, 40, R, 1961)

4690   If you talk harshly to a cow, she won't let down her milk.
(M, 48, R, 1958)

4691   If you sing while you are milking the cow, she will give more milk.
(F, 49, R, 1957)

4692   A cow can't kick straight behind her.
      (M, 63, R, 1961)

4693   Cattle will head into the wind while eating.
      (M, 70, R, 1959)

4694   A cow will not mourn when her calf is taken from her if the calf is taken out of the barn backwards.
      (M, 1962)

4695   On Christmas Eve, at midnight, the cows kneel down to pray.
      (F, 20, 1962, + 1 F and 1 M)

4696   On New Year's Eve the cows kneel down to pray at midnight.
      (F, 40, 1963, + 3 F)

4697   On New Year's Eve the cows roll over at midnight.
      (F, 21, R, 1959)

4698   If a baby calf is born head first, it will die before it is thirteen days old.
      (M, 14, R, 1958, + 1 M)

4699   If a calf is born head first, it will be runty or will die.
      (M, 55, R, 1958)

4700   If you breed your cattle in the morning, the calves will all be heifers.
      (F, 45, R, 1961)

4701   If you butcher beef in the light of the moon, the meat will be tender.
      (F, 1962)

4702   If a cow is unthrifty, she has wolf-in-the-tail. The cure is to split the skin on the tail and then to rub salt and pepper in the wound.
      (M, 70, 1961)

4703   When a cow is sick and down, if there is a hollow place at the end of her tail, split it and put salt and pepper in it to make her well.
      (M, 20, R, 1956, + 1 M)

4704   A cow with a blunt tail will never make a good milker.
      (M, 70, R, 1959)

4705   Calves will arrive at the change of the moon.
      (F, 30, R, 1958)

4706   You are supposed to feed your cattle and sheep real good on Christmas night, because that is the only night they will talk about you.
      (F, 40, R, 1961 [her parents])

4707   If a cow's tail reaches the ground, she is a good milker.
      (F, 19, R, 1958)

4708 Oxen only sweat on the ends of their noses.
      (M, 91, R, 1963)

CHICKENS AND BIRDS

4709 A bad thunderstorm kills chicks in their shells.
      (F, 35, 1958, + 1 F and 2 M)
4710 Chickens and other animals know when a storm is coming.
      (F, 50, 1959)
4711 When you are carrying eggs to be set, carry them in your
      apron, covered, before sunrise, and they will all hatch into
      roosters.
      (F, 20, 1959)
4712 Always set a hen on an uneven number of eggs; otherwise you
      will have a poor hatch.
      (F, 76, R, 1956, + 1 F)
4713 Don't set hens on Friday, because if you do, the eggs won't
      hatch.
      (F, 70, R, 1958)
4714 If you paint the windows in the brooder house red, the chicks
      won't peck at each other.
      (M, 69, R, 1956)
4715 Tobacco put in the nests of hens will kill the lice and other
      parasites on the chickens.
      (F, 50, R, 1957)
4716 To break a hen of setting, pen her in a box, and then hang the
      box in a tree where the wind will swing it.
      (M, 66, R, 1955)
4717 When a hen cackles, she has laid an egg.
      (F, 20, 1958)
4718 Chickens with yellow legs lay better than chickens with red
      legs.
      (M, 60, R, 1959)
4719 Chicks hatched with the new moon grow faster.
      (F, 72, R, 1961)
4720 Some people have a religious belief that you should eat only
      the yolk of the egg; the white is chicken feathers.
      (M, 55, 1959)
4721 Large eggs that have two yolks are rooster eggs.
      (F, 1961)

4722   If you feed red pepper to chickens, they will drink more water, eat less feed, and lay more eggs.
(F, 40, R, 1960 [her aunt])

4723   If a chicken doesn't lay, chase it up a slippery board.
(F, 56, R, 1958 [her grandmother])

4724   Put salt on a bird's tail so that you can catch it.
(F, 20, 1950, + 18 F and 12 M)

4725   A bird will be tame if you put salt on its tail.
(F, 20, R, 1957, + 2 F and 2 M)

4726   If you sight a stray albatross, land is near.
(F, 27, R, 1957)

4727   An early colonial belief was that migratory birds wintered on the moon.
(F, 1962)

4728   The return or appearance of money or the robins in March is a sign of an early spring.
(F, 20, 1957)

4729   The turkey buzzard has the power to kill snakes or other small animals by fluttering over their heads and releasing its horrible stench.
(M, 80, 1958)

4730   During World War II in the Aleutian Islands, there was a superstition that if the ravens talked to you, you would return home soon. The soldiers took every opportunity to "talk" to the ravens, hoping that the ravens would reply.
(M, 1963)

DOGS

4731   If you have a dog that you want to have stay at home, pull or cut hairs from its tail, and place them under a rock at the home site.
(M, 20, R, 1958, + 1 F)

4732   If your dog won't stay at home, cut some hairs off its tail, and bury them under the doorstep.
(F, 1961)

4733   When a dog's nose is dry, it is sick.
(M, 20, R, 1959)

4734   If a dog has a white spot anywhere else on it, there will also be one on the end of its tail.
(F, 20, R, 1956)

4735　A barking dog never bites.
　　　　(M, 37, 1959 [his grandfather], + 3 M)

4736　A cold nose indicates a healthy dog.
　　　　(F, 25, R, 1957)

4737　A dog with a cold nose is a good coon dog (has a good scent).
　　　　(M, 76, R, 1958)

4738　When a dog's nose is hot, the dog is probably not feeling well.
　　　　(F, 40, 1959)

4739　If a dog doesn't like a person, that person isn't any good.
　　　　(M, 48, 1958, + 1 F)

4740　Any person with whom either dogs or children make up to readily is sure to be a good person.
　　　　(F, 60, 1959)

4741　Dogs can smell fear on a person. If you act as if you are not afraid of a dog, it will never hurt you.
　　　　(F, 84, R, 1957)

4742　If a dog cries when you pull its ear, it will be a good dog.
　　　　(F, 58, R, 1958)

4743　A dog circles around and tramps down grass to prevent it from tickling him while he is in the process of relieving his body of waste products.
　　　　(M, 75, R, 1958)

4744　A dog always walks around before it lies down.
　　　　(F, 50, R, 1957)

4745　Bird dogs work best during moist weather.
　　　　(M, 60, 1964)

4746　If a dog won't lick a wound, the wound won't heal.
　　　　(F, 50, R, 1952)

4747　To get rid of a stray dog, tie a tin can on its tail.
　　　　(M, 50, R, 1957)

4748　If you hold a piece of bread in your hand until it is warm, then feed it to a dog, the dog will never leave you.
　　　　(F, 1961)

4749　If you give a pup some whiskey, it will never get much bigger than it is right then.
　　　　(M, 70, R, 1959)

4750　If a dog eats grass, it is sick.
　　　　(M, 20, R, 1959)

4751　A dog that is suffering from rabies will always go into a fit at the sight of water.
　　　　(M, 62, R, 1959)

4752   Dogs can bleed to death through their toenails.
      (F, 1962)

4753   If a dog howls at the moon, it is a sign of fire.
      (F, 1962, + 1 F)

4754   Dogs see the Devil when a bell rings or a whistle blows; that's
      why they howl.
      (M, 40, R, 1961)

4755   Never let a dog go into a haunted castle. If you do, it will come
      out with its skin wrong side out, hanging over its head.
      (F, 47, 1958)

4756   Man's best friend is his dog.
      (F, 42, R, 1964)

4757   A dog turns around three times before it lies down to sleep in
      order to determine the direction of the wind. By turning
      around, the dog can tell which direction the wind is from by
      feeling it on its wet nose. It will lie down facing the wind, so
      that if anyone approaches, the smell will be carried by the
      wind.
      (M, 1962)

4758   A good bird dog will honor another dog's point.
      (M, 55, R, 1964)

4759   A dog that has a spotted mouth will not be any good.
      (M, 40, R, 1961)

4760   A puppy that has a black mouth is going to be a good dog.
      (M, 15, R, 1958, + 1 F and 2 M)

4761   If the roof of a dog's mouth is black, the dog will be energetic.
      (M, 63, R, 1958)

4762   A dog that has a lot of black in his mouth is intelligent.
      (M, 20, R, 1959)

4763   A dog that has a black mouth is smarter than one that has a
      plain mouth.
      (M, 1959 [his mother])

4764   If your dog has the mange, put a copper wire around its neck,
      and the mange will go away.
      (F, 55, 1955)

4765   Feeding gunpowder to a dog will make it fierce.
      (F, 51, R, 1956)

4766   Put turpentine into an egg to break a dog of sucking them.
      (F, 50, R, 1960)

4767   You can cure a dog of sucking eggs by cutting off its tail.
      (M, 70, R, 1958)

HOGS

4768   If a black pig is born in a litter, you must kill it; otherwise all
the piglets will die.
(F, 20, 1957)

4769   A pig whose tail doesn't curl is unhealthy.
(M, 60, R, 1958 [his father])

4770   Hogs will head into the wind while eating.
(M, 70, R, 1959)

4771   To load a stubborn pig, put a bucket over its head, and back it
up the chute.
(M, 50, R, 1954)

4772   Wean calves and pigs when the signs of the zodiac are right.
(F, 60, R, 1959)

4773   Be sure to wean pigs or small animals on the first Tuesday
after a new moon. Everything seems to work better if started
under this sign.
(F, 30, R, 1961)

4774   Castrate calves and pigs according to the signs of the zodiac.
(M, 50, R, 1962, + 1 M)

4775   If you castrate a hog while the sign is in the hoof, the hog
won't swell.
(M, 32, R, 1959 [his friends])

4776   Only castrate hogs by the light of the full moon.
(M, 21, R, 1956, + 1 M)

4777   Hogs that are butchered in the light of the moon produce
more lard.
(F, 60, 1959)

4778   If hogs are butchered during the light of the moon, the meat
will shrink a great deal.
(M, 62, R, 1959)

4779   If you butcher a hog in the dark of the moon, your meat will
fry away.
(F, 53, R, 1960)

4780   If the fat fries out of your pork, the pork was butchered at the
wrong time of the moon.
(F, 50, R, 1962, + 1 M)

4781   If a hog was butchered during the wrong time of the moon,
the bacon will curl in the skillet.
(M, 31, 1959)

4782   If you butcher pork in the light of the moon, the meat will always curl when cooked.
     (M, 40, R, 1957, + 3 F)

4783   If pork has been killed in the light of the moon, it will curl up when fried.
     (M, 58, 1958, + 1 M)

4784   If you butcher in the light of the moon, the meat won't shrink as much as it will when butchered in the dark of the moon.
     (M, 50, R, 1960 [his father-in-law], + 3 F and 3 M)

4785   The best time to butcher hogs is the light of the moon. In the dark of the moon the meat will be tough and will not keep well.
     (M, 50, 1962)

4786   It is better to butcher in the full of the moon, as the meat will be more solid.
     (M, 79, R, 1962 [his parents])

4787   Don't butcher at the time of the full moon, or the lard won't be any good.
     (F, 45, R, 1960)

4788   Butcher three or four days after the new moon, so that the meat won't curl or shrink when cooked.
     (M, 94, 1957)

4789   Meat butchered in the last quarter of the moon will not shrivel up.
     (M, 60, R, 1957)

4790   Be sure to butcher your hogs under the right sign of the zodiac; otherwise the bacon will be flabby.
     (M, 50, 1956)

4791   A pig must squeal when it is being killed in order for the meat to be good.
     (M, 1962)

HORSES

4792   If you are lost, give your horse its head, and it will take you home.
     (M, 20, R, 1959)

4793   A horse can always find its way home in the dark or in a storm.
     (F, 84, R, 1957)

4794   When buying a horse: One stocking foot, buy it; two stocking

feet, try it; three stocking feet, look well about it; four stocking feet, do without it.

(F, 50, R, 1961)

4795 If a horse has a white eye, it will be a mean and wild horse.

(M, 26, R, 1957, + 1 M)

4796 A white ring around a horse's eye (between the pupil and the lid) means that the horse will be wild and untamable.

(M, 50, R, 1958)

4797 Blue-eyed horses are usually unpredictable.

(F, 21, 1956)

4798 One contributor's father always weaned his colts according to the signs in his almanac.

(F, 70, R, 1961)

4799 If you wean a colt before sunup, you'll never have to milk the mare.

(M, 1961)

4800 A farting horse never gets tired.

(M, 60, R, 1961)

4801 A horse that has four white feet, a white face, and a glass eye is wild and no good.

(M, 19, R, 1959 [his father])

4802 A horse that has four white-stocking feet is a good buy. A horse that has only three white-stocking feet is a bad buy.

(M, 56, R, 1958)

4803 A horse that has two white feet is a bad horse.

(F, 20, 1958)

4804 A horse with a roman nose is balky.

(M, 66, 1955)

4805 A cold-shouldered horse won't work.

(M, 66, 1956)

4806   If a mare conceives in the light of the moon, she will have a mare colt.
(M, 50, R, 1958)

4807   Never get on a horse from the right side.
(F, 20, R, 1960 [her grandmother])

4808   Get on a horse from the left side; otherwise it will kick the thunder out of you!
(F, 19, 1959)

4809   If a horse lays its ears back, don't try to ride it.
(F, 20, R, 1958)

4810   A horse that raises its tail while working cattle or running usually has a mean streak or was broken in wrong and now is not to be trusted.
(M, 50, R, 1961)

4811   If a horse is born backwards, you should kill it.
(M, 63, R, 1958)

4812   If a stranger crosses in front of a barn while a foal is being born, the foal's color will change.
(M, 63, R, 1968)

4813   You can't make a horse cross a railroad trestle.
(M, 60, R, 1959 [his father])

4814   White horses eat more hay than black horses eat.
(M, 19, R, 1956)

4815   If a horse rolls clear over, it is worth a hundred dollars; if it rolls clear over twice, it is worth two hundred dollars; and so forth. (A person who used to go with the polo team a lot picked up many such beliefs.)
(F, 20, 1957)

4816   A horse is worth fifty dollars for every time he can roll completely over.
(M, 40, R, 1963 [his father])

4817   To take warts off a horse, take a piece of binding twine, and tie it around the wart. Each day, pull the twine a little tighter. The wart will come off in approximately one week. (The informant raised mules and sold them to the army during World War I.)
(M, 1962)

4818   Cover a horse's head so that you can get it out of a burning barn.
(F, 29, R, 1958, + 2 F and 2 M)

4819   If you put a goat in the stable, you will prevent the horses from getting diseases.
(F, 18, 1955)

4820 During a storm, horses always stand with their tails to the wind, and cattle stand with their heads to the wind.
  (M, 20, R, 1958)

INSECTS AND SPIDERS

4821 A fly in the house on New Year's Day means that you will have prosperity all year.
  (F, 60, 1959)

4822 For every fly killed in the spring, there will be a thousand fewer in the summer.
  (F, 60, R, 1964 [her mother])

4823 The flies bite the hardest just before it rains; and the birds chirp the loudest just before a storm.
  (F, 47, 1961)

4824 Grasshoppers come only in dry years.
  (M, 83, R, 1961, + 1 M)

4825 When a centipede walks on you, his feet leave poison at every step.
  (F, 50, R, 1962 [her mother])

4826 If you make a chalk mark where ants run, they will never cross the chalk line.
  (F, 82, R, 1957)

4827 Sprinkle black pepper over cabbages to kill cabbage bugs.
  (F, 70, 1958)

4828 If you put a bedbug in a dead person's coffin and then bury it, all the bedbugs will leave your house.
  (F, R, 1948 [this came from Sweden])

4829 To kill bugs, put a hedge ball in the basement.
  (F, 40, 1961, + 1 F)

4830 To find the direction that the cows are in, hold a daddy-longlegs by one leg and ask him to point to the direction. With one of his free legs he will point to the right direction.
  (F, 49, R, 1959, + 2 F and 1 M)

4831 If you see a spider in the morning, you will have to work hard; a spider at noon is a sign of mourning; a spider at night is lucky.
  (F, 21, 1957)

4832 If you see a spider hanging on a web, you will get a letter.
  (F, 50, R, 1958, + 1 F and 1 M)

4833   If a spider web falls across your face in the dark, your
       enemies are working against you.
       (F, 50, R, 1959)

4834   If a spider drops down on you from its web, you will get a new
       dress.
       (F, 60, 1957)

4835   To kill a spider is to lose a friend.
       (F, 1959)

4836   If you kill a black widow spider on Sunday, two of them will
       appear on Monday.
       (F, 50, 1957)

RODENTS

4837   A plentiful crop of rats is an indication of war.
       (M, 60, R, 1957)

4838   To get rid of rats, feed them ground glass and cornmeal.
       (F, 70, 1960)

4839   If you want to get rid of rats, kill one, and let it lie.
       (M, 20, R, 1958)

4840   At a harbor, if all the rats leave the ship, it will sink on its
       next voyage.
       (M, 40, R, 1960 [his mother], + 2 F)

4841   If a rat leaves a boat when it comes to port, that boat is going
       to sink.
       (F, 50, R, 1957, + 1 M)

4842   If the rats jump off a ship, it is sinking.
       (M, 20, R, 1963, + 1 M and 1 F)

4843   If mice and rats leave a ship, the ship will be shipwrecked on
       its next voyage.
       (F, 21, R, 1957)

4844   If you put a dried apple in a jar, there will be no mice in your
       house.
       (F, 21, 1956)

4845   In order to catch an Easter bunny, put some salt on his tail.
       (F, 20, 1959)

4846   If you sprinkle salt on a rabbit's tail, you will be able to catch
       it.
       (F, 61, R, 1957)

4847   If you kill a rabbit in a cemetery and then take the left front foot, dry it, and rub the foot on somebody, that person will do whatever you want him to do.

(M, 90, 1958)

SNAKES

4848　The hoop snake is said to have a sting on the end of its tail that can kill a human being. The snake is said to take its tail in its mouth and roll like a hoop. It is thought to be able to travel faster in this way than a fast horse can run. However, it can only travel in a straight line; so, if a person sees one coming, he may be able to dodge it. If the snake runs into a green tree, its sting will be so deeply imbedded in the tree that it cannot get away, but the tree will die as a result of the sting.

(M, 75, 1961)

4849　Hoop snakes bite their tails and roll down a hill.

(M, 50, 1962, + 1 F)

4850　If a hoop snake hits a tree, the tree will die.

(M, 50, 1962 [his father])

4851　One informant said that he had heard of hoop snakes but had never seen one. He did say, however, that he had taken a bull-snake and had put its tail in its mouth so that the snake's fangs caught the tail. Then he had tried to roll it like a hoop.

(M, 60, 1962)

4852　Some people think that if one strikes a joint snake, it will break in two; then if it is left alone, the two parts will come back together, and the whole snake will go on its way. The truth is that only the tail can be broken off so easily. It will not join back on the snake, but the snake will grow a new tail in time. This is a protective measure that helps it to escape from its enemies if they seize the snake by its tail.

(M, 75, 1961)

4853　If you kill a snake, its mate will find it before sundown.

(M, 20, R, 1958, + 1 F and 2 M)

4854　When you see a snake, you know that there is another one nearby that will come to it even if you kill it.

(F, 35, 1958)

4855　If you kill a snake, its mate will try to bite you.

(M, 55, R, 1958)

4856   Whenever you see one big snake, you are sure to find its mate.
      (F, 68, R, 1958)

4857   Snakes always travel in pairs.
      (M, 1961, + 1 F)

4858   If you put hair from a horse's tail in water, it will turn into a snake.
      (F, 19, R, 1956, + 12 F and 4 M)

4859   If you drop a white hair from a horse's tail into a pond of water during any month, it will turn into a hair snake.
      (F, 70, R, 1963 [her mother], + 1 F and 1 M)

4860   If you pull a hair from a horse's tail and put it in a rain barrel, it will soon turn into a snake.
      (F, 78, R, 1958)

4861   A hair that has been put in a rain barrel will turn into a tadpole.
      (M, 50, R, 1958)

4862   If you tie a knot in a horse hair and place it in a jar, the hair will turn into a snake.
      (M, 50, 1959)

4863   A piece of hair from a horse's tail will turn into a snake if it is put in a bottle of water and left undisturbed for several weeks.
      (F, 80, R, 1960 [her parents])

4864   If, when you hit a joint snake, it breaks into several pieces and crawls away, the parts will rejoin later.
      (M, 20, 1955, + 2 F)

4865   A certain kind of snake, if hit with a stick, hoe, or such, will break into pieces, and each piece will grow into a new snake.
      (F, 20, R, 1961)

4866   A snake will not be completely dead until sundown.
      (M, 20, R, 1963, + 13 F and 20 M)

4867   When you try to kill a snake, it will keep on squirming as long as the sun is up.
      (M, 25, 1958, + 5 F)

4868   A dead snake's tail will live till sundown and will keep on wiggling until then.
      (M, 21, R, 1961, + 5 F and 3 M)

4869   Some people claim that snakes can take milk from a cow.
      (F, 60, R, 1962, + 2 F and 1 M)

4870   Snakes come out in springtime after the first thunderstorm.
      (F, 20, R, 1956, + 1 F)

4871   It is believed that rattlesnakes add only one rattle each year. Actually, they add two or three, depending upon the number of times they shed their skins.

(F, 16, R, 1963, + 1 F)

4872   When you kill a snake, always be sure to get its mate.

(M, 50, 1959, + 1 F)

4873   If you kill one snake, you will have to kill two, as its mate will be nearby.

(F, 34, 1958, + 1 F and 1 M)

4874   Snakes won't crawl over a hair rope. (Because of this belief, cowboys used to surround their beds with ropes made of horsehair or cow's hair.)

(F, 35, 1958, + 1 F and 3 M)

4875   When you are on a hunting trip, lay a horsehair rope around the tent to keep the snakes away.

(M, 35, 1963)

4876   If you are in a desert, draw a ring around you so that the snakes won't cross it.

(F, 40, 1959)

4877   A rattlesnake won't cross a rope.

(M, 50, 1957)

4878   If there are bullsnakes around your place, there will not be any rattlesnakes.

(F, 40, R, 1962)

4879   If you don't move, a rattlesnake will not strike you.

(F, 49, R, 1961)

4880   If you throw something that you have handled down close to a rattlesnake, it will stay there for a long time watching the object.

(F, 49, R, 1961)

4881   Rattlesnakes are drawn by ground vibrations.

(M, 20, R, 1958)

4882   A rattlesnake will always give a warning.

(F, 18, 1959)

4883   If a rattlesnake doesn't rattle, he won't bite.

(F, 20, R, 1958)

4884   A snake can spit poison in your eyes and thus blind you.

(F, 28, 1956)

4885   Kill a snake by spitting tobacco juice into its mouth.

(M, 35, 1964)

4886   A water snake can't strike while it is underwater.

(M, 21, R, 1961)

4887   Some people believe that snakes jump from the ground and that they have to strike from a coil.
(F, 66, R, 1963)

4888   A blue racer will chase you.
(M, 20, R, 1957)

4889   A snake will swallow its young if danger approaches.
(F, 71, 1961)

4890   Where you find snake fedders (dragonflies), you will find snakes.
(F, 50, R, 1959 [her mother], + 1 M)

4891   If you kill a snake, you conquer your enemy.
(F, 62, R, 1962 [her parents])

4892   If you kill the first snake you see in the spring, you have conquered your enemies.
(F, 59, R, 1957)

4893   If you cut a live snake in half, one part will go one way, while the other part will go the other way.
(F, 14, 1958)

4894   When you kill a snake, separate the head from the rest of the body, and bury the head separately. This will prevent the head from reattaching itself to the snake. This has to be done before dusk; otherwise the snake will continue to live.
(M, 1963)

4895   If you kill a snake on Friday, it won't be completely dead until Sunday morning.
(M, 40, 1958)

4896   When someone kills a snake, he should place it on its back until the sun goes down, so that it will quit wiggling.
(F, 40, R, 1960 [her father])

4897   Snakes can hypnotize birds.
(M, 20, R, 1959)

TURTLES

4898   If a turtle bites you, it will not let loose until it thunders.
(F, 20, R, 1960, + 9 F and 4 M)

4899   If a turtle bites you, it won't let go till sundown.
(F, 20, R, 1961, + 2 F and 6 M)

4900   If you chop the head off a turtle, it will blink its eyes the next day.
(F, 70, R, 1963)

4901   When the head of a turtle has been severed, the body will turn toward water.
          (M, 84, R, 1956)

MISCELLANEOUS

4902   Burying a possum under the door of a chicken house will keep other possums away.
          (M, 70, R, 1958 [his uncle])

4903   A porcupine can shoot its quills.
          (F, 28, 1956)

4904   All animals begin to talk at midnight on New Year's Eve.
          (M, 20, R, 1961)

4905   Animals can speak at midnight on Christmas.
          (F, 35, 1956)

4906   An animal will not harm a person who is praying.
          (F, 20, 1958)

4907   If an animal licks a wound, the wound will heal faster.
          (M, 50, R, 1958)

4908   When you hear coyote howls on a cold moonlight night, it may sound like there are five, but there is only one there.
          (M, 69, R, 1956)

4909   If you pick up a skunk by the tail, he won't squirt you.
          (F, 20, R, 1961 [her parents])

12

Hunting and Fishing

SUPERSTITION, AS WE THINK OF IT, IS PREVALENT IN THE lore of hunters and fishermen, and generally they do not personally consider these beliefs and practices necessarily as superstitions or as odd, but rather as worthwhile knowledge that has proved useful or beneficial in some way. A careful search through several volumes of popular hunting and fishing magazines showed very little concern on the part of their writer-specialists for folk beliefs other than the common safety practices. There is an avoidance of manifestations that are different from the reality of "our world." Scientific rationality is the dictator in these popular magazines; so, what goes on in the hunting and fishing world as far as folk beliefs are concerned must be "field collected," as a hunter must go to the field.

Of the 253 items in this chapter, 31 percent are concerned with animal-hunting, 25 percent with fishing, and 14 percent with bird- hunting. About 20 percent concern luck or how to be successful.

Some of the various practices to help ensure luck are carrying a twig of mistletoe, kissing shells, wearing red, or spitting on fish bait. Friday is considered a bad-luck day. The condition of the moon, the weather, the direction of the wind, and sometimes a chew of tobacco are practical considerations for the sportsman. More cosmic is the custom of taking blood from a slain deer and smearing the forehead of its vanquisher, or wearing claws of the animal strung around the neck, "to inherit an animal's strength."

Mid-America boasts major duck and geese flyways, some rare bird-hunting, such as the prairie chicken, and occasional big game along the western fringes. Literally scores of other kinds of wild game exist to excite the young and the old—the young, most of whom are trained by the old-timers, whose traditional lore is shared willingly.

HELPS TO ENSURING SUCCESS

4910   If you arise before the alarm goes off, you will have a good day's hunting.
(M, 23, 1964 [his uncle])

4911   If you make your mouth look a little bit more like a grin than like a frown, you will make a better shot; but the look has to be just right.
(M, 70, 1964)

4912   The sound of a gun does not scare an animal; only the movement of a person scares it.
(M, 20, 1964)

4913   The longer the barrel of a gun, the harder it will shoot.
(M, 54, 1964)

4914   Wrap the barrel of a gun to keep the sun from reflecting off the gun. Also, darken your face to stop the reflection. Reflection will scare animals.
(M, 20, 1964)

4915   When using a rifle scope on a hazy day, light a match and smudge the end of the scope, so that you will be able to see through the haze.
(M, 32, 1964)

4916   Lead your moving target.
(M, 35, R, 1964)

4917   The best time to hunt animals is at sunrise or sunset, because that is when they feed.
(M, 21, 1964)

4918   There is an Indian saying about a hunting moon: if there is a wet moon—when you can hang your powder horn on it—stay home; if there is a dry moon—when you can't hang your powder horn on it—go hunting.
(M, 66, 1964, + 1 M)

4919   If a crescent moon is tilted till Davy Crockett can hang his hat on it, the hunting will be bad. If it is tilted downward so that his hat won't stay on it, he is out hunting; therefore the hunting will be good.
(M, 22, 1964 [his grandfather])

4920   During the dark of the moon is the best time to hunt, fish, or trap. The light of the moon is the poorest time.
(M, 61, 1964)

4921   The more miserable the weather, the better the hunting.
      (M, 23, 1964)

4922   When you are ready to shoot, tie a string on the end of your gun barrel to see which way wind is blowing.
      (M, 20, 1964)

4923   When the wind is in the west, the huntin' is the best.
      (M, 25, 1964)

4924   "Rainbow in morning, / Hunters take warning; / Rainbow at night, / Hunters delight; / Rainbow to windward, / Foul fall the day; / Rainbow to leeward, / Damp runs away."
      (M, 22, 1964)

4925   All hunting is better in moist weather.
      (M, 47, 1964, + 1 M)

4926   Always hunt upwind, so that the game won't smell your scent.
      (M, 21, 1964, + 6 M)

4927   Hunt downwind from your game.
      (M, 40, 1964, + 1 M)

4928   If you can look the victim in the eye while you are hunting, it will stand still, and you will be able to shoot it.
      (M, 22, 1964)

4929   You can tell how far ahead of you an animal is by how much the grass has straightened up in his tracks.
      (M, 59, 1964)

4930   Some hunters use a salt lick to attract animals.
      (M, 35, 1964)

4931   Where the cover is the thickest and the going is the roughest, that is where the best and biggest game will be hiding.
(M, 23, 1964)

4932   An animal that dwells underground can be brought out by rapidly pouring enough water in its hole to fill the hole.
(M, 52, 1964)

4933   Animals are not as afraid of a man when he is down on all fours as when he is standing up.
(M, 20, 1964)

4934   A hunter should walk with the sun to his back. Thus the sun will be in the animal's eyes, not in the hunter's.
(M, 20, 1964, + 1 M)

4935   While you are hunting, walk at an irregular pace, and change directions at irregular times. Animals know the human step; it will cause them to run and hide.
(M, 20, 1964)

4936   To attract the attention of any animal and prevent it from fleeing, make a sharp whistle, a sound, or a clicking noise.
(M, 68, 1964)

4937   Whistle to make a woodchuck stand up so that you can get a shot at it.
(M, 21, R, 1964)

4938   A bird cannot spot a hat as well as it can spot a man's bare head.
(M, 46, 1964)

LUCK AND WARNINGS

4939   Carrying a twig of mistletoe while hunting will bring you good luck.
(M, 13, 1964)

4940   It is bad luck to see a stray dog or cat before firing the first shot of the day.
(M, 22, 1964)

4941   Carry a rabbit's foot for luck while you are hunting.
(M, 46, 1964)

4942   It is good luck when a guest gets the first shot when you are hunting.
(M, 20, R, 1964)

4943   Carry the empty case from a shotgun shell for good luck, if the case is from a good kill that you have made before.
(M, 20, 1964)

4944   Always throw over your left shoulder the first shell that you have shot.
        (M, 21, 1964)

4945   If you kiss the shell, your shot will be good.
        (M, 18, 1964)

4946   You will change your luck to the worse if you wash your hunting coat.
        (M, 46, 1964)

4947   Wear red laces in your shoes for luck.
        (M, 23, R, 1964)

4948   A good hunter always wears the same clothes—trousers, shirt, vest, cap, and boots—to bring luck. His clothes are not to be washed.
        (M, 23, R, 1964)

4949   Shoot only the male game; never the female.
        (M, 35, R, 1964, + 1 M)

4950   Never shoot an albino of any kind. If you should do so by accident, bury it, don't eat it.
        (M, 43, 1964)

4951   If your dog lets out a yell like a wolf when you start to hunt, you had better be careful; otherwise, you will get hurt.
        (M, 32, 1964)

4952   If on one day you do not use all of your shells, do not ever use the same shells the next day.
        (M, 45, 1964)

4953   Never shoot the first bird that you see on a hunting trip.
        (M, 20, R, 1964)

4954   Never hunt on Friday.
        (M, 38, 1964 [learned from an experienced hunter])

4955   Don't haul a bird dog in the trunk of your car; it won't be able to scent birds because of the carbon monoxide fumes.
        (M, 48, 1964)

4956   While hunting, always wear red for good luck.
        (M, 68, 1964)

SAFETY MEASURES

4957   Never stir gunpowder and alcohol together.
        (M, 80, 1964)

4958   Never use your last bullet.
        (M, 50, R, 1964)

4959   Never brush shoot—that is, never shoot in heavy brush or thick trees.
          (M, 45, 1964)

4960   Never track big game immediately after it has been shot.
          (M, 21, R, 1964)

4961   Do not shoot at the first noise that you hear.
          (M, 35, R, 1965)

4962   Always break the breech of a gun while you are walking.
          (M, 35, R, 1964)

4963   Always unload your gun before going through a fence.
          (M, 21, R, 1964, + 1 M)

4964   Always put your gun over a fence before you cross the fence yourself.
          (M, 22, R, 1964)

4965   Check the barrel of your gun for obstructions before you load it.
          (M, 22, R, 1964)

4966   Never point a gun at anything you don't intend to shoot.
          (M, 21, 1964, + 2 M)

4967   It's the empty gun that kills.
          (M, 42, R, 1964, + 1 M)

4968   A gun is *always* loaded.
          (M, 50, 1964, + 1 M)

4969   Always chew tobacco when you are out hunting in case you get bitten by a snake.
          (M, 81, 1964)

4970   Always step on a log or rock, not over it; there may be a snake on the shaded side.
          (M, 81, 1964)

4971   When you are on a hunting trip, lay a horsehair rope around the tent to keep the snakes away.
          (M, 30, 1964, + 3 M)

4972   Always wear bright red or yellow clothing when hunting to protect yourself from being mistakenly shot by another hunter. Deer are color blind, so this will not make you more easily seen by them.
          (M, 32, 1964, + 1 M)

4973   When you go hunting, always wear some bright wearing apparel, such as a red hat.
          (M, 45, R, 1964)

4974   Never shoot at a bird from the car, even when in the field.
          (M, 48, 1964)

HUNTING

Antelope and Deer

4975   Antelope are the hardest things on earth to get a shot at, and you'll find that they can make out a hunter miles away. If there is only one antelope, it will always keep its eyes peeled for something to get scared at.
(M, 68, 1964)

4976   Antelope meat can't be beaten for a few meals, but for a steady diet it is not so good as buffalo. It cloys the stomach when you get too much of it.
(M, 68, 1964)

4977   You should never shoot a white deer. (This is an old Indian belief.)
(M, 65, 1964)

4978   When a person kills his first deer, whoever is with him should cut the deer's throat and smear blood on the person's forehead and cheeks.
(M, 20, 1964)

4979   If you sit up high, the deer will never see you.
(M, 68, 1964)

4980   If the moon is bright, the deer run at night.
(F, 70, 1964)

4981   One shot, one deer; two shots, one deer; three shots, no deer.
(F, 70, 1964)

4982   Hunt deer on the slopes in the evening; hunt deer in the valley in the morning. The smell goes up.
(M, 20, 1964)

4983   To attract deer, hang a chewed piece of chewing tobacco upwind in a tree or bush. They will be attracted by the smell.
(M, 35, 1964)

4984   To bring deer to your position, rub old antlers together.
(M, 21, 1964)

4985   Deer are hard to shoot, because one of them always watches, and when it sees or hears anything suspicious, its tail turns up so that the white underside shows. This is a danger signal, and the whole herd will take off for safety.
(M, 23, 1964)

4986   Always bury the viscera of a deer after it has been shot.
(M, 19, 1964)

4987   To hunt deer, place a block of stock salt near your cabin about a month to six weeks before the hunting season and again when you arrive, for the deer will be attracted in this way.
  (M, 52, 1964)

4988   Remove the musk glands of a deer right after you kill it; otherwise the meat will not be good.
  (M, 28, 1964)

4989   When you are stalking deer, the wind must be blowing from the deer toward you, so that the deer don't get a scent from you.
  (M, 22, 1964)

4990   When hunting deer, it is customary to wait near a water hole on the downwind side until the deer come to drink, or to wait in a tree until the deer walk beneath it, rather than to trail the deer.
  (M, 20, 1964)

4991   You always miss your first shot in deer season because you have "buck fever."
  (M, 46, 1964)

Bears and Beavers

4992   After killing a bear or an eagle, take the claws and wear them around your neck in order to inherit the animal's strength.
  (M, 68, 1964)

4993   Always track down and kill a wounded bear.
  (M, 35, 1964)

4994   When a grizzly bear is killed, its eyes must be dug out and buried before the bear cools; otherwise the spirit of the guide will turn into a grizzly bear.
  (M, 30, 1964)

4995   Always dig out the eyes of a bear and bury them in order to keep the spirit of the Indians out of the bear.
  (M, 30, 1964 [learned from an Alaskan Indian])

4996   Set a beaver trap to one side or the other of the beaver's slide so that you get his feet.
  (M, 24, 1964)

Birds and Fowl

4997   Good hunting doesn't go with the cawing of the crow.
  (M, 56, 1964)

4998   When a lot of crows are hollering and fussing, there is an owl or a hawk in the tree.
        (M, 68, 1964)

4999   If a crow has been shot out of a flock and is lying crippled and dying on the ground, it will be honored by a funeral homage paid by the rest of the flock.
        (M, 46, 1964)

5000   If a storm comes from the south, the crows will go north.
        (M, 57, 1958)

5001   Never shoot a dove until you can see the color of its breast.
        (M, 47, 1964)

5002   The best time for hunting ducks is when it is snowing.
        (M, 20, R, 1964)

5003   The worst winter weather is the best for duck hunting.
        (M, 21, R, 1964)

5004   When you are duck hunting, always pick up your shells; otherwise the reflections off them will scare the ducks.
        (M, 20, 1964)

5005   Use narrow-leaf willow branches in constructing duck blinds; their leaves will not fall off.
        (M, 20, 1964)

5006   A dead duck should always be carried with its head down so that the evil spirits can leave.
        (M, 18, 1964 [his father])

5007   In the springtime, a good duck hunter will return to his blind and practice his duck-calling as the ducks fly back north.
        (M, 20, 1964)

5008   If you see many red-legged mallards while hunting ducks in the fall, it will turn colder in three days.
        (M, 61, 1964)

5009   Approach a flock of ducks from the downwind side.
        (M, 28, 1965)

5010   If you get three days of south winds at the end of February, the ducks will soon be coming back from the south.
        (M, 24, 1964)

5011   Ducks fly lower earlier in the morning.
        (M, 50, 1964)

5012   You will get more ducks on a warm morning just before a cold wave.
        (M, 50, 1964)

5013   A cold, overcast day is best for hunting ducks and geese.
        (M, 21, 1964)

5014   A duck that has been wounded by a hunter will dive down into the water and hang onto the roots of the water weeds to commit suicide or hide.
(M, 46, 1964)

5015   When hunting geese and ducks, never look up at them, because they will be able to see your face.
(M, 21, 1960)

5016   For best results, hunt geese when a very cold wind is blowing hard.
(M, 18, 1964)

5017   To kill an owl, walk up to the owl while it is sitting on a post, and then walk around and around the owl. It will always look at you, and eventually it will wring its own neck.
(M, 72, 1964)

5018   When hunting pheasant, tie a rope with bells on it between the hunters. This will cause the pheasants to fly.
(M, 22, 1964)

5019   When hunting pheasant, stop for a few seconds. The pheasants will fly when they can't hear the hunter.
(M, 41, 1964)

5020   A high shrill whistle that sounds like a hawk will keep pheasant, quail, and other flushing birds from flying very far.
(M, 40, 1964)

5021   If you scare a covey of quail, they will scatter; but if you wait for a while, you will hear them call themselves together, and you will get a chance at the whole covey.
(M, 23, 1964 [his uncle])

5022   During quail-hunting season, if you drive your car over the country and see a hawk sitting in a tree, this means that he is watching a covey of quail near him.
(M, 61, 1964 [learned from an old-timer])

5023   When hunting quail, if you approach the covey from behind, you can pick the quail off one by one by shooting the last one in the covey. If you shoot the ones in the lead, this will scare the others off.
(M, 51, 1964)

5024   If the weather is bad, quail always put their tails together so that they can see around them.
(M, 23, 1964)

5025   To ensure more hits, always walk into the wind when hunting quail.
(M, 21, 1964)

5026 If you put glass marbles in a small box (when hunting quail) and shake it in the vicinity of the quail's habitat, the quail will settle right down so that you can shoot them easily.
(M, 50, 1964)

5027 When hunting quail or doves, give a crow call. They will immediately fly up, giving the hunter a chance to shoot.
(M, 50, 1964)

5028 If a person eats at least one quail every day for a month, he will die.
(M, 18, 1964)

5029 When you are stalking turkeys, the warning "pit, pit" will tell you if you have been seen.
(M, 1964)

5030 If you hit a game bird in the head, it will fly straight up.
(M, 23, 1964)

5031 A wet bird will never fly at night.
(M, 23, 1964)

5032 When a group of men goes hunting, the one closest to the bird shoots first.
(M, 48, R, 1964)

Coyotes, Wolves, and Foxes

5033 To trap a coyote, put entrails or guts from a pig or cow on a straw pile or a haystack. Set several traps, some about one hundred feet away, all around the bait. A coyote will make several circles around the stack before approaching the bait and is apt to step on a trap and get caught.
(M, 52, 1964)

5034 Coyotes have one-track minds. They will run into cars instead of changing direction.
(M, 38, 1964)

5035 To bring a coyote within shooting range, make the sound of a wounded rabbit.
(M, 21, 1964)

5036 Male wolves and coyotes rule over a certain area or domain, which they mark out and designate by urinating on the trees or bushes. Another wolf or coyote may pass through the area, but it will not stay unless it can defeat the present occupant in battle.
(M, 38, 1964)

5037   If a coyote runs over a hill after you have shot it, don't leave, but walk over the hill, and the coyote will still be there waiting.
         (M, 20, 1964)

5038   If you "jump" a coyote, it will always stop running once to look back.
         (M, 50, 1964)

5039   Coyotes, when being chased by hounds, will run in a large circle if they have young.
         (M, 50, 1964)

5040   If you rub asafetida on the soles of your shoes, wolves will follow the smell and follow you to the traps.
         (F, 52, 1964)

5041   Where you find a grey fox you will not find a red fox.
         (M, 23, 1964)

Dogs

5042   Don't take your dogs out if the wind is high; they'll go in circles.
         (M, 65, 1964)

5043   Dogs can't smell game very well on dry and dusty days.
         (M, 21, 1964)

5044   If you cut off a piece of a hunting dog's tail and bury it under the doorstep, the dog will never stray.
         (M, 54, 1964)

5045   A black hunting dog is the symbol of sorrow, defeat, and mourning.
         (M, 54, 1964)

5046   A greyhound runs by sight, not by scent.
         (M, 25, 1964)

5047   It is natural for a greyhound to go in and fight to kill any animal that goes down.
         (M, 25, 1964)

5048   It is the natural instinct of a greyhound to run down anything that will run away from him.
         (M, 25, 1956)

5049   "Soft on the trail, solid on the tree" (this pertains to a dog's voice).
         (M, 25, 1964)

5050   A bawl-mouthed dog is usually a good fighter.
         (M, 24, 1964)

Rabbits

5051   Never kill a rabbit to eat until after the first snow.
        (M, 23, 1964, + 5 M)
5052   When skinning a rabbit, never let the fur touch the meat;
        otherwise the meat will be ruined.
        (M, 28, 1964)
5053   Don't shoot rabbits for eating except during months with an r
        in their names.
        (M, 28, 1964, + 2 M)
5054   Never shoot or eat a rabbit unless there have been fourteen
        nights of frost.
        (M, 48, 1964)
5055   Don't eat rabbits that have white spots on their livers.
        (M, 24, 1964)
5056   After shooting rabbits, or other wild game, be sure to soak
        them in salt water all night before eating them.
        (M, 44, 1964)
5057   When you are hunting rabbits, shine a light on them, and they
        will not move.
        (M, 19, 1964)
5058   When hunting rabbits in brush and the like, walk a while,
        then stop, and the rabbits will run away.
        (M, 19, 1964)
5059   A rabbit, when jumped, will follow rabbit lanes out of the
        field and know just how far to duck in order to clear the
        fence. Therefore, the hunter who hangs a broom wire loop
        below the fence and over the lane will snare the rabbit.
        (M, 60, 1964)
5060   Rabbits and coyotes will circle when being trailed.
        (M, 21, 1964, + 2 M)
5061   Never shoot a sitting rabbit; as the old-timers say, it is sick.
        (M, 48, 1964)
5062   Don't shoot a rabbit that doesn't run.
        (M, 24, 1964)
5063   Where there are a lot of rabbits, there are no quail.
        (M, 24, 1964)
5064   When hunting rabbits in snow or thick brush, stop every ten
        or fifteen feet. This makes a rabbit think that you have seen
        it, so it will run; otherwise you may walk right by it, and it will
        "hole up" and not move.
        (M, 19, 1964)

5065   While you are hunting rabbits, if one jumps up, be ready to shoot at another, because rabbits travel in pairs.
(M, 21, 1964)

5066   Hunt rabbits in the light of the moon.
(M, 32, 1964)

5067   A squeak-type of call will lure rabbits and coyotes. Rabbits will come running.
(M, 47, 1964)

5068   When you go rabbit hunting, you will find that if, when you see a rabbit nearby, you give short, low-pitched whistles, the rabbit will halt in his tracks and listen. Then you can take a shot at him.
(M, 25, 1964)

5069   When you are hunting jack rabbits, if a storm is approaching or is very near, they will run and continue to run without stopping and looking back; whereas, if it's a nice day, they will run a ways, and then stop and look back.
(M, 43, 1964)

5070   The rabbit hunting is poor where the coyotes are big and fat.
(M, 22, 1964, + 1 M)

5071   Don't handle a rabbit with your bare hands when you are skinning it and preparing it to eat.
(M, 45, 1964)

5072   When you are skinning a rabbit, great care must be taken to avoid scratching one's fingers on the bones. If one is scratched, rabbit fever may result.
(M, 21, 1964, + 1 M)

Raccoons and Opossums

5073   A coon won't tree when the moon is full.
(M, 21, 1964, + 1 M)

5074   When a coon is around a pond, it will usually skin and wash its prey before eating it.
(M, 25, 1964)

5075   "Casing a skin" means that the coons are skinned out without splitting and are stretched over a board.
(M, 22, 1964)

5076   The bigger and older a tree, the more likely it is to have a coon.
(M, 68, 1964)

5077   A coon won't run on frost-covered ground, and if the frost
        stays for thirty days, the coon will die.
        (M, 54, 1964)

5078   Possum-hunting is best on bright moonlit nights.
        (M, 21, 1964)

Skunks

5079   To trap a skunk, put a piece of tissue paper covered with dirt
        over the trap. The skunk won't be able to tell the difference
        between the trap and the ground.
        (M, 52, 1964)

5080   If you pick a skunk up by its tail, it can't squirt you.
        (M, 49, 1964)

5081   Never skin a skunk until after the first frost; it will shed.
        (M, 65, 1964)

Squirrels

5082   When two men are hunting squirrels, they should stand on
        opposite sides of the tree so that the squirrels can be shot at
        from either side.
        (M, 25, 1964)

5083   You have to keep walking to catch squirrels; you can't sit and
        wait for them to cross your path.
        (M, 45, 1964)

5084   To bring squirrels to your position, rub two coins together.
        (M, 21, 1964)

5085   To hunt squirrels, you must sit by a tree before sunrise and
        wait. To attract them, knock together stones gathered from a
        stream bed.
        (M, 19, 1964)

5086   When you go squirrel hunting, take along two hard objects
        that you can hit together to make a cracking sound. When the
        squirrels hear it, they will stop long enough for you to get a
        shot off.
        (M, 49, 1964)

5087   Where you find grey squirrels you will not find red squirrels.
        (M, 23, 1964)

5088   Hunt for squirrels in a grove of oak trees; this is where they
        are found most often.
        (M, 20, 1964)

5089   Rub a rough stick on tree bark to flush squirrels out of a nest. They will think that something is climbing up the tree after them.
(M, 40, 1964)

5090   Squirrel tails are good luck to hunters.
(M, 68, 1964)

Miscellaneous

5091   If there is extra-heavy fur on an animal, a cold winter is coming.
(M, 58, 1964, + 1 M)

5092   In a storm, a wild animal will always go into the wind.
(M, 28, 1964)

5093   Skunk scent can be used to "cover up" human scent when you are stalking animals while hunting. The animals will smell the skunk odor and pay no attention to the human.
(M, 47, 1964)

FISHING

5094   "With a wind in the north, / Fish won't go forth."
(M, 30, R, 1947, + 3 F and 1 M)

5095   "When the wind is in the south, / It will blow the bait into the fish's mouth."
(M, 20, R, 1962, + 3 F and 7 M)

5096   "When the wind is in the east, / Fishes bite the least."
(F, 18, R, 1956, + 10 F and 25 M)

5097   "Wind in the east, / Fish bite the least. / Wind in the west, / Fish bite the best."
(F, 20, R, 1957, + 5 M)

5098   "When the wind is in the east, / The fish bite the least. / When the wind is in the west, / The fish bite the best, / When the wind is in the south, / The bait blows in their mouth."
(F, 18, 1957, + 4 M)

5099   "When the wind is in the east, / The fish bite least. / When the wind is in the west, / The fish bite best. / When the wind is in the south, / They take it in the mouth. / When the wind is in the north, / You'd just as well stay home."
(M, 23, 1964)

5100 When the wind is in the east, it is neither good for man nor beast. (This is heeded by fishermen.)
   (M, 58, R, 1957, + 2 M)

5101 "When the wind's from the west, / Fish bite the best."
   (M, 21, 1956, + 11 F and 21 M)

5102 The best fishing season is the dark of the moon in May.
   (F, 58, R, 1958)

5103 Fish won't bite in the light of the full moon.
   (M, 39, R, 1958)

5104 When the moon is bright, the fish won't bite.
   (M, 1959)

5105 Don't go fishing until the moon is full.
   (M, 26, R, 1952, + 1 M)

5106 Fish bite best when the moon is on the rise; after it reaches a position directly overhead and starts down, you will not have any more luck.
   (M, 20, R, 1959)

5107 Fish always bite in the bright of the moon.
   (M, 38, 1954)

5108 Fish won't bite if the moon isn't right.
   (F, 1959)

5109 "A moon out at night; / A fisherman's delight."
   (F, 21, 1950)

5110 "When the mists begin to nod, / Fishermen, put away your rod."
   (M, 1958)

5111   "When the mist creeps up the hill, / Fishermen, up and try your skill. / When the mist begins to nod, / Fishermen, then put by your rod."
(M, 40, R, 1962)

5112   There is good fishing in the evening.
(M, 20, R, 1959)

5113   Fish are supposed to bite better in rainy weather.
(F, 21, 1950, + 1 F and 1 M)

5114   Fish will not bite when it is raining.
(F, 70, 1956)

5115   When rain comes from the east, the fish won't bite.
(F, 61, R, 1957)

5116   Fish bite best after a rain.
(M, 20, R, 1962)

5117   Fish won't bite after a rainstorm.
(M, 5, R, 1959)

5118   Fish bite best just before a rain.
(M, 20, R, 1958, + 5 F and 3 M)

5119   Fish will bite more frequently when a stream is rising due to heavy rains.
(M, 30, R, 1957, + 2 M)

5120   There is good fishing on the night before a rain.
(M, 20, R, 1958)

5121   Fish when it thunders.
(F, 40, 1959)

5122   A good time for a fish trap is during an electrical storm.
(M, 23, R, 1959)

5123   When the wind blows, the fish will bite.
(M, 20, R, 1958)

5124   Fish will not bite when it is windy.
(M, 80, 1959, + 1 M)

5125   It rains fish if the weather is right.
(M, 50, 1959)

5126   When the stream is up and running swiftly, the bigger fish bite better.
(M, 20, R, 1962)

5127   Some people will not go fishing if the barometer is going down.
(M, 56, 1962)

5128   A falling barometer indicates that there will be good fishing.
(M, 20, 1957)

5129   Fish only bite when the barometer is high.
       (F, college student)

5130   If the frogs jump into the water and then hop right back on the land, the fish are biting.
       (M, 20, 1959)

5131   Fish won't bite if flying insects are sluggish.
       (M, 60, R, 1958)

5132   If mosquitoes are biting, the fish will bite too.
       (F, 56, R, 1963, + 1 M)

5133   If you can see fish playing on top of the water, they will not bite on a hook.
       (M, 50, R, 1959)

5134   The fish will not bite on a day when an owl screeches early in the morning.
       (M, 60, R, 1957)

5135   If a horse fly lands on your fishing pole, the fish are biting.
       (F, 40, 1959)

5136   When you go fishing, always throw one fish back for seed.
       (M, 60, R, 1959, + 1 M)

5137   When there are worms on top of the ground, the fish aren't biting, because they find the worms and aren't hungry.
       (F, 20, 1962)

5138   If a fishworm breaks in half, the fish won't bite it.
       (M, 60, R, 1957)

5139   To get fishworms, hit the ground with a board. They'll come up, because they will think that the sound is being made by rain.
       (F, 82, 1958)

5140   When you are fishing, it is lucky to let doctor flies land on your pole and line.
       (M, 75, R, 1958)

5141   If you are fishing from a boat, take your shoes off for luck.
       (M, 35, R, 1960)

5142   A black cat is a sign of good luck only when you're going fishing.
       (F, 50, 1958)

5143   When you are fishing, it is lucky to say "Old Joe Bush."
       (M, 75, R, 1958)

5144   When you are fishing, it is lucky to cast pebbles into the water above the location of your bait.
       (M, 75, R, 1958)

5145   Don't talk or make noise when you are fishing; otherwise the fish won't bite.
        (F, 20, 1958)
5146   Fish will not bite if women are talking.
        (F, 60, 1958)
5147   If you talk when you are fishing, you will scare the fish away.
        (F, 50, 1958)
5148   If you count the number of fish that you have caught, you will not catch any more that day.
        (F, 27, 1960)
5149   After baiting a hook, spit on the bait (some say tobacco juice); this will ensure a bite.
        (M, 35, R, 1957, + 1 F and 1 M)
5150   If you spit on your bait, a fish will be certain to bite.
        (M, 50, R, 1958, + 7 M)
5151   Use a coin for a weight on a fishline to make the fish bite.
        (M, 50, R, 1958)
5152   If you use stink bait in running water, you will never fail to catch fish.
        (M, 21, R, 1958)
5153   A fire at the side of the stream will keep the fish from biting.
        (M, 48, R, 1958)
5154   Dough balls make good catfish bait.
        (M, 80, R, 1959)
5155   Fish can be kept fresh for several days by wrapping them in green walnut leaves.
        (F, 65, R, 1962)

MISCELLANEOUS ADVICE

5156   Always gut your game immediately after the kill.
        (M, 29, 1964)
5157   In preparing all wild game, soak it in salt water, and cook it with an apple and an onion.
        (M, 57, 1964)
5158   Soak wild game in milk to take away any strong odor and taste.
        (M, 38, 1969)
5159   To strengthen any weak part of your body, kill an animal, and eat that particular part of its body.
        (M, 57, 1964)

5160   Each animal that is hunted has a certain type of tree. When a hunter shoots an animal, he should break off a twig from that tree, dip it in the animal's blood, and put it in his hat.
(M, 20, 1964)

5161   When one hunter sees another hunter with a twig in his hat (indicating that he has shot something), the latter is obligated to buy the former hunter a drink.
(M, 20, 1964)

5162   A hunter can find his way by looking for the moss on a tree, as it is always on the north side.
(M, 60, 1964)

APPENDIX

Statistics, Contributors, Collectors

Distribution of Kansas Population by County

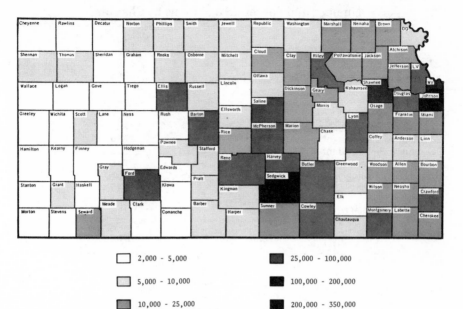

☐ 2,000 – 5,000   ■ 25,000 – 100,000

☐ 5,000 – 10,000   ■ 100,000 – 200,000

▨ 10,000 – 25,000   ■ 200,000 – 350,000

Based on population figures reported to Kansas State Board of
Agriculture by county appraisers, January 1, 1978.

Number of Items Collected in Each County

• 100   ● 500   ● 1,000   ● 1,500   ⬤ 2,000

TABLE 1
Number and Percentage of Items by Chapter

Chapter	Number of Items	Percentage
The Prevention and Cure of Illnesses and Injuries	1,018	20
The Weather	734	14
Luck	710	14
People	664	13
Death and Funeral Customs and Beliefs	345	7
Courtship and Marriage	339	7
Pregnancy, Birth, and Infancy	312	6
Animals, Birds, and Insects	268	5
Hunting and Fishing	253	5
Plants and Planting	245	5
Making Wishes	161	3
The Significance of Dreams	113	2
Total	5,162	

Subject Matter in Percentage by Chapter

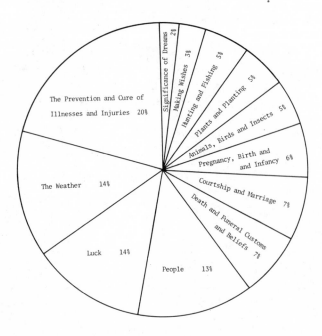

TABLE 2

Categories with Highest Percentages of Items

Chapter	Number of Categories	Number of Items	Percent of Total [5,162]	Category	Number of Items	Percent of Items in Chapter
1 Courtship and Marriage	12	339	7	Catching a Sweetheart	53	16
				Wedding Clothes	53	16
				Identifying One's Future Sweetheart	49	14
				Signs of Romance, Proposals, and Weddings	42	12
				Spinsterhood and Bachelorhood	29	9
				Signs of Success or Failure	28	8
				Remaining 6 categories*	85	25
2 Pregnancy, Birth, and Infancy	11	312	6	Things That Will Affect the Unborn Baby	78	25
				Determining the Sex and Number of Children	58	19
				Appearance and Growth	47	15
				Remaining 8 categories*	129	41
3 The Prevention and Cure of Illnesses and Injuries	28	1,018	20	Warts	114	11
				Miscellaneous	106	10
				The Common Cold	99	10
				Remaining 25 categories*	699	69
4 Death and Funeral Customs and Beliefs	8	345	7	Household Signs of Death	81	24
				Birds as Signs of Death	59	17
				Death, Miscellaneous	54	16
				Funerals, Graves, and the Dead	41	12
				Remaining 4 categories*	110	32

*See the Contents for the titles of the remaining categories.

TABLE 2—continued

Chapter	Number of Categories	Number of Items	Percent of Total (5,162)	Category	Number of Items	Percent of Items in Chapter
5 People	11	664	13	Advice Regarding Clothing, the Household, and Food	114	17
				Company	93	14
				Miscellaneous Advice and Observations	80	12
				The Meanings of Days and Seasons	73	11
				The Occult	72	11
				Things That Affect the Body	72	11
				Remaining 5 categories	160	24
6 Making Wishes	5	161	3	Miscellaneous	73	45
				Cars and Highways	28	17
				The Moon and the Stars	25	16
				Food	20	12
				Clothing	15	9
7 The Significance of Dreams	5	113	2	Miscellaneous	47	42
				Animals	24	21
				Death	18	16
				Remaining 2 categories*	24	21
8 Luck	32	710	14	Animals	76	11
				Household Items	57	8
				People	56	8
				Black Cats	48	7
				Remaining 28 categories*	473	67

*See the Contents for the titles of the remaining categories.

TABLE 2—continued

Chapter	Number of Categories	Number of Items	Percent of Total (5,162)	Category	Number of Items	Percent of Items in Chapter
9 The Weather	10	734	14	Animal Signs	320	44
				Nature in General	189	26
				Remaining 8 categories*	225	31
10 Plants and Planting	6	245	5	When to Plant	124	51
				The Care of Plants	38	16
				Signs of Success	33	13
				Remaining 3 categories*	50	20
11 Animals, Birds, and Insects	11	268	5	Cattle	53	20
				Snakes	50	19
				Dogs	37	14
				Horses	29	11
				Remaining 7 categories*	99	37
12 Hunting and Fishing	6	253	5	Hunting	119	47
				Fishing	62	25
				Helps to Ensuring Success	29	11
				Remaining 3 categories*	43	17

*See the Contents for the titles of the remaining categories.

TABLE 3
Frequency of Items by Number and Percentage

Chapter	Number of Items in Chapter	Items with Frequencies of 5 through 9		Items with Frequencies of 10 or More		Items with Frequencies of 5 or More	
		Number	Percent	Number	Percent	Number	Percent
1 Courtship and Marriage	339	24	7	23	7	47	14
2 Pregnancy, Birth, and Infancy	312	9	3	8	3	17	5
3 The Prevention and Cure of Illnesses and Injuries	1,018	41	4	41	4	82	8
4 Death and Funeral Customs and Beliefs	345	19	6	11	3	30	9
5 People	664	34	5	40	6	74	11
6 Making Wishes	161	15	9	10	6	25	15
7 The Significance of Dreams	113	10	9	7	6	17	15
8 Luck	710	44	6	45	6	89	13
9 The Weather	734	52	7	42	6	94	13
10 Plants and Planting	245	7	3	9	4	16	7
11 Animals, Birds, and Insects	268	7	3	7	3	14	5
12 Hunting and Fishing	253	7	3	3	1	10	4
Totals	5,162	269	5	246	5	515	10

List of Items with Frequencies of 5 through 9

Chapter
1 *Courtship and Marriage,* 24 items: nos. 28, 38, 40, 44, 45, 63, 65, 75, 98, 118, 121, 139, 164, 209, 210, 217, 238, 243, 259, 267, 287, 293, 300, 322
2 *Pregnancy, Birth, and Infancy,* 9 items: nos. 340, 343, 420, 446, 490, 545, 594, 595, 601
3 *The Prevention and Cure of Illnesses and Injuries,* 41 items: nos. 652, 657, 658, 666, 667, 695, 731, 782, 798, 806, 902, 915, 918, 922, 925, 938, 942, 1020, 1023, 1094, 1132, 1181, 1184, 1229, 1269, 1311, 1340, 1344, 1346, 1347, 1348, 1383, 1393, 1409, 1410, 1417, 1425, 1433, 1465, 1604, 1654
4 *Death and Funeral Customs and Beliefs,* 19 items: nos. 1677, 1690, 1701, 1713, 1714, 1734, 1759, 1763, 1764, 1806, 1819, 1837, 1848, 1853, 1882, 1895, 1928, 1965, 2012
5 *People,* 34 items: nos. 2026, 2033, 2037, 2040, 2041, 2084, 2085, 2089, 2091, 2092, 2105, 2112, 2113, 2150, 2163, 2182, 2208, 2209, 2340, 2394, 2443, 2446, 2471, 2494, 2497, 2504, 2510, 2515, 2531, 2548, 2561, 2643, 2676, 2677
6 *Making Wishes,* 15 items: nos. 2679, 2707, 2708, 2712, 2725, 2733, 2746, 2772, 2774, 2781, 2795, 2798, 2799, 2810, 2817
7 *The Significance of Dreams,* 10 items: nos. 2856, 2859, 2870, 2878, 2880, 2881, 2884, 2896, 2899, 2932
8 *Luck,* 44 items: nos. 2958, 2978, 2994, 3050, 3062, 3092, 3094, 3120, 3127, 3157, 3182, 3184, 3185, 3193, 3209, 3211, 3240, 3241, 3255, 3268, 3281, 3288, 3296, 3320, 3334, 3338, 3374, 3383, 3390, 3402, 3417, 3432, 3433, 3437, 3530, 3534, 3538, 3554, 3576, 3579, 3603, 3619, 3627, 3662
9 *The Weather,* 52 items: nos. 3678, 3684, 3685, 3689, 3726, 3731, 3758, 3764, 3788, 3789, 3792, 3795, 3799, 3800, 3832, 3848, 3850, 3853, 3883, 3884, 3926, 3937, 3950, 3984, 4064, 4099, 4115, 4126, 4179, 4183, 4184, 4195, 4208, 4216, 4229, 4233, 4237, 4240, 4272, 4307, 4310, 4312, 4318, 4319, 4321, 4322, 4331, 4362, 4382, 4387, 4394, 4396
10 *Plants and Planting,* 7 items: nos. 4399, 4464, 4494, 4504, 4507, 4510, 4556
11 *Animals, Birds, and Insects,* 7 items: nos. 4725, 4784, 4818, 4867, 4868, 4874, 4899
12 *Hunting and Fishing,* 7 items: nos. 4926, 5051, 5094, 5097, 5098, 5118, 5150

List of Items with Frequencies of 10 or More

Chapter
1 *Courtship and Marriage,* 23 items: nos. 1, 37, 106, 107, 204, 207, 230, 233, 237, 246, 247, 252, 258, 263, 264, 297, 302, 306, 308, 312, 319, 320, 339
2 *Pregnancy, Birth, and Infancy,* 8 items: nos. 341, 342, 347, 371, 462, 514, 559, 567
3 *The Prevention and Cure of Illnesses and Injuries,* 41 items: nos. 718, 730, 733, 734, 790, 792, 797, 837, 897, 898, 903, 909, 916, 920, 926, 927, 928, 929, 930, 931, 941, 946, 949, 950, 1019, 1130, 1131, 1142, 1145, 1153, 1154, 1226, 1376, 1384, 1394, 1397, 1411, 1649, 1650, 1653, 1667
4 *Death and Funeral Customs and Beliefs,* 11 items: nos. 1678, 1679, 1686, 1733, 1735, 1772, 1773, 1879, 1883, 1902, 1927
5 *People,* 40 items: nos. 2024, 2025, 2039, 2043, 2063, 2065, 2079, 2087, 2097, 2098, 2115, 2119, 2120, 2130, 2137, 2177, 2187, 2210, 2258, 2259, 2402, 2403, 2481, 2488, 2489, 2491, 2501, 2506, 2507, 2509, 2512, 2514, 2516, 2517, 2529, 2551, 2552, 2638, 2647, 2648
6 *Making Wishes,* 10 items: nos. 2711, 2718, 2724, 2732, 2748, 2756, 2757, 2775, 2776, 2785
7 *The Significance of Dreams,* 7 items: nos. 2868, 2874, 2877, 2897, 2898, 2905, 2929

8 *Luck,* 45 items: nos. 2977, 3007, 3022, 3041, 3044, 3045, 3063, 3123, 3181, 3220, 3221, 3242, 3244, 3272, 3285, 3290, 3323, 3331, 3338, 3339, 3361, 3363, 3380, 3398, 3401, 3403, 3414, 3416, 3441, 3443, 3447, 3531, 3532, 3574, 3575, 3577, 3578, 3580, 3581, 3582, 3613, 3617, 3618, 3630, 3636
9 *The Weather,* 42 items: nos. 3668, 3690, 3705, 3708, 3732, 3747, 3749, 3754, 3755, 3757, 3760, 3763, 3765, 3767, 3768, 3779, 3785, 3798, 3809, 3821, 3831, 3846, 3862, 3863, 3875, 4019, 4032, 4035, 4070, 4112, 4122, 4133, 4194, 4196, 4230, 4277, 4303, 4350, 4360, 4374, 4385, 4388
10 *Plants and Planting,* 9 items: nos. 4406, 4407, 4411, 4477, 4493, 4495, 4506, 4516, 4555
11 *Animals, Birds, and Insects,* 7 items: nos. 4642, 4652, 4679, 4724, 4858, 4866, 4898
12 *Hunting and Fishing,* 3 items: nos. 5095, 5096, 5101

List of Contributors

(An asterisk indicates that the person, usually a college student, also helped in the collecting project.)

Name	Town	County
Abernathy, T. L.	White City	Morris
Abernathy, Mrs. T. L.	White City	Morris
Ackard, Ethel	Colby	Thomas
Adams, Al	———	Riley
Adams, Don	Radium	Stafford
Adams, Edward	———	Riley
Adams, Mrs. Lydia	Dodge City	Ford
Adolph, Claude	Alma	Wabaunsee
Adrian, Peter	Newton	Harvey
Aebler, Muriel	Pratt	Pratt
Albert, Mrs. J.	Savonburg	Allen
Alenquist, Rose	Wichita	Sedgwick
Alexander, H.	Oakley	Logan
Allen, Billie	Ellis	Ellis
Allen, Marilyn	Wichita	Sedgwick
Allison, Mrs.	Hays	Ellis
Allison, Warren	Salina	Saline
Allison, Mrs. Warren	Salina	Saline
Almquist, Rose	Wichita	Sedgwick
Amerine, Bethel	Goodland	Sherman
Amerine, Gary	Syracuse	Hamilton
Anderson, Andy	Osage City	Osage
Anderson, Mrs. Barbara	Salina	Saline
Anderson, Bernice	Baxter Springs	Cherokee
*Anderson, Dale	Protection	Comanche
Anderson, Elden	Baxter Springs	Cherokee

Name	Town	County
Anderson, Esta	Manhattan	Riley
Anderson, Mrs. Ethel	Reece	Greenwood
Anderson, John	Hutchinson	Reno
Anderson, Karl	Scranton	Osage
Anderson, Mrs. Pete	Ellsworth	Ellsworth
Anderson, Mrs. Reba	Colby	Thomas
Anderson, Rhoda	Saint Francis	Cheyenne
Anderson, William	———	Ottawa
Andregg, Mrs. Kyle	Hoxie	Sheridan
Andrews, Paula	Piedmont	Greenwood
Appleton, Mrs. Roy	Manhattan	Riley
Arasmith, Grace	Densmore	Norton
Armstrong, Jack	Wichita	Sedgwick
Arned, Mrs.	Kingman	Kingman
Arned, Ray	Kingman	Kingman
Arnold, A. L.	Larned	Pawnee
Arnold, Lorraine	Hays	Ellis
Arnold, Richard	Johnson	Stanton
Arnold, Wilma	Rozel	Pawnee
Arrents, Nyla	Leonardville	Riley
Ash, Gladys	Medicine Lodge	Barber
Ash, Harry	Mankato	Jewell
*Ash, Lyla	Mankato	Jewell
Asher, Marc	Saint John	Stafford
Ate, Linda	Wellington	Sumner
Atherton, Nellie	Wichita	Sedgwick
Atlakson, Keith	Atchinson	Atchison
Aubel, Betty	Hays	Ellis
Auer, Mildred	El Dorado	Butler
Augustine, Glen	Lenora	Norton
Augustine, Shelia	Hays	Ellis
Ault, Linda	Manhattan	Riley
Aust, Fredis	Garden City	Finney
Austin, Hazel	Wichita	Sedgwick
Austin, Rosie	Salina	Saline
Aver, Mildred	El Dorado	Butler
Axline, Larry	Wichita	Sedgwick
Backhus, William	Tampa	Marion
Badgley, Georgia	Selden	Sheridan
Bailey, Bertha	La Crosse	Rush
Bailey, Lillian	Ellsworth	Ellsworth
Bailey, Rony	Sublette	Haskell
Bair, George	———	Stafford
Baird, Mary	Wichita	Sedgwick
Bairhart, Mrs.	Wichita	Sedgwick
Baker, Mrs. T. M.	Goodland	Sherman
Bakis, Marjie	Sterling	Rice
Balding, Robert	Medicine Lodge	Barber
Baldwin, Mrs. Lola	Hill City	Graham
Baldwin, Mrs. S. C.	New Salem	Cowley
Bale, Patsi	Sublette	Haskell
Ball, James	Hoxie	Sheridan
Ballard, Ethyle	Haviland	Kiowa
Balley, Eugena M.	Hutchinson	Reno
Balton, Dia	Frankfort	Marshall

Name	Town	County
Bandel, Herbert	Saint Francis	Cheyenne
Banhart, Mrs.	Wichita	Sedgwick
Bankey, Merry	El Dorado	Butler
Banks, Joyce	Effingham	Atchison
Barclay, Dennis	Manhattan	Riley
Barclay, Mrs. Dennis	Manhattan	Riley
Bardot, Ramona	Coldwater	Comanche
Bare, Charley	Kensington	Smith
*Bare, Thistle E.	Kensington	Smith
Barkert, Basil	Council Grove	Morris
Barley, Bertha	La Crosse	Rush
Barnaby, Lester	———	Woodson
Barnes, Bill	Pawnee Rock	Barton
Barnes, Mrs. Burrey	Wichita	Sedgwick
Barnes, Linda	Manhattan	Riley
Barnes, Wanda	Wichita	Sedgwick
Barragree, Nancy	McPherson	McPherson
Barrar, Janet	El Dorado	Butler
Bascom, Dr. K.	———	Riley
Base, Gladys	Atchison	Atchison
Basgall, George	Sharon Springs	Wallace
Bass, Richard	Hill City	Graham
Bauer, Katie	Radium	Stafford
Baumfolk, Mrs. Alice	Atwood	Rawlins
*Baumfolk, Clara	Atwood	Rawlins
Baus, Dorothy	La Crosse	Rush
Baus, Mrs. Raymond	La Crosse	Rush
*Baus, Wilma	La Crosse	Rush
Bay, Darrell	———	Riley
Beals, Mrs. Frank	Argonia	Sumner
Beamer, Emily	Russell	Russell
Beamer, S. J.	Russell	Russell
Beard, Tohy	———	Ford
Bearley, John	Atwood	Rawlins
Beatch, Mrs. Elsie	Hays	Ellis
Bechtel, Ethel M.	Russell	Russell
Beck, W. T.	Holton	Jackson
Beckley, Betty	Atwood	Rawlins
Beckley, Duane	Atwood	Rawlins
Beckman, Elaine	Kensington	Smith
Beedy, Mrs. Ethel	Agra	Phillips
Beedy, Sara Frances	Colby	Thomas
Beel, James	Manhattan	Riley
Behrens, Herman	Great Bend	Barton
Behrmann, Elsa	Buff City	Harper
Bell, James	Manhattan	Riley
Bell, Katy	Topeka	Shawnee
Bell, Leigh	Kansas City	Wyandotte
*Bell, Sandra	Fort Scott	Bourbon
Beltz, Esther	Haven	Reno
Beneda, Mrs. Jim	Oberlin	Decatur
Beng, Kay	Topeka	Shawnee
Benjamin, Harvey	Atwood	Rawlins
Bennett, George	Hoisington	Barton
Bennett, James	———	Dickinson

Name	Town	County
Benson, Fred	Manhattan	Riley
Berghardt, Gene	Meade	Meade
Berghaus, Frank	Meade	Meade
Berghaus, Mrs. Gertrude	Meade	Meade
Bergman, A. C.	Lillis	Marshall
Bergman, D. C.	Lillis	Marshall
Bergman, Mrs. Marge	Lillis	Marshall
Berkeley, Mrs. Eloise	Stockton	Rooks
Berland, Edna	Hays	Ellis
Berls, Jim	Selden	Sheridan
Bernhardt, Ted	Tampa	Marion
Bernhardt, Mrs. Ted	Tampa	Marion
Berry, Mrs. Rebecca	Yates Center	Woodson
Bethel, Judy	Sublette	Haskell
Betz, George	Asherville	Mitchell
Bevins, Charley	Alma	Wabaunsee
Biays, Mrs.	Hays	Ellis
Bieber, Margaret	Bison	Rush
Bieker, Tony	Leoti	Wichita
Bieker, Mrs. Tony	Leoti	Wichita
Bierman, Bonnie	Kensington	Smith
Bigge, Robin	Stockton	Rooks
Biggs, J.	Pittsburg	Crawford
Binder, Nora	Hays	Ellis
Binder, Virgie	Hays	Ellis
Binggeli, Bonnie	Marysville	Marshall
Bingham, Nannie	Sabetha	Nemaha
Bioys, Mrs.	Hays	Ellis
Bird, Galen	———	Saline
Bird, Mrs. John	Hays	Ellis
Birkenbaugh, George	———	Kingman
Birles, Beverly	Pomona	Franklin
Birney, Maxine	Sublette	Haskell
Bizek, Charlotte	La Crosse	Rush
Bizek, Mrs. Edith	La Crosse	Rush
Blackburn, Mr.	Goodland	Sherman
Blackburn, Bill	Leoti	Wichita
Blackwell, Mrs. Mary	Kansas City	Wyandotte
Blair, Gilbert	Collison	Pratt
Blakeman, Mrs. Ellis	Wellsville	Franklin
Blalack, Audy	Wichita	Sedgwick
Blankenburg, A.	Oakley	Logan
Blankenburg, Edna	Oakley	Logan
Blankenship, Marilyn	Great Bend	Barton
Blattner, Varena	Esbon	Jewell
Bloor, Arthur	Bucklin	Ford
Blossom, Marilyn	Horton	Brown
Blum, Mrs. Carl	Menlo	Thomas
Bodes, Carl	Dorrance	Russell
Boettaher, Mrs. William	Lindsborg	McPherson
Bogart, Jane	Prairie View	Phillips
Bogart, Kate	Oakley	Logan
Bohata, Mary Frances	Brookville	Saline
Bokelman, Mr.	Greenleaf	Washington
Bokelman, Mrs.	Greenleaf	Washington

Name	Town	County
Bokelmann, Mrs. Emma	Linn	Washington
Bolch, Larry	Manhattan	Riley
Bolding, Robert	Medicine Lodge	Barber
Bolin, Susan	Shawnee Mission	Johnson
Boll, Bruce	Manhattan	Riley
Boller, Len	Bunker Hill	Russell
Bolt, Albert	Hoisington	Barton
Bolte, Betty	Council Grove	Morris
Bolton, Dia	Frankfort	Marshall
Bolze, Mrs. Clarence	Kansas City	Wyandotte
Bonner, Orville	Leoti	Wichita
Booth, Mrs. J. C.	Osage City	Osage
Booth, Ray	Lyndon	Osage
Borgman, Mrs. Carl	Goodland	Sherman
Bormet, Robert	Cuba	Republic
Boss, Richard	Hill City	Graham
Bott, Mrs. Albert	Hoisington	Barton
Bottger, Perle	———	Riley
Bourne, Patricia	Delphos	Ottawa
Bowe, Mary	Prairie View	Phillips
Bowen, Terry	Lenexa	Johnson
Bower, Carl	Norton	Norton
*Bower, Lona	Norton	Norton
Bowers, Mabel	Osborne	Osborne
Bowers, Mrs. Maxine	Hill City	Graham
Bowman, Mrs. Ed	White City	Morris
Bowman, Joe	———	Douglas
Bowman, Mrs. Karl	Russell	Russell
Boyd, Betsy	Waterville	Marshall
Boyd, Mrs. Norman	Page City	Logan
Boyd, Roscoe	Page City	Logan
Boyd, Mrs. Roscoe	Monument	Logan
Boyer, Wilma	Hutchinson	Reno
Boys, Nixie	Hoisington	Barton
Bradley, Elmer	Arrington	Atchison
Bradley, Mrs. Elmer	Arrington	Atchison
Bradley, Jean	Salina	Saline
Brady, John	Osawatomie	Miami
Brand, Robert	Sharon Springs	Wallace
Branda, Edith	Wilson	Ellsworth
Brassfield, Laurean	Osawatomie	Miami
Breit, Mrs. Elizabeth	Hays	Ellis
Brent, Bertha	Alton	Osborne
Brent, Ross	Baylord	Osborne
Brewer, Marilyn	Wichita	Sedgwick
Bricker, Mary	Marysville	Marshall
Brightenburg, Mrs. Melisa	Phillipsburg	Phillips
Briles, Beverly	Pomona	Franklin
Briles, Virginia	Manhattan	Riley
Brilis, Floyd	Wichita	Sedgwick
Brink, Meredith	LeRoy	Coffey
Britt, Jeinell	Bloomington	Osborne
Broadstock, Bert	Augusta	Butler
Broadstock, Mrs. Lucy	Augusta	Butler
Brock, Mrs. Evelyn	Blue Mound	Linn

Name	Town	County
Broers, Lawrence	Wichita	Sedgwick
Brokes, Mrs. Anna	Wilson	Ellsworth
Brolund, Jean	Wichita	Sedgwick
Brooks, Mrs. Anna	Brewster	Thomas
Brooks, Irene	Logan	Phillips
Brose, Mr.	Wichita	Sedgwick
Brower, Joyce	El Dorado	Butler
Brown, Bill	Minneapolis	Ottawa
*Brown, Carole	Hays	Ellis
Brown, Mrs. Dale	Delphos	Ottawa
Brown, Dennis	.Oberlin	Decatur
Brown, Fred	Manhattan	Riley
Brown, G. C.	Liberal	Seward
Brown, Mrs. Harold	Manhattan	Riley
Brown, J. R.	Cawker City	Mitchell
Brown, Janis	Oberlin	Decatur
Brown, John	Collyer	Trego
Brown, Leslie	Gove	Gove
Brown, Mrs. Leslie	Gove	Gove
Brown, Liela	Lebanon	Smith
Brown, Mrs. Lola	Hays	Ellis
Brown, Mike	Horton	Brown
Brown, Mrs. Pearl	Wilson	Ellsworth
Brown, Shirley	Colby	Thomas
Brown, Valeta	Manhattan	Riley
Brown, Vernon	Hays	Ellis
Browning, Mrs. Hazel	Scott City	Scott
Brubaker, Esther	Ellsworth	Ellsworth
Brubaker, Louis	Ellsworth	Ellsworth
Brueggeman, Walter	Linn	Washington
Brueggeman, Mrs. Walter	Linn	Washington
Brungardt, Ambrose	Hays	Ellis
Brungardt, Frank	Victoria	Ellis
Brungardt, Lawrence	Victoria	Ellis
Brungardt, Margery	Gorham	Russell
Bryan, Bonnie	White Cloud	Doniphan
Bryan, Joel	Manhattan	Riley
Bryant, Austin	Haviland	Kiowa
Bryant, Julia	Quinter	Gove
Buck, Mrs. Louis	Lawrence	Douglas
Buckles, Marene	Kansas City	Wyandotte
Buffington, Barbara	Saffordville	Chase
*Bula, Joe	Hays	Ellis
Bundy, Mrs. Fred	Manhattan	Riley
Bunyan, Bill	Manhattan	Riley
Burden, Martha	Manhattan	Riley
Burditt, Margaret	Partridge	Reno
*Burdorf, Phyllis	Mount Hope	Sedgwick
Burgat, Mrs. Gary	Hoisington	Barton
Burgess, Mrs. Ivy	Wamego	Pottawatomie
Burgess, Jim	Wamego	Pottawatomie
Burgess, Sandra	Sublette	Haskell
Burgess, Veda	Manhattan	Riley
Burghaus, Gene	Meade	Meade
Burka, Lee	Little River	Rice

Name	Town	County
Burke, Maridel	Council Grove	Morris
*Burnham, Betsy	Junction City	Geary
Burns, Mrs. Emma	Wilson	Ellsworth
Burns, Mary	Dodge City	Ford
*Burns, Walter	Dodge City	Ford
Burrell, Ralph	Dighton	Lane
Burrow, Mrs. Frank	Manhattan	Riley
Butcher, Nancy	Abilene	Dickinson
Butler, Mrs. Esther	La Crosse	Rush
Butler, Mabel	Stockton	Rooks
Butler, Marcia	Glasco	Cloud
Byers, Doris	Logan	Phillips
Byler, Jane	Newton	Harvey
Byrne, Henry	———	Cloud
Cain, Catherine	La Crosse	Rush
Cain, Elizabeth	Topeka	Shawnee
*Cain, Judie	Wichita	Sedgwick
Cain, Louise	Wa Keeney	Trego
Cain, Park	———	Shawnee
Caldwell, Blanche	Russell	Russell
Caldwell, J. H.	Russell	Russell
Calvert, Paul	———	Riley
Cambern, Joan	Hugoton	Stevens
Campbell, Art	Saint John	Stafford
Campbell, Mrs. Charles	Norton	Norton
Cannon, Kitty	Kansas City	Wyandotte
Carey, J. Paul	Valley Center	Sedgwick
Carl, Mrs. Lena	Garden City	Finney
Carlson, Eldine	Courtland	Republic
Carlson, Mrs. H. E.	Kansas City	Wyandotte
Carlton, Mrs. Joe	Cullison	Pratt
Carney, Charles	Manhattan	Riley
Carpenter, Frank	———	Riley
Carpenter, Glennis	Goodland	Sherman
Carpenter, Thaine	Manhattan	Riley
Carson, Mrs. C. R.	Concordia	Cloud
Carson, John	———	Riley
Carstens, Mrs. Dick	Kensington	Smith
Carstens, Lottie	Norton	Norton
Carter, Barbara	Dodge City	Ford
Carter, Sarah	Garden City	Finney
Carver, Mrs. Ardin	Smith Center	Smith
Casey, Mrs.	Zurich	Rooks
Caspers, Herman	Smith Center	Smith
Cernasky, Maurice	Colby	Thomas
Chance, Floyd	Selden	Sheridan
*Chance, Mary	Selden	Sheridan
Chandler, Alice	Lyons	Rice
Chandler, Ira	Phillipsburg	Phillips
Chandler, Mrs. Nell	Phillipsburg	Phillips
Chapin, Mrs. George	Glasco	Cloud
Chapin, Irene	Glasco	Cloud
Chapman, Mrs. John	Great Bend	Barton
Chapman, Mrs. Manalow	Hays	Ellis
Charlson, Sam	Manhattan	Riley

Name	Town	County
Chase, Kenneth	Salina	Saline
Chastain, Neal	Topeka	Shawnee
Chegwidden, H. A.	Bunker Hill	Russell
Chesley, Mrs. K. E.	Minneola	Clark
Cheuvront, Steve	Mulvane	Sumner
Childers, Mrs. Nellie	Bird City	Cheyenne
Childs, Mrs. Birdie	Selden	Sheridan
Chipman, Jim	Hill City	Graham
Chockley, Mrs. W. O.	Wilson	Ellsworth
*Chopman, Karen	Oakley	Logan
Christian, Alma	Linn	Washington
Christian, Elaine	Wellington	Sumner
Christie, Mr.	Fostoria	Pottawatomie
Christine, Mrs. Jack	Sabetha	Nemaha
Cisneros, Pete	Kanopolis	Ellsworth
Claar, Lawrence	Oberlin	Decatur
Clapp, Mrs. A. L.	Manhattan	Riley
Clark, Barbara	Leoti	Wichita
Clark, Clarence	Hays	Ellis
Clark, Mrs. Don	Bendena	Doniphan
Clark, Jesse	Hill City	Graham
Clark, Mrs. Ladene	Hays	Ellis
*Clark, Laura	Leoti	Wichita
Clark, Mrs. Lois	Hays	Ellis
Clark, Mrs. Marguerite	Hays	Ellis
Clark, Marilyn	Barnes	Washington
*Clark, Nancy	Russell	Russell
Clark, Nancÿ	Munden	Republican
Clark, Richard	Hays	Ellis
Clark, Vida	Morland	Graham
Clark, Vona	Ashland	Clark
Classen, R. Dwight	Newton	Harvey
Clemensen, Julia	Haviland	Kiowa
Clements, Mrs. A. C.	Wichita	Sedgwick
Clements, Archie	Yates Center	Woodson
Clements, Roberta	Wichita	Sedgwick
Cless, Gene	Hutchinson	Reno
Clothier, Mrs.	Wichita	Sedgwick
Cluster, Colleen	Hays	Ellis
Cobb, Mrs. Ida	Hutchinson	Reno
Coberly, David	Winfield	Cowley
Cochran, Mary Jo	Bonner Springs	Wyandotte
Coder, Ralph	Hays	Ellis
Coffey, Mrs. Anna	Wilson	Ellsworth
Coffey, Mary	Wichita	Sedgwick
Colburn, W. C.	Emporia	Lyon
Colgalizer, Mrs. Molly	Neosho Rapids	Lyon
Collins, Carroll	Mankato	Jewell
*Colyer, Mrs. Frank	Elkhart	Morton
Combs, Carolyn	Wichita	Sedgwick
Commer, Leo	Utica	Ness
*Compton, Bernice	Manhattan	Riley
Compton, H.	———	Brown
Compton, Steve	———	Brown
Conant, Bernice	Atwood	Rawlins

Name	*Town*	*County*
Conard, Edith	Hazelton	Barber
Conard, Karen	Larned	Pawnee
Conboy, Phyllis	Larned	Pawnee
Condon, Anna	Hale	Chautauqua
Condon, R. H.	Hale	Chautauqua
Confield, Merle	Satanta	Haskell
Conger, W. T.	Natoma	Osborne
Conger, Mrs. W. T.	Natoma	Osborne
Conins, Shirley	Scott City	Scott
Conner, Leo	Utica	Ness
Conner, Mrs. Oral	Utica	Ness
Conrad, Josephine	Mound City	Linn
Cook, Mrs. Florence	Wilson	Ellsworth
Cook, Lillian	El Dorado	Butler
Cook, Robert	Manhattan	Riley
Cooke, Laura	Medicine Lodge	Barber
Coolbaugh, Dorothy	Dodge City	Ford
Cooley, Everett	Alton	Osborne
Cooper, Bob	Hoxie	Sheridan
Cooper, Joe	———	Sedgwick
Cooper, Karen	Hoxie	Sheridan
Cooper, Mary	Hoxie	Sheridan
Cooper, Sandra	Hoxie	Sheridan
Coover, C. R.	Lakin	Kearny
Copeland, Charles	Wichita	Sedgwick
Copeland, Constance	Great Bend	Barton
Cordry, Mrs. Barton	Manhattan	Riley
Cornell, C. E.	Mission	Johnson
Costa, Beth	Wichita	Sedgwick
Coughlin, Robert	Manhattan	Riley
Coulter, Sylvia	Oberlin	Decatur
Cowan, Elsie	Clyde	Cloud
*Cox, Billy	El Dorado	Butler
Cox, Joanne	Sedan	Chautauqua
Cozad, Suki	Manhattan	Riley
*Cozine, Eileen	Greenleaf	Washington
Crabtree, Norma	Saint Francis	Cheyenne
*Craft, Dorothy	Kinsley	Edwards
Craft, Joe	Kinsley	Edwards
Cram, Bonnie	Saint Francis	Cheyenne
Creever, Selma	Oberlin	Decatur
Crews, Pat	Hiawatha	Brown
Crist, Floyd	Quinter	Gove
Crist, Mrs. Nellie	Quinter	Gove
Crist, Virginia	Syracuse	Hamilton
Cromwell, Mrs. Desta	Dodge City	Ford
Crow, Harriett	Topeka	Shawnee
Crow, Virgil	Topeka	Shawnee
Crowe, Jim	Osawatomie	Miami
Crownwell, Shelia	Hays	Ellis
Crumbaker, Mrs. Claire	Beloit	Mitchell
Cruver, Selma	Oberlin	Decatur
Cummer, Betty	Junction City	Geary
Cummerford, Jackie	Tampa	Marion
Cunningham, Marilyn	Wichita	Sedgwick

Name	Town	County
Cunningham, Mona	Wichita	Sedgwick
Curley, Frank	Mildred	Allen
Curran, Mildred	Hays	Ellis
Curran, Orville	Hays	Ellis
Currey, Mrs. Enas	Kensington	Smith
Currey, Gene	Coldwater	Comanche
Currey, Linda	Kensington	Smith
Currey, Mrs. Mary	Kensington	Smith
Curtain, Mrs. C.	Derby	Sedgwick
Curtis, Mrs. Cline	Colby	Thomas
Cussin, Mike	Hays	Ellis
Cyra, John	Radium	Stafford
Dagel, Alberta	Augusta	Butler
*Dagel, K.	Augusta	Butler
Dahl, Jake	Colby	Thomas
Dahl, Marie	Colby	Thomas
Dale, Sally	Wichita	Sedgwick
Damewood, Jim	Logan	Phillips
Damon, Mrs. Esther	Turon	Reno
Daniels, Mrs. Oren	Page City	Logan
Darnell, Dale	Kansas City	Wyandotte
Davenport, William	———	Riley
Davidson, Mrs. Nellie	Rush Center	Rush
Davies, Leona	Valley Falls	Jefferson
Davis, Mrs.	Wichita	Sedgwick
Davis, Mrs. A. L.	Colby	Thomas
Davis, Mrs. E. L.	Neodesha	Wilson
*Davis, Eula	Colby	Thomas
Davis, Florence	Manhattan	Riley
Davis, Forest	Wichita	Sedgwick
Davis, Genevieve	Abilene	Dickinson
Davis, Mrs. Lula	Manhattan	Riley
Davis, Mrs. Lula	Lewis	Edwards
Davis, Mabel	Medicine Lodge	Barber
Davis, Mabel	Norton	Norton
Davis, Nathan	Phillipsburg	Phillips
Davis, Rogene	Harper	Harper
Dawe, Curtis	———	———
*Dawkins, Myrtice	Bucklin	Ford
Dawson, Mrs. Frank	Manhattan	Riley
Dawson, Haskell	———	Leavenworth
Dawson, Helen	Russell	Russell
Dawson, Lois	Wichita	Sedgwick
Day, Mayme	Satanta	Haskell
De Agva, Steve	Wichita	Sedgwick
Deal, Fred	Colby	Thomas
Dean, Mrs. Isabelle	Wamego	Pottawatomie
Dearmond, J.	———	Cowley
DeBoer, Jean	Hays	Ellis
DeBoer, John	Prairie View	Phillips
*Decker, Treva	Saint Marys	Pottawatomie
Deese, Mrs. John	Newton	Harvey
Deeter, Marvin	Isabel	Barber
Deets, Katherine	———	Sumner
Deets, Leonard	———	Sumner

Name	Town	County
Deewall, Mary Lynne	El Dorado	Butler
Degeer, Charles	———	Barber
Degeer, Katherine	Lake City	Barber
Degner, Jo Ann	Sylvan Grove	Lincoln
Delp, Ruby	Saint John	Stafford
Deming, Hazel	Newton	Harvey
Demuth, Jean	Junction City	Geary
Denberge, Mrs. Edith	Russell	Russell
Denchfield, Marleen	Hays	Ellis
Denholm, Wilma	Tonganoxie	Leavenworth
Denison, Mable	Hoxie	Sheridan
Denk, Bernie	———	Johnson
Denks, Rosemary	Norton	Norton
Dennison, Jerry	Wichita	Sedgwick
Denton, Donna	Kanorado	Sherman
Denton, Kay	Manhattan	Riley
Denton, Sally	Wichita	Sedgwick
DePuy, Percy	Manhattan	Riley
Desbien, Mary	Palco	Rooks
Des Jardins, Dixie	Manhattan	Riley
Deuser, Kathy	Overland Park	Johnson
Deutsch, Dean	———	Barton
Dewater, Mrs. O. J.	Hutchinson	Reno
Dickens, Charlotte	Manhattan	Riley
Dickerson, Dana	Topeka	Shawnee
Dicks, Rosemary	Norton	Norton
Dickson, Mr.	Wichita	Sedgwick
Dickson, Diane	Manhattan	Riley
Dielman, Ted	Canton	McPherson
Dies, Ed	Hays	Ellis
Dietz, Mrs.	Bunker Hill	Russell
Dimitt, Mrs. Ermine	Johnson	Stanton
Dimmitt, Frank	Goodland	Sherman
Dinkel, Clemens	Victoria	Ellis
Dinkel, John	Victoria	Ellis
Dirk, Charles	Albert	Barton
Ditcock, Bill	Russell	Russell
Doak, Ruth	Topeka	Shawnee
Dodson, Janice	Wichita	Sedgwick
Dolecek, Phyllis	Ellsworth	Ellsworth
Donauan, Marcia	Belpre	Edwards
Donbek, Mary	Wilson	Ellsworth
Dorman, Orval	Wa Keeney	Trego
Dorn, Lola	Ulysses	Grant
Dorrel, Cleya	———	Meade
Doubek, Mary	Wilson	Ellsworth
Doubrava, Goretta	Bushton	Rice
Dougherty, E. L.	Dorrance	Russell
Douglass, Bob	———	Coffey
Douthit, Emily	Saint Francis	Cheyenne
Dowdell, Billie	Junction City	Geary
Dower, Lona	Norton	Norton
Downs, Charles	Council Grove	Morris
Doyle, Michael	Manhattan	Riley
Dozier, Mrs. J. D.	Manhattan	Riley

Name	Town	County
Drake, Mrs. Ted	Saint John	Stafford
Draut, Bill	Manhattan	Riley
Dreher, Sylvester	Schoenchen	Ellis
Dreiling, Margaret	Fowler	Meade
Dreiling, Sena	Victoria	Ellis
Drumm, Frank	Longford	Clay
Dudley, Nona	Osawatomie	Miami
Duncan, Barbara	Westmoreland	Pottawatomie
Dunn, Mrs. Rebecca	Arkansas City	Cowley
Dunning, Clara	Bison	Rush
Dunton, Eris	Smith Center	Smith
Dyatt, Lynn	Goodland	Sherman
Dyche, Lewis	———	Riley
Dyer, Mrs. Pearl	Lincoln	Lincoln
Dyer, Vic	Lincoln	Lincoln
Eagon, Mrs. Madeline	Stockton	Rooks
Eakin, Ronnie	Syracuse	Hamilton
Eakle, George	Fort Scott	Bourbon
Ealy, Robert	———	Riley
Earl, Don	Lawrence	Douglas
Earl, Jean	Lawrence	Douglas
Early, Ada	Valley Falls	Jefferson
Eastman, Mrs.	Wichita	Sedgwick
Eckel, Roy	Hill City	Graham
Eckhardt, Billy	Bazaar	Chase
Edgell, Vern	Bernard	Lincoln
Edwards, Barbara	Wichita	Sedgwick
Edwards, Ester	Goodland	Sherman
Edwards, Mable	Emporia	Lyon
Edwards, Maude	Atwood	Rawlins
Edwards, Murray	Atwood	Rawlins
Edwards, Mrs. Naomi	Hays	Ellis
Edwards, Neva	Atwood	Rawlins
Ehrlich, Bernard	Atwood	Rawlins
Ehrlich, Juanita	Russell	Russell
Ehrlich, Larry	Russell	Russell
Ehrlich, Mrs. Maurine	Atwood	Rawlins
Ehrlich, Mildred	Russell	Russell
Ehrlich, Regina	Russell	Russell
Eibert, Rudolph	Hays	Ellis
Eicholtz, Ruth	Abilene	Dickinson
Eilts, Mrs. Betty	Rush Center	Rush
Eishinberger, Mrs. Walter	Scott City	Scott
Elder, Betty	Smith Center	Smith
Elder, Minnie	Bison	Rush
Eldridge, June	Lenora	Norton
Elferas, Mrs. J. C.	Hartford	Lyon
Eliot, Mrs. Percy	Clay Center	Clay
Elleman, Paul	———	Johnson
Elliott, Eunice	Leavenworth	Leavenworth
Elliott, Mrs. Marvin	Wichita	Sedgwick
Elliott, Mrs. W. C.	Oakley	Logan
Ellsworth, E. E.	Formoso	Jewell
Emigh, Flora	Selden	Sheridan
Endsley, Mrs.	Wichita	Sedgwick

Name	Town	County
Engle, Carol	Ellsworth	Ellsworth
Engle, Kermit	Ellsworth	Ellsworth
Engle, Mrs. Mildred	Ellsworth	Ellsworth
Engleman, Mrs. Jessie	Hill City	Graham
Engwall, Nina	Courtland	Republic
Erbert, Shirley	Hays	Ellis
Erin, Mrs. Clara	Bison	Rush
Erskin, Mrs. Anna	Cimarron	Gray
*Esslinger, Mildred	Broughton	Clay
Estes, Ann	Abilene	Dickinson
Estes, Aurice	Radium	Stafford
Eurich, Jane	Wichita	Sedgwick
Eussin, Mike	Hays	Ellis
Evanhoe, Clara	Topeka	Shawnee
Evanlene, Bernard	Topeka	Shawnee
Evans, Claralyn	Kansas City	Wyandotte
Evans, Larry	Kansas City	Wyandotte
Evans, Margaret	Kansas City	Wyandotte
Evel, Bryan	Utica	Ness
*Evel, Della	Utica	Ness
Evel, Mrs. Esther	Utica	Ness
*Evel, Vernon	Utica	Ness
Everhart, Mrs. Irma	Brownell	Ness
Eversole, Hazel	Mahaska	Washington
Ewing, Barbara	Saint Francis	Cheyenne
Ewing, Jill	Wa Keeney	Trego
Fabrizius, S. P.	Wa Keeney	Trego
Fall, Mrs. Helen	Burdett	Pawnee
Falls, Arclith	Leavenworth	Leavenworth
Farr, Alice	Eureka	Greenwood
Farr, Susie	Lenora	Norton
Farrand, Judy	Asherville	Mitchell
Farrar, Janet	El Dorado	Butler
Farrell, Katherine	Palco	Rooks
Farrell, Louise	Lawrence	Douglas
Farrow, Mrs. C. E.	Leavenworth	Leavenworth
Feil, Mrs. Dave	Russell	Russell
Feist, Aaron	Ellinwood	Barton
Feist, Iura	Spearville	Ford
Feist, John	Spearville	Ford
Feldkamp, Alan	Baileyville	Nemaha
Feldkamp, Blanche	Lincoln	Lincoln
Feldt, Leo	Victoria	Ellis
Felzien, Elmer	Saint Francis	Cheyenne
Fenwick, Larry	Macksville	Stafford
Fenwick, Mrs. Linda	Macksville	Stafford
Fergus, Orvileine	Garfield	Pawnee
Ferguson, Frances	Kensington	Smith
Ferguson, Lula	Bazine	Ness
Fertig, Harry	Larned	Pawnee
Fertig, Mrs. Harry	Larned	Pawnee
Fesler, Myrtle	Palco	Rooks
Fetrow, H. B.	Cedar	Smith
Fetrow, Velma	Cedar	Smith
Fetsch, Gloria	Marienthal	Wichita

Name	*Town*	*County*
Finch, Mrs. Harley	Ottawa	Franklin
Findley, Howard	Sharon Springs	Wallace
Fink, Joan	Utica	Ness
Finney, Mike	Seneca	Nemaha
Fisher, Mrs. Harold	McPherson	McPherson
Fisher, Mrs. Ora	Lewis	Edwards
Fisher, Mrs. Pearl	Mankato	Jewell
Fisher, Wilda	Wichita	Sedgwick
Fitus, E. L.	Wellington	Sumner
Fitzgerald, Mrs. E. A.	Ellis	Ellis
Flesher, Robert	———	Cloud
Flesher, Walter	Wa Keeney	Trego
Fletcher, B. C.	Wichita	Sedgwick
Fletcher, Irene	Wichita	Sedgwick
Fletcher, Mrs. Lloyd	Marienthal	Wichita
Fletcher, Mrs. Sam	Wichita	Sedgwick
Flicker, Emma	Bogue	Graham
Fliess, Mrs. B. A.	Lyons	Rice
Flint, Steve	Smith Center	Smith
Flowers, Mary	Wichita	Sedgwick
Flowers, Ruth	Russell	Russell
Flummerfelt, Mrs. Ed	Hugoton	Stevens
Flummerfelt, Ross	Hugoton	Stevens
Fobes, Darrell	Beloit	Mitchell
Foland, Nancy	Almena	Norton
Folck, Wilbur	Geneseo	Rice
*Foley, Alice	Norton	Norton
Foley, Carrie	Norton	Norton
Folkert, Minnie	Rush Center	Rush
Folkerts, Charlotte	Hays	Ellis
Folkerts, Gerald	Hays	Ellis
Fonts, Madge	Wichita	Sedgwick
Force, Lois	Topeka	Shawnee
Ford, Sebastian	Wichita	Sedgwick
Forester, Oscar	Emporia	Lyon
Fortin, Glifford	Manhattan	Riley
Fouts, Mrs. L. D.	Wichita	Sedgwick
Fraley, Donna	Concordia	Cloud
Fraley, Kent	Hays	Ellis
Frank, Dena	Norton	Norton
Frantz, Verlee	Hays	Ellis
Frantz, Mrs. William	Hays	Ellis
Fraser, Jerry	———	Sedgwick
Fraser, Thory	Colby	Thomas
Freeland, Kent	———	Riley
Frick, Barbara	Atwood	Rawlins
Frick, Dr. E. J.	———	Riley
Fritschen, Larry	Dorrance	Russell
Fritschen, Lila	Dorrance	Russell
Frutiger, Albert	Cedar	Smith
Fuller, Fred	Ellis	Ellis
Fuller, Katie	Salina	Saline
Fuller, Ruth	Dighton	Lane
Gallion, Mrs. Wilfred	Grinnell	Gove
Galster, Hilda	Marienthal	Wichita

Name	Town	County
Gangel, Herman	Louisburg	Miami
Gangel, Paul	———	Riley
Gardner, Goldie	Wa Keeney	Trego
Gardner, Pat	Wa Keeney	Trego
Garland, John	Wellington	Sumner
Garlow, Mrs. J. B.	Hays	Ellis
Garrett, Frank	———	Riley
Garrett, Rosalie	———	Riley
Garrison, Barbara	Wichita	Sedgwick
Garst, Carrie	Quinter	Gove
Gary, Garrat	———	Thomas
Gaskill, F. C.	Hutchinson	Reno
Gaskill, Mrs. F. C.	Hutchinson	Reno
Gatz, Thomas	Newton	Harvey
Geer, Mrs. Howard	Clay Center	Clay
Geiger, Milton	Robinson	Brown
Geist, Joe	Hoxie	Sheridan
George, Mollie	La Crosse	Rush
German, Roy	Protection	Comanche
German, Mrs. Roy	Protection	Comanche
Getz, Irvin	Hoxie	Sheridan
Gibbons, Mrs. Thomas	Russell	Russell
Gibson, Earlene	Leoti	Wichita
Gienger, Clayton	Saint Francis	Cheyenne
Gilbert, Blair	Council Grove	Morris
Gilbert, Molly	Plainsville	Rooks
Gilbert, Ray	Ludell	Rawlins
Gilbert, Robert	Clifton	Washington
Gile, Mr.	Hays	Ellis
Ginest, Joan	Wichita	Sedgwick
Gish, Mrs. Faye	Saint George	Pottawatomie
Gladfelter, H. Lee	———	Riley
Gladfelter, Harold	———	Shawnee
Gladsen, Harvey	———	Riley
Glanville, Mrs. John	Leoti	Wichita
Glaum, Allan	Phillipsburg	Phillips
Gleason, Oma	Radium	Stafford
Glick, Luella	Great Bend	Barton
Gliss, Mrs. B. A.	Lyons	Rice
Glotzbach, Carl	Paxico	Wabaunsee
Goddard, Mrs. Merle	Liberal	Seward
Godfrey, Malenda	Wa Keeney	Trego
Godlin, Ellen	Wichita	Sedgwick
Goedwasser, Pat	Prairie Village	Johnson
Goetzinger, Charles	Manhattan	Riley
Goin, Gail	Gem	Thomas
Goin, Maye	Gem	Thomas
Gomez, Eddie	Lawrence	Douglas
Gonzolis, William	Kansas City	Wyandotte
Good, Emerson	Barnard	Lincoln
Good, Mrs. Emerson	Barnard	Lincoln
Goodell, Mrs. Virginia	Abilene	Dickinson
Goodman, Mrs.	Ness City	Ness
Goodwin, Mrs. G. H.	Parsons	Labette
Gore, Gary	Oberlin	Decatur

Name	Town	County
Goss, Sue	Larned	Pawnee
Gotschall, R. J.	Plainville	Rooks
*Graber, Harriet	Hays	Ellis
Grabhorn, Fred	Hoisington	Barton
Graham, Elsie	Manhattan	Riley
Graham, Merideth	Wichita	Sedgwick
Grant, Mrs. Beulah	Goodland	Sherman
Grant, Frank	Palco	Rooks
Grant, Lucille	Palco	Rooks
Graves, Don	Manhattan	Riley
Graves, Florence	Manhattan	Riley
Gray, Darrell	———	Johnson
Gray, Marcia	Wichita	Sedgwick
Gray, Twila	Geneseo	Rice
Graybill, Annie	Kanorado	Sherman
Green, Mrs.	Wichita	Sedgwick
Green, Dixie	Ludell	Rawlins
Green, Jack	———	Wichita
Green, La Verne	Saint John	Stafford
Green, Wayne	———	Cowley
Greenfield, Pearl	Norton	Norton
Greenwood, Mrs. Minnie	Cimarron	Gray
Greer, Mrs.	Wichita	Sedgwick
Greer, Mrs. Howard	Clay Center	Clay
Greer, Jack	Selkirk	Wichita
Greer, Margaret	Selkirk	Wichita
Griere, Mrs. John	Osborne	Osborne
Griggs, Mrs. Anna	Meade	Meade
Grimm, Anita	Caldwell	Sumner
*Griswold, Virginia	Marysville	Marshall
Gross, William	Friend	Finney
Grumbein, Al	Ness City	Ness
Grutzmacher, Lance	Westmoreland	Pottawatomie
Guard, Carolyn	Asherville	Mitchell
Guenther, David	Yates Center	Woodson
Gugler, Ben	Woodbine	Dickinson
Gulley, Hazel	Fowler	Meade
*Gunckel, Edith	Wa Keeney	Trego
Gundy, Elmer	Oberlin	Decatur
Gustauson, Nancy	Lawrence	Douglas
Guthrie, LaReta	Walton	Harvey
Gutshall, Jerry	Meade	Meade
Haden, William	———	Jewell
Haflich, Mrs. Ralph	Garden City	Finney
Hagen, Carlene	Cimarron	Gray
Hagenmaier, Mrs. Melvin	Randolph	Riley
Hain, Anna	La Crosse	Rush
Hair, Ruth	Ness City	Ness
Hale, Mrs. Dean	Bloomington	Osborne
Hale, William	Alton	Osborne
Hale, Mrs. William	Alton	Osborne
Haley, Mrs.	Wichita	Sedgwick
Halfman, August	Tribune	Greeley
Hall, Mary	Salina	Saline
Hallagin, Joan	McDonald	Rawlins

Name	Town	County
Halling, Mrs. Lois	Hanston	Hodgeman
Hallsted, Mrs. A. L.	La Crosse	Rush
Hamburg, Fred	Ellis	Ellis
Hamburg, Lydia	Ellis	Ellis
Hamburg, Ora	Bison	Rush
Hamby, Barbara	Hays	Ellis
Hamey, Erma	Wichita	Sedgwick
Hamlin, Eurma	Syracuse	Hamilton
Hamm, Linda	Salina	Saline
Hammer, Mrs. Frank	Eureka	Greenwood
Hammer, Ruth	Manhattan	Riley
Hammerschmidt, Joe	Victoria	Ellis
Hammond, Mrs. Emma	Stockton	Rooks
Hanson, Clarence	Herndon	Rawlins
Hanson, Garry	———	Riley
Hanson, James	Lawrence	Douglas
*Hanson, Sonja	Wichita	Sedgwick
Haramore, Lena	Wichita	Sedgwick
Harbaugh, Art	Great Bend	Barton
Harbaugh, Mrs. Art	Great Bend	Barton
Harbaugh, Jerry	———	Sedgwick
Harden, Len	Tampa	Marion
Harden, Mrs. Len	Tampa	Marion
Harder, Roy	Inman	McPherson
Hardesty, John	Jennings	Decatur
Harding, Ina	Lawrence	Douglas
Harkins, Katherine	Saint Francis	Cheyenne
Harmon, Edna	La Harpe	Allen
Harmon, Nancy	Wichita	Sedgwick
Harmon, S. W.	La Harpe	Allen
Harning, Louise	Ransom	Ness
Harper, Dee	Hays	Ellis
Harper, Mrs. G. E.	Weskan	Wallace
Harper, Harold	Bird City	Cheyenne
Harper, Mrs. Jessie	Hays	Ellis
Harper, Lee	Hays	Ellis
Harper, Margaret	Syracuse	Hamilton
*Harper, Mrs. Norman	Manning	Scott
Harper, Ronnie	Weskan	Wallace
Harri, Macey	Brookville	Saline
Harris, Leamar	Cunningham	Kingman
Harris, M. B.	Topeka	Shawnee
Harris, Timothy	Coffeyville	Montgomery
Harrison, Mrs. Daze	Norton	Norton
Hart, Deane	Ulysses	Grant
Hart, Mrs. Grace	Tribune	Greeley
Hartford, Maedeen	Kansas City	Wyandotte
Hartley, Mrs. Robert	Winfield	Cowley
Harvey, Nora	Bison	Rush
Haryna, Mrs. E.	Hanston	Hodgeman
*Hastings, Charles	Jetmore	Hodgeman
Hatfield, Roy	Kinsley	Edwards
Hatton, Bernice	Syracuse	Hamilton
Hattrup, Rita	Kinsley	Edwards
Hauck, Dana	Delphos	Ottawa

Name	Town	County
Haun, Adelia	Jetmore	Hodgeman
Haun, Mrs. K. B.	Jetmore	Hodgeman
Hauschild, Mrs. De Etta	Oakley	Logan
Hauserman, Mrs. Beulah	Great Bend	Barton
Havel, Mary	Cuba	Republic
Havlik, Mr.	Tampa	Marion
Hawley, Lula	Wichita	Sedgwick
Hayden, Mrs.	Lincoln	Lincoln
Hayden, Mrs. Peggy	Ensign	Gray
Hayden, Ruth	Atwood	Rawlins
Hayes, Jo Nell	Little River	Rice
Hayes, Laberta	Hutchinson	Reno
Hayes, Pat	Colby	Thomas
Hayes, Sue	Manhattan	Riley
Haymaker, Unis	Wichita	Sedgwick
Haynes, Gary	Salina	Saline
Hays, Mrs. Ethel	Cottonwood Falls	Chase
Hays, Mrs. Harriet	Gaylord	Smith
Head, Barbara	Manhattan	Riley
Heath, Mrs. Hazel	Junction City	Geary
Heaton, Carol	Woodston	Rooks
Hecht, Winnie	Wichita	Sedgwick
Hecox, Roberta	Sharon Springs	Wallace
Hedge, Mrs. Eva	Hoxie	Sheridan
*Hedge, Mary	Hoxie	Sheridan
Hedge, Mrs. Susie	Hoxie	Sheridan
Hedlind, Judy	Manhattan	Riley
Hefling, Dorothy	Hutchinson	Reno
Heft, Mrs. Jimmie	Dodge City	Ford
Heibert, Marilyn	McPherson	McPherson
Heidebracht, Carol	Hutchinson	Reno
Heiland, Mary	Bucklin	Ford
Heilman, Leila	Norton	Norton
Heinen, Stephen	Osborne	Osborne
Helfirch, Virginia	Coolidge	Hamilton
Heller, George	Pittsburg	Crawford
Heller, Thelma	Pittsburg	Crawford
Heller, Vivian	Manhattan	Riley
Helm, Jeanne	Stockton	Rooks
Helmke, Scott	Iola	Allen
*Helmle, Marie	Garden City	Finney
Helms, Mary	Larned	Pawnee
Hemes, Lonnie	———	Riley
Henderson, Keno	Lakin	Kearny
Henderson, Ruth	Atchison	Atchison
Hendrix, Mrs. Jennie	Brownell	Ness
Henerson, Mrs. M. L.	Abilene	Dickinson
Henkle, Betty	Great Bend	Barton
Herman, Mrs. Elizabeth	Marienthal	Wichita
Herman, Stephen	Osborne	Osborne
Herndon, Charlet	Leoti	Wichita
Herron, Charles	Junction City	Geary
Hess, Helen	Peabody	Marion
Hesse, Mrs. Leo	Paxico	Wabaunsee
Heutz, Alma	Montezuma	Gray

Name	*Town*	*County*
Hewes, Mrs. Mary	Ingalls	Gray
Hibler, Muriel	Pratt	Pratt
Hicks, Dave	Dodge City	Ford
Hicks, Mrs. Dave	Dodge City	Ford
Hicks, Michael	Kansas City	Wyandotte
*Higerd, Larry	Gem	Thomas
Higerd, Roy	Gem	Thomas
*Higgins, Mary	Manhattan	Riley
Hill, Mrs. Annie	Hays	Ellis
*Hill, Mrs. Frances	Bellaire	Smith
Hill, Frank	Bucklin	Ford
Hill, Dr. H. T.	Manhattan	Riley
*Hill, Ione	Logan	Phillips
Hill, Irma	Manhattan	Riley
Hill, James	Lawrence	Douglas
Hill, Jean	Manhattan	Riley
Hillgren, David	Lindsborg	McPherson
Hilman, Leila	Norton	Norton
Hindman, Georgia	Minneola	Clark
Hindman, Hyla	Medicine Lodge	Barber
Hindman, Maxine	Junction City	Geary
Hinkhouse, Lola	Hays	Ellis
Hiott, Mrs. Curtis	Hartford	Lyon
Hipple, Janice	Hutchinson	Reno
Hirskler, E. E.	Hanston	Hodgeman
Hirt, Joe	Dorrance	Russell
Hirt, Mrs. Joe	Dorrance	Russell
Hirt, Mary	Dorrance	Russell
Hobrock, Mildred	Haviland	Kiowa
Hochman, Rose	Ellsworth	Ellsworth
Hochman, Shirley	Ellsworth	Ellsworth
Hochstatler, Mrs. Maude	Hoisington	Barton
Hockett, Mary	Haviland	Kiowa
Hoema, Mrs. Julius	Preston	Pratt
Hoff, Henry	Gorham	Russell
Hoff, Mary	Gorham	Russell
*Hoff, Ruth	Hays	Ellis
Hofman, Mrs. Marth	Wichita	Sedgwick
Hollinger, Jim	Lyons	Rice
Hollingsworth, Mrs. J. I.	Newton	Harvey
Holmer, Nancy	Junction City	Geary
Holmes, Maud	Woodston	Rooks
Holmes, Roberta	Manhattan	Riley
*Holmquish, Carole	Hutchinson	Reno
Holste, Charles	Ludell	Rawlins
Holt, Mrs. F. R.	Great Bend	Barton
Holt, Nancy	Uniontown	Bourbon
Holthus, Mrs. Fred	Smith Center	Smith
Holymann, Tom	Mission	Johnson
Homer, Orvilla	Junction City	Geary
Hooker, Jack	———	Wichita
Hopkins, Charlotte	La Crosse	Rush
Hopkins, Mrs. John	Warning	Scott
Hopps, Mrs. John	Wichita	Sedgwick
Hopps, Mrs. Jolen	Wichita	Sedgwick

Name	Town	County
Hopson, Neil	Phillipsburg	Phillips
*Hopson, Virginia	Phillipsburg	Phillips
Horigan, Peggy	Marysville	Marshall
Hornbaker, Mrs. Lee	Junction City	Geary
Horning, Albert	Ransom	Ness
Horning, Louise	Ransom	Ness
Hornor, Garnetta	Wichita	Sedgwick
Horvath, Linda	Manhattan	Riley
Horwege, Lois	Saint Francis	Cheyenne
Houchin, Minnie	Downs	Osborne
Hough, Arthur	Coldwater	Comanche
*Hough, Bernice	Coldwater	Comanche
Hough, Elsie	Coldwater	Comanche
Hougland, Robert	———	Geary
House, Isaac	Bogue	Graham
Houseman, Mrs. Beulah	Great Bend	Barton
Houseman, Leonard	Great Bend	Barton
Housholder, Mrs. D. F.	Belleville	Republic
Housholder, Mrs. Glenn	Belleville	Republic
Howard, Louis	Topeka	Shawnee
Hoy, Jim	———	Butler
Hoyt, Janet	Manhattan	Riley
Hoyt, Rodger	Manhattan	Riley
Hubbard, Mr.	Wichita	Sedgwick
Hubbard, Ann	Hutchinson	Reno
Hubbard, Molly	Wichita	Sedgwick
Hubbart, Pearl	Lincoln	Lincoln
Hubbs, Anna	Dorrance	Russell
Hudelson, Nick	Pomona	Franklin
*Hudson, Carol	Hays	Ellis
Hudson, Clarence	Oakley	Logan
Hudson, John	Oakley	Logan
Hudson, Lila	Oakley	Logan
Huffman, Red	Hays	Ellis
Hughan, Mrs. Bill	Plains	Meade
Huhn, Roy	Ottawa	Franklin
Hulse, Gladys	Topeka	Shawnee
Humberg, Ora	Bison	Rush
Hurd, Mrs. Sidney	Pretty Prairie	Reno
Hurley, Mrs. John	Manhattan	Riley
Ideker, Vergie	Rozel	Pawnee
Imler, Mrs. Nora	Montrose	Jewell
Ingemann, Miss	Lawrence	Douglas
Ioeger, Karen	Harper	Harper
Irby, Inez	Bogue	Graham
Isom, Elizabeth	Manhattan	Riley
Isom, James	Manhattan	Riley
Jackman, Mrs. Oscar	Lakin	Kearny
Jackson, Fern	Wichita	Sedgwick
Jackson, Nora	Holton	Jackson
Jackson, Orval	El Dorado	Butler
Jacobs, Mrs. Ruth	Hays	Ellis
Jacobs, John	Hays	Ellis
*Jacobs, Ruth	Manhattan	Riley
Jacobson, Jane	Manhattan	Riley

Name	Town	County
Jamison, Violet	Stockton	Rooks
Janisch, Ed	Hays	Ellis
Jantz, Elizabeth	Dodge City	Ford
Jecha, Mrs. Elma	Timken	Rush
Jellison, Mrs. C. R.	Wilson	Ellsworth
Jenkins, Mrs. Elsie	Kinsley	Edwards
Jennings, Ruth	Wichita	Sedgwick
*Jensen, Julie	Kinsley	Edwards
Jepson, Marla	Manhattan	Riley
*Jilg, Eudella	La Crosse	Rush
Johnson, Mrs. Adeline	Lindsborg	McPherson
*Johnson, Alma	Shields	Lane
Johnson, Barbara	Fredonia	Wilson
Johnson, Mrs. Carl	Great Bend	Barton
Johnson, Charles	Gove	Gove
Johnson, Mrs. Charles	Gove	Gove
Johnson, Darrell	Manhattan	Riley
Johnson, Joe	Preston	Pratt
Johnson, Lowell	Manhattan	Riley
Johnson, Marline	Lindsborg	McPherson
Johnson, Mollie	Rush Center	Rush
Johnson, Norman	Manhattan	Riley
Johnson, Orpha	Sharon Springs	Wallace
Johnson, Rhonda	Larned	Pawnee
Johnson, Sue	Wichita	Sedgwick
Johnston, Mary	Manhattan	Riley
Johnston, Mrs. Velma	Fort Scott	Bourbon
Jollison, Mrs. C. R.	Wilson	Ellsworth
Jones, Mrs.	Newton	Harvey
Jones, Allice	Lawrence	Douglas
Jones, Carol	Jewell	Jewell
Jones, Mrs. Charles	Wichita	Sedgwick
Jones, Frank	Manhattan	Riley
Jones, Ike	Oberlin	Decatur
Jones, John	Goodland	Sherman
Jones, Judy	Kansas City	Wyandotte
Jones, Mrs. Kevin	Lawrence	Douglas
Jones, Lucina	Emporia	Lyon
Jones, Marjory	Kensington	Smith
Jones, Marlyn	Kanorado	Sherman
Jones, Molly	Mankato	Jewell
Jones, Oke	Oberlin	Decatur
Jones, Robert	Mankato	Jewell
Jones, Mrs. Rosa	Hoisington	Barton
Jones, Sandra	Dodge City	Ford
Jordon, Perry	Pratt	Pratt
Jorgensen, Mrs. Maude	Beloit	Mitchell
Josiafiak, Rosie	Rush Center	Rush
Joy, Denni	Mission	Johnson
Judd, Mary	Osawatomie	Miami
Jump, Gordon	Manhattan	Riley
Junge, Telse	Manhattan	Riley
Justus, Mr.	Wichita	Sedgwick
Kalb, Mrs. Ralph	Wellsville	Franklin
Kappleman, Cletus	Augusta	Butler

Name	Town	County
Karban, Mrs. Neva	Wilson	Ellsworth
Karls, Audrey	Leoville	Decatur
Karstenson, Elmer	Haven	Reno
Kasselder, Charles	————	Riley
Kauffman, E. Gerald	————	Riley
Kaufman, Cheryl	Moundridge	McPherson
Kaufman, Kay	Medicine Lodge	Barber
Kear, V. A.	Colby	Thomas
Keaslin, Mrs. Dale	Protection	Comanche
Keen, Oleta	Medicine Lodge	Barber
Keen, Ray	————	Riley
Keiper, Kenneth	Prairie View	Phillips
Keller, Mrs. Mary	Pierceville	Finney
Keller, Ronald	Hill City	Graham
Kellogg, Mrs. Charles	Niles	Ottawa
Kelly, Winnie	Woodston	Rooks
Kelty, Father Leo	Marienthal	Wichita
Kempthorne, Charles	Manhattan	Riley
Kempthorne, Lillian	Manhattan	Riley
Kennedy, Binton	Russell	Russell
Kennedy, Margaret	Russell	Russell
Kenton, Mrs. Lucille	Lawrence	Douglas
Kentzel, Grace	Hudson	Stafford
Kenyon, Melvin	Bogue	Graham
Kern, George	————	Saline
Kerns, Naomi	Syracuse	Hamilton
Kersenbrock, Glenn	Colby	Thomas
Kershner, Craig	————	Riley
*Kethcart, Barbara	Beloit	Mitchell
Keyser, Anna	Wa Keeney	Trego
Keyser, Howard	Wa Keeney	Trego
Keyser, Wilma	Wa Keeney	Trego
Kich, Lenard	Wichita	Sedgwick
Kile, Larkin	Satanta	Haskell
Kimsey, Elsie	Goodland	Sherman
King, Amelie	Wichita	Sedgwick
King, Charley	Hays	Ellis
King, Dale	Norton	Norton
King, Florence	Agra	Phillips
King, Grace	Portis	Osborne
King, Jack	————	Reno
King, Johnny	————	Riley
King, L. R.	Almena	Norton
King, Mrs. Ruth	Manhattan	Riley
King, Thomas	Portis	Osborne
Kingsley, Larry	————	Sumner
Kingsley, Thomas	————	Sumner
Kinter, Dean	Speed	Phillips
Kinter, Mrs. John	Speed	Phillips
Kinzie, Mrs. A. E.	Quinter	Gove
*Kinzie, Rachel	Quinter	Gove
Kipp, Harry	Prairie View	Phillips
Kirk, Hazel	Newton	Harvey
Kirkeminde, W. P.	Wamego	Pottawatomie
Kissick, C. Jay	Beverly	Lincoln

Name	Town	County
Kliervet, Lorena	Pawnee Rock	Barton
Kline, Irene	Lenora	Norton
Kline, Stella	Emporia	Lyon
Klotz, Paul	Norton	Norton
Knight, Mrs. Wilbur	Manhattan	Riley
*Knoll, Donna	Hays	Ellis
Kobler, Mrs. C. H.	Hays	Ellis
Kobler, Elma	Hays	Ellis
Kobler, L.	Hays	Ellis
Kobs, Charlene	Meade	Meade
Koch, Marion	Scott City	Scott
Koch, Raymond	Scott City	Scott
Koch, Mrs. Raymond	Scott City	Scott
Koefod, Mrs. Jane	Junction City	Geary
Koelling, Will	Alton	Osborne
Koelsch, Dorothy	Saint John	Stafford
Kohler, Julia	White City	Morris
Kohls, Mrs. Jack	Ellsworth	Ellsworth
Kolb, Emma	Hays	Ellis
Kolde, Mrs. Joe	Paxico	Wabaunsee
Komoroske, Mrs. B. E.	Cimarron	Gray
Koontz, Dixie	Osawatomie	Miami
Korf, Lona	Hanston	Hodgeman
Kramer, Judy	Osawatomie	Miami
Kranz, Mrs. Fred	Brownell	Ness
Kraus, Carl	Hays	Ellis
Krentzel, Grace	Hudson	Stafford
Krentzel, Hope	Hudson	Stafford
Kreutzer, Alvy	Marienthal	Wichita
Kreutzer, John	Marienthal	Wichita
Kristner, Pete	Ulysses	Grant
Krug, Ivan	La Crosse	Rush
Krug, Ruth	La Crosse	Rush
Kruse, Chester	Hepler	Crawford
*Kuhlman, Dorothy	Wichita	Sedgwick
Kuhn, Elizabeth	Hays	Ellis
Kuhn, John	Ellis	Ellis
Kuhn, Mrs. John	Victoria	Ellis
Kuhn, Norman	Gorham	Russell
Kuhrt, Emilie	Edson	Sherman
*Kuiper, Mrs. Alice	Prairie View	Phillips
Kurt, Mary	Attica	Harper
Kuttler, Clara	Tribune	Greeley
Kuttn, Mike	Manhattan	Riley
Lackett, George	———	Riley
Lackley, Jo Ann	Mattfield Green	Chase
Lageese, Jake	———	Rooks
Lagerberg, Mrs. Roger	Ottawa	Franklin
Lakey, Ruth	Council Grove	Morris
Lally, Frank	Russell	Russell
Lambert, Mrs. Amy	Liberal	Seward
Lammers, Ned	———	Riley
Land, Mrs. Edith	Manhattan	Riley
Lane, Gala	Zurich	Rooks
Lanning, Lorraine	Osawatomie	Miami

Name	Town	County
Lantz, Mrs. B. R.	Concordia	Cloud
Larmer, Lyda	Russell	Russell
Larson, Mrs. C. R.	Concordia	Cloud
Larson, Cynthia	Colby	Thomas
Larson, Mrs. Martin	Scandia	Republic
Larson, Mrs. Paul	Riley	Riley
Larson, Rosa	Concordia	Cloud
Lasater, Clifton	Garden City	Finney
Latta, Bonnie	Topeka	Shawnee
Lauber, Charles	Kinsley	Edwards
Lawrence, Lena	Great Bend	Barton
Lawrence, Marilyn	Nashville	Kingman
Lawson, Ila	Norton	Norton
Lawver, Alma	Atwood	Rawlins
Layman, Gladys	Kingman	Kingman
Leas, Arthur	Hays	Ellis
*Lederer, Margaret	Valley Falls	Jefferson
Lee, Christine	Hays	Ellis
Lee, Denny	Hays	Ellis
Lee, Floyd	Hays	Ellis
Lee, Freda	Hays	Ellis
Lee, Jack	Hudson	Stafford
Lee, Mary	Wichita	Sedgwick
Leece, E. S.	Lovewell	Jewell
Leevis, Steve	Hanston	Hodgeman
Legan, Burney	Clearwater	Sedgwick
Lehew, Harry	Hiawatha	Brown
Leighton, Isa	Lakin	Kearny
Leiker, Harvey	Hays	Ellis
Leiker, Roberts	Spearville	Ford
Leisure, Mrs. T. L.	Lawrence	Douglas
Lennartz, Jerald	La Crosse	Rush
Lenz, Mrs. Berl	Scott City	Scott
Ler, Mary	Wichita	Sedgwick
Leslie, Mrs. J. D.	Junction City	Geary
Lessig, Mrs. Ruth	Hays	Ellis
Leuze, Mudlyn	Sabetha	Nemaha
Lewick, Mrs. Leahmae	Lincoln	Lincoln
Lewis, Mrs. Carl	Liberal	Seward
Lewis, Mrs. Cecil	Mount Hope	Sedgwick
Lewis, Donald	Kansas City	Wyandotte
Lewis, Donna	Colby	Thomas
Lewis, James	Belleville	Republic
Lewis, Kep	Hanston	Hodgeman
Lewis, Mrs. Steven	Hanston	Hodgeman
Lewman, Victor	———	Johnson
Lilak, Mrs. Frank	Wilson	Ellsworth
Linch, Charles	Huron	Atchison
Lind, Dale	Manhattan	Riley
Lindburg, R. N.	Lucas	Russell
Lindley, Eileen	Hill City	Graham
Lisenly, Mary	Wichita	Sedgwick
Littler, Eugene	La Crosse	Rush
Livingston, Annaruth	Sublette	Haskell
Livingston, Mrs. Bill	Pawnee Rock	Barton

Name	Town	County
Livingston, W. M.	Pawnee Rock	Barton
Lockard, Mrs. Margaret	Lawrence	Douglas
Locke, Mrs. Jessie	Larned	Pawnee
Lockman, Mrs. A. A.	Ford	Ford
Lockman, Archie	Ford	Ford
Lockman, Nellie	Ford	Ford
Loeppke, Bernice	Lakin	Kearny
Loeske, Phyllis	Gem	Thomas
Logue, Lona	Stafford	Stafford
Loller, Betty	Wichita	Sedgwick
Lolly, Frank	Russell	Russell
*Lolly, Jerry	Russell	Russell
London, R.	Hale	Chautauqua
Long, Mrs.	Greenleaf	Washington
Long, Esther	Wichita	Sedgwick
Long, Helen	Atwood	Rawlins
Long, Mrs. Jesse	Ellis	Ellis
Long, Mrs. La Verne	Liberal	Seward
Long, Mrs. Thelma	Winfield	Cowley
Loreditsch, Clarence	Hays	Ellis
*Losey, Jessie	Kinsley	Edwards
Loucks, Martin	———	Wilson
Loughridge, Ann	Palco	Rooks
Lounsbary, Mrs. Ruth	Lincoln	Lincoln
Love, Juanita	Zurich	Rooks
Lowe, Bob	Winona	Logan
Lowe, Dave	———	Washington
Lowell, Dean	Concordia	Cloud
Lower, Beverly	Hays	Ellis
Lowman, Bill	———	Riley
Loyd, Mrs.	Wichita	Sedgwick
Lucas, Mrs. Visa	Cimarron	Gray
Luhman, Ray	Woodston	Rooks
Luken, Anna	Goodland	Sherman
Lukert, Dolores	Manhattan	Riley
Lumpkins, Nevella	Plainville	Rooks
Lundin, Mildrid	Saint Francis	Cheyenne
Lundquist, Marcia	Belle Plaine	Sumner
Lusker, John	Wichita	Sedgwick
Lynam, Mary	Burdett	Pawnee
Lyon, Anne	Wichita	Sedgwick
Lyons, Lowell	Ottawa	Franklin
Mace, Mrs. Mary	Lebanon	Smith
Mackabu, M. G.	Concordia	Cloud
MacNaughton, Paula	Manhattan	Riley
Maddox, Gwendolyn Lou	Manhattan	Riley
Mai, Richard	Hays	Ellis
Makinas, Mrs. Nellie	Atwood	Rawlins
Mallows, Oscar	Wathena	Doniphan
Malone, Mrs. Helen	Medicine Lodge	Barber
Manahan, Mrs. Esta	La Crosse	Rush
Mann, Mike	Toronto	Woodson
Manners, Mrs. Wesley	Norton	Norton
Manny, Evelyn	Bogue	Graham
Marando, Ben	Wichita	Sedgwick

Name	*Town*	*County*
Marietta, Judith	Manhattan	Riley
Marlor, John	Salina	Saline
Marsh, Betty	Great Bend	Barton
Marsh, Mrs. Louise	Bunker Hill	Russell
Martin, Fred	Goodland	Sherman
Martin, Mrs. Helen	Overland Park	Johnson
Martin, Jim	Saint John	Stafford
Martin, Karen	Glasco	Cloud
Martin, Marilyn	Augusta	Butler
Martin, Martha	Hoisington	Barton
Marty, Etta Bradley	Courtland	Republic
Massey, Gary	———	Riley
Massey, Richard James	Wichita	Sedgwick
Mathias, W. J.	Belleville	Republic
Mattes, Mrs. E. M.	Kansas City	Wyandotte
Mauch, Mrs. Gene	Wichita	Sedgwick
Maxwell, Pauline	Hays	Ellis
May, Mrs. William	Wichita	Sedgwick
Mayer, Sally	Goddard	Sedgwick
McAdoo, Mrs. D. A.	Larned	Pawnee
McAdoo, H. M.	Larned	Pawnee
McAllaster, Pearl	Tribune	Greeley
McAllaster, Rollin	Tribune	Greeley
McBee, Muriel	Utica	Ness
McBride, Michael A.	Great Bend	Barton
McCabe, Mae	Zurich	Rooks
McCabe, William	Lawrence	Douglas
McCall, Mrs. Grace	Goodland	Sherman
McCall, Mrs. H. F.	Ulysses	Grant
McCammond, Mrs. Roy	Stafford	Stafford
McCandless, Alice	Stafford	Stafford
McCarey, Pat	Manhattan	Riley
McCartney, Mrs. Bess	Kensington	Smith
McClelland, Darleen	Almena	Norton
McConnell, Faith	Manhattan	Riley
McCurry, Mrs. Walter	Sedgwick	Harvey
McDonald, Mrs. Norma	Lucas	Russell
McDougal, Hal	Colby	Thomas
McDougal, Leone	Copeland	Gray
McElferas, J. C.	Hartford	Lyon
McGee, Ann	Great Bend	Barton
McGhee, Mrs. W. A.	Langdon	Reno
McGinnis, Mrs. Forest	Manhattan	Riley
McGowne, Lois	Oberlin	Decatur
McGuire, Mrs. Gracie	Wa Keeney	Trego
McGuire, Paul	Saint Francis	Cheyenne
McGuire, Richard	Parsons	Labette
McJunkins, Mrs. B. I.	Bazine	Ness
McKee, Mrs. George	Colby	Thomas
McKeen, Shirley	Manhattan	Riley
McKenzie, Virgie	Ransom	Ness
McKiney, Mary Ett	Hartford	Lyon
McKinstry, Ethel	Hoisington	Barton
McKinstry, Harrison	Hoisington	Barton
McLean, Martha	Wichita	Sedgwick

Name	Town	County
*McMillan, E. D.	Randall	Jewell
*McMillan, Mary Jo	Randall	Jewell
McNeil, Cenzil	Hays	Ellis
McNeil, Mary	Hays	Ellis
McNitt, Dale	Syracuse	Hamilton
McNutt, Freeman	Colby	Thomas
McQueen, Nancy	Phillipsburg	Phillips
McVicar, Linda	Wichita	Sedgwick
McWilliams, Dennis	Sharon Springs	Wallace
Medley, Walter L.	Coffeyville	Montgomery
Medley, Mrs. Walter L.	Coffeyville	Montgomery
Medley, William Perry	Coffeyville	Montgomery
Meehan, Dennis J.	Manhattan	Riley
*Meeks, Sandra	Wichita	Sedgwick
Mellisee, Mrs.	Wichita	Sedgwick
Mendenhall, Mrs. Ina	Gove	Gove
Mermis, Bernard	Hays	Ellis
Merritt, Bud	Ellis	Ellis
*Merritt, George	Ellis	Ellis
Merritt, Hazel A.	Ellis	Ellis
Merryfield, Mrs. L. T.	Minneapolis	Ottawa
Merten, Mrs. Arthur	Pratt	Pratt
Mesa, Albina	Kanopolis	Ellsworth
Mesa, Joe	Kanopolis	Ellsworth
Messmer, Harley	———	Kingman
Mettler, Mrs. Della	Atwood	Rawlins
Metz, Minnie	Lincoln	Lincoln
Meyer, Charles	Manhattan	Riley
Meyer, Ruby	Norton	Norton
Meyer, Sandra	Council Grove	Morris
Michaelis, Ruth Ann	Lincoln	Lincoln
Michel, Carl	Wichita	Sedgwick
Miesse, John V.	Kansas City	Wyandotte
Miller, Mrs. Amy	Hanston	Hodgeman
Miller, Blanche	Agra	Phillips
*Miller, Carolyn	Manhattan	Riley
Miller, Cecil A.	Hanston	Hodgeman
Miller, Darrell	Manhattan	Riley
Miller, Dianne	Fellsburg	Edwards
Miller, Mrs. Edna	Greenleaf	Washington
Miller, Frank	Hays	Ellis
Miller, Gene	Manhattan	Riley
Miller, George F.	Phillipsburg	Phillips
Miller, Mrs. L. R.	Ellis	Ellis
*Miller, Mrs. Lloyd	Wichita	Sedgwick
Miller, Marvin	Victoria	Ellis
Miller, Mary	Jetmore	Hodgeman
Miller, Minne	Saint Francis	Cheyenne
Miller, Myrtle	Bucklin	Ford
Miller, Raymond	———	Riley
Miller, S. Ann	Stuttgart	Phillips
*Miller, Shirley	Phillipsburg	Phillips
Miller, Suzanne	Claflin	Barton
Miller, Tom	Canton	McPherson
Miller, Verna	Sublette	Haskell

Name	Town	County
Miller, Victor H.	Pawnee Rock	Barton
Miller, Virgil	Hanston	Hodgeman
Mills, Gene	Manhattan	Riley
Miner, Paul	Sublette	Haskell
Mitchell, Mrs. Marie	Stockton	Rooks
Mitchell, O. R.	Russell	Russell
Mitchell, Mrs. Ray	Wichita	Sedgwick
Mitchell, Mrs. Virginia J.	Lawrence	Douglas
Moberg, Sue	Alta Vista	Wabaunsee
Moe, Glenn	———	Riley
Moffatt, Carrie	Manhattan	Riley
Moffit, Mrs. Fred	Tampa	Marion
Mohr, James	Hutchinson	Reno
Moll, Mrs. A. B.	Little River	Rice
Mollhagen, Tony	Lorraine	Ellsworth
Montgomery, J. R.	Wichita	Sedgwick
Mooney, Annie	Burdett	Pawnee
*Moore, Betty	Gardner	Johnson
Moore, Edna	Tribune	Greeley
Moore, Esther	Wichita	Sedgwick
Moore, Joan	Hays	Ellis
Moore, Mrs. Maurice	Waverly	Coffey
Moore, Nora	Hill City	Graham
Moore, Ronald	Hays	Ellis
Morehead, Marie	Earlton	Neosho
*Morgan, Lora	Ogallah	Trego
Morgan, Mrs. Minnie	Scott City	Scott
Morhor, Dick	———	Riley
Moritz, Gelane	Manhattan	Riley
Morris, Mrs. Benjamin	Quinter	Gove
Morris, Mrs. Clyde	Manhattan	Riley
Morris, Jean	Kanopolis	Ellsworth
Morris, Lucille	Quinter	Gove
Morrison, Agnes	Oberlin	Decatur
*Morrison, Janet	La Harpe	Allen
Morrison, Joan	Manhattan	Riley
Morse, Mrs. Nettie	Howard	Elk
Moscher, O. W.	Emporia	Lyon
Moser, Janet	Sublette	Haskell
Moshier, Alice	Manhattan	Riley
Moshier, Walt	Manhattan	Riley
Moss, A. H.	Hoxie	Sheridan
Moss, Joy	Hays	Ellis
Mousley, Clarence	Long Island	Phillips
Mowery, Dr. W.	———	Saline
Muellen, Sandra	Wichita	Sedgwick
Mueller, Rodney	Hoisington	Barton
Muller, Eugene	Hays	Ellis
Mulnix, Dr. Frank	Scott City	Scott
Munk, Mary	Walker	Ellis
Munsinger, Roy	Speed	Phillips
Murphy, Mrs. George	Gorham	Russell
*Murphy, Jan	Gorham	Russell
Murphy, Mary Anne	Sublette	Haskell
Musselman, Charles	Clay Center	Clay

Name	Town	County
Mutchussom, Reba	Osawatomie	Miami
Muth, Jim	———	Republic
Mutschler, Charlotte	Manhattan	Riley
Myers, Earl	Norwich	Kingman
Myers, Francis	Smith Center	Smith
Myers, Mollie	Ellsworth	Ellsworth
Myers, Pearl	Selden	Sheridan
Naegele, Mrs. William	Lucas	Russell
Naiman, F. L.	Wa Keeney	Trego
Neaderhiser, Lou Ann	Abilene	Dickinson
*Nebergall, Bettie	La Crosse	Rush
Neelly, Ann	Hopewell	Pratt
*Neelly, C. J.	Hopewell	Pratt
Neelly, Ethel E.	Hopewell	Pratt
Neelly, Norma	Johnson	Stanton
Neilsen, Chris	Russell	Russell
Nelson, Bob J.	Manhattan	Riley
Nelson, Dick	Hays	Ellis
Nelson, Mrs. Dick	Hays	Ellis
Nelson, Ethel	Marysville	Marshall
Nelson, Jean	Wichita	Sedgwick
Nelson, Luella	Manhattan	Riley
Neoses, Don	Wichita	Sedgwick
Nesbitt, Mrs. Alice	Morland	Graham
Nevins, Arnetta	Osborne	Osborne
Newbold, Will	Edmond	Norton
Newbrey, Mrs. E. C.	Stockton	Rooks
Newbrey, Francis	Downs	Osborne
Newbrey, Helen	Norton	Norton
Newbury, Linnea	———	Norton
Newby, Elizabeth	Manhattan	Riley
Newman, Nancy	Wichita	Sedgwick
Newman, Ralph	———	Shawnee
Newman, Vina	Sabetha	Nemaha
Newsom, Charles	Wichita	Sedgwick
Niccum, Barbara	Oxford	Sumner
Nichols, Duane	Manter	Stanton
Nichols, Mike	Lawrence	Douglas
Nickels, Cameron	Kinsley	Edwards
Nickels, Charlie	Corning	Nemaha
Nickels, Vinn	Kinsley	Edwards
Nickolls, Elsie	Burdett	Pawnee
Nickum, Barbara	Oxford	Sumner
Nieman, Mike	———	Jefferson
Nihl, Mrs. William	Colby	Thomas
Noble, Bessie	Fowler	Meade
Noble, Steve	Manhattan	Riley
Noely, Mrs. George	Wichita	Sedgwick
Noland, Mrs. Donna	Dodge City	Ford
Nolte, Mrs. Bertha	Seneca	Nemaha
Nolte, R. R.	Cawker City	Mitchell
Norberg, Esther	Lindsborg	McPherson
Nordstrom, Mrs. Ruth	Overland Park	Johnson
Norstrom, Carl	Larned	Pawnee
*Norstrom, Helen	Larned	Pawnee

Name	Town	County
Northup, Amy	Woodston	Rooks
Nuckolls, Elsie G.	Burdett	Pawnee
Nuse, Charles	Salina	Saline
Nystrom, Mrs. Alma	Axtell	Marshall
Oberg, Melba	Saint John	Stafford
Oberholser, Mrs. Ray	Lindsborg	McPherson
Oborny, Dolores	Timken	Rush
O'Connell, Edith	Marquette	McPherson
O'Connor, John	Herington	Dickinson
Odenweller, Avis	Winfield	Cowley
Oelke, John	Hoxie	Sheridan
Oglevie, Narvelle	Norton	Norton
O'Hara, Laura	Blue Mound	Linn
Ohman, Mrs. Ernie	Hill City	Graham
Olivering, Mrs. Jim	Timken	Rush
Oller, Lola	McCracken	Rush
Olsen, Diana	Burdett	Pawnee
Olson, Agnes	Lindsborg	McPherson
Olson, Catherine	Wichita	Sedgwick
Olson, Edith	Junction City	Geary
Olson, Elaine	Council Grove	Morris
Olson, Oscar	Horton	Brown
Oltjen, Nadine	Robinson	Brown
Oltjen, Mrs. William	Robinson	Brown
O'Neill, Norman	Lyons	Rice
Opdyke, Mrs. A.	Russell	Russell
Opitz, Edna	Garden City	Finney
*Orr, Grace	Woodston	Rooks
Orr, Mrs. Ina	Anthony	Harper
Orr, William	Woodston	Rooks
Osborne, Mrs. Agnes	Hanston	Hodgeman
Osborne, Larry	Council Grove	Morris
Osterman, Mrs.	Wichita	Sedgwick
Oswald, Donald	Greeley	Anderson
Oswald, Irma	Gorham	Russell
Ottaway, Robert	Wichita	Sedgwick
Ottem, Martha	Syracuse	Hamilton
Ottman, Donna	Manhattan	Riley
Owens, Ruth	Belleville	Republic
Owenzer, Mrs. Eunice	Utica	Ness
Owsley, C. L.	Manhattan	Riley
Page, Mrs. Ella	Formoso	Jewell
Palmer, Mrs. Edith	Russell	Russell
Palmer, Russell	Meade	Meade
Paramore, Evelyn	Topeka	Shawnee
Parcells, Mrs. Bill	Wichita	Sedgwick
Parker, Bud	Hays	Ellis
Parker, Mrs. Lenore	Goodland	Sherman
Parker, Mrs. Lucile	Kinsley	Edwards
Parker, M. C.	Goodland	Sherman
Parkinson, Mrs. Elma	Scott City	Scott
Parks, Mrs. Ruth	Fort Scott	Bourbon
Parsons, Mrs. James	Hays	Ellis
Parsons, Lola	Wichita	Sedgwick
Pasek, Leo	Dorrance	Russell

Name	*Town*	*County*
Patterson, Kay	Salina	Saline
Pattie, Shetty L.	Manhattan	Riley
Patton, T. J.	Scott City	Scott
Patton, Mrs. Thelma	Scott City	Scott
Patton, Mrs. Vera	Scott City	Scott
Paul, William	Weskan	Wallace
Paustian, Elva	La Crosse	Rush
Paxton, Mark	Wheeler	Cheyenne
Payne, Bess S.	Syracuse	Hamilton
Payton, Mrs. George	Ellsworth	Ellsworth
Peak, Emma V.	Larned	Pawnee
Pearson, Mrs. Lizzie	Plainville	Rooks
Pearson, Nelda	Lawrence	Douglas
*Pearson, Sara	Logan	Phillips
Pellett, Mrs. C. E.	Topeka	Shawnee
Pellett, Earl	Topeka	Shawnee
Pence, Mrs. Homer	Colby	Thomas
Pennington, Mrs. Cynthia	Pretty Prairie	Reno
Penrod, Mrs. Ralph	Manhattan	Riley
Perevial, Grace	Tescott	Ottawa
Perkins, Phillip	Manhattan	Riley
Perona, James	Colby	Thomas
Perry, Jim	Independence	Montgomery
Perry, Martha	Pittsburg	Crawford
*Perry, Miriam	Hays	Ellis
Peterie, Pearl	Kinsley	Edwards
Peters, Joan	Edson	Sherman
Peterson, Carl	Garfield	Pawnee
Peterson, Doris	Hugoton	Stevens
Peterson, Fern	Garfield	Pawnee
Peterson, Freda	Osage City	Osage
Peterson, Gary	Arcadia	Crawford
Peterson, Lynn	Larned	Pawnee
Peterson, Myrtle	Hugoton	Stevens
Peterson, Mrs. Ralph	Osage City	Osage
Petrick, Julia	La Crosse	Rush
Peuce, Mrs. Howard	Colby	Thomas
Pfalser, Ivan L.	Caney	Montgomery
Phelps, Mrs. Zenobia	Cimarron	Gray
Philip, Sara	Wichita	Sedgwick
Phillips, Kim	Colby	Thomas
Phillips, Wallace	Plainville	Rooks
Pickins, Miriam	Abilene	Dickinson
Pierson, Kristi	McPherson	McPherson
Pince, Mrs. Homer	Colby	Thomas
Piper, Mrs. Pete	Wichita	Sedgwick
Pishny, Mrs. Ben	Waterville	Marshall
Pitcock, Bill	Russell	Russell
Plenninger, Howard	Nekama	Rush
Ploeger, Wayne	Horton	Brown
Plomondon, Doris	Sun City	Kiowa
Plummer, Ward	Oakley	Logan
Plunkett, Viva	Manhattan	Riley
Poage, Mrs. Valeta	Lincoln	Lincoln
Polk, Louise	Lawrence	Douglas

Name	Town	County
Porge, Mrs. Valeta	Lincoln	Lincoln
Porter, Clark	Moran	Allen
Porter, Dian	Chanute	Neosho
*Porter, Don B.	Chanute	Neosho
Porter, Geneva	Chanute	Neosho
Porter, Mrs. Lila	Little River	Rice
Porter, Perry	Wichita	Sedgwick
Portschy, Mrs. Gertrud	Oberlin	Decatur
Post, Mrs. William	Spring Hill	Johnson
Powell, Jenny	Newton	Harvey
Powers, Mrs. Ella	Wa Keeney	Trego
Preston, Richard	Lawrence	Douglas
Preusch, Harriet	Healy	Lane
Price, Alfred	Winfield	Cowley
Price, Barry	Reading	Osage
*Price, Donald Harrison	Winfield	Cowley
Price, Terry	Reading	Lyon
Prouty, Mrs.	Wichita	Sedgwick
Pryor, Mrs. Caroline	Garden City	Finney
Pufahl, Don	Wichita	Sedgwick
*Pulliam, Barbara	Attica	Harper
Pults, Joyce	Holton	Jackson
Purma, Mrs. Anna	Wilson	Ellsworth
*Purma, Betty	Scott City	Scott
Purvis, Debby	Baldwin City	Douglas
Pyle, Donald	Manhattan	Riley
Quenzer, Mrs. Eunice	Utica	Ness
Querbach, John	Hanston	Hodgeman
Ragan, Rebecca	Hays	Ellis
Rainley, Mrs. Kate	Ellis	Ellis
Rajewski, Mrs. Joe	Victoria	Ellis
Ramsey, Mrs. Glenn	Manning	Scott
Ramsey, Robert	Manhattan	Riley
Ranker, Mrs. Robert	Ellsworth	Ellsworth
Ranson, Mrs. Willis	Wichita	Sedgwick
*Raser, Margaret Haun	Jetmore	Hodgeman
Ravens, Elizabeth	Kingman	Kingman
Ravens, John	Kingman	Kingman
Rawley, Mrs.	Ellis	Ellis
Rawson, Mrs. Willis	Wichita	Sedgwick
Rayberg, Grace	Leoti	Wichita
Reager, Mrs. Ollie	Mankato	Jewell
Rech, Karl	Brookville	Saline
Ree, Jack	Hudson	Stafford
Reed, Beverly	Topeka	Shawnee
Reed, George F.	Medicine Lodge	Barber
Reed, Mrs. Helen	Circleville	Jackson
Reed, John	Goodland	Sherman
Reed, Laura	Lucas	Russell
Reedy, Mrs. Charley	Norton	Norton
Reener, Harve	Manhattan	Riley
Reese, Mrs. Joe	Jetmore	Hodgeman
Reese, Mrs. John	Newton	Harvey
Reese, Royston	Newton	Harvey
Reeves, Florence	Almena	Norton

Name	*Town*	*County*
Reich, Mrs. Carl	Russell	Russell
Reid, Laura	Lucas	Russell
Reid, Mrs. Lola Mae	Newton	Harvey
Reid, Ray	———	Osage
Reid, Sybil	Wichita	Sedgwick
*Reimer, Janie	Selkirk	Wichita
Reimer, Karl	Selkirk	Wichita
Reinert, Karen	Cimarron	Gray
Reinhardt, Mrs. Lydia	Bison	Rush
Renner, Mrs. Bessie	La Crosse	Rush
Renner, Harve	Manhattan	Riley
Renure, Helen Ward	Montezuma	Gray
Rexroad, Glen	Dodge City	Ford
Rhea, Glen	Salina	Saline
Rhoades, Shirley	Williamsburg	Atchison
Rhodes, Donald	Protection	Comanche
Ricci, Orlando	Osawatomie	Miami
Rice, Berry	Reading	Lyon
Rich, Margaret	Wichita	Sedgwick
Richard, Homer	Johnson	Stanton
Richard, Lucille	Johnson	Stanton
Richard, Sylvia	Johnson	Stanton
Richards, Dr.	Goodland	Sherman
Richards, Mrs. Dorothy	Hays	Ellis
Richards, Mrs. Roy	Goodland	Sherman
Richardson, Barbara	Arkansas City	Cowley
Richardson, Beverly	Howard	Elk
Richmond, Dee	Wichita	Sedgwick
Richmond, Joe	Alma	Wabaunsee
Richmond, Mrs. Joe	Alma	Wabaunsee
Richmond, Mrs. Samuel P.	Wichita	Sedgwick
Richmond, Shirley	Codell	Rooks
Richner, Mrs. Earnest	Randolph	Riley
Rickford, W. B.	Marienthal	Wichita
Rickford, Mrs. W. B.	Marienthal	Wichita
Riddlen, Gertie	Tribune	Greeley
Riech, Mrs. Carl	Russell	Russell
Rietcheck, Carolyn Ann	Hoxie	Sheridan
Rietcheck, Mrs. Rose	Hoxie	Sheridan
Riffel, Jerris L.	Manhattan	Riley
Riley, Bridgie	Lawrence	Douglas
Rinner, Mrs. Bessie	La Crosse	Rush
Riseman, Louis	Manhattan	Riley
Ritts, Lorene	Stafford	Stafford
Roach, Gerald	Kansas City	Wyandotte
Robbin, Bert	Hoxie	Sheridan
Robel, Robert	———	Riley
*Roberts, Elaine	Hutchinson	Reno
Roberts, Emily	Palco	Rooks
Roberts, Mrs. Glenn	Hutchinson	Reno
Roberts, Mrs. Karel	Garden City	Finney
*Roberts, M. E.	Manhattan	Riley
Roberts, Mrs. Mary	Jetmore	Hodgeman
Roberts, Merle	Liberal	Seward
Roberts, Oliver	Jetmore	Hodgeman

Name	Town	County
Robinson, Mrs. Mildred	Hill City	Graham
Robinson, Mrs. O. H.	Wichita	Sedgwick
Robison, Mrs. W. T.	Winfield	Cowley
Rodenberg, Louise	Halstead	Harvey
Roeder, Eulalia	Almena	Norton
*Roeder, Mervin	Almena	Norton
*Rogers, Anet	Minneola	Clark
Rogers, Mrs. Charles	Sedgwick	Harvey
Rogers, James	Minneola	Clark
Rogers, Virgie	Saint Francis	Cheyenne
Rogg, Deanna	Wichita	Sedgwick
Rogg, Ray	Bunker Hill	Russell
Rohrbaugh, Bryce	Great Bend	Barton
Rohrbaugh, E. C.	Great Bend	Barton
Rohrbaugh, Mrs. Evalyn	Great Bend	Barton
Rohrer, Ruth	Junction City	Geary
Romeiser, Mrs. Pearl	Rush Center	Rush
Roniger, Frank	Bazaar	Chase
Rose, Mrs. A. R.	Newton	Harvey
Rose, Mrs. Alec	Lincoln	Lincoln
Rose, Arthur	Lincoln	Lincoln
Rose, Grace	Lincoln	Lincoln
Rose, Ruth	Lincoln	Lincoln
Roseboom, Beulah	Hiawatha	Brown
Ross, Dorothy	Alton	Osborne
*Ross, Francis	Alton	Osborne
Ross, Frank	Haviland	Kiowa
Ross, Jay	Council Grove	Morris
*Ross, John	Sabetha	Nemaha
Ross, Kent	Satanta	Haskell
Ross, Marcia	Sabetha	Nemaha
Ross, Mrs. Toni	Wellington	Sumner
Ross, Mrs. W. M.	Sabetha	Nemaha
Roth, Mrs. Rose	Junction City	Geary
Rothbun, Gordon	Oberlin	Decatur
Rouse, Mrs.	Hays	Ellis
Rouse, James E.	Hays	Ellis
Rowley, J. G.	Hoisington	Barton
Rowley, Mrs. J. G.	Hoisington	Barton
Rowley, Kate	Hays	Ellis
Rowley, Pearl	Hoisington	Barton
Rowley, Roland	Hoisington	Barton
Rozar, Lily B.	Howard	Elk
Ruby, Mrs. Clara	Lincoln	Lincoln
Ruder, Geo.	Hays	Ellis
Rudman, Mrs. Katie	Palco	Rooks
Rudman, Mrs. Laroy	Palco	Rooks
Ruffenthal, Margaret	Russell	Russell
Ruffman, Ralph	Hays	Ellis
Rumbaugh, Mrs. Earl	Haven	Reno
*Rumford, Clair	Manter	Stanton
Rumford, Mrs. Leland	Hanston	Hodgeman
Rummel, Kay	Atwood	Rawlins
Rundberg, James	Manhattan	Riley
Rundell, G. A.	Pierceville	Gray

Name	Town	County
Rundell, Irma	Bucklin	Ford
Rundell, Mrs. J. J.	Garden City	Finney
Rupp, Mrs. Ben	Ellis	Ellis
Rusho, Leilani	Wichita	Sedgwick
Russ, Mrs. Charles	Logan	Phillips
Russell, Donna	Cimarron	Gray
Russell, Katie	Oakley	Logan
Russell, Mrs. Lee	Cimarron	Gray
Ruth, Darrel	Johnson	Stanton
Ruth, Don	Johnson	Stanton
Ruth, Jeanine	Lakin	Kearny
Ruth, Verle	Johnson	Stanton
Ruth, Mrs. Vila	Johnson	Stanton
Ryan, Flora	Salina	Saline
Ryan, George	Junction City	Geary
Ryan, Jean	McCracken	Rush
Ryan, Mrs. P. B.	Solomon	Dickinson
Ryan, Stella	La Crosse	Rush
Ryckman, Gordon	Kansas City	Wyandotte
*Ryman, Beverly	Cuba	Republic
Ryman, Ed	Cuba	Republic
Ryman, Mrs. Ed	Cuba	Republic
Saddler, Leota	Colby	Thomas
Salem, Mrs. Roy	Cimarron	Gray
Salem, Ruth	Cimarron	Gray
*Salley, Mrs. Ira	Liberal	Seward
*Samples, Joan	Minneapolis	Ottawa
Samuelson, Mary Ellen	Weskan	Wallace
Sander, Alois	Victoria	Ellis
Sander, Lucina M.	La Crosse	Rush
Sanders, Betty	Wichita	Sedgwick
Sanders, Gerald	Mankato	Jewell
Sands, Andy	Cimarron	Gray
Sandstrom, Josephine	Bison	Rush
Sangster, Mrs. Lucy	Protection	Comanche
Sapp, Odes	Fowler	Meade
Sapp, Mrs. Odes	Fowler	Meade
Saunders, Mrs. Boyd	Bogue	Graham
Saunders, Joe Ann	Dwight	Morris
Sawyer, Alice	Kensington	Smith
Sawyer, B. M.	Topeka	Shawnee
Sawyer, Mrs. B. M.	Topeka	Shawnee
*Sawyer, Pat	Manhattan	Riley
Schaake, William	Abilene	Dickinson
Schadel, Levi	Rush	Rush
Schank, Mrs. Dee	Hanover	Washington
Schecher, Charles	Horton	Brown
Scheer, Maria	Kansas City	Wyandotte
Schellenger, Dr. Waldo	Manhattan	Riley
Scheuerman, Mrs. Grace	Manning	Scott
Schimpf, Mary	Marion	Marion
Schlagel, Mrs. Conrad	Hoisington	Barton
Schlingloff, Marie	Hill City	Graham
Schmedemann, Marjorie	Manhattan	Riley
*Schmeidler, Mrs. N. J.	Hays	Ellis

Name	Town	County
Schmeidler, Mrs. Regina	Hays	Ellis
Schmidt, Clarice	Copeland	Gray
Schmidt, Jacob	Hays	Ellis
Schmidtberger, Mrs. Eddie	Victoria	Ellis
Schmitt, Ada	Rexford	Thomas
*Schnatterly, Sally	Hays	Ellis
Schnieder, Clara	Ellsworth	Ellsworth
Schnieder, Helen	Manhattan	Riley
Schnoebelen, Jane	Lewis	Edwards
Schoonhoven, Dr. R. G.	Manhattan	Riley
Schreiber, Carl	Traer	Decatur
*Schreiner, Bob	Hays	Ellis
Schroeder, Mrs. Herb	Wichita	Sedgwick
Schroeder, Jerry	Wichita	Sedgwick
Schroer, Mrs. Anna	Dresden	Decatur
*Schubert, Eunice	Ulysses	Grant
Schuette, Mrs. Stella	Greenleaf	Washington
Schulte, Luke	Plainville	Rooks
Schulz, Lonnie	Norton	Norton
Schumacher, Maxine	Hays	Ellis
Schumacher, Mrs. Wilma	Ellis	Ellis
Schurle, Raymond	———	Riley
Schutte, Mrs. A. H.	Ellis	Ellis
Schwindt, Mrs.	Le Roy	Coffey
Schwinn, Gene	Leavenworth	Leavenworth
Scott, Florence	Atchison	Atchison
Scott, Mrs. Frank	Argonia	Sumner
Scott, Fred	Liberal	Seward
*Scott, Jeanette	Manhattan	Riley
Scott, Laura	Larned	Pawnee
Scott, Minnie	Pratt	Pratt
Scott, Robert	Hays	Ellis
Scrogin, Dick	Wichita	Sedgwick
Scrogin, Rick	Saint John	Stafford
Sealock, Mrs. Vern	Hoxie	Sheridan
Seaman, Hazel J.	Natoma	Osborne
Seaton, Kathy	Manhattan	Riley
See, Lottie	Great Bend	Barton
Self, Doris	Manhattan	Riley
Sellers, Mrs. August	Florence	Marion
Seltman, John	Rush	Rush
Shadid, Billie	Wichita	Sedgwick
Shamburg, Ronald	Syracuse	Hamilton
Shane, Tom	———	Sedgwick
Shannon, C. E.	Lincoln	Lincoln
Shaw, Jay	Council Grove	Morris
Shaw, Lorna	Albert	Barton
Shawver, Norman	———	Sedgwick
Sheets, Mrs. Pearl	Wa Keeney	Trego
Shepard, Ella	Lenora	Norton
Sherman, A. M.	Sitka	Clark
Sherman, Mrs. Mary	Sitka	Clark
Sherman, Roger	———	Riley
Shink, Jean	Merriam	Johnson
Shipley, Thelma	Osawatomie	Miami

Name	Town	County
Shirley, Margarette	Ottawa	Franklin
*Shockey, Mrs. Gilbert	Wichita	Sedgwick
Shoemaker, Mrs. Edna	———	Sumner
Sholtz, Lester Van	Council Grove	Morris
Short, Beatrice	Blue Rapids	Marshall
Shoup, Jack	Manhattan	Riley
Showalter, Oscar	La Crosse	Rush
Shumate, Denis	Garfield	Pawnee
Shuttleworth, Mrs. Sharon	Codell	Rooks
Sidlow, Isabel	La Crosse	Rush
Siegle, Barbara	Manhattan	Riley
Sigler, Millie	Hays	Ellis
Simmons, Mrs. Frank	Gove	Gove
Simpson, Cliff	———	Riley
Simpson, Marjorie	Howard	Elk
*Simpson, Wesley	Everest	Brown
Sims, Agnes	Bunker Hill	Russell
Sims, Alice	Lyndon	Osage
Sims, Kenneth	Meade	Meade
Sims, Mrs. Neva	Meade	Meade
Sinclair, Geo. E.	Jetmore	Hodgeman
Sinclair, Mrs. George	Jetmore	Hodgeman
*Sinclair, Norma	Wichita	Sedgwick
.Sinclair, Ruth V.	Plains	Meade
Sinnet, Arthur	Rush Center	Rush
Sis, Jan	Manhattan	Riley
Sites, Mrs. Russell	Grinnell	Gove
Skinner, Mrs. Gladys	Peabody	Marion
Skinner, Mary Lou	Fairview	Brown
Skinner, Mrs. R. E.	Topeka	Shawnee
Slater, Mrs. M.	Axtell	Marshall
Smades, Helen	Leoti	Wichita
Smith, Alice	Lenora	Norton
Smith, Mrs. Ardna L.	Belleville	Republic
Smith, Bernice	Ellinwood	Barton
Smith, Mrs. Betty	Bogue	Graham
Smith, Coralie	Little River	Rice
Smith, Don	Larned	Pawnee
Smith, Dorothy	Hays	Ellis
Smith, Mrs. Eliza	Great Bend	Barton
Smith, Elizabeth	Satanta	Haskell
Smith, Eva	Manhattan	Riley
Smith, Grace	Densmore	Norton
Smith, Mrs. J. A.	Oberlin	Decatur
Smith, Janice	Stockton	Rooks
Smith, Jeanne	Topeka	Shawnee
Smith, Mrs. Laura	Meade	Meade
Smith, L. Lee	Codell	Rooks
Smith, Lena	Bogue	Graham
Smith, Lennice	Codell	Rooks
Smith, Mrs. Luella Sutton	Ensign	Gray
Smith, Marcene	Codell	Rooks
Smith, Marianne	Leoti	Wichita
Smith, Myrtle	Manhattan	Riley
Smith, Mrs. Paul	Shawnee	Johnson

Name	*Town*	*County*
Smith, Mrs. Ray	Great Bend	Barton
Smith, Mrs. Robert E.	Belleville	Republic
Smith, Rush	Agra	Phillips
Smith, Sally	Topeka	Shawnee
Smith, Mrs. Sylvia	Oberlin	Decatur
Smith, Ted	Little River	Rice
Smith, Thos. B.	Ellinwood	Barton
Smoll, Kent	Wichita	Sedgwick
Sneath, Elizabeth	Kanopolis	Ellsworth
Snodgrass, Alberta	Council Grove	Morris
Snook, Iva	Ford	Ford
Snyder, David	Saint John	Stafford
Snyder, Mildred	Medicine Lodge	Barber
Snyder, Russell	Dodge City	Ford
Snyder, Mrs. Russell	Dodge City	Ford
Soden, George	Robinson	Brown
Soliday, Martha	Cimarron	Gray
*Soliday, Phyllis	Cimarron	Gray
Sontact, Judy	Kansas City	Wyandotte
Soper, Dorothy	Palco	Rooks
Souchek, Leonard	Ludell	Rawlins
Soverns, Mrs. P. M.	Wa Keeney	Trego
Spain, Nelle	Haviland	Kiowa
Spangler, Robert	Hays	Ellis
Sparks, Mrs. Carl	Minneola	Clark
Sparks, Mrs. Mabel	Cullison	Pratt
Spencer, Minnie	Saint John	Stafford
Spiker, Robert	———	Riley
Spitsnangle, Mrs. Lee	Wa Keeney	Trego
Spittles, Mrs.	Junction City	Geary
Sprague, Bob	Leavenworth	Leavenworth
Sprinkle, Mrs.	Hutchinson	Reno
Sprout, Philip	Sublette	Haskell
Sprout, Sharon	Copeland	Gray
Sramek, Philip	———	Scott
*Stacey, Mr. Lowell	Jennings	Decatur
Stagewood, Mrs. M. W.	Lewis	Edwards
Staggs, Jean	Wichita	Sedgwick
Stanford, Lee	Concordia	Cloud
Stanford, Mrs. L. R.	Concordia	Cloud
Stanley, Leland	Manhattan	Riley
Stansbury, George	———	Pawnee
Stansbury, Mrs. G.	———	Pawnee
Stanton, Doris	Hays	Ellis
*Staples, Charles J.	Plains	Meade
Staples, Mrs. J. W.	Plains	Meade
Start, James	Hays	Ellis
Staub, Mrs. Godfrey	Saint John	Stafford
Stauffer, Freda	Nickerson	Reno
Stauth, Frank	Dodge City	Ford
Stauth, Mrs. Olive	Dodge City	Ford
Steel, Marjorie	Ellis	Ellis
Steele, Jeanie	Leoti	Wichita
Stein, Jim	———	Ford
Steinert, Wayne	Hays	Ellis

Name	*Town*	*County*
Steinshouer, Terry	Downs	Osborne
Stephenson, Paul	Elkhart	Morton
Stephenson, Mrs. Paul	Elkhart	Morton
Sterling, Bill Warner	Dodge City	Ford
Sterling, Mrs. Elsie Wagonseller	Dodge City	Ford
Steuber, Mrs. Alice	McPherson	McPherson
Steven, Mrs.	Wichita	Sedgwick
Stevens, Goleta	Wichita	Sedgwick
Stevenson, Gene	Ashland	Clark
Stever, Mrs.	Wichita	Sedgwick
Stewart, James	Selden	Sheridan
Stewart, Lee	Healy	Lane
Stewart, Sarah	Weskan	Wallace
Stewart, William H.	Densmore	Norton
Stienbarger, Blance	Medicine Lodge	Barber
Stillwell, Robert	Scotsville	Mitchell
Stineburg, Larry	Hays	Ellis
*Stites, Elvena	Hill City	Graham
Stites, Mrs. Floyd	Wa Keeney	Trego
Stites, Mrs. Lawrence	Wa Keeney	Trego
Stoever, Henry	Frankfort	Marshall
Stone, Pat	Wichita	Sedgwick
Storer, Florence	Hoxie	Sheridan
Storer, Harley	Hoxie	Sheridan
Storer, Opal	Hoxie	Sheridan
Stoskopf, Ina	Hoisington	Barton
Stoskopf, John	Hoisington	Barton
Stout, Mrs. Elizabeth	Hays	Ellis
Strain, Jennifer	Overland Park	Johnson
Strathman, Joe	Seneca	Nemaha
Strathman, Mrs. Joe	Seneca	Nemaha
Strecker, Mrs. John	Russell	Russell
Strong, Mrs.	Hill City	Graham
Strumfa, Mrs. Rudolph	Belleville	Republic
Stuckey, Mrs. Gilbert	Wichita	Sedgwick
Stuckey, Larry	———	Leavenworth
Studer, Sharon	Beloit	Mitchell
Suelter, Alfred	Manhattan	Riley
Suelter, Mrs. Alfred	Manhattan	Riley
Sullivan, Joyce	Wichita	Sedgwick
Sullivan, Martha	Lawrence	Douglas
Summers, Mrs. Ralph	Scott City	Scott
Surber, Maudie	Yates Center	Woodson
Sutor, Leola	Palco	Rooks
Svoboda, Gregg	Wichita	Sedgwick
Svoboda, Mrs. L. V.	Pawnee Rock	Barton
Swafford, Mrs. Bertha	Fort Scott	Bourbon
Swan, David	Wichita	Sedgwick
Swanson, Joyce	Elsmore	Allen
Swiggett, Margaret	Wa Keeney	Trego
Swink, Marlene	Satanta	Haskell
Taylor, Allen	Yates Center	Woodson
Taylor, Carl	Medicine Lodge	Barber
Taylor, Clayton	Hugoton	Stevens
Taylor, Dennis	Council Grove	Morris

Name	Town	County
Taylor, Elizabeth	Winfield	Cowley
Taylor, Esther	Kansas City	Wyandotte
Taylor, Guy	———	Riley
*Taylor, Mary Sue	Kansas City	Wyandotte
Taylor, Mrs. William	Manhattan	Riley
Teas, Chester	———	Riley
Teed, Carol	Weskan	Wallace
Teichman, Cibyl	Stafford	Stafford
Telson, Louise	Ulysses	Grant
Temple, Mrs. Clyde	Axtell	Marshall
Templeton, Nancy	Atwood	Rawlins
Terman, Mrs. Roy	Protection	Comanche
Terrill, Mrs.	Ulysses	Grant
Thelen, Mrs. Daisy	Stockton	Rooks
Thiele, Patti	Scott City	Scott
Thomas, Art	Cimarron	Gray
Thomas, Mrs. Ina	Sharon	Barber
Thomas, Mrs. L. E.	Topeka	Shawnee
Thomas, Mrs. Rose	Gove	Gove
Thomas, Ruth E.	Osawatomie	Miami
Thomi, Mrs. Marie	Junction City	Geary
Thomm, Juneil	Kensington	Smith
*Thompson, Esther	Garden City	Finney
Thompson, Harry	Minneola	Clark
Thompson, Mrs. Harry	Minneola	Clark
Thompson, Laura	Pratt	Pratt
Thompson, Marilyn	Almena	Norton
Thomson, Edith	Moscow	Stevens
Thonhoff, John	Meade	Meade
Thornhill, Gladys	Protection	Comanche
Thorpe, Mrs. Bernard	Manhattan	Riley
Thouvenelle, Mrs. Geo.	Russell	Russell
*Tien, Dorothy	Prairie View	Phillips
Tillotson, Peggy	Dighton	Lane
Tilson, Louise	Ulysses	Grant
Tinkler, Mrs. Nedra	Russell	Russell
Tipling, Barbara	Arrington	Atchison
Titus, E. L.	Wellington	Sumner
Todd, Frank	Wilmore	Comanche
Todd, Mrs. Frank	Wilmore	Comanche
Todd, Minnie	Wilmore	Comanche
Todd, Sherrill	Kansas City	Wyandotte
Toley, John	Norton	Norton
Tomanek, Mrs. Hazel	Collyer	Trego
Tomasheck, Carol	Zurich	Rooks
Tomilson, Mary	Rush	Rush
Ton, Ella	Haven	Reno
Toole, Walter	Arnold	Ness
Torrez, Joe	Kanopolis	Ellsworth
Townsley, Helen	Blue Mound	Linn
Travis, Gerald	Norton	Norton
Tremmer, W. B.	Wa Keeney	Trego
Trerking, Margaret	Potwin	Butler
Trexler, Edna	Hill City	Graham
Triplett, Myrtle	Bogue	Graham

Name	Town	County
Troell, Dick	———	Sedgwick
*Troydon, Joyce	Hugoton	Stevens
Troydon, L. R.	Hugoton	Stevens
Tucker, Deb	Manhattan	Riley
Tucker, Tom	Tribune	Greeley
Turley, L. W.	La Harpe	Allen
Turnbull, Donna	Manhattan	Riley
*Turner, Donna	Valley Center	Sedgwick
Turner, Edwin	Tonganoxie	Leavenworth
Turner, Mrs. Glenn	Valley Center	Sedgwick
Turner, J. R.	Mullinville	Kiowa
Turner, Marten	La Crosse	Rush
Turner, Zula Mae	Mullinville	Kiowa
Tweed, Alice	Norton	Norton
Twyman, Hazel	———	Kingman
Tyler, Gary	Sabetha	Nemaha
Tyler, Mrs. Gary	Sabetha	Nemaha
Uht, Jim	Hays	Ellis
Ukele, Clyde	———	Norton
Underhill, Deanna	Ulysses	Grant
Underwood, Gertrude	Hoisington	Barton
Unruh, Mrs.	Montezuma	Gray
Utt, Maxine	Satanta	Haskell
Valliere, Mrs. Julia	Osawatomie	Miami
Van Doren, J. P.	———	Ellis
Van Doren, L. M.	———	Shawnee
Vang, Mrs. Mary	Kinsley	Edwards
Van Hoozer, Mrs. L. D.	Yates Center	Woodson
Van Winkle, Gail	Saint John	Stafford
Venneberg, Nancy A.	Havensville	Pottawatomie
Vesecky, Mary Lou	Hays	Ellis
Veverka, Mrs. Albie	Wichita	Sedgwick
Vilander, Mrs. V. E.	Manhattan	Riley
Vincent, Thomas	———	Rice
Vink, Mary	Fowler	Meade
Vogt, Fred	Meade	Meade
Vogt, Mrs. Irvin	Meade	Meade
Volok, Susie	Dorrance	Russell
Vopat, Mrs. Mildred	Brookville	Saline
Vosseler, Nancy	Leavenworth	Leavenworth
Voth, Mrs. Pete	Little River	Rice
Waddle, Mrs. R. E.	Junction City	Geary
Waggoner, Mrs. A. S.	Hoisington	Barton
Wagner, Gary	Manhattan	Riley
Wagner, Judy	Wichita	Sedgwick
Wakeman, Don	———	Shawnee
Waldman, Barbara	Grinnell	Gove
Walker, Carl	Stockton	Rooks
Walker, Harry	Garden City	Finney
Walker, J. O.	Fowler	Meade
Walker, Mrs. J. O.	Fowler	Meade
Walker, Mrs. Nellie	Cimarron	Gray
Wallace, D.	Barnard	Lincoln
Wallon, Marylyn	Wichita	Sedgwick
Walt, Mrs. Tony	Collyer	Trego

Name	Town	County
Walter, Nancy	Montezuma	Gray
Walters, Jan	———	Geary
Walters, W. K.	Valley Falls	Jefferson
Walton, Marylyn	Wichita	Sedgwick
*Wampler, Vera Mae	Garden City	Finney
Ward, Blanche	Liberal	Seward
Ward, Mrs. Kenneth	Waldo	Russell
Ward, Mrs. May	Wellington	Sumner
Warner, Cliff	———	Sedgwick
Wasinger, John	Hays	Ellis
Waterman, Joan	Plainville	Rooks
Waters, Mrs. Anna Mae	Wichita	Sedgwick
Watrons, Aileen	Wichita	Sedgwick
Watson, B.	Sublette	Haskell
Wear, Mrs. Flora	Dighton	Lane
Wear, Will	Dighton	Lane
Weathers, Emma	Great Bend	Barton
Weaver, Juanita	Wichita	Sedgwick
*Weber, Betty	Fowler	Meade
Weber, Gay	Larned	Pawnee
Weber, Harold	La Crosse	Rush
Weber, Mary	Fowler	Meade
Weber, William	La Crosse	Rush
Weber, Mrs. William	La Crosse	Rush
Webster, Edna May	Protection	Comanche
Webster, Monty	———	Stafford
Wehking, Betty	Lancaster	Atchison
Weigand, Jon	La Crosse	Rush
Weigel, Kenny	Hays	Ellis
Weigel, Lorena	Gorham	Russell
*Weigel, Mrs. Vera	Oakley	Logan
Weiland, Mrs. Sarah	Gridley	Coffey
*Weinhold, Leann	Belleville	Republic
Weinhold, Mrs. Lester	Sylvan Grove	Lincoln
Weir, L. A.	Ulysses	Grant
Weirich, Jim	Council Grove	Morris
Weis, Judy	Hays	Ellis
Welch, Buddy	———	Dickinson
Welch, Vinnie	Cedar	Smith
Wellbrock, Leo	Hays	Ellis
Wellbrock, Rosann	Victoria	Ellis
Wells, Carl	Hays	Ellis
Wells, Mr. George	———	Sumner
Wells, Golda	Marysville	Marshall
Wells, R. L.	Sublette	Haskell
Welmbold, R. L.	Tribune	Greeley
Weltz, Amy Jo	La Crosse	Rush
Wenger, Mrs. La Von	Sabetha	Nemaha
Wenger, Mrs. Ollie	Selden	Sheridan
Werner, Marvin	Kinsley	Edwards
Werner, Matilda	Paxico	Wabaunsee
Wertz, Dan	Quinter	Gove
Wesley, Walter	Minneapolis	Ottawa
Wesley, Mrs. Walter	Minneapolis	Ottawa
Westbrook, Mae	Wichita	Sedgwick

Name	Town	County
Westerhaus, Ivah	Marion	Marion
Westerhaus, Leo	Marion	Marion
Westerman, O. W.	Hays	Ellis
Westhoff, Vivian	Morse	Wyandotte
*Whaley, Rosa Lee	Attica	Harper
Wharton, Phyllis	Hutchinson	Reno
Wheeler, Fred	Norton	Norton
Whipple, Dorothy	Jetmore	Hodgeman
Whipple, Lawrence	Jetmore	Hodgeman
White, Mrs. A. D.	Ottawa	Franklin
White, Mrs. Alice	Coldwater	Comanche
White, Anne	Goodland	Sherman
White, Florence	Satanta	Haskell
White, Mrs. Jerome	Manhattan	Riley
White, Mrs. L.	Ottawa	Franklin
White, Mary	Hutchinson	Reno
White, Mrs. Phyllis	Kinsley	Edwards
White, Rayma	Garden City	Finney
White, S. D.	Ottawa	Franklin
*White, Sandra	Ottawa	Franklin
White, Steve	Manhattan	Riley
White, Wilber	Goodland	Sherman
White, Mrs. Wilber	Goodland	Sherman
Whitmer, Ella	Wilson	Ellsworth
Whitney, Nancy	Manhattan	Riley
Wieck, Ellen	Goodland	Sherman
Wieland, Mrs. Sarah	Gridley	Coffey
Wiesner, Mrs. Josephine	Ellis	Ellis
Wiklund, Mrs. Geo.	Stockton	Rooks
Wikoff, Nettie	Leoti	Wichita
Wilcox, Sally	Holton	Jackson
Wiles, Helen	Beloit	Mitchell
Wiley, Gary D.	Hays	Ellis
Wilkerson, Pat	Manhattan	Riley
Willard, Julia	Lawrence	Douglas
Willett, Peggy	Manhattan	Riley
Williams, Chester	Nekoma	Rush
Williams, David	Caldwell	Sumner
Williams, Edgar	Norton	Norton
*Williams, Mrs. Edgar	Norton	Norton
Williams, Hazel B.	Lakin	Kearny
Williams, Jennie	Manhattan	Riley
Williams, Judy Jean	Hutchinson	Reno
Williams, Lois	Lindsborg	McPherson
Williams, Rose	Hoxie	Sheridan
Williams, Walter	Brewster	Thomas
Willis, Mrs. Alice	Kirwin	Phillips
Willis, James	———	Brown
Willt, Kathy	Saint Francis	Cheyenne
Wilson, Bill	Hays	Ellis
Wilson, Cinda	Liberal	Seward
Wilson, Esther	Marienthal	Wichita
Wilson, Francis	Marienthal	Wichita
Wilson, Hallie	Marienthal	Wichita
Wilson, Mrs. Henry	Nicodemus	Graham

Name	Town	County
Wilson, Mrs. John	Marienthal	Wichita
Wilson, Kenneth	Wichita	Sedgwick
Wilson, Richard	———	Norton
Wilson, Wanda	Bucklin	Ford
Windholz, Bernard	Hays	Ellis
Windhorst, Alona	Manhattan	Riley
Winfrey, Iola	Manhattan	Riley
Wingett, Virginia	Kansas City	Wyandotte
Winkelman, Don	Pratt	Pratt
Winkle, Mrs. Dale	Glen Elder	Mitchell
Winkler, Mrs. F. R.	Oberlin	Decatur
Winsted, Vira	Satanta	Haskell
Winston, Linda	Wichita	Sedgwick
Winter, Barbara	Medicine Lodge	Barber
Winters, George	———	Riley
Wise, Karen	Linwood	Leavenworth
Wolfe, Mrs. Bertha	Blue Mound	Linn
Wolfe, Z. M.	La Crosse	Rush
Wolff, Mrs. Fred	Everest	Brown
Wonder, Dorothy	Manhattan	Riley
Wonderlich, Mrs. J. C.	Osborne	Osborne
Wonderlich, Nellie	Osborne	Osborne
Wonnell, Dallas	Hays	Ellis
Woodall, Horace	Manhattan	Riley
Woodall, Janie	Manhattan	Riley
Woodbury, Fred	Olivet	Osage
Woodmansee, Phil	Ellsworth	Ellsworth
Woods, Cris	Hays	Ellis
Woodson, Sandra	Penalosa	Kingman
Woofter, Glenda	Colby	Thomas
Woolley, Sarah	Oberlin	Decatur
Workman, Esther	Pratt	Pratt
Worley, Dave	Manhattan	Riley
Wright, Charlie	Wichita	Sedgwick
Wright, Mrs. Ernest	Saint John	Stafford
Wright, Harry	Kinsley	Edwards
Wright, Laura	Rush Center	Rush
Wright, Mary	Great Bend	Barton
Wright, Mrs. Merritt	Saint John	Stafford
Wulfkuhle, Noell	Lecompton	Douglas
*Wurm, Kay	Bazine	Ness
Wylie, Bertha	Jennings	Decatur
Wyman, Claude	Seward	Stafford
Yeakley, Charles	Hoyt	Jackson
Yeakley, Marguerite	Hoyt	Jackson
Yeakley, Susan	Hoyt	Jackson
Yohe, Mary	Plainville	Rooks
*Yonse, Mrs. Clarence	Dodge City	Ford
Yoos, Henry	Arcadia	Crawford
Yoos, Lottie	Pittsburg	Crawford
York, Ben	Manhattan	Riley
York, Raymond	———	Geary
*Young, Ardene	Washington	Washington
Young, Mrs. Ernie	Saint John	Stafford
Younger, Felix	Goodland	Sherman

Name	Town	County
Youngquist, M.	Kensington	Smith
Yowell, Mrs. Clyde	Palco	Rooks
Yunk, Mrs. Anna	Hays	Ellis
Zerbe, Norleen	Syracuse	Hamilton
Ziegler, Gary	Grainfield	Gove
Ziegler, Mrs. Leo	Collyer	Trego
Ziegler, Mrs. Sylva	Natoma	Osborne
Zieske, Truman	Lawrence	Douglas
Zimbelman, Eldon	Saint Francis	Cheyenne
Zimmerman, Hester	Edmond	Norton
Zimmerman, Homer	Hays	Ellis
Zimmerman, Mrs. Leroy	Haggard	Gray
Zimmerman, Lydia	Hays	Ellis
Zimmerman, Mrs. Ted	Ellinwood	Barton
Zoeller, Mrs. Henry	Manhattan	Riley
Zonts, Madge	Wichita	Sedgwick
Zorn, Mrs.	Wilson	Ellsworth
Zvolanek, Mrs. Irene	Bogue	Graham

List of Collectors

(These individuals are former students who took folklore courses at Kansas State University, Manhattan, and at Fort Hays Kansas State College, Hays, Kansas.)

Akasofer, T.	Bairhart, Julie	Bauhart, Julie
Allison, Jerry	Baker, Emmett	Bechtel, Jerry
Alson, Lynne	Ballard, Cherel	Beechert, Lowell
Anderson, Gail	Banhart, Julie	Behrmann, Paula
Anderson, J. Fadonna	Barrier, John	Beirly, Zula
Anderson, Larry	Barry, John	Bender, Gary
Antic, Carol	Barstow, Henry	Bennett, Beverly
Armstrong, Nancy	Bauer, Karen	Berghaus, Kay

Berry, Carol
Bigler, Jane
Binder, Sarah
Bizek, S.
Blackwell, Ruth
Blain, Steve
Blankenburg, Judith
Boettaher, Bill
Bolze, Martha
Bomgardner, John
Boyd, Agnes
Boyd, Norma
Boys, Sandra
Bozer, Beth
Brandenburg, Betty
Bremyer, Jill
Brent, Lanny
Bridgees, LaVonne
Broach, Doris
Brose, Jim
Brotemarkle, Gladye
Brown, Alice
Brown, James
Brown, Lois
Brown, Sonie
Brownlee, Lola
Brubaker, Mona
Bruton, Leathrine
Bukacek, Donale
Burrell, Emma
Burton, Catherine
Cain, Jim
Cain, Judith
Caldwell, Jean
Caldwell, Malcolm
Candes, Richard
Carlson, Donna
Carlson, Laura
Carroll, Connie
Carter, Lola
Chandler, Don
Chapin, Sandra
Chapman, Karen
Chappell, K.
Chegwidden, Don
Clapp, Geraldine
Clar, Paul
Clark, Laura
Clark, Paul
Cleveland, Gretchen
Clifton, Rose
Cobb, Beverly
Coldwell, Jean
Coldwell, Malcolm
Conrad, Bob
Conrad, Gray

Conred, Bob
Cook, Ann
Cook, Ronnie
Cooke, D.
Cordry, Barbara
Cowen, Leone
Crist, Gary
Cromwell, Larry
Crow, Jane
Curry, Linda
Davis, Carolyn
Davis, Ray
Denio, Alberta
Dennis, Carolyn
Desbien, Freda
Deyoz, Mrs. Fred
Dickens, Robert
Dierks, Gloria
Dinkel, Marlene
Dinkel, Phyllie
Dodd, Dixie
Downing, Michelle
Doxon, Evereth
Doxon, Everetta
Drees, Francis
Drumm, Marjorie
Dyatt, Donna
Edwards, Betty
Edwards, Cliff
Edwards, Lolita
Edwards, Sue
Ehrlich, Edward
Elder, Frances
Elliott, Jim
Emigh, Keith
Engler, Gretchen
Engwall, Janet
Eulert, Don
Eversole, Norma
Fally, Jerry
Farrell, Jerome
Farrow, Pat
Feaker, Kay
Feist, Marion
Feist, Myrna
Ferguson, Kenneth
Fetsch, Marquita
Fletcher, L.
Flowers, Jean
Floyd, John
Flummerfelt, James
Foekerts, Charlotte
Foiteschen, Ischelle
Folds, Eunice
Folkert, Charlotte
Franks, John

Fraser, Gloria
Frederick, Carol
Fritschen, Isabelle
Fritz, Sharon
Gangel, Paul
Garnder, Goldie
Gaskill, Rex
Gatschet, Paul
Gilbert, Bob
Glick, Gary
Goddard, Joan
Goddard, Suzanna
Goreham, Ann
Graham, Janice
Graham, Nancy
Green, Laveta
Greenwood, Georgia
Grim, Dorothy
Hale, Winton
Hamburg, Jim
Hamill, Mary
Hanson, Claude
Harbaugh, Bonnie
Harden, Kathleen
Harmon, M. A.
Harper, Marcalene
Harting, Genola
Hartle, Jack
Hartley, Mary
Haun, Virginia
Hauptli, Esther
Hauschild, Karen
Hawk, Kay
Heath, J.
Helimer, Leonard
Heller, Judy
Henning, Kay
Hepburn, R.
Hester, Betty
Hewett, Geneva
Higgins, Elizabeth
Higgins, Lucille
Higgins, Mary Jo
Hilda, M.
Hildebrand, A.
Hilgers, Herbert
Hill, Jim
Hiltz, Howard
Hindman, Judy
Hinkhouse, Emily
Holeman, Robert
Holinquist, Carole
Holliday, Sheri
Holmes, Richard
Holmquist, Carole
Holthus, Sharleen

Hond, Margaret
Hopkins, Cynthia
Hopson, Edna
Horning, Mary
Hough, David
Housholder, Nancy
Howard, Barbara
Howard, Nancy
Hubbard, M.
Hubert, Craig
Hulse, J.
Hund, Margaret
Hutchinson, Cathy
Jellison, Alice
Jimerfield, Tom
Johnson, Bernice
Johnson, Jim
Jones, George
Jones, Mina
Justic, Karen
Kaiser, Sylvia
Kalb, Mary
Keen, Gary
Keen, Roy
Keiper, Alice
Keller, Dave
Kempthorne, Elizabeth
Kenyon, Barbara
Kethcart, Barbara
Kinter, Mary
Kissick, Kay
Knoll, Carroll
Knoll, Devon
Knoll, Lorena
Knowless, Ruth
Koch, William
Koelling, Ruth
Koerner, Jean
Kohler, Phyllis
La Barr, C.
Laird, Mary
Lally, Jerry
Landes, Ricardo
Leas, Judy
Lederen, Margaret
Ledeser, Margaret
Leikam, Mildred
Lester, Jerry
Lewis, Richard
Lindquist, Mrs. D.
Lindsay, Richard
Lockman, Donna
Loeppke, Doris
Lofstead, Ruby
Long, Gary
Loughridge, Mary Ann

Lusk, Carolyn
Maee, Jackie
Mall, Jackie
Martin, S.
Maxwell, Louise
May, Marilyn
Mayfield, Velma
McAdoo, William
McCalmont, Clarice
McCormick, F.
McCormick, Mike
McCormick, William
Meca, Phillip
Medley, R.
Meehan, Coleen
Melleson, Bette
Mellisee, Tom
Mermis, Patty
Merritt, Georgette
Merten, Bob
Mettler, Rae
Miller, Floyd
Miller, Virginia
Milleson, Bette
Mills, Carolyn
Mitchell, Margaret
Mitchell, William
Moritz, Gelane
Morris, Ben
Morris, Billy
Morris, Gordon
Munsell, Darrell
Munsinger, Larry
Myers, Pat
Naiman, D.
Neal, Shirley
Newbrey, Agnes
Newton, Ray
Nickels, Helen
Nickels, Vina
Nikergall, Bettie
Nordstrom, Gretchen
Norman, Kay
Norton, Ben
Oberg, Dee
Oberg, Del
Oberg, Dru
Olson, Mrs. Egla
Olson, Judy
Olson, Lynne
Opitz, Glenda
Oswald, Lloyd
Owenzer, Doris
Palmer, Barbara
Parcels, Bill
Patterson, Helen

Patterson, Ward
Patton, Marilyn
Paukon, John
Paulson, Arnold
Paulson, John
Paustian, Gay
Pellett, David
Penrod, Marge
Perren, Betty
Perry, Roger
Petterson, John
Pickering, Kathleen
Pierantoni, Sally
Pivonka, Joan
Poling, Terry
Porter, Gerald
Potoski, R.
Prouty, Diana
Quenzer, Doris
Querbach, Mary
Rameiser, Betty
Randall, Sally
Redin, Eva
Reed, Dennis
Remple, Lucy
Render, Gary
Richard, Marilyn
Richards, Barbara
Richards, Loren
Richards, Vickie
Rickford, Lionel
Riggs, Leann
Riley, Esta
Riley, Kenneth
Ringer, Roberta
Robertson, Rodney
Robinson, Carol
Rohrbaugh, Yvonne
Romeiser, Betty
Rose, Adelaide
Rose, Margaret
Ross, Nancy
Rothenberger, Alma
Rothwell, Edna
Rowland, Lucille
Rowley, Marilyn
Rucken, Joe
Rundell, Jo Anne
Rupp, Mary
Ruth, Marylin
Sackett, S. J.
Schlagel, Wilma
Schmidt, Mary
Schmidt, Paul
Schmidt, Sheila
Schneidler, N. J.

Schroder, Harriet
Schroeder, Sandra
Schwindt, Paul
Scott, Charles
Scott, Erma
Scott, Mary
Seitz, Jane
Sevser, Edna
Seybold, Francis
Shacklett, Susan
Shaffer, Leola
Shields, Joel
Shumate, Karen
Simpson, W.
Smith, Joyce
Smith, La Dean
Smith, Patricia
Smith, Robert
Smith, Rona
Smith, Ross
Spillman, Betty
Squier, Luella
Staab, Clare
Staats, Donita
Stadelara, Mary
Stanford, Julie
Staples, Jim
States, Eluena
Steeples, Marie
Stephenson, Richard
Stevens, Joanne
Stineburg, Gail

Stone, Tom
Storer, Donald
Strecker, Wilmer
Subert, Don
Svoboda, Bill
Taisley, Charlene
Tangeman, John
Teaker, Kay
Thelen, William
Tobin, Mary
Toland, Pauline
Toley, Alice
Towsley, Charlene
Trump, Sharon
Turner, Norma
Underwood, J. T.
Vonfeldt, L.
Voth, Dwight
Waddle, Nancy
Walker, Diana
Walker, Margaret
Ward, Karen
Ware, James
Watson, Diane
Webber, Phil
Weber, Leila
Wedin, Judy
Weigand, Sharon
Weis, Bill
Weker, Betty
Wells, Edith
Wells, Jerry

Whipple, Gerald
White, Andy
White, Isandra
White, Jerry
White, Judy
White, Sandra
Wiklund, Donna
Wilcox, Joe
Wilkie, Cherrie
Williams, Edgar
Williams, J. D.
Williams, Kay
Wilmore, Carol
Wilson, Anita
Wilson, Barbara
Wingate, Dixie
Winkelman, Madelyne
Winslow, Elizabeth
Wonder, Bertha
Wonderlich, Claudene
Woodall, Walter
Woods, Peggie
Wright, Duane
Wright, Linda
Wunsch, Mayme
Yoos, Fred
Young, Donald
Young, Rena
Younger, Roger
Youngs, Sylvia
Ziegler, Marvin
Zyskowski, Alex